FOCUS
ON
GRAMMAR

AN INTEGRATED SKILLS APPROACH

THIRD EDITION

MARJORIE FUCHS
MARGARET BONNER

PEARSON
Longman

To the memory of my parents, Edith and Joseph Fuchs—MF

To my parents, Marie and Joseph Maus, and to my son, Luke Frances—MB

FOCUS ON GRAMMAR 4: An Integrated Skills Approach

Copyright © 2006, 2000, 1995 by Pearson Education, Inc.
All rights reserved.
No part of this publication may be reproduced,
stored in a retrieval system, or transmitted
in any form or by any means, electronic, mechanical,
photocopying, recording, or otherwise,
without the prior permission of the publisher.

Pearson Education, 10 Bank Street, White Plains, NY 10606

Vice president, multimedia and skills: Sherry Preiss
Executive editor: Laura Le Dréan
Senior development editor: Andrea Bryant
Production supervisor: Christine Edmonds
Marketing manager, higher education: Timothy P. Benell
Senior production editor: Kathleen Silloway
Art director: Ann France
Manufacturing manager: Nancy Flaggman
Photo research: Aerin Csigay
Cover design: Rhea Banker
Cover images: Large shell, background, Nick Koudis, RF; large shell, center image, Kaz Chiba; background, Comstock Images, RF
Text design: Quorum Creative Services, Rhea Banker
Text composition: ElectraGraphics, Inc.
Text font: 11/13 Sabon, 10/13 Myriad Roman
Illustrators: Steve Attoe pp. 108, 201; Burmar Technical Corporation pp. 320, 379; Ron Chironna pp. 162, 336, 337; Chris Gash pp. 170, 373, 413; David Klug, pp. 52, 53, 396; Suzanne Mogensen, pp. 41, 130; Andy Myer pp. 168, 240, 342, 346; Dusan Petricic pp. 246, 294; Steven Schulman p. 304; Susan Scott pp. 17, 256; Meryl Treatner pp. 72, 114; PC&F 59, 62.
Text credits: **p. 191,** based on information from Margaret Mead and Rhoda Metraux, *A Way of Seeing* (New York: McCall, 1970); **p. 210,** Eva Hoffman, *Lost in Translation: A Life in a New Language* (New York: Penguin, 1989); **p. 239,** based on information from *Psychology Today,* October 1979; **p. 286,** based on information from Judith Stone, "It's a Small World after All," *Discover* (February 1992), pp. 23–25.
Photo credits: see p. x.

Library of Congress Cataloging-in-Publication Data

Focus on grammar. An integrated skills approach — 3rd ed.
    p. cm.
  ISBN 0-13-147466-9 (v. 1 : student book : alk. paper) — ISBN 0-13-189971-6 (v. 2 : student book : alk. paper) — ISBN 0-13-189984-8 (v. 3 : student book : alk. paper) — ISBN 0-13-190008-0 (v. 4 : student book : alk. paper) — ISBN 0-13-191273-9 (v. 5 : student book : alk. paper)
  1. English language—Textbooks for foreign speakers. 2. English language—Grammar—Problems, exercises, etc.
PE1128.F555 2005
428.2'4—dc22

2005007655

ISBNs: 0-13-190008-0 (Student Book)
        0-13-190009-9 (Student Book with Audio CD)

LONGMAN ON THE **WEB**

Longman.com offers online resources for teachers and students. Access our Companion Websites, our online catalog, and our local offices around the world.

Visit us at **longman.com.**

Printed in the United States of America
10 11 12 13 14 15 VO64 15 14 13 12 11 10   (Student Book)

13 14 15 16 17 18 VO64 15 14 13 12 11 10   (Student Book with Audio CD)

CONTENTS

PART X   INDIRECT SPEECH AND EMBEDDED QUESTIONS

APPENDICES

GLOSSARY OF GRAMMAR TERMS

REVIEW TESTS ANSWER KEY

INDEX

ABOUT THE AUTHORS

Marjorie Fuchs has taught ESL at New York City Technical College and LaGuardia Community College of the City University of New York and EFL at the Sprach Studio Lingua Nova in Munich, Germany. She has a master's degree in Applied English Linguistics and a Certificate in TESOL from the University of Wisconsin–Madison. She has authored and co-authored many widely used books and multimedia materials, notably *Crossroads, Top Twenty ESL Word Games: Beginning Vocabulary Development, Families: Ten Card Games for Language Learners, Focus on Grammar 3: An Integrated Skills Approach, Focus on Grammar 3 CD-ROM, Focus on Grammar 4 CD-ROM, Longman English Interactive 3* and *4, Grammar Express Basic, Grammar Express Basic CD-ROM, Grammar Express Intermediate,* and the workbooks to the *Longman Dictionary of American English, the Longman Photo Dictionary, The Oxford Picture Dictionary, Focus on Grammar 3* and *4,* and *Grammar Express Basic.*

Margaret Bonner has taught ESL at Hunter College and the Borough of Manhattan Community College of the City University of New York, at Taiwan National University in Taipei, and at Virginia Commonwealth University in Richmond. She holds a master's degree in Library Science from Columbia University; and she has done work toward a Ph.D. in English Literature at the Graduate Center of the City University of New York. She has authored and co-authored numerous ESL and EFL print and multimedia materials, including textbooks for the national school system of Oman, *Step into Writing: A Basic Writing Text, Focus on Grammar 3: An Integrated Skills Approach, Focus on Grammar 4 Workbook, Grammar Express Basic, Grammar Express Basic CD-ROM, Grammar Express Basic Workbook, Grammar Express Intermediate, Focus on Grammar 3 CD-ROM, Focus on Grammar 4 CD-ROM, Longman English Interactive 4,* and *The Oxford Picture Dictionary Intermediate Workbook.*

CREDITS

Grateful acknowledgment is given to the following for providing photographs:

INTRODUCTION

The *Focus on Grammar* series

Written by ESL/EFL professionals, *Focus on Grammar: An Integrated Skills Approach* helps students to understand and practice English grammar. The primary aim of the course is for students to gain confidence in their ability to speak and write English accurately and fluently.

The **third edition** retains this popular series' focus on English grammar through lively listening, speaking, reading, and writing activities. The new *Focus on Grammar* also maintains the same five-level progression as the second edition:

- Level 1 (Beginning, formerly Introductory)
- Level 2 (High-Beginning, formerly Basic)
- Level 3 (Intermediate)
- Level 4 (High-Intermediate)
- Level 5 (Advanced)

What is the *Focus on Grammar* methodology?

Both controlled and communicative practice

While students expect and need to learn the formal rules of a language, it is crucial that they also practice new structures in a variety of contexts in order to internalize and master them. To this end, *Focus on Grammar* provides an abundance of both controlled and communicative exercises so that students can bridge the gap between knowing grammatical structures and using them. The many communicative activities in each Student Book unit provide opportunity for critical thinking while enabling students to personalize what they have learned in order to talk to one another with ease about hundreds of everyday issues.

A unique four-step approach

The series follows a four-step approach:

Step 1: Grammar in Context shows the new structures in natural contexts, such as articles and conversations.

Step 2: Grammar Presentation presents the structures in clear and accessible grammar charts, notes, and examples.

Step 3: Focused Practice of both form and meaning of the new structures is provided in numerous and varied controlled exercises.

Step 4: Communication Practice allows students to use the new structures freely and creatively in motivating, open-ended activities.

Thorough recycling

Underpinning the scope and sequence of the *Focus on Grammar* series is the belief that students need to use target structures many times, in different contexts, and at increasing levels of difficulty. For this reason, new grammar is constantly recycled throughout the book so that students have maximum exposure to the target forms and become comfortable using them in speech and in writing.

A complete classroom text and reference guide

A major goal in the development of *Focus on Grammar* has been to provide students with books that serve not only as vehicles for classroom instruction but also as resources for reference and self-study. In each Student Book, the combination of grammar charts, grammar notes, a glossary of grammar terms, and extensive appendices provides a complete and invaluable reference guide for students.

Ongoing assessment

Review Tests at the end of each part of the Student Book allow for continual self-assessment. In addition, the tests in the new *Focus on Grammar* Assessment Package provide teachers with a valid, reliable, and practical means of determining students' appropriate levels of placement in the course and of assessing students' achievement throughout the course. At Levels 4 (High-Intermediate) and 5 (Advanced), Proficiency Tests give teachers an overview of their students' general grammar knowledge.

What are the components of each level of *Focus on Grammar*?

Student Book

The Student Book is divided into eight or more parts, depending on the level. Each part contains grammatically related units, with each unit focusing on specific grammatical structures; where appropriate, units present contrasting forms. The exercises in each unit are thematically related to one another, and all units have the same clear, easy-to-follow format.

Teacher's Manual

The Teacher's Manual contains a variety of suggestions and information to enrich the material in the Student Book. It includes general teaching suggestions for each section of a typical unit, answers to frequently asked questions, unit-by-unit teaching tips with ideas for further communicative practice, and a supplementary activity section. Answers to the Student Book exercises and audioscripts of the listening activities are found at the back of the Teacher's Manual. Also included in the Teacher's Manual is a CD-ROM of teaching tools, including PowerPoint presentations that offer alternative ways of presenting selected grammar structures.

Workbook

The Workbook accompanying each level of *Focus on Grammar* provides additional exercises appropriate for self-study of the target grammar for each Student Book unit. Tests included in each Workbook provide students with additional opportunities for self-assessment.

Audio Program

All of the listening exercises from the Student Book, as well as the Grammar in Context passages and other appropriate exercises, are included on the program's CDs. In the book, the symbol ⌒ appears next to the listening exercises. Another symbol ⌒, indicating that listening is optional, appears next to the Grammar in Context passages and some exercises. All of these scripts appear in the Teacher's Manual and may be used as an alternative way of presenting the activities.

Some Student Books are packaged with a separate Student Audio CD. This CD includes the listening exercise from each unit.

CD-ROM

The *Focus on Grammar* CD-ROM provides students with individualized practice and immediate feedback. Fully contextualized and interactive, the activities broaden and extend practice of the grammatical structures in the reading, writing, speaking, and listening skills areas. The CD-ROM includes grammar review, review tests, score-based remedial practice, games, and all relevant reference material from the Student Book. It can also be used in conjunction with the *Longman Interactive American Dictionary* CD-ROM.

Assessment Package (NEW)

An extensive, comprehensive Assessment Package has been developed for each level of the third edition of *Focus on Grammar*. The components of the Assessment Package are:

1. **Placement, Diagnostic, and Achievement Tests**

   - a Placement Test to screen students and place them into the correct level
   - Diagnostic Tests for each part of the Student Book
   - Unit Achievement Tests for each unit of the Student Book
   - Part Achievement Tests for each part of the Student Book

2. **General Proficiency Tests**

   - two Proficiency Tests at Level 4 (High-Intermediate)
   - two Proficiency Tests at Level 5 (Advanced)

   These tests can be administered at any point in the course.

3. **Audio CD**

   The listening portions of the Placement, Diagnostic, and Achievement Tests are recorded on CDs. The scripts appear in the Assessment Package.

4. **Test-Generating Software**

   The test-bank software provides thousands of questions from which teachers can create class-appropriate tests. All items are labeled according to the grammar structure they are testing, so teachers can easily select relevant items; they can also design their own items to add to the tests.

Transparencies (NEW)

Transparencies of all the grammar charts in the Student Book are also available. These transparencies are a classroom visual aid that will help instructors point out important patterns and structures of grammar.

Companion Website

The companion website contains a wealth of information and activities for both teachers and students. In addition to general information about the course pedagogy, the website provides extensive practice exercises for the classroom, a language lab, or at home.

What's new in the third edition of the Student Book?

In response to users' requests, this edition has:

- a new four-color design
- easy-to-read color coding for the four steps
- new and updated reading texts for Grammar in Context
- post-reading activities (in addition to the pre-reading questions)
- more exercise items
- an editing (error analysis) exercise in each unit
- an Internet activity in each unit
- a Glossary of Grammar Terms
- expanded Appendices

References

Alexander, L. G. (1988). *Longman English Grammar.* White Plains: Longman.

Biber, D., S. Conrad, E. Finegan, S. Johansson, and G. Leech (1999). *Longman Grammar of Spoken and Written English.* White Plains: Longman.

Celce-Murcia, M., and D. Freeman (1999). *The Grammar Book.* Boston: Heinle and Heinle.

Celce-Murcia, M., and S. Hilles (1988). *Techniques and Resources in Teaching Grammar.* New York: Oxford University Press.

Firsten, R. (2002). *The ELT Grammar Book.* Burlingame, CA: Alta Book Center Publishers.

Garner, B. (2003). *Garner's Modern American Usage.* New York: Oxford University Press.

Greenbaum, S. (1996). *The Oxford English Grammar.* New York: Oxford University Press.

Leech, G. (2004). *Meaning and the English Verb.* Harlow, UK: Pearson.

Lewis, M. (1997). *Implementing the Lexical Approach.* Hove East Sussex, UK: Language Teaching Publications.

Longman (2002). *Longman Dictionary of English Language and Culture.* Harlow, UK: Longman.

Willis, D. (2003). *Rules, Patterns and Words.* New York: Cambridge University Press.

TOUR OF A UNIT

Each unit in the *Focus on Grammar* series presents a specific grammar structure (or two, in case of a contrast) and develops a major theme, which is set by the opening text. All units follow the same unique **four-step approach**.

Step 1: Grammar in Context

The **conversation** or **reading** in this section shows the grammar structure in a natural context. The high-interest text presents authentic language in a variety of real-life formats: magazine articles, web pages, questionnaires, and more. Students can listen to the text on an audio CD to get accustomed to the sound of the grammar structure in a natural context.

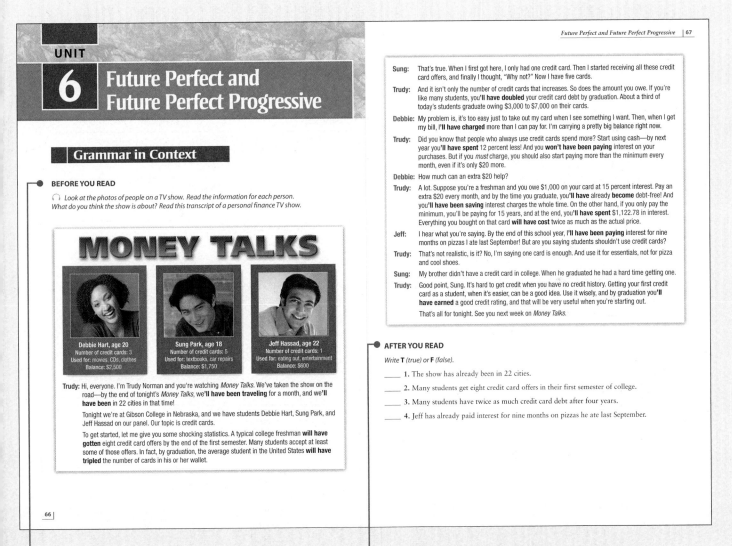

Pre-reading questions *create interest, elicit students' knowledge about the topic, and lead students to make predictions about the text.*

A post-reading activity *helps students understand the text and focus on the grammar structure.*

Step 2: Grammar Presentation

This section is made up of grammar charts, notes, and examples. The **grammar charts** focus on the forms of the grammar structure. The **grammar notes** and **examples** focus on the meanings and uses of the structure.

Clear and easy-to-read **grammar charts** present the grammar structure in all its forms and combinations.

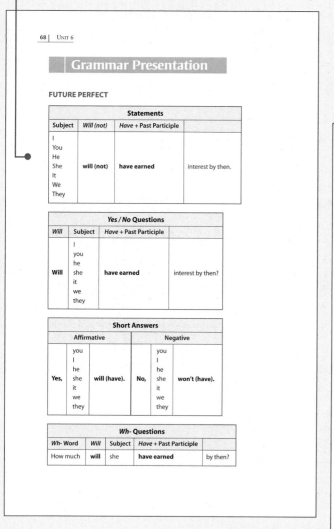

Each **grammar note** gives a short, simple explanation of one use of the structure. The accompanying **examples** ensure students' understanding of the point.

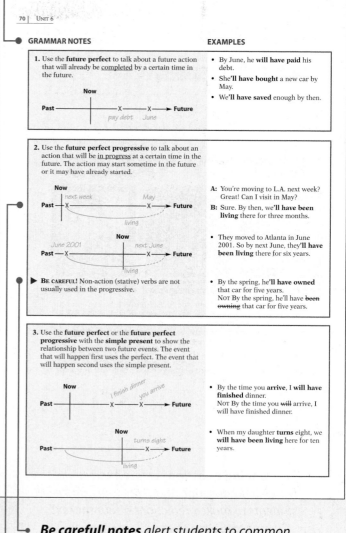

Be careful! notes alert students to common errors made by students of English.

Time lines clarify the meaning of verb forms and their relationship to one another.

Step 3: Focused Practice

This section provides students with a variety of contextualized **controlled exercises** to practice both the forms and the uses of the grammar structure.

*Focused Practice always begins with a "for recognition only" exercise called **Discover the Grammar**.*

Focused Practice

1 DISCOVER THE GRAMMAR

Read this magazine article about lying on the job. Circle the reporting verbs. Underline the examples of direct speech once. Underline the examples of indirect speech twice.

"Lying during a job interview is risky business," (says) Martha Toledo, director of the management consulting firm Maxwell. "The truth has a funny way of coming out." Toledo tells the story of one woman applying for a job as an office manager. The woman told the interviewer that she had a B.A. degree. Actually, she was eight credits short. She also said that she had made $50,000 at her last job. The truth was $10,000 less. "Many firms really do check facts," warns Toledo. In this case, a call to the applicant's company revealed the discrepancies.

Toledo relates a story about another job applicant, George. During an interview, George reported that he had quit his last job. George landed the new job and was doing well until the company hired another employee, Pete. George and Pete had worked at the same company. Pete eventually told his boss that his old company had fired George.

2 CONFESSIONS
Grammar Notes 3, 6–7

Complete the student's essay with the correct words.

Once when I was a teenager, I went to my Aunt Leah's house. Aunt Leah collected pottery, and
as soon as I got there, she _____told_____ me she _____ to show me
          1. (said / told)   2. (wants / wanted)
_____ new bowl. _____ she _____ just bought it.
3. (my / her)   4. (said / told)   5. (has / had)
It was beautiful. When Aunt Leah went to answer the door, I picked up the bowl to examine it. It
slipped from my hands and smashed to pieces on the floor. As Aunt Leah walked back into the
room, I screamed and _____ that the cat had just broken _____ new
                         6. (said / told)   7. (her / your)
bowl. Aunt Leah got this funny look on her face and _____ me that it really
                                                        8. (said / told)
_____ very important.
9. (isn't / wasn't)
I didn't sleep at all that night, and the next morning I called my aunt and _____
                                                                              10. (said / told)
her that I had broken _____ bowl. She said _____ 'd known that all
                        11. (her / your)   12. (I / she)
along. We still laugh about the story today.

*Exercises are **cross-referenced** to the appropriate grammar notes to provide a quick review.*

---

*A **variety of exercise types** guide students from recognition to accurate production of the grammar structure.*

4 TIME LINE
Grammar Notes 3–5

*This time line shows some important events in Monique's life. Use the time line and the cues below to write sentences about her. Use **when** or **while**.*

born in Canada	moves to Australia	meets Paul	starts medical school	marries	gets medical degree	gets first job	starts practice at Lenox Hospital	has son; starts book	finishes book; does TV interview	book becomes a success; quits job
1973	1988	1989	1995	1996	1999	2000	2002	2003	2004	2005

1. moves to Australia / meets Paul   *She met Paul when she moved to Australia.*

2. gets married / studies medicine   *She got married while she was studying medicine.*

3. lives in Australia / gets married _____

4. receives medical degree / gets her first job _____

5. practices medicine at Lenox Hospital / has a son _____

6. writes a book / works at Lenox Hospital _____

7. does a TV interview / finishes her book _____

8. leaves job / her book becomes a success _____

5 EDITING

Read Monique's letter to a friend. There are eleven mistakes in the use of the simple past and the past progressive. The first mistake is already corrected. Find and correct ten more.

Dear Crystal,
                                          thought
   I was writing chapter two of my new book when I was thinking of you. The last time I saw you, you walked down the aisle to
marry Dave. That was more than two years ago. How are you? How is married life?
   A lot has happened in my life since that time. While I worked at Lenox Hospital, I began writing. In 2004, I was publishing a
book on women's health issues. It was quite successful here in Australia. I even got interviewed on TV. When I was getting a
contract to write a second book, I decided to quit my hospital job to write full-time. That's what I'm doing now. Paul, too, has had
a career change. While I was writing, he was attending law school. He was getting his degree last summer.
   Oh, the reason I thought of you while I wrote was because the chapter was about rashes. Remember the time you were getting
that terrible rash? We rode our bikes when you were falling into a patch of poison ivy. And that's how you met Dave! When you
were falling off the bike, he offered to give us a ride home. Life's funny, isn't it?
   Well, please write soon, and send my love to Dave. I miss you!

                                                            Monique

*Focused Practice always ends with an **editing** exercise to teach students to find and correct typical mistakes.*

Step 4: Communication Practice

This section provides open-ended **communicative activities** giving students the opportunity to use the grammar structure appropriately and fluently.

A **listening** activity gives students the opportunity to check their aural comprehension.

Adjective Clauses with Subject Relative Pronouns | 201

Communication Practice

6 | LISTENING

🎧 Some friends are at a high school reunion. They haven't seen one another for 25 years. Look at the picture and listen to the friends talk about the people at the table. Then listen again and write the correct name next to each person.

Ann	Asha	Bob	Kado	Pat	Pete

Many exercises and activities are **art based** to provide visual cues and an interesting context and springboard for meaningful conversations.

A **writing** activity allows students to use the grammar structure in a variety of formats.

64 | UNIT 5

10 | LET'S GET TOGETHER

Complete the schedule below. Write in all your plans for next week. Then work with a partner. Without showing each other your schedules, find a time to get together by asking and answering questions using the future progressive.

Example: A: What will you be doing at 11:00 on Tuesday?
B: I'll be taking a history test.

	MONDAY	TUESDAY	WEDNESDAY	THURSDAY	FRIDAY
9:00					
11:00					
1:00					
3:00					
5:00					
7:00					

11 | WRITING

Write a paragraph about your life 10 years from now. What will you be doing for a living? What kind of family life will you have? What hobbies will you be enjoying? What will you do to achieve these things? Use the future and future progressive.

Example: In 10 years, I will be working for the space program. I am going to be planning the first colony on Mars. First I will have to graduate from college.

12 | ON THE INTERNET

🌐 Do a search on space activities. Find information about what will be happening during the 21st century. For example, will tourists be traveling to the moon or Mars? Will scientists "terraform" Mars (make the Martian atmosphere safe for people from Earth)? Are there going to be farms and factories in space?

Work with a small group. Find your own organization or look at information from these:

SEDS (Students for the Exploration and Development of Space)
The Mars Society
The Planetary Society
Space.com

Present your predictions to the class.

Example: A lot of different countries are going to be developing space. China will probably be sending people to the moon. The European countries and Japan will work together to explore the planet Mercury . . .

An **Internet** activity gives students the opportunity to expand on the content of the unit and interact with their classmates creatively and fluently.

TOUR BEYOND THE UNIT

In the *Focus on Grammar* series, the grammatically related units are grouped into parts, and each part concludes with a section called **From Grammar to Writing** and a **Review Test** section.

From Grammar to Writing

This section presents a point which applies specifically to writing, for example, avoiding sentence fragments. Students are guided to practice the point in a **piece of extended writing**.

● An **introduction** relates the grammar point to the writing focus.

● Students practice **pre-writing strategies** such as brainstorming, word-mapping, and outlining.

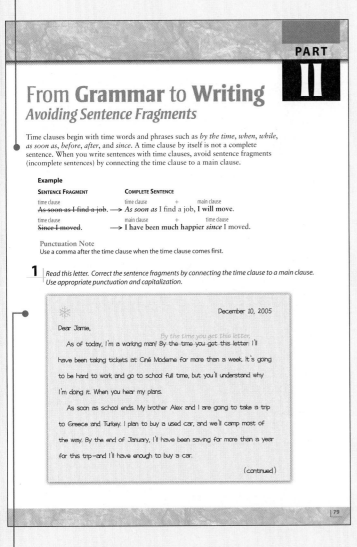

PART II

From **Grammar** to **Writing**
Avoiding Sentence Fragments

Time clauses begin with time words and phrases such as *by the time*, *when*, *while*, *as soon as*, *before*, *after*, and *since*. A time clause by itself is not a complete sentence. When you write sentences with time clauses, avoid sentence fragments (incomplete sentences) by connecting the time clause to a main clause.

Example

SENTENCE FRAGMENT	COMPLETE SENTENCE
time clause	time clause + main clause
As soon as I find a job. →	*As soon as* I find a job, **I will move.**
time clause	main clause + time clause
Since I moved. →	**I have been much happier** *since* I moved.

Punctuation Note
Use a comma after the time clause when the time clause comes first.

1 Read this letter. Correct the sentence fragments by connecting the time clause to a main clause. Use appropriate punctuation and capitalization.

December 10, 2005

Dear Jamie,

By the time you get this letter,
As of today, I'm a working man! By the time you get this letter. I'll have been taking tickets at Ciné Moderne for more than a week. It's going to be hard to work and go to school full time, but you'll understand why I'm doing it. When you hear my plans.

As soon as school ends. My brother Alex and I are going to take a trip to Greece and Turkey. I plan to buy a used car, and we'll camp most of the way. By the end of January, I'll have been saving for more than a year for this trip—and I'll have enough to buy a car.

(continued)

79

From Grammar to Writing | 117

2 Before writing the essay in Exercise 1, the student made a Venn diagram showing the things that Brasília and Washington, D.C. have in common, and the things that are different. Complete the student's diagram.

Brasília   Washington, D.C.

in South America   national capital   in North America

3 Before you write . . .

1. Work with a partner. Agree on a topic for an essay of comparison and contrast. For example, you can compare two places, two people, two types of food, or two TV programs.
2. Brainstorm ideas and complete a Venn diagram like the one in Exercise 2.

4 Write an essay of comparison and contrast using your diagram in Exercise 3.

5 Exchange essays with a different partner. Underline once all the additions that show similarity. Underline twice the additions that show difference. Write a question mark (**?**) above the places where something seems wrong. Then answer the following questions.

	Yes	No
1. Did the writer use the correct auxiliary verbs in the additions?	☐	☐
2. Did the writer use correct word order?	☐	☐
3. Do the examples show important similarities and differences?	☐	☐

4. What are some details you would like to know about the two things the writer compared? _____

_____

6 Work with your partner. Discuss each other's editing questions from Exercise 5. Then rewrite your own paragraph and make any necessary corrections.

● **Writing formats** include business letters, personal letters, notes, instructions, paragraphs, reports, and essays.

● The section includes **peer review** and **editing** of the students' writing.

Review Test

This review section, covering all the grammar structures presented in the part, can be used as a test. An **Answer Key** is provided at the back of the book.

PART IX

Review Test

I *Circle the letter of the correct word(s) to complete each sentence.*

1. I _____ late for work if the bus doesn't arrive soon.   A B Ⓒ D
   (**A**) am   (**C**) 'll be
   (**B**) was   (**D**) 've been

2. I _____ a flight attendant if I didn't get airsick.   A B C D
   (**A**) would become   (**C**) become
   (**B**) became   (**D**) had become

3. What do you do when your bus _____ late?   A B C D
   (**A**) were   (**C**) would be
   (**B**) is   (**D**) had been

4. If the teacher cancels class today, I _____ you.   A B C D
   (**A**) have joined   (**C**) 'll join
   (**B**) could have joined   (**D**) join

5. This flight is full. _____ someone gives up a seat,   A B C D
   you won't get on this flight today.
   (**A**) If   (**C**) When
   (**B**) Unless   (**D**) Where

6. If you _____ early enough, we can't save a seat for you.   A B C D
   (**A**) 'll check in   (**C**) don't check in
   (**B**) check in   (**D**) have checked in

7. If I hadn't been fascinated with flying, I _____ a pilot.   A B C D
   (**A**) would become   (**C**) won't become
   (**B**) became   (**D**) wouldn't have become

8. I'm going to Gerry's for Thanksgiving, but I can't stand to eat turkey.   A B C D
   What _____ if that happened to you?
   (**A**) would you do   (**C**) do you do
   (**B**) did you do   (**D**) will you do

(continued)

361

The Review Tests *include* **multiple-choice questions** *in standardized test formats, giving students practice in test taking.*

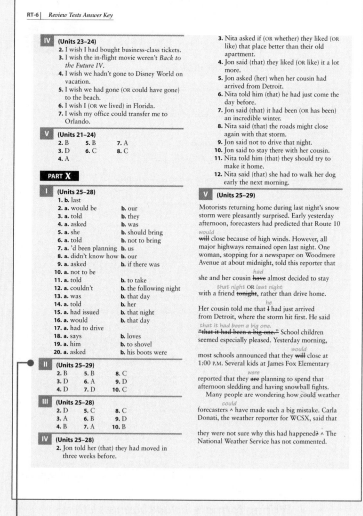

IV **(Units 23–24)**
2. I wish I had bought business-class tickets.
3. I wish the in-flight movie weren't *Back to the Future IV*.
4. I wish we hadn't gone to Disney World on vacation.
5. I wish we had gone (OR could have gone) to the beach.
6. I wish I (OR we lived) in Florida.
7. I wish my office could transfer me to Orlando.

V **(Units 21–24)**
2. B   5. B   7. A
3. D   6. C   8. C
4. A

PART X

I **(Units 25–28)**
1. **b.** last
2. **a.** would be   **b.** our
3. **a.** told   **b.** they
4. **a.** asked   **b.** was
5. **a.** she   **b.** should bring
6. **a.** told   **b.** not to bring
7. **a.** 'd been planning **b.** us
8. **a.** didn't know how **b.** our
9. **a.** asked   **b.** if there was
10. **a.** not to be
11. **a.** told   **b.** to take
12. **a.** couldn't   **b.** the following night
13. **a.** was   **b.** that day
14. **a.** told   **b.** her
15. **a.** had issued   **b.** that night
16. **a.** would   **b.** that day
17. **a.** had to drive
18. **a.** says   **b.** loves
19. **a.** him   **b.** to shovel
20. **a.** asked   **b.** his boots were

II **(Units 25–29)**
2. B   5. B   8. C
3. D   6. A   9. D
4. D   7. D   10. C

III **(Units 25–28)**
2. D   5. C   8. C
3. A   6. B   9. D
4. B   7. A   10. B

IV **(Units 25–28)**
2. Jon told her (that) they had moved in three weeks before.

3. Nita asked if (OR whether) they liked (OR like) that place better than their old apartment.
4. Jon said (that) they liked (OR like) it a lot more.
5. Jon asked (her) when her cousin had arrived from Detroit.
6. Nita told him (that) he had just come the day before.
7. Jon said (that) it had been (OR has been) an incredible winter.
8. Nita said (that) the roads might close again with that storm.
9. Jon said not to drive that night.
10. Jon said to stay there with her cousin.
11. Nita told him (that) they should try to make it home.
12. Nita said (that) she had to walk her dog early the next morning.

V **(Units 25–29)**

Motorists returning home during last night's snow storm were pleasantly surprised. Early yesterday afternoon, forecasters had predicted that Route 10 *would* ~~will~~ close because of high winds. However, all major highways remained open last night. One woman, stopping for a newspaper on Woodmere Avenue at about midnight, told this reporter that *had* she and her cousin ~~have~~ almost decided to stay *that night* OR *last night* with a friend ~~tonight~~, rather than drive home. *he* Her cousin told me that ~~I~~ had just arrived from Detroit, where the storm hit first. He said *that it had been a big one.* ~~"that it had been a big one."~~ School children seemed especially pleased. Yesterday morning, *would* most schools announced that they ~~will~~ close at 1:00 P.M. Several kids at James Fox Elementary *were* reported that they ~~are~~ planning to spend that afternoon sledding and having snowball fights.
   Many people are wondering how ~~could~~ weather *could* forecasters ^ have made such a big mistake. Carla Donati, the weather reporter for WCSX, said that they were not sure why this had happened~~?~~ ^ The National Weather Service has not commented.

The Review Tests Answer Key *provides* **cross-references** *to the appropriate unit(s) for easy review.*

ACKNOWLEDGMENTS

Before acknowledging the many people who have contributed to the third edition of *Focus on Grammar*, we wish to express our gratitude to those who worked on the first and second editions and whose influence is still present in the new work.

Our continuing thanks to:

- Joanne Dresner, who initiated the project and helped conceptualize the general approach of *Focus on Grammar*.

- Joan Saslow, our editor for the first edition, and Françoise Leffler, our editor for the second edition, for helping to bring the books to fruition.

- Sharon Hilles, our grammar consultant, for her insight and advice on the first edition.

In the third edition, *Focus on Grammar* has continued to evolve as we update materials and respond to the valuable feedback from teachers and students who have been using the series. We are grateful to the following editors and colleagues:

- Laura Le Dréan, Executive Editor, for her dedication and commitment. In spite of an incredibly full schedule, she looked at every page of manuscript and offered excellent suggestions. In addition, she was always available and responsive to authors' concerns.

- Andrea Bryant, Senior Development Editor, for her enthusiasm and energy and her excellent ear for natural language. Her sense of contemporary culture helped us to reflect the spirit of the new millennium.

- Kathleen Silloway, Senior Production Editor, for piloting the book through its many stages of production and for always giving us a heads up when more *FOG* was about to roll in.

- Irene Schoenberg, for generously sharing her experience in teaching our first two editions and for her enthusiastic support.

Finally, we are grateful, as always, to Rick Smith and Luke Frances for their helpful input and for standing by and supporting us as we navigated our way through our third *FOG*.

We also wish to acknowledge the many reviewers for reading the manuscript and offering many useful suggestions.

Elizabeth Ackerman, California State University at Los Angeles, Los Angeles, CA; **Mary Ann Archbold,** South Bay Adult School, Redondo Beach, CA; **Larisa Álvarez Ávila,** Centro Educativo Renacimiento, Mérida, Yucatán, Mexico; **Vahania Carvajal García,** Instituto Cultural Regina Teresiano, Hermosillo, Sonora, Mexico; **Marilyn De Liro Álvarez,** Instituto "Las Brisas" Nuevo León, Mexico; **Amelia Chávez Ruiz,** Lake Forest School Mexico State, Mexico; **Elizabeth Clemente,** Instituto Tecnológico de Estudios Superiores de Monterrey, Atizapan, Mexico State, Mexico; **Stephen M. Drinane,** Rockland Community College, Suffern, NY; **Susanna Eguren,** Instituto Cultural Peruano Norteamericano, Lima, Peru; **Barbara Fields,** Beverly Hills Adult School,

Beverly Hills, CA; **Carolyn Flores,** University of Texas–Pan American, Edinburg, TX; **Leon Geyer,** Bell Language School, Brooklyn, NY; **Anthony Halderman,** Cuesta College, San Luis Obispo, CA; **M. Martha Hall,** The New England School of English, Cambridge, MA; **Heather Hein,** University of Denver, Denver, CO; **Mary Hill,** North Shore Community College, Danvers, MA; **Angela Hughes,** Instituto Tecnológico de Estudios Superiores de Monterrey, Atizapan, Mexico State, Mexico; **Peggy Hull,** Dodge City Community College, Dodge City, KS; **Silvia Icela Espinoza Galvez,** Colegio Lux, Hermosillo, Sonora, Mexico; **Alice Jarvis,** Glendale Community College, Glendale, CA; **Jennifer Johnston,** Southwest Missouri State University, Springfield, MO; **Melanie Joy,** Roxbury Community College, Roxbury Crossing, MA; **Lisa Krol,** University of Saskatchewan, Saskatoon, Saskatchewan, Canada; **Jeanne Lachowski,** University of Salt Lake City, Salt Lake City, UT; **David Lane,** Puente Learning Center, Los Angeles, CA; **Elena Lattarulo,** Cuesta College, San Luis Obispo, CA; **Anik Low,** Collège Jean-de-Brébeuf, Montreal, Québec, Canada; **Craig Machado,** Norwalk Community College, Norwalk, CT; **Vanessa Marín de Cervantes,** Ladies' World, Guadalajara, Jalisco, Mexico; **Javier Martínez García,** Instituto Las Américas, Mexico City, D.F., Mexico; **Louis Mavalankar,** Truman College–Chicago, Chicago, IL; **Sheryl Meyer,** University of Denver, Denver, CO; **Irina Morgunova,** Roxbury Community College, Roxbury Crossing, MA; **Georgina Orozco,** Instituto Cumbre, Ciudad Obregón, Sonora, Mexico; **Kathleen Pierce,** Bell Language School, Brooklyn, NY; **Melissa Powers Lee,** University of Texas at Austin, Austin, TX; **Kate Price,** University of Denver, Denver, CO; **Rachel Robbins,** Red River College, Winnipeg, Manitoba, Canada; **Maria Roche,** Housatonic Community College, Bridgeport, CT; **Ernesto Romo,** Lake Forest School, Mexico State, Mexico; **Karen Roth,** University of British Columbia, Vancouver, B.C., Canada; **Fernando Rujeles,** Centro Colombo Americano, Bogotá, Colombia; **René Sandoval,** Martin Luther King, Jr. School, Guadalajara, Jalisco, Mexico; **Anne-Marie Schlender,** Austin Community College, Austin, TX; **Rusten Seven,** Dokuz Eylul University School of Languages, Izmir, Turkey; **Judy Tanka,** American Language Center–University of California, Los Angeles, Los Angeles, CA; **Modesto L. Tollison,** Tarrant County College, Fort Worth, TX; **Jacqueline Torres Ramírez,** Instituto Horland Johnson, Guadalajara, Jalisco, Mexico; **María Elena Vera de la Rosa,** Lake Forest School, Mexico State, Mexico; **Magneli Villanueva Morales,** Universidad Regiomontana, Monterrey, Nuevo León, Mexico; **Essio Zamora,** Instituto Carlos Gracido, Oaxaca, Mexico; **Ian Zapp,** Colegio México Irlandés, Guadalajara, Jalisco, Mexico.

PART I

Present and Past:
Review and Expansion

Simple Present and Present Progressive

Grammar in Context

BEFORE YOU READ

🎧 *Think about the meaning of these terms: nickname, title, given name, surname. Can you give an example of each from your first language? Can you guess the meanings of the words you don't know? Read this school newsletter article about names.*

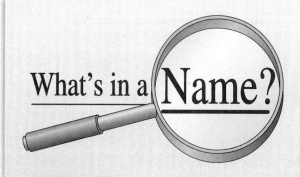

What's in a Name?

Hola! My name **is** Jorge Santiago García de Gonzalez, and I**'m** from Mexico City. I**'m studying** English here at the language institute. Jorge **is** my first, or given, name; Santiago, my middle name; García **comes** from my father (it**'s** his surname); and Gonzalez from my mother (it**'s** her surname). People often **think** my name **is** Mr. Gonzalez, but it**'s** actually Mr. García. Of course in class, everyone just **calls** me Jorge. People here **find** my name a "mouthful," but to me it **seems** perfectly normal. Some of my new friends **are trying** to convince me to call myself "George" while I**'m** here, but I **like** my name, and I **don't want** to lose my identity.

Hi. My name **is** Yevdokiya Ivanova. I**'m** from Russia, but this year I**'m living** and **working** in Canada. Yevdokiya **is** an old-fashioned name, but it**'s** **coming back** into style. My classmates **find** it difficult to pronounce, so they **call** me by my nickname—Dusya. In my country, people always **call** their teachers by a first and a middle name, for example, Viktor Antonovich. The middle name **comes** from the father's first name and **means** "son of Anton." We **don't use** titles like "Mr." or "Professor." Here, some teachers actually **prefer** to be called by just their first name. At first, this was very hard for me to do. It still **seems** a little disrespectful, but I**'m getting** used to it.

Common Last Names Around the World	
ARABIC	Ali, Ahmed, Haddad
CHINESE	Zhang, Wang, Chen
ENGLISH	Smith, Jones, Williams
JAPANESE	Satou, Suzuki, Takahashi
KOREAN	Kim, Lee, Park
RUSSIAN	Ivanov, Smirnov, Vasilev
SPANISH	García, Fernandez, Lopez
TURKISH	Özkan, Akcan, Gürbüz

AFTER YOU READ

Write **T** *(true) or* **F** *(false).*

_____ **1.** Yevdokiya is now in Canada.

_____ **2.** In Russia, she uses only her teacher's first name.

_____ **3.** Jorge is in Mexico City.

_____ **4.** He's going to change his first name.

Grammar Presentation

SIMPLE PRESENT

Affirmative Statements

They **live** in Mexico.
She always **works** here.

Negative Statements

They **don't live** in Mexico.
She **doesn't work** here.

***Yes / No* Questions**

Do they **live** in Mexico?
Does she **work** here?

Short Answers

Yes, they **do**.
Yes, she **does**.

No, they **don't**.
No, she **doesn't**.

***Wh-* Questions**

Where **do** they **live**?
Why **does** she **work** so hard?

PRESENT PROGRESSIVE

Affirmative Statements

Now, they**'re living** in Mexico.
She**'s working** here today.

Negative Statements

They **aren't living** in Mexico now.
She **isn't working** here now.

***Yes / No* Questions**

Are they **living** in Mexico now?
Is she **working** here now?

Short Answers

Yes, they **are**.
Yes, she **is**.

No, they **aren't**.
No, she **isn't**.

***Wh-* Questions**

Where **are** they **living** these days?
Why **is** she **working** so hard?

GRAMMAR NOTES   **EXAMPLES**

---

1. Use the **simple present** to describe what <u>generally happens</u> (but not necessarily right now).

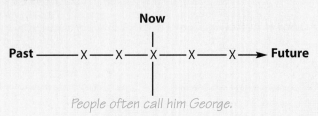

People often call him George.

Use the **present progressive** to describe what is happening <u>right now</u> or in the <u>extended present</u> (for example, *nowadays, this month, these days, this year*).

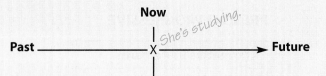

She's studying.

- People *often* **call** him George.
- We *never* **use** nicknames.
- The paper *usually* **arrives** at 7:00 A.M.

A: Where's Dusya?
B: At the library. She**'s studying**.
A: What's Jorge **doing** *these days*?
B: He**'s working** on a new project.

---

2. Remember that **non-action verbs** (also called *stative verbs*) are <u>not usually used in the progressive</u> even when they describe a situation that exists at the moment of speaking.

   Non-action verbs describe emotions *(love, hate)*; mental states *(remember, understand)*; wants *(need, want)*; perceptions *(hear, see)*; appearance *(look, seem)*; and possession *(have, own)*.

- I **want** to have a special name. NOT I'm wanting to have a special name.

- I **hate** my nickname.
- **Do** you **remember** her name?
- Jan **wants** to change her name.

---

3. Use the **simple present** to talk about situations that are <u>not connected to time</u>—for example, scientific facts and physical laws.

- Water **freezes** at 32°F (0°C).
- The Earth **orbits** the sun.

---

4. The **simple present** is often used in book or movie <u>reviews</u>.

- This book **gives** information about names. It also **talks** about giving gifts.

---

5. The **present progressive** is often used with *always* to express a <u>repeated action</u>.

   USAGE NOTE: We often use the present progressive to express a negative reaction to a situation.

- She**'s** *always* **smiling**. That's why we call her "Sunshine."

- He**'s** *always* **calling** me "Sweetie." I hate that name.

Reference Notes

For definitions and examples of **grammar terms**, see the Glossary.
For a list of **non-action verbs**, see Appendix 2 on page A-2.
For **spelling rules** on forming the **present progressive**, see Appendix 22 on page A-11.
For **spelling rules** on forming the third person singular of the **simple present**, see Appendix 21 on page A-11.
For **pronunciation rules** for the **simple present**, see Appendix 28 on page A-14.

Focused Practice

1 | DISCOVER THE GRAMMAR

Read this book review. Underline all the present progressive verbs and circle all the simple present verbs.

Are you <u>living</u> or <u>working</u> in a foreign country? (Do you worry) about making a mistake with someone's name? You are right to be concerned. Naming systems vary a lot from culture to culture, and people tend to have very strong feelings about their names. Well, now help is available in the form of an interesting and practical book by Terri Morrison. *Kiss, Bow, or Shake Hands: How to Do Business in Sixty Countries* gives information on cross-cultural naming customs and much more. And it's not just for businesspeople. In today's shrinking world, people are traveling abroad in record numbers. They're flying to all corners of the world, and they're e-mailing people they've never met. So, if you're doing business abroad **or** making friends across cultures, I recommend this book.

2 | PARTY TALK   *Grammar Notes 1–3, 5*

🎧 *Complete the conversations. Use the correct form of the verbs in parentheses—simple present or present progressive.*

A. IANTHA: Hi, I'm Iantha.

    AL: Nice to meet you, Iantha. I'm Alan, but my friends _____*call*_____ me Al.
                                           1. (call)

            Iantha is an unusual name. Where _____ it _____ from?
                                                           2. (come)

IANTHA: It's Greek. It _____ "violet-colored flower."
                        3. (mean)

    AL: That's pretty. What _____ you _____, Iantha?
                                               4. (do)

IANTHA: Well, I usually _____ computer equipment, but right now
                         5. (sell)

        I _____ at a flower shop. My uncle _____ it.
          6. (work)   **7. (own)**

    AL: You _____! I _____ it's true that names
               8. (joke)   **9. (guess)**

        _____ our lives!
        10. (influence)

B. MARIO: I _____ to find Greg Costanza. _____ you
             1. (try)

       _____ him?
       2. (know)

   BELLA: Greg? Oh, you _____ Lucky. That's his nickname. Everyone
                        3. (mean)

       _____ him Lucky because he _____ things.
       4. (call)   **5. (always win)**

(continued)

C. **LOLA:** I _____ that you _____ a baby. Have you decided on a
1. (hear)　　　　　　　　2. (expect)

name yet?

VANYA: We _____ naming the baby Mangena. What _____ you
3. (think of)

_____ that name?
4. (think about)

LOLA: It _____ pretty. How _____ you _____ it?
5. (sound)　　　　　　　　　　　　　　　6. (spell)

D. **ROSA:** Would you like a cup of coffee, Dr. Ho?

DR. HO: Oh. No, thanks. It _____ delicious, but I _____ coffee.
1. (smell)　　　　　　　　　　　　2. (not drink)

ROSA: Well, how about a cup of tea, then? The water _____. Why
3. (boil)

_____ water _____ so quickly here, Dr. Ho?
4. (boil)

DR. HO: In the mountains, water _____ at a lower temperature.
5. (boil)

3 | EDITING

Read this post to a class electronic bulletin board. There are eleven mistakes in the use of the present progressive and the simple present. The first mistake is already corrected. Find and correct ten more.

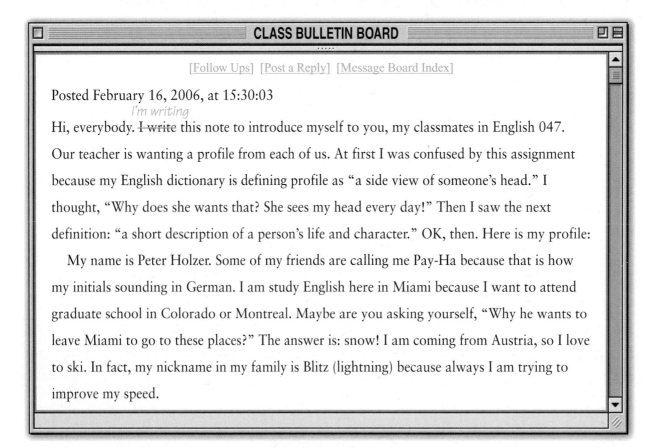

CLASS BULLETIN BOARD

[Follow Ups] [Post a Reply] [Message Board Index]

Posted February 16, 2006, at 15:30:03

I'm writing

Hi, everybody. ~~I write~~ this note to introduce myself to you, my classmates in English 047.

Our teacher is wanting a profile from each of us. At first I was confused by this assignment

because my English dictionary is defining profile as "a side view of someone's head." I

thought, "Why does she wants that? She sees my head every day!" Then I saw the next

definition: "a short description of a person's life and character." OK, then. Here is my profile:

　　My name is Peter Holzer. Some of my friends are calling me Pay-Ha because that is how

my initials sounding in German. I am study English here in Miami because I want to attend

graduate school in Colorado or Montreal. Maybe are you asking yourself, "Why he wants to

leave Miami to go to these places?" The answer is: snow! I am coming from Austria, so I love

to ski. In fact, my nickname in my family is Blitz (lightning) because always I am trying to

improve my speed.

Communication Practice

4 | LISTENING

🎧 *Listen to two classmates discuss these photos. Then listen again and label each photo with the correct name(s) from the box.*

~~Alex~~	Bertha	"Bozo"	Karl	Red	"Sunshine"	Vicki

a. _____

d. _____

b. _____ *Alex* _____

e. _____

c. _____

f. _____ and _____

5 | GETTING TO KNOW YOU

A *Write down your full name on a piece of paper. Your teacher will collect all the papers and redistribute them. Walk around the room. Introduce yourself to other students and try to find the person whose name you have on your piece of paper.*

Example: **A:** Hi. I'm Jelena.
B: I'm Eddy.
A: I'm looking for Kadin Al-Tattany. Do you know him?
B: I think that's him over there. OR Sorry, I don't.

B *When you find the person you are looking for, find out about his or her name. You can ask some of these questions:*

What does your name mean?

Which part of your name is your family name?

Do you use a title? (for example, Ms., Miss, Mrs., Mr.)

What do your friends call you?

Do you have a nickname?

What do you prefer to be called?

How do you feel about your name?

Other: _____

Example: **A:** What does Kadin mean?
B: It means "friend" or "companion." It's Arabic.
OR I don't know what it means.

You can also ask some general questions such as:

Where do you come from?

Where are you living now?

Why are you studying English?

Other: _____

C *Finally, introduce your classmate to the rest of the class.*

Example: **A:** This is Henka Krol. Henka comes from Poland. Her name means "ruler of the house or home."

6 | WRITING

Write a profile to introduce yourself to your class. Write about your name, your interests and hobbies, and your plans. Use the simple present and present progressive. You can use the profile in Exercise 3 as a model.

Example: My name is Thuy Nguyen, but my American friends call me Tina.

7 | ON THE INTERNET

C *There are many websites about names. Do a search to find out information about a name—your own name or another person's name. Use key words such as **Russian first names** or **Mexican surnames**. Share your information with a group.*

Simple Past and Past Progressive

Grammar in Context

BEFORE YOU READ

🎧 *Look at the photos here and on the next page. Which couples do you recognize? What do you know about them? Do you know how they met? Read this article about four famous couples.*

BEARING LOIS IN HIS ARMS SUPERMAN HEADS TOWARD THE CITY — —

Superman and Lois Lane

SUPER COUPLES

Cover Story by Dennis Brooks

It's a bird, . . . it's a plane, . . . it's Superman! Disguised as Clark Kent, this world-famous character **met** Lois Lane while the two **were working** as newspaper reporters for the *Daily Planet*. At first Lois **wasn't** interested in mild-mannered Kent—she **wanted** to cover stories about "The Man of Steel." In time, she **changed** her mind. When Kent **proposed**, Lois **accepted**. (And she **didn't** even **know** he **was** Superman!)

Like Superman and Lois Lane, some names just seem to belong together: Marie and Pierre Curie, Gloria and Emilio Estefan, or Ekaterina Gordeeva and Sergei Grinkov. What **were** these other super couples **doing** when they **met**? What **did** they **accomplish** together? Let's find out.

(continued)

SUPER COUPLES

When she **was** 24, Maria Sklodowska **left** Poland and **moved** to Paris. While she **was studying** at the Sorbonne, she **met** physicist Pierre Curie. She **was planning** to return to Poland after her studies, but the two scientists **fell** in love and **got** married. While they **were raising** their daughters, they **were** also **doing** research on radioactivity. In 1903, the Curies **won** the Nobel Prize in physics. Then, in 1906, a horse-drawn carriage **hit** and **killed** Pierre while he **was** out **walking**. When Marie **recovered** from the shock, she **continued** their work. In 1911, she **received** her second Nobel Prize.

Marie and Pierre Curie

Gloria and Emilio Estefan

CONGA! In 1985, millions of people **were listening** to this hit song. It **made** singer Gloria Estefan and bandleader Emilio Estefan international stars. Born in Cuba, Gloria **was** only 16 months old when she and her family **moved** to the United States. By that time she **was** already **showing** musical talent. She **met** Emilio when he **spoke** to her high school music class. Soon after, she **joined** his group. The two **married** a few years later. They **were enjoying** their success in the music business when Gloria **broke** her back in a 1990 traffic accident. She **recovered** and **went on** to win many awards for her Spanish and English songs.

She **was** only 11 and he **was** 15 when their coaches **brought** them together as skating partners. Off the ice, Sergei **didn't pay** much attention to "Katia." However, that **changed** in 1988 when the pair **won** their first Olympic gold medal for the former Soviet Union. World-famous skaters Ekaterina Gordeeva and Sergei Grinkov **thrilled** their fans when they **married** two years later. A baby girl and another Olympic gold medal **followed**. Their lives **seemed** perfect. Then one day Sergei **collapsed** while they **were practicing**. He **died** an hour later. Today Gordeeva is remarried and has a new skating partner.

*Ekaterina Gordeeva
and Sergei Grinkov*

AFTER YOU READ

Answer these questions.

1. Look at the information about Superman and Lois Lane. Find a sentence that describes two events that happened one after the other.

   _____

2. Look at the information about the Curies. Find a sentence that describes two things that were happening at the same time.

   _____

3. Look at the information about Gloria and Emilio Estefan. Find a sentence that describes something that was happening at a specific time.

_____

4. Look at the information about Gordeeva and Grinkov. Find a sentence that describes one event that happened while something else was going on.

_____

Grammar Presentation

SIMPLE PAST

Affirmative Statements
Marie **studied** at the Sorbonne.

Negative Statements
Lois **didn't plan** to marry Clark at first.

Yes / No Questions	Short Answers
Did he **teach**?	**Yes**, he **did**. **No**, he **didn't**.

Wh- Questions
Where **did** they **practice**?

Simple Past and Simple Past
We **won** when we **skated** there.

Simple Past and Past Progressive
She **met** him while she **was studying**.

PAST PROGRESSIVE

Affirmative Statements
She **was studying** at the Sorbonne in 1892.

Negative Statements
She **wasn't planning** to get married.

Yes / No Questions	Short Answers
Was he **doing** research?	**Yes**, he **was**. **No**, he **wasn't**.

Wh- Questions
Where **were** they **practicing**?

Past Progressive and Past Progressive
We **were winning** while we **were skating** there.

Past Progressive and Simple Past
She **was studying** when she **met** him.

GRAMMAR NOTES   **EXAMPLES**

---

1. Use the **simple past** to describe an action that was <u>completed</u> at a specific time in the past.

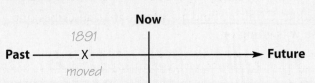

- Marie **moved** to Paris in 1891.
- The Curies **won** the Nobel Prize in 1903.

---

2. Use the **past progressive** to describe an action that was <u>in progress</u> at a specific time in the past. The action began before the specific time and may or may not continue after the specific time.

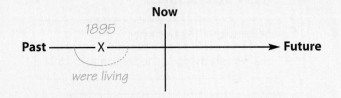

REMEMBER! Non-action verbs are not usually used in the progressive.

- The Curies **were living** in Paris in 1895.
- She **was studying** at the Sorbonne.

- Marie **had** a degree in physics. NOT Marie ~~was having~~ a degree in physics.

---

3. Use the **past progressive** with the **simple past** to talk about an action that was <u>interrupted by another action</u>. Use the simple past for the interrupting action.

Connect the two actions with:

> *while* + past progressive

> OR

> *when* + simple past

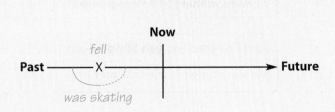

- They **were driving** when the accident **occurred**.

- *While* he **was skating**, he **fell**.

  OR

- He **was skating** *when* he **fell**.

4. You can use the **past progressive** with *while* or *when* to talk about two actions <u>in progress at the same time</u> in the past. Use the past progressive in both clauses.

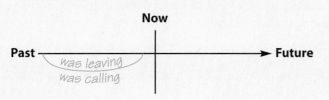

- *While* Clark **was leaving** the newsroom, Lois **was calling** the police.
- *When* she **wasn't looking**, he **was changing** into Superman.

5. **BE CAREFUL!** Sentences with two clauses in the simple past have a very different meaning from sentences with one clause in the simple past and one clause in the past progressive.

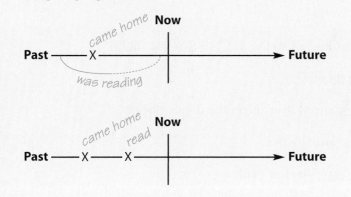

- When he **came** home, she **was reading** the paper.
  (First she started reading the paper. Then he came home.)

- When he **came** home, she **read** the paper.
  (First he came home. Then she read the paper.)

Reference Note
For a list of **irregular past verbs**, see Appendix 1 on pages A-1–A-2.

Focused Practice

1 | DISCOVER THE GRAMMAR

Read these people's descriptions of how they met important people in their lives. Decide if the statement that follows is true (T) or false (F).

1. **LUCKY:** I was riding home on my bike when I saw Elena on a park bench.

   __F__ Lucky saw Elena before he got on his bike.

2. **ROD:** I was climbing a mountain when I met my best friend, Ian.

   _____ Ian was on the mountain.

3. **MARIE:** How did I meet Philippe? I was sitting at home when the phone rang. When I answered it, it was the wrong number, but we spoke for an hour!

   _____ Marie knew Philippe before they spoke on the phone.

(continued)

4. **DON:** When I first met Ana, I was working in a restaurant. She was a customer.

_____ Don started his restaurant job after he met Ana.

5. **TONY:** How did I meet my wife? Actually, it was kind of like a blind date. My cousins invited her to dinner while I was living at their place.

_____ Tony moved in with his cousins after he met his wife.

6. **MONICA:** I was taking an English class while Dania was taking Spanish. We met in the hall during a break.

_____ Monica and Dania were students at the same time.

2 | SAD ENDINGS

Grammar Notes 1–5

Complete the conversations. Circle the correct verbs.

A. **LILY:** Guess what! I <u>was seeing</u> / (saw) Gloria Estefan at Club Rio last night.
1.

   TONY: What <u>was</u> / <u>did</u> she <u>do</u> / <u>doing</u> there?
   2.   3.

   LILY: She and Emilio <u>were dancing</u> / <u>danced</u> near us on the dance floor.
   4.

   TONY: <u>Were</u> / <u>Did</u> you <u>getting</u> / <u>get</u> her autograph?
   5.   6.

   LILY: Yes. And then she <u>was giving</u> / <u>gave</u> me her pen!
   7.

   TONY: <u>Were</u> / <u>Did</u> you <u>bringing</u> / <u>bring</u> it with you? I want to see it!
   8.   9.

   LILY: No. It <u>was falling</u> / <u>fell</u> out of my pocket when someone <u>was bumping</u> / <u>bumped</u> into
   10.   11.

   me. I never <u>was finding</u> / <u>found</u> it.
   12.

B. **TARO:** What <u>were</u> / <u>did</u> you <u>doing</u> / <u>do</u> when you <u>were breaking</u> / <u>broke</u> your arm?
   1.   2.   3.

   KIWA: I <u>was skating</u> / <u>skated</u> with my boyfriend. We <u>were pretending</u> / <u>pretended</u> to be
   4.   5.

   Gordeeva and Grinkov. Jon <u>was dropping</u> / <u>dropped</u> me while he <u>was lifting</u> / <u>lifted</u>
   6.   7.

   me over his head!

C. **JASON:** Are you OK, Erin? <u>Were</u> / <u>Did</u> you <u>crying</u> / <u>cry</u>?
   1.   2.

   ERIN: Yes, but how <u>were</u> / <u>did</u> you <u>knowing</u> / <u>know</u>? I <u>wasn't crying</u> / <u>didn't cry</u> when you
   3.   4.   5.

   <u>were coming</u> / <u>came</u> in.
   6.

   JASON: Your eyes are red.

   ERIN: The ice-skating competition was on TV. While I <u>was watching</u> / <u>watched</u>,
   7.

   I <u>was thinking</u> / <u>thought</u> about Sergei Grinkov.
   8.

3 | HAPPY ENDINGS

Complete the conversations. Use the correct form of the verbs in parentheses—simple past or past progressive.

A. PAZ: What _____ *were* _____ you _____ *looking* _____ at just then? You

               1. (look)

        _____.

           2. (smile)

  EVA: I _____ the video of Nicole's wedding. She _____ so

           3. (watch)   4. (look)

    excited and happy.

  PAZ: How _____ she and Matt _____?

                        5. (meet)

  EVA: At my graduation party. Matt almost _____. He _____ for

                   6. (not come)   7. (study)

    a big exam. Luckily, he _____ his mind. The rest is history.

                   8. (change)

B. DAN: I _____ your Superman web page while I _____ the

          1. (find)   2. (surf)

    Internet. It's great.

  DEE: Thanks. When _____ you _____ a Superman fan?

                      3. (become)

  DAN: Years ago. I _____ a comic book when I _____ to marry

           4. (read)   5. (decide)

    Lois Lane! Just kidding. I _____ to *draw* Lois Lane—and Superman and

                 6. (want)

    Wonder Woman.

  DEE: Me too. In fact, I _____ graphic arts when I _____ my

             7. (study)   8. (start)

    web page.

C. LARA: _____ Jason _____ you when he _____

                 1. (surprise)   2. (come)

    over last night?

  ERIN: Yes! I _____ some ice skaters on TV when he _____ on

           3. (watch)   4. (knock)

    the door. When the show _____, we _____ a delicious

                   5. (end)   6. (have)

    dinner. And while we _____, Jason _____ me to marry

               7. (eat)   8. (ask)

    him!

  LARA: That's great. Congratulations!

4 | TIME LINE
Grammar Notes 3–5

*This time line shows some important events in Monique's life. Use the time line and the cues below to write sentences about her. Use **when** or **while**.*

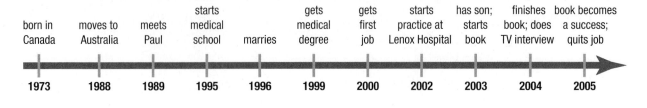

born in Canada	moves to Australia	meets Paul	starts medical school	marries	gets medical degree	gets first job	starts practice at Lenox Hospital	has son; starts book	finishes book; does TV interview	book becomes a success; quits job
1973	1988	1989	1995	1996	1999	2000	2002	2003	2004	2005

1. moves to Australia / meets Paul   *She met Paul when she moved to Australia.*

2. gets married / studies medicine   *She got married while she was studying medicine.*

3. lives in Australia / gets married _____

4. receives medical degree / gets her first job _____

5. practices medicine at Lenox Hospital / has a son _____

6. writes a book / works at Lenox Hospital _____

7. does a TV interview / finishes her book _____

8. leaves job / her book becomes a success _____

5 | EDITING

Read Monique's letter to a friend. There are eleven mistakes in the use of the simple past and the past progressive. The first mistake is already corrected. Find and correct ten more.

Dear Crystal,

    I was writing chapter two of my new book when I ~~was thinking~~ *thought* of you. The last time I saw you, you walked down the aisle to marry Dave. That was more than two years ago. How are you? How is married life?

    A lot has happened in my life since that time. While I worked at Lenox Hospital, I began writing. In 2004, I was publishing a book on women's health issues. It was quite successful here in Australia. I even got interviewed on TV. When I was getting a contract to write a second book, I decided to quit my hospital job to write full-time. That's what I'm doing now. Paul, too, has had a career change. While I was writing, he was attending law school. He was getting his degree last summer.

    Oh, the reason I thought of you while I wrote was because the chapter was about rashes. Remember the time you were getting that terrible rash? We rode our bikes when you were falling into a patch of poison ivy. And that's how you met Dave! When you were falling off the bike, he offered to give us a ride home. Life's funny, isn't it?

    Well, please write soon, and send my love to Dave. I miss you!

                                      Monique

Communication Practice

6 | LISTENING

🎧 *Listen to a woman explain how she met her husband. Then listen again and circle the letter of the series of pictures that illustrate her story.*

a.

b.

c.

7 | FIRST ENCOUNTERS

Work in small groups. Think about the first time you met someone important to you: a best friend, teacher, boyfriend or girlfriend, husband or wife. Tell your classmates about the meeting. What were you doing? What happened then?

Example: I was walking to class when this guy came over and asked me for the time . . .

8 | THE TIMES OF YOUR LIFE

Complete the time line with some important events in your life. Show it to a classmate. Answer your classmate's questions.

Event

Year

Example: A: Why did you move to Mexico City?
B: I was studying medicine, and I wanted to work in a big hospital.

9 | WRITING

Write a paragraph about a relationship that is important to you. How did you meet? What were you doing when you met? Describe some events in the relationship. Use the simple past and past progressive.

Example: I met my friend Dania while I was living in Germany . . .

10 | ON THE INTERNET

Do a search on a famous couple. Choose a pair you know about or one of these:

Lian Shanbo and Zhu Yingtai	Romeo and Juliet
Yuri Malenchenko and Ekaterina Dmitriev	Torville and Dean
Antony and Cleopatra	Eva Duarte and Juan Perón

*Make notes about some important events in their lives. What were they doing before they met? How did they meet? What happened after they met? Use **when** and **while** in your notes. Compare notes with a partner or in a small group.*

Simple Past, Present Perfect, and Present Perfect Progressive

Grammar in Context

BEFORE YOU READ

🎧 *Look at the photo. What are the people doing? Have you ever participated in an adventure sport? Read this personal website.*

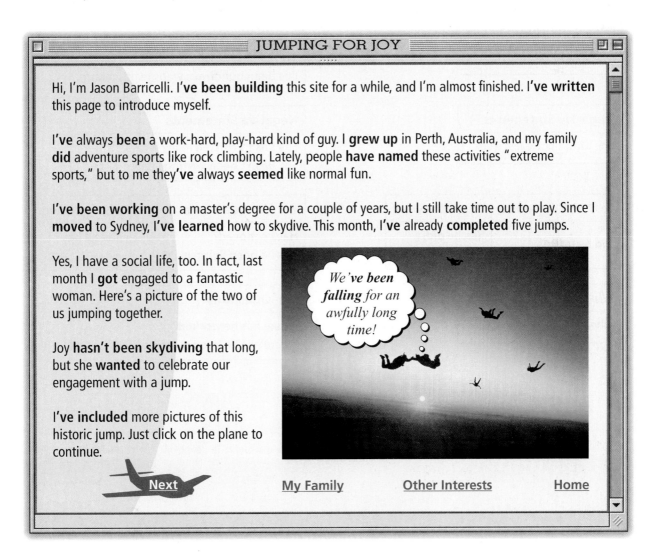

> ═══ JUMPING FOR JOY ═══
>
> Hi, I'm Jason Barricelli. I**'ve been building** this site for a while, and I'm almost finished. I**'ve written** this page to introduce myself.
>
> I**'ve** always **been** a work-hard, play-hard kind of guy. I **grew up** in Perth, Australia, and my family **did** adventure sports like rock climbing. Lately, people **have named** these activities "extreme sports," but to me they**'ve** always **seemed** like normal fun.
>
> I**'ve been working** on a master's degree for a couple of years, but I still take time out to play. Since I **moved** to Sydney, I**'ve learned** how to skydive. This month, I**'ve** already **completed** five jumps.
>
> Yes, I have a social life, too. In fact, last month I **got** engaged to a fantastic woman. Here's a picture of the two of us jumping together.
>
> *We've been falling for an awfully long time!*
>
> Joy **hasn't been skydiving** that long, but she **wanted** to celebrate our engagement with a jump.
>
> I**'ve included** more pictures of this historic jump. Just click on the plane to continue.
>
> Next   **My Family**   **Other Interests**   **Home**

AFTER YOU READ

Write **T** *(true) or* **F** *(false).*

_____ 1. Jason is still building his website.

_____ 2. Jason has a master's degree.

_____ 3. He was living in Perth when he started skydiving.

_____ 4. Jason is married.

Grammar Presentation

SIMPLE PAST

Affirmative Statements
I **built** a website last month.

Negative Statements
She **didn't write** last week.

Yes / No Questions	Short Answers
Did he **move**?	**Yes**, he **did**. **No**, he **didn't**.

Wh- Questions
Where **did** he **work**?

PRESENT PERFECT
PRESENT PERFECT PROGRESSIVE

Affirmative Statements
I**'ve built** a website.   I**'ve been building** a website this month.

Negative Statements
She **hasn't written** many letters.   She **hasn't been writing** lately.

Yes / No Questions	Short Answers
Has he **moved**? **Has** he **been living** in Perth?	**Yes**, he **has**. **No**, he **hasn't**.

Wh- Questions
Where **has** he **worked**?   Where **has** he **been working**?

GRAMMAR NOTES   **EXAMPLES**

---

1. Use the **simple past** to talk about things that happened and were <u>completed in the past</u>.

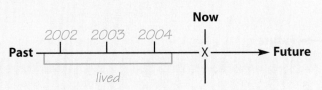

Use the **simple past** with *ago* to show when something started.

- I **lived** in Perth for three years.
  (I don't live in Perth now.)

- I **moved** there five years *ago*.

---

2. Use the **present perfect** and the **present perfect progressive** to talk about things that started in the past but were <u>not completed</u>. These things continue up to the present and may continue into the future.

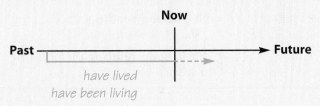

REMEMBER! Non-action (stative) verbs are not usually used in the progressive.

- I**'ve lived** in Perth my whole life.
  OR
- I**'ve been living** in Perth my whole life.
  (I was born in Perth, and I'm still living there today.)

- I**'ve known** Joy for a long time.
  NOT I've ~~been knowing~~ Joy for a long time.

---

3. We often use the **present perfect** and the **present perfect progressive** with *for* and *since*.

Use *for* **+ a length of time** to show <u>how long</u> a present condition has been true.

Use *since* **+ a point of time** to show <u>when</u> a present condition <u>started</u>.

- He**'s lived** in Sydney *for two years*.

- He**'s lived** in Sydney *since 2004*.
- He**'s been living** there *since he graduated*.

---

4. Use the **simple past** with <u>past time expressions</u>.

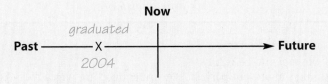

▶ BE CAREFUL! Don't use specific time expressions with the present perfect except after *since*.

- He **graduated** *in 2004*.
- He **moved** to Sydney *last year*.

- He**'s known** his wife *since 2003*.
- He **met** his wife *in 2003*.
  NOT He ~~has met~~ his wife in 2003.

(continued)

5. Use the **present perfect** <u>without time expressions</u> to talk about things that happened at some indefinite time in the past.

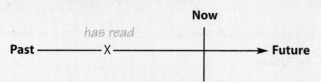

BE CAREFUL! *She's read a book* and *She's been reading a book* have very different meanings.

a. The **present perfect** without *for* or *since* shows that an activity is <u>finished</u>. We often say *how many* or *how many times* with this use of the present perfect.

b. The **present perfect progressive** shows that an activity is <u>unfinished</u>. We often say *how long* with the present perfect progressive.

- She**'s read** a book about skydiving. *(We don't know when she read the book, or the time is not important.)*

- She**'s read** the book. *(She's finished the book.)*
- She**'s read** *three books* about skydiving.
- She**'s read** that book *three times*.

- She**'s been reading** a book. *(She's still reading it.)*
- She**'s been reading** the book *for a week*.

6. Use the **present perfect** or the **simple past** with <u>unfinished time periods</u> such as *today, this week, this month,* and *this year.*

Use the **present perfect** for things that <u>might happen again</u> in that time period.

Use the **simple past** for things that <u>probably won't happen again</u> in that period.

BE CAREFUL! *This morning, this afternoon,* and *this evening* can be either unfinished or finished. Use the **simple past** if the time period is <u>finished</u>.

- He**'s jumped** three times *this month*. *(The month isn't over. He might jump again.)*

- He **jumped** three times *this month*. *(The month isn't over, but he probably won't jump again this month.)*

- I**'ve had** three cups of coffee *this morning*. *(It's still morning.)*

- I **had** three cups of coffee *this morning*. *(It's now afternoon.)*

Reference Notes

For a list of **irregular past verbs**, see Appendix 1 on pages A-1–A-2.

For a list of **irregular past participles** used in forming the **present perfect**, see Appendix 1 on pages A-1–A-2.

Focused Practice

1 | DISCOVER THE GRAMMAR

A *Read this newspaper article about a wedding. Circle all the simple past verbs.
Underline all the present perfect verbs.*

Nancy Board and Erden Erduc of Seattle, Washington, have always loved the outdoors, so Alaska was a natural choice for their wedding. Nancy flew there for the June 7 ceremony, but Erden started in February and rode his bike. Then he climbed Mt. Denali. Unfortunately, he ran into some bad weather, so the wedding was a week late. Nancy understood. She has been an adventure athlete for years.

The wedding was a Native American ceremony on the beach of Lake Wonder. The couple told a reporter, "We wanted . . . a combination of meeting new people, meeting new cultures, and experiencing history and nature."

Erden, an engineer, has earned degrees from universities in Turkey and the United States. He has been climbing since he was 11, and for years he's been dreaming about an around-the-world climbing trip. In 2003, he left his job to begin the adventure. Mt. Denali was the first of six climbs on six continents. Erden has been living in Seattle since 1999.

Nancy, a psychotherapist, has been president of her own business in Seattle since 2003. In the last few years, she has been using her outdoor experience to teach leadership skills.

B *Now read the statements and write* **T** *(true),* **F** *(false), or* **?** *(the information isn't in the article).*

___F___ **1.** In the past, Nancy and Erden loved the outdoors.

_____ **2.** Nancy and Erden got married on June 7.

_____ **3.** Erden left for Alaska before Nancy.

_____ **4.** Nancy started adventure sports a year ago.

_____ **5.** Erden started climbing at the age of 11.

_____ **6.** He got his degree in Turkey in 1989.

_____ **7.** He started dreaming about this trip in 2001.

_____ **8.** He moved to Seattle in 1999.

_____ **9.** Nancy started her business in 2003.

_____ **10.** She teaches leadership skills.

2 | DOWN-TO-EARTH HOBBIES
Grammar Notes 1–6

Complete the article about another hobby. Circle the correct verbs.

MOVE OVER, BARBIE!

Ty Warner has been making / made toys since
1.
1986. In 1992, he has gotten / got the idea to make
2.
stuffed animals that children could afford. The first

nine Beanie Babies® have appeared / appeared in
3.
stores just one year later. Pattie the Platypus and

her eight companions have sold out / sold out
4.
immediately. Ever since then, store owners have been having / had a hard time keeping
5.
Beanies on the shelves. In the 1990s, the fad has become / became an international craze,
6.
and the Babies are still popular around the world today. More than 2 billion fans

have visited / have been visiting Ty's website, and not long ago, one toy collector
7.
has been paying / paid an amazing $24,000 for a Beanie. Which reminds me—I'd like to
8.
discuss some trades. Have you found / Have you been finding Iggy the Iguana yet?
9.

3 | OTHER PEOPLE, OTHER INTERESTS
Grammar Notes 1–6

Complete the paragraphs about other people's interests. Use the correct form of the verbs in parentheses—simple past, present perfect, or present perfect progressive.

A.   May __has been taking__ photos ever since her parents _____ her a camera
1. (take)   2. (buy)

when she _____ only 10. At first she only _____ color snapshots
3. (be)   4. (take)

of friends and family, but then she _____ to black and white. Lately she
5. (change)

_____ a lot of nature photographs. This year she _____ in three
6. (shoot)   7. (compete)

amateur photography contests. In fact, last month she _____ second prize for
8. (win)

her nighttime photo of a lightning storm.

B. Carlos _____ playing music when he _____ an electric guitar
               1. (begin)   **2. (get)**

for his twelfth birthday. He _____ playing since. In fact, the guitar
                                      3. (not stop)

_____ more than just a way of having some fun with his friends. Last year he
     4. (become)

_____ a local band. Since then, they _____ all over town. So far
     5. (join)   **6. (perform)**

this year, they _____ six concerts, and they have plans for many more.
               7. (give)

C. Kate _____ a beautiful old stamp last month. It is now part of the collection
             1. (find)

she _____ on for the past two years. At first she just _____
      2. (work)   **3. (save)**

stamps from letters that she _____ from friends. After a while, though, she
                         4. (get)

_____ to look more actively for stamps. Lately, she _____ them
     5. (begin)   **6. (buy)**

from special stores and _____ stamps with other collectors. So far she
                   7. (trade)

_____ over 200 stamps from all over the world.
     8. (find)

4 | EDITING

Read this e-mail message. There are nine mistakes in the use of the present perfect, present perfect progressive, and the simple past. The first mistake is already corrected. Find and correct eight more.

Dear Erden,

have been doing
I ~~am doing~~ adventure sports for about two years, and this year I've been joining a

climbing club. All the members followed your trip on the *Around-n-Over* website since

last January, but I haven't been written to you before. I have a few questions. I know

you have been climbing Mt. Erciyes in Turkey many years ago. Will you climb it again

on this project? Also, you have traveling to different continents. How have you

communicated with people? Did you study other languages before your trip? Last

month, I have seen an article about your project in *Hooked on the Outdoors Magazine.*

You've became famous! Have you received many e-mails since you start your project?

Thanks for answering my questions, and good luck!

Lise Bettmann

Communication Practice

🎧 *Jason and Joy have been planning their honeymoon trip. Look at their* To Do *list and listen to their phone conversation. Then listen again and check the things that they've already done.*

TO DO

- ☐ renew passports
- ☑ pick up plane tickets
- ☐ read skydiving guide
- ☐ make reservations at Hotel Splendor
- ☐ stop mail for two weeks
- ☐ buy bathing suit (Joy)

What did you plan to accomplish last week? Make a list. Include things you did and things that you still haven't done. Do not check any of the items. Exchange lists with a partner.

> **Example:** Write to my aunt.
> Clean out the car.

Now ask questions about your partner's list. Check the things that your partner has already done. Answer your partner's questions about your list. When you are done, compare your answers.

> **Example:** A: Have you written to your aunt?
> B: Yes. I wrote her a letter last weekend, but I haven't mailed it yet.

Work in small groups. Ask and answer questions about your hobbies and interests. Compare your experiences.

> **Example:** A: I've been collecting stamps since I was 11.
> B: Me too. Have you ever found a very rare stamp?
> A: Yes, once I . . .
> B: I've never found a rare stamp, but I've . . .

8 | WRITING

Write a few paragraphs about yourself for a personal website like the one on page 19. Tell about your interests and hobbies. Use the simple past, present perfect, and present perfect progressive.

Example: Welcome! I'm Steffie Hart. I've been living in Tokyo since 2004. I built this website to record my experience here. I've posted a lot of photos. I hope you enjoy them.

9 | ON THE INTERNET

© *Do a search on an adventure travel team. Choose one you know about or one of these:*

Ergen Erduc and his Around-n-Over team

Ann Bancroft and Liv Arneson

Make notes about what you learn. What is their current project? What have they accomplished so far? What did they do last year? What have they been doing lately? Discuss the information with a partner.

You and your partner can send an e-mail to the team with your questions.

Example: Dear Ann and Liv,
We've been reading about your new project and we have some questions. Why did you decide to go to the Arctic? How did you get there? How long have you been training for this trip?

Past Perfect and Past Perfect Progressive

Grammar in Context

BEFORE YOU READ

🎧 *Look at the photo. What do you think happened before the photo was taken? Read this article about film director Ang Lee.*

and the winner is . . .

It was March 2001, and Ang Lee was accepting his Oscar for the Best Foreign Film of 2000. *Crouching Tiger, Hidden Dragon* **had received** ten Oscar nominations (more than any foreign language film **had** ever **gotten**). By the end of the evening, it **had won** four Oscars.

Before this, Lee **had made** big, successful English language movies and small, award-winning Chinese language films. But this film was something new—a big, successful, Chinese-language film with an international audience and both Chinese and Hollywood producers.

Ang Lee is a brilliant director, but amazingly, his career almost didn't happen. Lee started college in Taiwan and then transferred to a college in the United States. By 1985, he **had gotten married** and **finished** his studies, but he had no job. He was ready to return to Taiwan when he learned that his student film **had won** an award. Lee and his wife stayed in the United States.

By 1991, Lee was desperate. He **had had** no success. For six years, his wife **had been working** as a researcher, and he **had been writing** scripts and **taking care** of their son. It was the lowest point of his life, he recalls. They **had** just **had** their second son, and when Lee went to the bank to get some money for diapers, the screen showed $26 left. But Lee **had entered** two scripts in a competition, and soon after that awful day, they both won. He directed both films, and one of them, *The Wedding Banquet*, earned millions. Lee **had become** a successful director.

Oscars, March 2001
*Making a martial arts film **had always been** Taiwanese director Ang Lee's dream.*

and the winner is . . .

Lee went on to direct *Eat, Drink, Man, Woman* in Taiwan, *Sense and Sensibility* in England, two more movies in the United States, and *Crouching Tiger* in China. When he picked up his Oscar in 2001, he **had achieved** his boyhood dream of making a martial arts movie— but he **had** also **brought** together cultures, languages, and styles in a way no filmmaker **had** ever **done** before.

Entertainment Today

AFTER YOU READ

*Put these events in Ang Lee's career in the correct chronological order (***1** = first, **4** = last).*

_____ Lee finished his studies in the United States.

_____ *The Wedding Banquet* won a competition.

_____ The Lees had their second child.

_____ Lee started to write scripts.

Grammar Presentation

PAST PERFECT

Statements			
Subject	*Had (not)*	**Past Participle**	
I You He She It We You They	**had (not)**	**received** **gotten**	awards.

Contractions		
I had	=	**I'd**
you had	=	**you'd**
he had	=	**he'd**
she had	=	**she'd**
we had	=	**we'd**
they had	=	**they'd**
had not	=	**hadn't**

Yes / No Questions			
Had	**Subject**	**Past Participle**	
Had	I you he she it we you they	**received** **gotten**	awards by then?

(continued)

Short Answers					
Affirmative			**Negative**		
Yes,	you I he she it we you they	**had**.	**No**,	you I he she it we you they	**hadn't**.

Wh- Questions				
Wh- Word	*Had*	Subject	Past Participle	
When	**had**	he	**received**	awards?

PAST PERFECT PROGRESSIVE

Statements		
Subject	*Had (not) been*	Base Form + *-ing*
I You He She It We You They	**had (not) been**	**working** regularly.

Yes / No Questions			
Had	Subject	*Been* + Base Form + *-ing*	
Had	I you he she it we you they	**been working**	regularly?

Short Answers					
Affirmative			**Negative**		
Yes,	you I he she it we you they	**had**.	**No**,	you I he she it we you they	**hadn't**.

Wh- Questions			
Wh- Word	*Had*	Subject	*Been* + Base Form + *-ing*
How long	**had**	he	**been working**?

GRAMMAR NOTES

EXAMPLES

1. Use the **past perfect** to show that something happened <u>before a specific time</u> in the past.

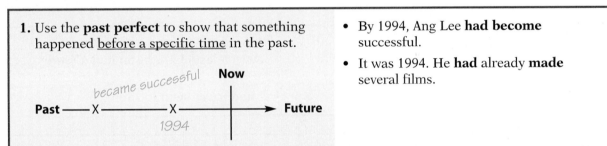

- By 1994, Ang Lee **had become** successful.
- It was 1994. He **had** already **made** several films.

2. Use the **past perfect progressive** to talk about an action that was <u>in progress before a specific time</u> in the past. The progressive emphasizes the continuing activity, not the end result.

Now

1992   2000

Past ─────────────────────→ Future

directing films

REMEMBER! Non-action (stative) verbs are not usually used in the progressive.

- **By** 2000, Lee **had been directing** films for eight years.

- It was 5:00 P.M. He **had had** a headache all day.
  NOT He ~~had been having~~ a headache all day.

3. We often use the **past perfect progressive** to <u>draw conclusions</u> based on evidence.

- She was out of breath. It was clear that she **had been running**.

(continued)

4. Use the **past perfect** and the **past perfect progressive** to show a relationship with a past time or another past event.

Use the **past perfect** or the **past perfect progressive** for the <u>earlier event</u>. Use the **simple past** for the <u>later time or event</u>.

▶ **BE CAREFUL!** In sentences with *when*, notice the difference in meaning between:

  a. the **simple past** and the **past perfect**

  b. the **past progressive** and the **past perfect progressive**

- It **was** 1980. She **had been** an author for two years.
  (She was an author before 1980.)

- He **had been working** at home when his scripts **won** a competition.
  (He was working at home. Then his scripts won a competition.)

- *When* the movie ended, she **left**.
  (First the movie ended. Then she left.)
- *When* the movie ended, she **had left**.
  (First she left. Then the movie ended.)

- *When* the filming started, it **was raining**.
  (It was still raining during the filming.)
- *When* the filming started, it **had been raining** and the streets were wet.
  (It wasn't raining during the filming. It had already stopped.)

---

5. Use *already*, *yet*, *ever*, *never*, and *just* with the **past perfect** to emphasize the event which occurred first.

- Jason and I saw *Crouching Tiger, Hidden Dragon* last night. Jason **had** *already* **seen** it.
- I **had** *never* **seen** it before.

---

6. When the time relationship between two past events is clear (as with *before*, *after*, and *as soon as*), we often use the **simple past for both events**.

- *After* Lee **had directed** *Eat, Drink, Man, Woman*, he **worked** on Hollywood movies.

                    OR

- *After* Lee **directed** *Eat, Drink, Man, Woman*, he **worked** on Hollywood movies.

---

7. We often use the **past perfect** and the **past perfect progressive** with *by* (a certain time).

- *By 1985*, Lee **had gotten** married.
- *By the time I got home*, he **had been waiting** for an hour.

Reference Notes
For a list of **irregular past participles**, see Appendix 1 on pages A-1–A-2.
For **spelling rules for progressive forms**, see Appendix 22 on page A-11.

Focused Practice

1 | DISCOVER THE GRAMMAR

Read each numbered situation. Decide if the description that follows is true (T) or false (F).
If there is not enough information to know, write a question mark (?).

1. When I found a seat, the movie started.

   ___F___ First the movie started. Then I found a seat.

2. When I found a seat, the movie had started.

   _____ First the movie started. Then I found a seat.

3. Cristina invited the director on her show because he had won an Oscar.

   _____ The guest won the Oscar after his appearance on the show.

4. Before the break, the guest had been explaining why he had made the film.

   _____ The guest's explanation was finished.

5. When I saw Mei Ling, her eyes were red. She had been crying.

   _____ She wasn't crying when I saw her.

2 | TIME LINE

Grammar Notes 1, 4–5, and 7

Look at some important events in Ang Lee's career. Then complete the sentences below.
Use the past perfect with **already** *or* **not yet**.

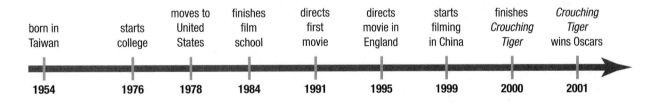

born in Taiwan	starts college	moves to United States	finishes film school	directs first movie	directs movie in England	starts filming in China	finishes *Crouching Tiger*	*Crouching Tiger* wins Oscars
1954	1976	1978	1984	1991	1995	1999	2000	2001

1. It was 1974. Lee _____*had not yet started*_____ college.

2. By 1985, he _____ film school.

3. By 1990, he _____ his first movie.

4. It was 1996. He _____ a movie in England.

5. By 1998, he _____ filming in China.

6. It was 1999. He _____ an Oscar.

7. By the end of 2000, he _____ *Crouching Tiger, Hidden Dragon.*

8. By 2002, *Crouching Tiger, Hidden Dragon* _____ four Oscars.

3 | **A BUSY DAY**   *Grammar Notes 1 and 5*

Carly worked as an "extra" actor in several movies last year. Read her journal notes about one job she had. Then complete the questions about her day and give short answers. Use the past perfect.

> DATE: *August 20, 2006*
>
> 6:00 A.M.   *My agent called about a job—she said to be there by 7 A.M.*
>
> 6:55   *Arrived at film location. Signed in, put on costume. I'm a farmer!*
>
> 7:30   *Waited for assignment—50 extras came today.*
>
> 10:30   *We all got jobs—running through a field. We did this 25 times.*
>
> 3:30 P.M.   *Lunch at last. Extras must eat after the regular crew finishes lunch.*
>
> 4:00   *We started running again.*
>
> 8:00   *We did it right! The director said to go home. He liked the scene!*
>
> 9:30   *Fell asleep before I ate dinner.*

1. It was 5:30 A.M. and Carly was awake.

    A: _____*Had her agent called*_____ about a job yet?

    B: _____*No, she hadn't.*_____

2. It was 7:00. Carly was on time.

    A: _____ at the film location yet?

    B: _____

3. At 8:00 she was waiting for an assignment.

    A: _____ her costume by that time?

    B: _____

4. At 2:30 she was running through a field.

    A: _____ lunch yet?

    B: _____

5. It was 4:00. The regular crew had finished lunch.

    A: _____ lunch yet?

    B: _____

6. It was 4:30 and lunch was over.

A: _____ running again yet?

B: _____

7. It was 7:30 and the extras were tired.

A: _____ it right yet?

B: _____

8. At 8:30. Carly was driving home.

A: _____ the scene?

B: _____

9. It was 10:00 and Carly was sleeping.

A: _____ dinner before she fell asleep?

B: _____

4 | HIDDEN LIVES

Complete the summary of the movie Crouching Tiger, Hidden Dragon. *Use the past perfect progressive form of the verbs in parentheses.*

In the early 1800s, three women traveled from western China to Beijing. The three women, Jen, Yu, and Jade Fox, _____*had been hiding*_____ the
1. (hide)
truth about their lives for years before their journey.

Jen, the daughter of a powerful family, traveled to Beijing for her wedding. For a long time, Jen

_____ martial arts secretly.
2. (practice)

Her parents _____ her
3. (plan)

marriage, but Jen _____ of a
4. (dream)

life as a fighter. Jen brought another secret with her

to Beijing—the family _____
5. (travel)

(continued)

across the desert when a group of bandits stopped their carriage and robbed them. Jen and the bandit leader Dark Cloud had fallen in love.

Yu, a skilled fighter, went to Beijing to deliver a valuable sword. She and the warrior Li Mu Bai were in love, but they _____ their feelings secret from each other for
6. (keep)

many years. Meanwhile, Yu _____ her family's business with great
7. (manage)

success.

Jade Fox, the third woman, had killed Li Mu Bai's martial arts teacher years before. Li

_____ for her for a long time. He hadn't found her because Jade Fox
8. (look)

_____ as a servant in Jen's home, where she _____
9. (hide)   10. (teach)

Jen martial arts.

All these warriors met in Beijing. Dark Cloud _____ the city for Jen.
11. (search)

He found her just before her wedding day. Li Mu Bai _____ to forget his
12. (try)

feelings for Yu, but he had failed. He found her in Beijing, but he also found Jade Fox. The ending

is tragic.

---

5 | BACKGROUND INFORMATION   *Grammar Notes 2–3 and 7*

*A talk-show host is trying to get some background information on a guest she is going to interview. Use **before** or **when** and the words in parentheses to write questions with the past perfect progressive.*

1. She won the Oscar for best actress. (she / act a long time?)

   Had she been acting a long time before she won the Oscar for best actress?

2. She acted in her first kung fu movie. (she / train long?)

   _____

3. She had a bad fall. (How long / they / filming?)

   _____

4. Newspaper reporters took pictures of her fall. (they / follow her?)

   _____

5. She married her director. (How long / they / date?)

   _____

6. She and her husband moved to Rome. (Where / they / live?)

_____

7. She quit her old job to act full-time. (What kind of work / she / do?)

_____

8. At the post-Oscar party her eyes were red. (she / cry?)

_____

6 | TROUBLED TEEN

Grammar Notes 1–3

Complete this description of a movie scene. Use the past perfect or past perfect progressive form of the appropriate verbs in the box. Use the progressive form when possible.

arrest	become	bring	have	hurt
leave	lose	recommend	~~see~~	

   The psychologist _____ _had seen_ _____ a hundred like him before. He sat on the
                                      1.
couch and stared out the window. He was only sixteen. His mother sat next to him. She

_____ him to see the psychologist.
            2.
She _____ control of her son. Ever
            3.
since his father _____ them four
                            4.
years before, she _____ trouble
                          5.
with her son. He _____ more and
                        6.
more angry and depressed.

   Recently he _____ someone in a
                          7.
school fight. The police _____ him
                                8.
and _____ psychological
          9.
counseling. The mother was afraid that he was going to run

away from home.

7 | LUCKY BREAKS

A talk-show host is interviewing an actor about her career. Complete the interview. Determine the correct order of the sentences in parentheses and use the past perfect or past perfect progressive to express the event that occurred first. Use the progressive form when possible.

HOST: When did you decide to work in films?

GUEST: (I made up my mind to work in films. / I was 10.)

  _____*I had made up my mind to work in films*_____ by the time _____*I was 10*_____.
  1.

HOST: How did you get your first paying job?

GUEST: (I was working with a student director. / He got a job.)

  _____ when _____.
  2.

  Then he hired *me*.

HOST: That was lucky! Did you work a lot after that?

GUEST: Yes, but not in films.

  (I worked in a restaurant for five years. / I got my next film job.)

  Before _____,
  3.

  _____ .

HOST: Did you do any acting at all in that time?

GUEST: Well, I got some jobs in TV ads.

  (I was selling cars on TV. / Louis Mille called me.)

  _____ when _____.
  4.

  (I almost decided to quit acting. / I hated that job.)

  _____ because _____.
  5.

HOST: The famous Louis Mille. What was that conversation like?

GUEST: Well, it's a good thing he couldn't see me.

  (He hung up. / I was jumping up and down for 10 minutes.)

  By the time _____, _____
  6.

  _____ .

8 | EDITING

Read this article about a martial arts expert. There are nine mistakes in the use of the past perfect and the past perfect progressive. The first mistake is already corrected. Find and correct eight more.

||||||||||||||||||||||||||||| MOVIES |||||||||||||||||||||||||||||||||||

In 1999, moviegoers gasped at the fighting sequences in *The Matrix* and were

                                                              had
amazed to learn that Keanu Reeves ~~has~~ actually performed those scenes himself.

Hong Kong director Yuen Wo Ping had trained the actors and designing the scenes.

At that time, Yuen was almost unknown in the United States, but he had already

have a long career.

Yuen was born in China in 1945. His father had been a kung fu actor, and he

trained Yuen in martial arts. When he was 25, Yuen began to design fight scenes

(by then, he had already been acted for 10 years). In 1978, he directed his first

film. *Snake in the Eagle's Shadow*, starring Jackie Chan, was a huge success.

Before he worked with Yuen, Chan had struggling to start his career. Yuen's films

made him famous.

In the 1980s, kung fu movies became less popular. Yuen turned to modern

action films, but with little success. By the end of the '90s, two things have happened:

Yuen had almost disappears from the movie business while Hollywood directors

have finally discovered high-flying Hong Kong fighting styles. When *The Matrix*

exploded on the screen, Western audiences saw something they had never been

seeing before, and Yuen was back in business. In 2001, Yuen repeated his success

in *Crouching Tiger, Hidden Dragon*, the first kung fu movie ever to receive

multiple Oscars.

Communication Practice

9 | LISTENING

🎧 *A talk-show host is interviewing a successful movie producer. Listen to the producer talk about some events in his life. Then read the list. Listen again and put the events in the correct chronological order.*

_____ Richard and Molly moved to New York.

__1__ Richard started selling newspaper advertising.

_____ Richard and Molly found an apartment in New York.

_____ They talked about returning to Utica.

_____ Lynn Costello called Richard and Molly.

10 | ACCOMPLISHMENTS

Think about what you did yesterday. Indicate whether it was or wasn't a busy day. Complete the sentences. Then compare your day with a classmate's.

> **Example:** **A:** By 9:00 A.M., I had made breakfast and taken the kids to school.
> **B:** By 9:00 A.M., I hadn't even gotten up!

Yesterday was / wasn't a busy day for me.

1. By 9:00 A.M., _____

2. By the time I got to work / school, _____

3. By the time I had lunch, _____

4. By the time I left work / school, _____

5. By the time I had dinner, _____

6. By 9:00 P.M., I _____

7. By the time I went to bed, I had done so much / little that I felt _____

11 | THERE'S ALWAYS A FIRST TIME

Think about things you had never done before you began living here (or before a certain year). Have a class discussion and write some of the results on the board. Possible topics: food, sports, clothing, entertainment, transportation.

> **Example:** Before I moved here, I had never eaten pizza or popcorn.

12 | THE NIGHT BEFORE

Imagine some friends stayed in your apartment when you were gone. When you came home, this is what you found. Work with a partner. Take turns describing what you saw and making guesses about what had been happening the night before you came home.

Example: There were CDs on the floor. They had been listening to music.

13 | WRITING

Write a journal entry explaining an achievement, for example, getting your driver's license, learning a new skill, or getting a job. In your journal entry, answer some of these questions: What had you been doing before your achievement? How did you prepare for it? Had you considered giving up before you succeeded? Use the past perfect and past perfect progressive.

Example: I got my driver's license yesterday. Before I got behind the wheel, I'd been worrying about the road test. But as soon as I started the car, I knew I could pass.

14 | ON THE INTERNET

Write a list of questions about an actor or director that you like. Then do a search and try to find the answers. Report your answers to a group.

Example: Questions about Michelle Yeoh

What problems did she have before she became successful?

What had she been doing before she made her first movie?

Has she won any awards?

What had she accomplished before she was in the award-winning film?

From **Grammar** to **Writing**
Editing for Verb Forms

When a paragraph includes more than one time frame (both present and past, for example), use correct verb forms to keep your meaning clear. You should also use transitional words and phrases such as *now*, *at that time*, and *since then*, to signal a change in time.

Example

simple past   present perfect
I **decided** to change my behavior. I **have been** much happier. ⟶
One day I **decided** to change my behavior. *Since then* I **have been** much happier.

1 | *Complete this student's paragraph about a* phase *in her life (a temporary period when she had particular kinds of behavior and feelings). Use the correct form of the verbs in parentheses.*

MY "STUPID" PHASE

Today my friends _____*think*_____ of me as a serious student,
            1. (think)

but they _____ about my "stupid" phase. Until two years
            2. (not know)

ago, I _____ mostly about clothes and makeup, and I usually
            3. (think)

_____ people by their appearance and possessions. In that
            4. (judge)

period of my life, my friends and I always _____ in
                                            5. (speak)

stereotyped phrases. We _____ "Hel-LO?" when something
                        6. (say)

_____ obvious, and "Whatever" when we _____
   7. (seem)   **8. (not care)**

about something. I never _____ anyone to realize that I
                          9. (want)

_____ interested in school. Sometimes I _____ the
   10. (be)   **11. (read)**

newspaper secretly and _____ to be unprepared for tests.
                        12. (pretend)

One day, my older brother _____ into my room while I
                           13. (come)

(continued)

_____ a serious novel. No one _____ ever
    14. (read)

_____ me do that before even though I _____ an
    15. (see)   16. (be)

avid reader for years. He thought I _____ to be interested
                                        17. (pretend)

in the book in order to impress a new boyfriend. I _____
                                                        18. (get)

angry when he _____ at me, so I _____ a
                    19. (laugh)   20. (make)

decision. I _____ hiding my real interests. Since that day, I
                21. (stop)

_____ my news magazines proudly and _____
    22. (carry)   23. (express)

opinions in class. For the last two years I _____ for tests
                                                24. (prepare)

openly. Now I _____ for college, and I _____
                    25. (apply)   26. (feel)

proud of being a good student.

2 | Look at the paragraph in Exercise 1. Find the transitional words and phrases that signal a change in time.

1. the simple present to the simple past _____ *Until two years ago* _____

2. the simple past to the present perfect (progressive) _____

3. the present perfect (progressive) to the present progressive _____

3 | Complete the chart with information from the paragraph in Exercise 1.

Paragraph Section	Information	Form of the Verb
Topic Sentence • what the writer is like now	*a serious student*	*simple present*
Body of the Paragraph • habits and feelings during the phase		
• the event that ended the phase		
• behavior since the phase ended		
Conclusion • the results of the change		

4 *Before you write . . .*

    1. Work with a partner. Discuss a phase that each of you has experienced.

    2. Make a chart like the one in Exercise 3 about your own phase.

5 *Write a paragraph about a phase you went through. Use information from the chart you made in Exercise 4. Remember to use transitional words or phrases when you shift from one time to another.*

6 *Exchange paragraphs with a different partner. Underline the verbs in your partner's paragraph. Circle the transitional words and phrases. Write a question mark (?) where something seems wrong or missing. Then answer the following questions.*

	Yes	No
1. Does each verb correctly express the time the author is writing about?	☐	☐
2. Is each verb formed correctly?	☐	☐
3. Are the shifts from one time to another time clearly marked with transitional words or phrases?	☐	☐

7 *Work with your partner. Discuss each other's editing questions from Exercise 6. Then rewrite your own paragraph and make any necessary corrections.*

Review Test

I *Complete this magazine article by circling the correct verb forms.*

The rainy spring is over and the nice weather arrived / (has arrived.) On all the TV food
                                                                1.

channels, celebrity chefs from Bobby Flay to Emeril Lagasse have discussed / are discussing
                                                                                    2.

their favorite barbecue sauce recipes. Are you thinking / Do you think of having a barbecue?
                                                        3.

Have you ever wondered / been wondering about the origin of the term?
                    4.

Even though North Americans love / are loving this suburban ritual, food historians
                                    5.

agree / are agreeing that the term *barbecue* is not strictly American. They argue / are arguing
6.   **7.**

about the origin of the name, however. Some historians claim / are claiming that the word
                                                            8.

has / is having Spanish and Haitian origins. In the past, people in those cultures
9.

used / were using a rack to roast meat or to dry it. They called / were calling this framework
10.   **11.**

of sticks and posts *barbaco.*

The word sounds / is sounding close to the modern word *barbecue,* but not everyone
          12.

accepted / has accepted this explanation. Other historians think / are thinking that the origin
13.   **14.**

of the term is the French phrase *barbe à queue,* which means / is meaning "from whisker
                                                        15.

(*barbe*) to tail (*queue*)." They point out that people in the 1700s roasted / have roasted
                                                                16.

whole animals outdoors as well as indoors. By 1733 this process of cooking meat

had become / had been becoming a party. People stood / have stood around the fire and
17.   **18.**

talked / had talked until the food was / had been ready.
19.   **20.**

That, with the addition of barbecue sauce, seems / is seeming pretty much like a modern
                                                21.

barbecue. Whatever the origin of the term, a barbecue is / has been now not only a means of
                                                        22.

cooking, but an event.

II *Complete these conversations that take place at a barbecue by circling the correct verb forms.*

1. **A:** George! How are you? I (haven't seen) / haven't been seeing you for a long time. What
   a.
   happens / 's been happening?
   b.

   B: Oh. I have / 'm having news. Betty and I moved / have moved last month.
   c. **d.**
   We bought / were buying a house.
   e.

   A: Congratulations! I didn't know you had looked / had been looking for one. So, where are
   f.
   you now?

   B: In Rockport County. We have been planning / had been planning to move to Putnam
   g.
   County, but we have decided / decided on Rockport instead.
   h.

   A: Oh, how come?

   B: The school district is / has been better there. Have you ever been / Had you ever been to
   i. **j.**
   Rockport?

   A: No. It's near Putnam, isn't it?

   B: Uh-huh. Listen, we have / 're having a barbecue almost every weekend. You'll have to
   k.
   come to one.

   A: Thanks. I'd love to.

2. **A:** Have you tried / Have you been trying the hot dogs? They're delicious.
   a.

   B: Yes. I 've already eaten / 've been eating four! The hamburgers smell / are smelling good
   b. **c.**
   too. I 'm thinking / think of having some of those.
   d.

   A: Well, just save some room for dessert. When I saw / see Betty in the kitchen a few minutes
   e.
   ago, she was taking some pies out of the oven. They looked /were looking great.
   f.

3. **A:** Have you met / Have you been meeting Jack's new wife?
   a.

   B: No. What's her name?

   A: Alice, but everyone calls / is calling her Al.
   b.

   B: What does she do / is she doing?
   c.

   A: Well, she's "between jobs." She was working / worked for a health insurance company
   d.
   when they laid off / had laid off a lot of employees. She was one of the people who
   e.
   lost / was losing their jobs.
   f.

(continued)

B: A lot of companies <u>have been cutting / had been cutting</u> their staff. That's too bad.
g.

A: Yes. And she really <u>likes / liked</u> her job. Now she <u>'s trying / tries</u> to change careers.
h.   i.

4. **A:** <u>Have Al and Jack / Had Al and Jack</u> left for their honeymoon yet?
a.

B: Yes. As a matter of fact, I <u>got / 've gotten</u> a postcard from them yesterday.
b.

They <u>stay / 're staying</u> at the Hotel Splendor. It <u>sounds / 's sounding</u> great.
c.   d.

A: Well, they really <u>need / are needing</u> a vacation. This is the first time that they
e.

<u>had been / have been</u> away since they <u>met / were meeting</u> each other.
f.   g.

B: I know. What <u>are they doing / do they do</u> there?
h.

A: Oh, they've got so many plans. They <u>'re taking / take</u> scuba diving lessons, and they also
i.

<u>have been learning / had been learning</u> to water-ski.
j.

B: Sounds like fun.

III *Circle the letter of the correct word(s) to complete each sentence.*

1. It was 1990, and I _____ in Denver for a year.   **A** (**B**) **C D**
   (**A**) have been living   (**C**) was living
   (**B**) had been living   (**D**) lived

2. I met my wife, Meri, while I _____ some classes at the local college.   **A B C D**
   (**A**) was taking   (**C**) have been taking
   (**B**) had been taking   (**D**) am taking

3. She _____ a ski instructor at a resort at that time, and she was working   **A B C D**
   every weekend.
   (**A**) is   (**C**) was
   (**B**) has been   (**D**) had been

4. As soon as my friend introduced us, I _____ her about her name.   **A B C D**
   (**A**) asked   (**C**) had asked
   (**B**) have asked (**D**) was asking

5. It _____ from *la mer*, the French word for *sea*.   **A B C D**
   (**A**) has come   (**C**) was coming
   (**B**) comes   (**D**) is coming

6. Her parents _____ her after their profession.   **A B C D**
   (**A**) name   (**C**) were naming
   (**B**) are naming (**D**) had named

7. Before they _____, they had both been diving instructors. **A B C D**
   (**A**) had retired   (**C**) have retired
   (**B**) retired   (**D**) retire

8. After Meri turned eighteen, they _____ to give her diving lessons. **A B C D**
   (**A**) always try   (**C**) were always trying
   (**B**) are always trying   (**D**) have always been trying

9. Meri has loved skiing _____ she was ten. **A B C D**
   (**A**) from   (**C**) since
   (**B**) for   (**D**) while

10. When we _____ married, we had been dating about a year. **A B C D**
    (**A**) get   (**C**) have gotten
    (**B**) had gotten   (**D**) got

11. We named our first daughter *Neige*, which _____ *snow* in French. **A B C D**
    (**A**) is meaning   (**C**) means
    (**B**) meant   (**D**) has meant

12. Meri _____ to name our daughter *Snowflake*, but she changed her mind. **A B C D**
    (**A**) is planning   (**C**) had been planning
    (**B**) plans   (**D**) has been planning

13. We _____ our third child now. **A B C D**
    (**A**) are expecting   (**C**) expected
    (**B**) were expecting   (**D**) have expected

14. We've been reading baby-name books for weeks, but we _____ a name yet. **A B C D**
    (**A**) didn't choose   (**C**) hadn't chosen
    (**B**) don't choose   (**D**) haven't chosen

IV *Complete this conversation with the correct form of the verbs in parentheses.*

    A: Hi, I __'m_____ Matt Rotell, a friend of Alice's.
              1. (be)

    B: Oh, yes. Alice _____ you the other day. Gee, you _____ like
                    2. (mention)   **3. (not look)**

     a detective.

    A: Well, that's good, I _____.
                        4. (guess)

    B: I'm curious. Tell me, how _____ you _____ to become an
                                              5. (decide)

     undercover cop?

(continued)

A: Well, when I _____ a kid, I _____ to read detective novels.
6. (be)   7. (love)

By the time I _____ ten, I _____ every book in the *Hardy*
8. (be)   9. (read)

Boys series. I _____ then that I _____ to go into law
10. (know)   11. (want)

enforcement.

B: But according to Alice, you _____ law school nowadays.
12. (attend)

A: Right. I _____ married last month. I _____ being on the
13. (get)   14. (not mind)

police force when I _____ single, but ever since I _____
15. (be)   16. (meet)

Nicole—that's my wife—I _____ to do something less dangerous.
17. (want)

B: I _____. By the way, _____ you _____ any
18. (understand)   19. (have)

luck yet with those counterfeiters?

A: Well, I _____ them for more than a month now, but so far I
20. (follow)

_____ catch them in the act. Sometimes I _____ that by the
21. (not be able to)   22. (worry)

time they're caught, I'll have my law degree and I'll be defending them!

V *Read this letter from Al. There are ten mistakes in the use of verb forms. The first mistake is already corrected. Find and correct nine more.*

Dear Nicole,

    have been staying

Jack and I ~~are staying~~ at the Splendor for almost a week already. We've been spending a lot of time at the beach swimming and water-skiing, and I was taking scuba lessons in the hotel pool for several days now. Yesterday, I've been planning to take my first dive from a boat. Unfortunately, by the time we left shore, the weather has changed. We had to cancel the dive. This morning it was still a little cloudy, so we did something different. We were deciding to visit the Castle, an old pirate stronghold in Hideaway Bay. We had both read a little about it before we left, and it really sounded fascinating. So we've rented a motorbike and took off. They aren't having any road signs here outside of town, so by the time we found the Castle, we've been driving for about an hour. It was fun, though. When we were seeing the Castle, dark clouds were drifting over it. It really looked spooky and beautiful.

    Well, the weather has cleared, and Jack gets ready to go for a dive. I think I'll join him. See you soon.

Love,
Al

▶ *To check your answers, go to the Answer Key on page RT-1.*

PART II

Future:
Review and Expansion

5 Future and Future Progressive

Grammar in Context

BEFORE YOU READ

🎧 *Look at the pictures. What topics do you think the article will discuss? Read this article about the future.*

PRESENTING THE FUTURE!

by Will Hapin

A new millennium has begun as well as a new century, and it's bringing new developments in all areas of our lives. Where **will** we **be working** in this new era? What **will** we **be wearing**? How **will** we **be traveling**, **studying**, and **relating** to our families? Let's follow Dr. Nouvella Eon on a typical day in 2115.

Dr. Eon's day begins at 7:00 A.M. when her bedroom lights turn themselves on. Her son **will be waking up** soon, so Dr. E. dresses quickly. She usually works from her home office, but today she**'s going to be teaching**, so she**'ll wear** a business suit. She doesn't bother to check the weather report—the high-tech material of her clothing **will keep** her comfortably warm or cool.

"Hi, Mom!" Her son greets her over the home communications system. She goes to his room to say good morning. While she**'s helping** Rocky get ready for his day, the household robot **will be preparing** breakfast.

PRESENTING THE FUTURE!

"When **will** Dad **be** home?" Rocky wants to know. Mr. Eon is a captain of the Mars shuttle.

"The shuttle **leaves** Mars at 6:00 P.M. today and it **arrives** tomorrow afternoon. He**'ll be** here by the time you **get** home from school tomorrow."

"These oranges are really good," Rocky says at breakfast. "All Mars fruits are delicious," Nouvella replies. "I've ordered some bananas, too. They**'re going to be arriving** on the shuttle tomorrow." (Years ago, Earth scientists changed the atmosphere on Mars, and now farmers are growing all kinds of fruits and vegetables there.)

"Don't forget your backpack," Nouvella tells Rocky as they leave. "You**'ll need** it to send me pictures of the zoo." Rocky's class **is going** on a field trip today, and he**'ll be carrying** a backpack with a built-in computer, camera, and cell phone. She **won't worry** about his getting lost. All the children's jackets have GPDs (Global Positioning Devices), so she**'ll be able** to see where he is at any time on her wristwatch computer.

Nouvella **is going to drive** Rocky to school and then drive to the freeway. There, she**'ll connect** with a freeway guidance system, so she **won't** actually **be driving** her car most of the way to the university. Instead, she**'s going to listen** to music and **prepare** to teach her class.

Many of these changes have already begun, and we**'ll be seeing** others very soon. The future **is arriving** any minute now. Are you ready for it?

AFTER YOU READ

Write **T** *(true) or* **F** *(false).*

_____ **1.** The robot will prepare breakfast after Nouvella helps Rocky.

_____ **2.** The Mars shuttle will leave Mars in the evening.

_____ **3.** Nouvella will drive all the way to the university.

Grammar Presentation

FUTURE

Affirmative Statements

We **are going to leave**	
We **will leave**	for Mars soon.
We **are leaving**	
We **leave**	

Negative Statements

We **are not going to leave**	
We **will not leave**	for Mars yet.
We **are not leaving**	
We **don't leave**	

Yes / No Questions

Is she **going to leave**	
Will she **leave**	for Mars soon?
Is she **leaving**	
Does she **leave**	

Short Answers

	Affirmative		Negative
	she **is**.		she **isn't**.
Yes,	she **will**.	**No,**	she **won't**.
	she **is**.		she **isn't**.
	she **does**.		she **doesn't**.

Wh- Questions

When **is** she **going to leave**	
When **will** she **leave**	for Mars?
When **is** she **leaving**	
When **does** she **leave**	

FUTURE PROGRESSIVE

Statements			
Subject	*Be (not) going to / Will (not)*	*Be* + Base Form + *-ing*	
People	**are (not) going to** **will (not)**	**be living**	on Mars by 2050.

Yes / No Questions				
Be / Will	Subject	*Going to*	*Be* + Base Form + *-ing*	
Are	they	**going to**	**be living**	on Mars by then?
Will	you			

Short Answers			
Affirmative		Negative	
Yes,	they **are**.	**No**,	they**'re not**.
	I **will**.		I **won't**.

Wh- Questions					
Wh- Word	*Be / Will*	Subject	*Going to*	*Be* + Base Form + *-ing*	
When	**are**	they	**going to**	**be living**	on Mars?
	will	you			

GRAMMAR NOTES   **EXAMPLES**

1. Use *be going to*, *will*, the **present progressive**, and the **simple present** to talk about actions and states in the future.

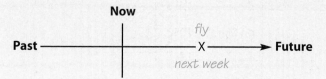

USAGE NOTE: Sometimes only one form of the future is appropriate, but in many cases more than one form is possible.

a. Use *be going to* or *will* for **predictions**.

b. Use *be going to* (not *will*) when something in the present leads to a prediction.

c. Use *be going to*, *will*, or the **present progressive** to talk about **future intentions or plans**.

d. We often use *will* when we decide something at the <u>moment of speaking</u>.

e. We often use *will* for **invitations**.

f. Use the **simple present** to talk about **scheduled future events** such as timetables, programs, and schedules.

- I'm **going to fly** to Mars next week.
- I **will fly** to Mars next week.
- I'm **flying** to Mars next week.
- I **fly** to Mars next week.

- Commuting **is going to be** easier in the year 2020.
- Commuting **will be** easier.

- Look at those dark storm clouds! It**'s going to rain**!
  NOT It will rain.

- Dr. Eon **is going to speak** tomorrow.
- Dr. Eon **will speak** tomorrow.
- Dr. Eon **is speaking** tomorrow.

A: Dr. Eon is giving a talk tomorrow.
B: Oh! Maybe I**'ll go**.

A: Will you **join** us for coffee?
B: Thanks. I'd love to.

- The shuttle **leaves** at 10:00 A.M. tomorrow.
- It **lands** at midnight.

2. Use the **future progressive** with *be going to* or *will* to talk about actions that will be in progress at a specific time in the future.

- At this time tomorrow, **I'm going to be flying** to Mars.

- At this time tomorrow, **I'll be flying** to Mars.

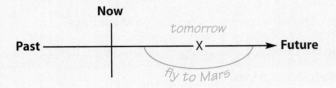

USAGE NOTES

a. We often use the **future progressive** instead of the future to make a question <u>more polite</u>.

- When **will** you **hand in** your paper? *(teacher to student)*

- When **will** you **be grading** our tests? *(student to teacher)*

b. People often use the **future progressive** to ask indirectly for a favor. This makes the request <u>more polite</u>.

A: **Will** you **be going** by the post office tomorrow?

B: Yes. Do you need stamps?

A: Yes. Could you get some?

---

3. In sentences with a **future time clause**:

a. Use the future or the future progressive in the main clause.

main clause   time clause
- **I'll call** when the robot **finishes** the laundry.

b. Use the simple present or the present progressive in the time clause.

▶ **BE CAREFUL!** Do not use the future or the future progressive in the time clause.

- I'll be making lunch while the robot **is cleaning**.

  NOT I'll be making lunch while the robot ~~will be cleaning~~.

Focused Practice

1 | DISCOVER THE GRAMMAR

🎧 *Dr. Eon is attending a conference this week. Read the conversation, and circle all the verbs that refer to the future.*

ROVER: Nouvella! It's nice to see you. (Are you presenting) a paper today?

EON: Hi, Rick. Yes. In fact my talk starts at two o'clock.

ROVER: Oh. I think I'll go. Will you be talking about robots?

(continued)

EON: Yes. I'm focusing on personal robots for household work.

ROVER: I'd like one of those! Where's your son, by the way? Is he with you?

EON: No. Rocky stays in Denver with his grandparents in the summer. I'm going to visit him when I leave the conference. So, what are you working on these days?

ROVER: I'm still with the Mars Association. In fact, we're going to be holding a news conference next month about tourists on Mars.

EON: That's exciting. Maybe I'll see you there!

2 | AT THE CONFERENCE   *Grammar Note 1*

Circle the best words to complete these conversations.

1.   EON: Which project <u>do you work</u> / <u>are you going to work</u> on?

    ROVER: I haven't decided for sure. Probably the Spacemobile.

2. ROVER: Look at those dark clouds!

    EON: Yes. It looks like <u>it's raining</u> / <u>it's going to rain</u> any minute.

3.   EON: I'd better get back to my hotel room before it starts to rain.

    ROVER: OK. <u>I'm seeing</u> / <u>I'll see</u> you later.

4.   DESK: Dr. Eon, your son just called.

    EON: Oh, good. I think <u>I'll call</u> / <u>I'm calling</u> him back right away.

5.   EON: Hi, honey. How's it going?

    ROCKY: Great. <u>I go</u> / <u>I'm going</u> fishing with Grandpa tomorrow.

6.   EON: Have fun, but don't forget. You still have to finish that paper.

    ROCKY: I know, Mom. <u>I send</u> / <u>I'm sending</u> it to my teacher tomorrow. I already discussed it with her.

7. ROCKY: How's the conference?

    EON: Good. <u>I'm giving</u> / <u>I'll give</u> my talk this afternoon.

8. ROCKY: Good luck. When <u>are you</u> / <u>will you be</u> here?

    EON: Tomorrow. My plane <u>lands</u> / <u>will land</u> at 7:00, so <u>I see</u> / <u>I'll see</u> you about 8:00.

3 | ROBO'S SCHEDULE

Dr. Eon's family uses a robot for household chores. Look at Robo the Robot's schedule for tomorrow. Write sentences, using the words in parentheses and the future progressive.

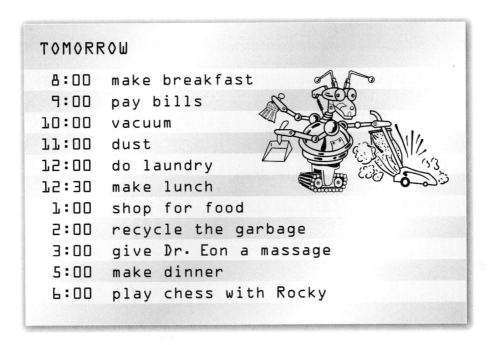

```
TOMORROW
 8:00   make breakfast
 9:00   pay bills
10:00   vacuum
11:00   dust
12:00   do laundry
12:30   make lunch
 1:00   shop for food
 2:00   recycle the garbage
 3:00   give Dr. Eon a massage
 5:00   make dinner
 6:00   play chess with Rocky
```

1. *At 8:05 Robo won't be paying bills. He'll be making breakfast.*
   (8:05 / pay bills)

2. *At 9:05 he'll be paying bills.*
   (9:05 / pay bills)

3. _____
   (10:05 / vacuum)

4. _____
   (11:05 / do laundry)

5. _____
   (12:05 / make lunch)

6. _____
   (12:35 / make lunch)

7. _____
   (1:05 / shop for food)

8. _____
   (2:05 / recycle the garbage)

9. _____
   (3:05 / give Dr. Eon a massage)

10. _____
    (5:05 / make dinner)

11. _____
    (6:05 / play cards with Rocky)

4 | ON CAMPUS

Complete the conversations. Use the future progressive form of the words in parentheses or short answers where appropriate.

1. STUDENT: _____*Will*_____ you _____*be having*_____ office hours today? I'd like to
   (Will / have)

   talk to you about my term paper.

   DR. EON: I _____ to lunch at two o'clock. Stop in any time before then.
   (will / go)

2. DR. GUPTA: _____ you _____ us for lunch? Dr. Rover from
   (Will / join)

   the Mars Association is going to be there.

   DR. EON: _____. I've been looking forward to seeing him.

3. MR. EON: When _____ you _____ the office?
   (be going to / leave)

   DR. EON: At two o'clock. Why? Do we need something?

   MR. EON: Would you mind picking up some milk? Robo forgot.

4. REPORTER: I'm calling from the *Times-Dispatch*. We've heard that the Mars Association

   _____ a tourist service to Mars soon.
   (will / start)

   DR. EON: I can't comment now. But I think you _____ a lot more about it
   (be going to / hear)

   in the next few weeks.

5. DR. EON: _____ you _____ an announcement about the
   (be going to / make)

   Mars shuttle soon? Everyone is very curious.

   DR. ROVER: _____. We've decided not to say anything until our plans are

   more certain.

6. DANNY: Dad? I need some help on my science project. What time _____

   you _____ home today?
   (will / get)

   DR. ROVER: I'll be there by 4:00.

7. TELEMARKETER: Hi. I'm calling from Robotronics, Inc. I _____ your
   (be going to / visit)

   neighborhood soon to demonstrate our new robot.

   ROBO: The Eon family _____ a new robot for a while.
   (will not / buy)

5 | **LEAVING EARTH**   *Grammar Notes 2–3*

Complete the ad for the Mars shuttle. Use the correct form of the verbs in parentheses—
future progressive or simple present.

The Sky's Not the Limit

Leave all your earthly problems behind. Call today and in just one week

you ___'ll be flying___ on the new shuttle to Mars! Imagine—while everyone _____
       1. (fly)   **2. (be)**

stuck back here on Earth, you _____ gravity in our spacious, comfortable,
                                   3. (defy)

modern spaceship. You _____ in your own compartment when one of our
                                 4. (float)

friendly flight robots _____ you a meal straight from the microwave.
                                 5. (offer)

You _____ your complimentary copy of *Star Magazine* while the
                          6. (read)

gentle swaying of the spacecraft _____ you to sleep. And before you
                                   7. (rock)

know it, you _____ to land on the planet of your dreams. So don't delay!
                8. (get ready)

Call for a reservation. Once aboard, we guarantee it—you _____ about
                                                 9. (not think)

anything except returning again and again and again. . . .

6 | **EDITING**

Read this flight announcement that was made on the shuttle to Mars. The captain has
made seven mistakes in the use of the future and future progressive. The first mistake is
already corrected. Find and correct six more. (Note: There is often more than one way to
correct a mistake.)

"Good evening, ladies and gentlemen. This ~~will be~~ *is* Captain Eon speaking. We are going

to be leave the Earth's gravity field in about five minutes. When you will hear the

announcement, you'll be able to unbuckle your seat belts and float around the cabin. Host

robots take orders for dinner soon. They'll serving from 6:30 to 7:30. The shuttle arrives

on Mars tomorrow morning at 9:00. Tonight's temperature on the planet is a mild minus

20 degrees Celsius. When you arrive tomorrow morning, the temperature is 18 degrees,

but it will be feeling more like 20 degrees. Enjoy your flight."

Communication Practice

7 | LISTENING

🎧 *Four members of the Mars Association are trying to organize a conference on Venus. Listen to their conversation. Then listen again. Mark the chart below to help you figure out when they are all available.*

	July				August			
Weeks:	1	2	3	4	1	2	3	4
Jennifer							X	X
Brian								
Lorna								
Tranh								
When they're all available: _____								

X = not available

8 | ROBOTS OF THE FUTURE

Robots will be doing many things in the near future. Look at the list of activities and decide which ones you think robots will or won't be doing. In small groups, share and explain your opinions. Do you think robots will be doing too much for humans? Why?

make dinner   plant gardens

go shopping   take a vacation

write letters   answer the phone

teach English   clean houses

take care of children paint walls

sew clothes   knit sweaters

read books   drive a car

Example: Robots will be cleaning houses, but they won't be taking care of children. Children need human contact to help them develop emotional security.

9 | INFORMATION GAP: DR. EON'S CALENDAR

Work in pairs (A and B). Student B, look at the Information Gap on page 65 and follow the instructions there. Student A, complete Dr. Eon's calendar below. Get information from Student B. Ask questions and fill in the calendar. Answer Student B's questions.

Example: **A:** What will Dr. Eon be doing on Sunday, the first?
B: She'll be flying to Tokyo. What about on the second? Will she be attending a conference then?
A: No, she'll be meeting with Dr. Kato.

FEBRUARY						2115
SUNDAY	MONDAY	TUESDAY	WEDNESDAY	THURSDAY	FRIDAY	SATURDAY
1 *fly to Tokyo*	2 meet with Dr. Kato	3	4	5	6	7
8 take Bullet Train to Osaka	9 sightseeing	10	11	12	13	14
15 fly home	16	17	18 attend energy seminar	19	20	21 shop with Rocky and Robo
22	23	24	25	26	27	28 take shuttle to Mars

When you are finished, compare calendars. Do they have the same information?

10 | LET'S GET TOGETHER

Complete the schedule below. Write in all your plans for next week. Then work with a partner. Without showing each other your schedules, find a time to get together by asking and answering questions using the future progressive.

Example: **A:** What will you be doing at 11:00 on Tuesday?
B: I'll be taking a history test.

	MONDAY	TUESDAY	WEDNESDAY	THURSDAY	FRIDAY
9:00					
11:00					
1:00					
3:00					
5:00					
7:00					

11 | WRITING

Write a paragraph about your life 10 years from now. What will you be doing for a living? What kind of family life will you have? What hobbies will you be enjoying? What will you do to achieve these things? Use the future and future progressive.

Example: In 10 years, I will be working for the space program. I am going to be planning the first colony on Mars. First I will have to graduate from college.

12 | ON THE INTERNET

Do a search on space activities. Find information about what will be happening during the 21st century. For example, will tourists be traveling to the moon or Mars? Will scientists "terraform" Mars (make the Martian atmosphere safe for people from Earth)? Are there going to be farms and factories in space?

Work with a small group. Find your own organization or look at information from these:

SEDS (Students for the Exploration and Development of Space)
The Mars Society
The Planetary Society
Space.com

Present your predictions to the class.

Example: A lot of different countries are going to be developing space. China will probably be sending people to the moon. The European countries and Japan will work together to explore the planet Mercury . . .

INFORMATION GAP FOR STUDENT B

Student B, complete Dr. Eon's calendar below. Answer Student A's questions. Then ask Student A questions and fill in the information.

Example: **A:** What will Dr. Eon be doing on Sunday, the first?
B: She'll be flying to Tokyo. What about on the second? Will she be attending a conference then?
A: No, she'll be meeting with Dr. Kato.

FEBRUARY						2115
SUNDAY	**MONDAY**	**TUESDAY**	**WEDNESDAY**	**THURSDAY**	**FRIDAY**	**SATURDAY**
1 fly to Tokyo	2 *meet with Dr. Kato*	3 attend World Future Conference	4 ————————	5	6	7 ——→
8	9 ————————	10	11 ——→	12 fly to Denver	13 visit Mom and Dad	14 ——→
15	16 give speech at Harvard University	17 meet with Dr. Rover	18 ————————	19	20 ——→	21
22 relax!	23 work at home ————————	24	25	26	27 ——→	28

When you are finished, compare calendars. Do they have the same information?

6 Future Perfect and Future Perfect Progressive

Grammar in Context

BEFORE YOU READ

🎧 *Look at the photos of people on a TV show. Read the information for each person. What do you think the show is about? Read this transcript of a personal finance TV show.*

MONEY TALKS

Debbie Hart, age 20
Number of credit cards: 3
Used for: movies, CDs, clothes
Balance: $2,500

Sung Park, age 18
Number of credit cards: 5
Used for: textbooks, car repairs
Balance: $1,750

Jeff Hassad, age 22
Number of credit cards: 1
Used for: eating out, entertainment
Balance: $600

Trudy: Hi, everyone. I'm Trudy Norman and you're watching *Money Talks*. We've taken the show on the road—by the end of tonight's *Money Talks*, we**'ll have been traveling** for a month, and we**'ll have been** in 22 cities in that time!

Tonight we're at Gibson College in Nebraska, and we have students Debbie Hart, Sung Park, and Jeff Hassad on our panel. Our topic is credit cards.

To get started, let me give you some shocking statistics. A typical college freshman **will have gotten** eight credit card offers by the end of the first semester. Many students accept at least some of those offers. In fact, by graduation, the average student in the United States **will have tripled** the number of cards in his or her wallet.

Sung: That's true. When I first got here, I only had one credit card. Then I started receiving all these credit card offers, and finally I thought, "Why not?" Now I have five cards.

Trudy: And it isn't only the number of credit cards that increases. So does the amount you owe. If you're like many students, you**'ll have doubled** your credit card debt by graduation. About a third of today's students graduate owing $3,000 to $7,000 on their cards.

Debbie: My problem is, it's too easy just to take out my card when I see something I want. Then, when I get my bill, I**'ll have charged** more than I can pay for. I'm carrying a pretty big balance right now.

Trudy: Did you know that people who always use credit cards spend more? Start using cash—by next year you**'ll have spent** 12 percent less! And you **won't have been paying** interest on your purchases. But if you *must* charge, you should also start paying more than the minimum every month, even if it's only $20 more.

Debbie: How much can an extra $20 help?

Trudy: A lot. Suppose you're a freshman and you owe $1,000 on your card at 15 percent interest. Pay an extra $20 every month, and by the time you graduate, you**'ll have** already **become** debt-free! And you**'ll have been saving** interest charges the whole time. On the other hand, if you only pay the minimum, you'll be paying for 15 years, and at the end, you**'ll have spent** $1,122.78 in interest. Everything you bought on that card **will have cost** twice as much as the actual price.

Jeff: I hear what you're saying. By the end of this school year, I**'ll have been paying** interest for nine months on pizzas I ate last September! But are you saying students shouldn't use credit cards?

Trudy: That's not realistic, is it? No, I'm saying one card is enough. And use it for essentials, not for pizza and cool shoes.

Sung: My brother didn't have a credit card in college. When he graduated he had a hard time getting one.

Trudy: Good point, Sung. It's hard to get credit when you have no credit history. Getting your first credit card as a student, when it's easier, can be a good idea. Use it wisely, and by graduation you**'ll have earned** a good credit rating, and that will be very useful when you're starting out.

That's all for tonight. See you next week on *Money Talks*.

AFTER YOU READ

Write **T** *(true) or* **F** *(false).*

_____ **1.** The show has now been in 22 cities.

_____ **2.** Many students get eight credit card offers in their first semester of college.

_____ **3.** Many students have twice as much credit card debt after four years.

_____ **4.** Jeff has already paid interest for nine months on pizzas he ate last September.

Grammar Presentation

FUTURE PERFECT

Statements			
Subject	***Will (not)***	***Have* + Past Participle**	
I You He She It We They	**will (not)**	**have earned**	interest by then.

Yes / No Questions			
Will	**Subject**	***Have* + Past Participle**	
Will	I you he she it we they	**have earned**	interest by then?

Short Answers					
Affirmative			**Negative**		
Yes,	you I he she it we they	**will (have).**	**No,**	you I he she it we they	**won't (have).**

Wh- Questions				
***Wh-* Word**	***Will***	**Subject**	***Have* + Past Participle**	
How much	**will**	she	**have earned**	by then?

FUTURE PERFECT PROGRESSIVE

Statements			
Subject	*Will (not)*	*Have been* + Base Form + *-ing*	
I You He She It We They	**will (not)**	**have been earning**	interest for a month.

Yes / No Questions			
Will	**Subject**	*Have been* + Base Form + *-ing*	
Will	I you he she it we they	**have been earning**	interest for a month?

Short Answers					
Affirmative			**Negative**		
Yes,	you I he she it we they	**will (have).**	**No,**	you I he she it we they	**won't (have).**

Wh- Questions				
Wh- Word	*Will*	**Subject**	*Have been* + Base Form + *-ing*	
How long	**will**	she	**have been earning**	interest?

GRAMMAR NOTES	EXAMPLES
1. Use the **future perfect** to talk about a future action that will already be <u>completed</u> by a certain time in the future. 	• By June, he **will have paid** his debt. • She**'ll have bought** a new car by May. • We**'ll have saved** enough by then.
2. Use the **future perfect progressive** to talk about an action that will be <u>in progress</u> at a certain time in the future. The action may start sometime in the future or it may have already started. 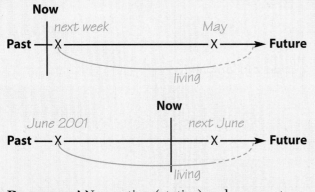 ▶ **BE CAREFUL!** Non-action (stative) verbs are not usually used in the progressive.	**A:** You're moving to L.A. next week? Great! Can I visit in May? **B:** Sure. By then, we**'ll have been living** there for three months. • They moved to Atlanta in June 2001. So by next June, they**'ll have been living** there for six years. • By the spring, he**'ll have owned** that car for five years. NOT By the spring, he'll have ~~been owning~~ that car for five years.
3. Use the **future perfect** or the **future perfect progressive** with the **simple present** to show the relationship between two future events. The event that will happen first uses the perfect. The event that will happen second uses the simple present. 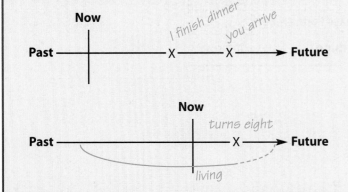	• By the time you **arrive**, I **will have finished** dinner. NOT By the time you ~~will~~ arrive, I will have finished dinner. • When my daughter **turns** eight, we **will have been living** here for ten years.

4. We often use *already* and *yet* with the **future perfect** to emphasize which event will <u>happen first</u>.

- By the time he graduates, he**'ll have** *already* **saved** $1,000.
- By the time he graduates, he **won't have saved** $5,000 *yet*.

Focused Practice

1 | DISCOVER THE GRAMMAR

Read each numbered statement. Then circle the letter of the sentence that is similar in meaning.

1. By next year, Trudy will have been doing her show *Money Talks* for five years.
   a. Next year, Trudy will no longer be doing her show.
   (b.) Next year, Trudy can celebrate the fifth anniversary of *Money Talks*.

2. By this time tomorrow, I'll have decided which car to buy.
   a. I know which car I'm going to buy.
   b. I haven't decided yet.

3. By the time you get home, we'll have finished studying.
   a. You will get home while we are studying.
   b. You will get home after we finish studying.

4. They won't have finished taping the show by ten o'clock.
   a. They will still be taping at ten o'clock.
   b. They will finish taping at ten o'clock.

5. By the year 2011, we will have moved to a larger office.
   a. We will move to a larger office before the year 2011.
   b. We will move to a larger office after the year 2011.

6. They will have finished Trudy's e-mail newsletter by five o'clock.
   a. They'll be finished by five o'clock.
   b. They'll still be working at five o'clock.

2 | FUTURE PLANS

Grammar Note 1

Look at the time line. Write sentences describing what Debbie Hart **will have done** *or* **won't have done** *by the year 2015.*

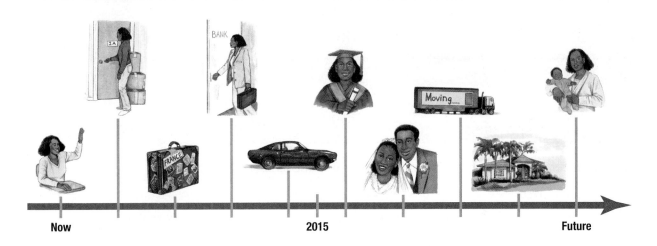

Now   2015   Future

1. (start college)

   By 2015, Debbie will have started college.

2. (get married)

   _____

3. (move into an apartment)

   _____

4. (move to Miami)

   _____

5. (spend a summer in France)

   _____

6. (start working at a bank)

   _____

7. (buy a used car)

   _____

8. (buy a house)

   _____

9. (graduate from college)

   _____

10. (become a parent)

    _____

3 | BY THE TIME . . .

Read the events in Debbie's life. What will or won't have happened by the time the first event occurs? Use the information in the time line from Exercise 2. Write sentences using **already** *and* **yet**.

1. move into an apartment / start college

   By the time Debbie moves into an apartment, she'll have already started college.

2. move into an apartment / get married

   _____

3. start college / buy a used car

   _____

4. graduate from college / move into an apartment

   _____

5. spend a summer in France / find a job at a bank

   _____

6. graduate from college / spend a summer in France

   _____

7. get married / graduate from college

   _____

8. move to Miami / buy a home

   _____

9. become a parent / graduate from college

   _____

10. buy a home / become a parent

    _____

4 | ACCOMPLISHMENTS

Ask and answer questions about these people's accomplishments. Choose between the future perfect and the future perfect progressive. Use the calendar to answer the questions.

January						
S	M	T	W	T	F	S
					1	2
3	4	5	6	7	8	9
10	11	12	13	14	15	16
17	18	19	20	21	22	23
24	25	26	27	28	29	30
31						

February						
S	M	T	W	T	F	S
	1	2	3	4	5	6
7	8	9	10	11	12	13
14	15	16	17	18	19	20
21	22	23	24	25	26	27
28						

March						
S	M	T	W	T	F	S
	1	2	3	4	5	6
7	8	9	10	11	12	13
14	15	16	17	18	19	20
21	22	23	24	25	26	27
28	29	30	31			

April						
S	M	T	W	T	F	S
				1	2	3
4	5	6	7	8	9	10
11	12	13	14	15	16	17
18	19	20	21	22	23	24
25	26	27	28	29	30	

May						
S	M	T	W	T	F	S
						1
2	3	4	5	6	7	8
9	10	11	12	13	14	15
16	17	18	19	20	21	22
23	24	25	26	27	28	29
30	31					

June						
S	M	T	W	T	F	S
		1	2	3	4	5
6	7	8	9	10	11	12
13	14	15	16	17	18	19
20	21	22	23	24	25	26
27	28	29	30			

1. On January 1, Debbie Hart started saving $15 a week.

   QUESTION: (By February 19 / how long / save?)

   By February 19, how long will Debbie have been saving?

   ANSWER: *By February 19, she'll have been saving for seven weeks.*

2. On March 1, Valerie Morgan started saving $5 a week.

   QUESTION: (By April 19 / how much / save?)

   _____

   ANSWER: _____

3. On March 3, Sung Park began reading a book a week.

   QUESTION: (By June 16 / how many books / read?)

   _____

   ANSWER: _____

4. On April 24, Don Caputo began running two miles a day.

   QUESTION: (How long / run / by May 29?)

   _____

   ANSWER: _____

5. On April 24, Tania Zakov began running two miles a day.

   QUESTION: (How many miles / run / by May 29?)

   _____

   ANSWER: _____

6. On February 6, Rick Gregory began saving $10 a week.

   QUESTION: (save $100 / by March 27?)

   _____

   ANSWER: _____

7. On May 8, Tim Rigg began painting two apartments a week in his building.

   QUESTION: (How many apartments / paint / by May 29?)

   _____

   ANSWER: _____

8. Tim's building has 12 apartments.

   QUESTION: (finish / by June 19?)

   _____

   ANSWER: _____

9. Talia began a fitness program on January 1. She is losing one pound a week.

   QUESTION: (lose 20 pounds / by May 21?)

   _____

   ANSWER: _____

10. Erik enrolled in a Spanish class on February 22.

    QUESTION: (How long / study / by April 26?)

    _____

    ANSWER: _____

5 | EDITING

Read this journal entry. There are nine mistakes in the use of the future perfect and future perfect progressive. The first mistake is already corrected. Find and correct eight more.

January 1

have been
By August, I'll ~~be~~ a word processor for ten years. And I'll earn

almost the same salary for three years! That's why I've just

made a New Year's resolution to go back to school this year.

First I'm going to write for school catalogs and start saving for

tuition. By March, I'll have figure out how much tuition will cost.

Then I'll start applying. By summer, I had received acceptance

letters. In August, when I will have my annual review with my

boss, I'll have already been decided on a school. I will talk to

her about working part-time and going to school part-time. By

that time, I'll also have saving enough to pay for a semester's

tuition. My cousin will had graduated by that time, so he might

move in with me and share the rent. By next New Year's Day, I'll

have finish the first semester!

Communication Practice

6 | LISTENING

🎧 *Don and Thea Caputo want to save for a summer vacation with their two children. Listen to their conversation about how to cut back on their spending. Then listen again, and write the amount they will have saved in each category by next summer.*

Amount They Will Have Saved by Next Summer	
Food	*$750*
Clothing	
Transportation	
Entertainment	
Total of all categories	

With their savings, where can they go for a two-week vacation?

☐ **1.** a car trip to British Columbia, camping on the way $1,000

☐ **2.** a car trip to British Columbia, staying in motels $2,000

☐ **3.** a trip to Disneyland $3,000

☐ **4.** a trip by airplane to Mexico and two weeks in a hotel $4,500

7 | SAVVY CONSUMERS

Write down some tips for saving money and share your tips with a group. Choose the best tips for yourself, and figure how much you will have saved by the end of the year if you use the tips.

> **Example:** I can save $10 a week by parking farther from my office.
> By the end of the year, I'll have saved $500.

8 | GOALS

Work in small groups. Conduct a survey to find out how many of your classmates will have done the following things one year from now. Complete this chart, and report back to the class.

Event	Number of Students
1. take a vacation	
2. get married	
3. move	
4. buy a car	
5. graduate	
6. get a new job	
7. decide on a career	
8. start a business	

Example: None of the students in our group will have moved by this time next year. Three of the students will have gotten new jobs.

9 | ON THE INTERNET

*Do a search on goals. Use the key words **goals worksheet**, and find a worksheet that you can use to plan one of your goals. Complete the worksheet and explain it to your group. Answer any questions. Then discuss your worksheet in a small group.*

Example: A: I'm going to buy a used car next year. Right now I'm reading consumer information. I'll have finished that step in about two weeks. Then I'll spend four or five weekends looking at cars. In about two months, I'll have decided which type of car I'll buy.

B: How much will you have saved for your car by next year?

10 | WRITING

Write a paragraph about a goal that you are working toward. What steps will you take to achieve your goal? When will you have completed each step? Use the future perfect and future perfect progressive.

Example: My goal is to buy a used car next year. By next year, I will have saved $4,000, so I'm looking for a car in that price range. My first step is to read consumer information. I'll have done that by June 2nd. The next step will be looking at cars.

From **Grammar** to **Writing**
Avoiding Sentence Fragments

Time clauses begin with time words and phrases such as *by the time*, *when*, *while*, *as soon as*, *before*, *after*, and *since*. A time clause by itself is not a complete sentence. When you write sentences with time clauses, avoid sentence fragments (incomplete sentences) by connecting the time clause to a main clause.

Example

SENTENCE FRAGMENT	**COMPLETE SENTENCE**
time clause	time clause + main clause
~~As soon as I find a job.~~ ⟶	*As soon as* I find a job, **I will move.**
time clause	main clause + time clause
~~Since I moved.~~ ⟶	**I have been much happier** *since* I moved.

Punctuation Note
Use a comma after the time clause when the time clause comes first.

1 | *Read this letter. Correct the sentence fragments by connecting the time clause to a main clause. Use appropriate punctuation and capitalization.*

December 10, 2005

Dear Jamie,

By the time you get this letter,

As of today, I'm a working man! ~~By the time you get this letter.~~ I'll

have been taking tickets at Ciné Moderne for more than a week. It's going

to be hard to work and go to school full time, but you'll understand why

I'm doing it. When you hear my plans.

As soon as school ends. My brother Alex and I are going to take a trip

to Greece and Turkey. I plan to buy a used car, and we'll camp most of

the way. By the end of January, I'll have been saving for more than a year

for this trip—and I'll have enough to buy a car.

(continued)

Why don't you come with us? I don't finish my finals until June 10. You'll already have finished your exams. While I'm still taking mine. Maybe you can come early and do some sightseeing until I'm ready to leave. Alex has some business to complete. Before he goes on vacation. He won't have finished until July 15, but he can join us then.

I'm leaving Paris on June 17. I'll drive through Italy and take the ferry from Brindisi to Greece. I'll stay in Greece. Until Alex joins me. Just think—while your friends are in summer school, you could be swimming in the Aegean! We'll be leaving Greece. As soon as Alex arrives so we'll have a month in Turkey. We'll start back around August 20. Your classes won't have started by then, will they?

I hope you will be able to join us for this trip. Alex is looking forward to seeing you again too.

Your friend,

Philippe

2 | *Complete the time line with information from the letter in Exercise 1.*

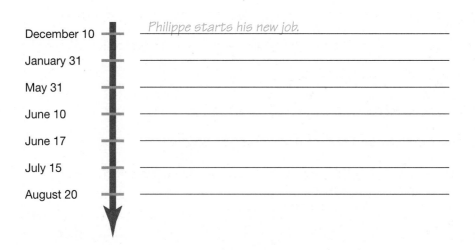

December 10	*Philippe starts his new job.*
January 31	
May 31	
June 10	
June 17	
July 15	
August 20	

3 | *Before you write . . .*

1. Think about some plans you are making for the future.

2. Make a time line about your plans like the one in Exercise 2.

3. Work with a partner. Discuss each other's plans. Use time clauses.

4 | *Write a letter to a friend about some plans you are making. Use information from your time line. Remember to connect some of the events with time clauses.*

5 | *Exchange letters with a different partner. Underline the time clauses. Write a question mark (?) above any time clauses that seem wrong. Then answer the questions.*

	Yes	No
1. Are the time clauses parts of complete sentences?	☐	☐
2. Are the sentences with time clauses punctuated correctly?	☐	☐
3. Are the verb forms correct in the sentences with time clauses?	☐	☐
4. Is the sequence of events clear?	☐	☐

5. What are some details you would like information about? _____

_____

_____

6 | *Work with your partner. Discuss each other's editing questions from Exercise 5. Then rewrite your own letter and make any necessary corrections.*

Review Test

I *Circle the correct words to complete each conversation.*

1. **A:** *Lord of the Rings* is playing at the Ciné tonight.

   B: Great. I think I go / (I'll go).

2. **A:** Please don't forget to pay the phone bill.

   B: I'll mail / I mail the check when I leave for work today.

3. **A:** What are your plans for the weekend?

   B: We'll go / We're going to go to the Moe concert. We just got our tickets.

4. **A:** What's wrong?

   B: Look at those two cars! They will crash / They're going to crash!

5. **A:** You look happy. What's up?

   B: I'm graduating / I will graduate next week.

6. **A:** What are you going to do after graduation?

   B: I'm starting a new job as soon as I'm getting / I get my degree.

7. **A:** I'd better get back to the library.

   B: OK. I'll see / I'm seeing you later.

8. **A:** I'll call you after I finished / I finish my exams.

   B: Great. I'm going to stay in town until I start / I'll start my new job.

9. **A:** Tracy promised to call tomorrow, but I won't be / I'm not home.

   B: Don't worry. I'll take / I take a message for you.

10. **A:** I have to do my homework now.

    B: OK. I'll cook dinner while you do / you'll do that.

II *Complete this conversation by circling the correct words.*

A: Graduation ceremonies were this afternoon. I can't believe this year is over already.

B: Me neither. Do you realize that in September we'll live / (we'll have been living) in this
   1.
apartment for two years?

A: Amazing! And you'll have been studying / you'll be studying here for four years.
   2.

B: I know. Next year at this time I'll have been graduating / I'll have graduated already.
   3.

A: So, what'll you be doing / what'll you have done next June? Any plans?
   4.

B: That's easy. Next June I'll be looking / I'll have been looking for a job. How about you?
   5.

A: I won't have graduated / I'll have graduated yet. I plan to go home at the beginning of
   6.
July next year, so during June, I guess I'm going to be getting ready / I'll have gotten ready
   7.
to travel to Greece.

B: Lucky you. Next summer you sit / you'll be sitting on beautiful beaches while
   8.
I go / I'll go to job interviews.
   9.

A: But just think. By the time I'll be getting / I get back, you'll find / you'll have found
   10.   11.
a good job. So while I'm learning / I will learn all about verb tenses in school,
   12.
you start / you'll be starting your career.
   13.

III *Circle the letter of the correct word(s) to complete each conversation.*

1. —Are you free tonight? The NBA playoffs are on TV at nine.   **A** (**B**) **C** **D**
   —I have to study first, but I _____ by then.
   (**A**) finished   (**C**) finish
   (**B**) 'll have finished   (**D**) 'll have been finishing

2. —How will I recognize your brother when I get to the airport?   **A** **B** **C** **D**
   —He has short dark hair, and he _____ a black leather jacket.
   (**A**) 'll be wearing   (**C**) 'll have been wearing
   (**B**) wore   (**D**) 'll have worn

3. —Do you think Mustafa should take the TOEFL in June?   **A** **B** **C** **D**
   —Sure. By that time, he _____ for more than six months.
   (**A**) 'll prepare   (**C**) 's prepared
   (**B**) prepared   (**D**) 'll have been preparing

(continued)

4. —Are you still reading Jack Francis novels?

    —Yes, but when I _____ this one, I'll have read all his books.

    (**A**) 'll finish   (**C**) finished

    (**B**) finish   (**D**) 'll have finished

    A B C D

5. —Will we be delayed here in Boston for long?

    —I'm afraid so. The train _____ the station for an hour.

    (**A**) won't be leaving   (**C**) won't have been leaving

    (**B**) won't have left   (**D**) didn't leave

    A B C D

6. —Should we go to Anna's before the party?

    —No. By the time we get there, she _____ already.

    (**A**) leaves   (**C**) 'll leave

    (**B**) 'll have left   (**D**) has left

    A B C D

7. —I hear that Jason is planning to buy a car.

    —I know. By next month, he _____ enough for a used one.

    (**A**) 'll have been saving   (**C**) saved

    (**B**) save   (**D**) 'll have saved

    A B C D

8. —It's your turn to do the dishes, right?

    —I _____ them in a minute. I'm busy right now.

    (**A**) do   (**C**) 'll do

    (**B**) 'll have done   (**D**) 've done

    A B C D

9. —Have you heard a weather report?

    —Yes. It _____ this afternoon.

    (**A**) 's going to snow   (**C**) snows

    (**B**) 's going to have been (**D**) 's snowing

    A B C D

10. —This job is endless.

    —I know. By the end of May, we _____ the house for two months.

    (**A**) 'll have painted   (**C**) 'll have been painting

    (**B**) 'll paint   (**D**) painted

    A B C D

IV *Complete this conversation. Use the correct form of the verbs in parentheses—future progressive, future perfect, or future perfect progressive.*

A: It says in this article that in the next ten years, electric cars _____*will have become*_____
1. (become)

cheap enough for most people to afford. That means we _____
2. (not drive)

gasoline-powered cars too much longer.

B: Great. By then, we _____ this gasoline-powered car for more
3. (drive)

than 150,000 miles. We'll be ready to buy a new car.

A: Right. And think of the benefit to the environment. We _____ the
4. (not pollute)

atmosphere the way we do now. And we _____ all that money
5. (not spend)

for fuel every year.

B: Speaking of driving, _____ you _____
6. (take)

Rocky to school tomorrow?

A: Yes. Why? Do you need the car?

B: No, but he has to bring in his science project, and it's huge. He _____
7. (work)

on it tonight. With luck, he _____ it by the time he goes to
8. (complete)

school tomorrow.

A: I can help him carry it in. No problem.

B: Tomorrow is an anniversary for me. I _____ at the university for
9. (teach)

five years.

A: I'll be home at seven. Let's go out for dinner and celebrate.

B: I've got to grade final exams tomorrow. I'm afraid I _____ all of
10. (not grade)

them by seven.

A: OK. The next day then.

> **V** Each sentence has four underlined words or phrases. The four underlined parts of the sentences are marked A, B, C, or D. Circle the letter of the <u>one</u> underlined part that is NOT CORRECT.

1. <u>By the time</u> you <u>will read</u> this, we'<u>ll</u> <u>already</u> have left.   **A** (**B**) **C** **D**
    A   B   C D

2. We'll <u>traveling</u> <u>for</u> a couple of days, so you <u>won't</u> <u>be able to</u> call us.   **A** **B** **C** **D**
       A   B   C   D

3. We'<u>ll call</u> you <u>as soon as</u> we'<u>re going to</u> <u>get home</u>.   **A** **B** **C** **D**
     A   B   C   D

4. By then, we'<u>ll have been</u> <u>traveled</u> since July, so we'<u>ll</u> <u>be</u> tired.   **A** **B** **C** **D**
             A   B   C D

5. Yukio <u>finished</u> school <u>by</u> next summer, so we'<u>re going to</u> <u>visit</u> her.   **A** **B** **C** **D**
        A   B   C   D

6. You'<u>ll have been</u> <u>studying</u> Japanese <u>for</u> three years, so you'<u>re speaking</u>   **A** **B** **C** **D**
      A   B   C   D

fluently by then.

7. We'<u>ll</u> <u>be have</u> a great time <u>when</u> we <u>get</u> together.   **A** **B** **C** **D**
  A   B   C   D

▶ *To check your answers, go to the Answer Key on page RT-2.*

PART III

Negative Questions and
Tag Questions,
Additions and Responses

7 Negative *Yes / No* Questions and Tag Questions

Grammar in Context

BEFORE YOU READ

🎧 *What do you like about the town or city where you live? What don't you like? Would you like to live in another country? Why or why not? Read these on-the-street interviews reported in a popular magazine.*

● **International Living Magazine**

IT'S A GREAT PLACE TO LIVE, **ISN'T IT?**

Our reporters around the world interviewed people working and studying in foreign countries. Our question: How do you like living here? Here's what we learned from Lydia Sousa, Anton Kada, Kinoro Okaya, and Tessa Bradley.

*Ipanema Beach,
Rio de Janeiro, Brazil*

Reporter: Hello. It's a beautiful day, **isn't it**? Do you mind if I ask you a few questions?

Sousa: Hi. **Haven't I** seen you on TV? You're Paulo Lopes, **aren't you**?

Reporter: That's right. I'm conducting a survey for *International Living Magazine.* You're not from Rio, **are you**?

Sousa: No, I'm not. I'm originally from Portugal. You could tell right away by my accent, **couldn't you**?

Reporter: How do you like living here?

Sousa: I love it. Just look around you—the beach, the bay, the mountains, the sky. It's fantastic looking, **isn't it**? I walk along this beach every day on the way to my office.

Reporter: It's not a bad way to get to work, **is it**?

Sousa: It's not a bad place to play either! Besides this beautiful beach, there are so many restaurants and clubs. It's a great place to live, **isn't it**?

IT'S A GREAT PLACE TO LIVE, **ISN'T IT?**

Seoul, South Korea

Reporter: You're a student, **aren't you**?

Kada: Yes, I am. I'm studying architecture at the Kaywon School of Art and Design.

Reporter: That's not in Seoul, **is it**?

Kada: No, it's not. But it's not far.

Reporter: So, how do you like living here? **Doesn't the cold weather** bother you?

Kada: No, I'm from Berlin, so I'm used to cold winters. I love this city. You can find modern skyscrapers right next to ancient structures.

Reporter: That's true. That's the old city gate over there, **isn't it**?

Kada: Yes. And there are several beautiful palaces nearby.

● ●

Reporter: This is one of the oldest markets in Cairo, **isn't it**?

Okaya: Yes, and one of the most interesting.

Reporter: **Don't they** have markets like this in Nairobi?

Okaya: Not this big. Hey, **didn't you** buy anything?

Reporter: Not today. So, what brought you to Cairo?

Okaya: My job. I work for an Internet provider that does a lot of business in Africa.

Reporter: It gets awfully hot here in the summer, **doesn't it**?

Okaya: Yes, but the winters are mild. And it almost never rains. You can't beat that, **can you**?

● ●

Cairo, Egypt

Reporter: You're from England, **aren't you**?

Bradley: Yes. I moved to Toronto 10 years ago.

Reporter: Was it a difficult adjustment?

Bradley: No, not really. First of all, having the same language makes things easy, **doesn't it**? And people here are very friendly.

Reporter: Why Canada?

Bradley: England's a small country. I was attracted by Canada's wide-open spaces. It seems to offer endless possibilities.

Reporter: **Don't you** miss your family back home?

Bradley: Sometimes, but the Internet keeps us connected. And they visit every year.

Reporter: It doesn't take long to cross the Atlantic, **does it**?

Bradley: No, that's why they call it "the Pond." It really *is* a small world now, **isn't it**?

Reporter: It sure is.

Toronto, Canada

AFTER YOU READ

Check the correct answers.

1. At the end of the first interview, Sousa is saying:
   ☐ I think Rio is a great place to live.
   ☐ Do you think Rio is a great place to live?

2. At the end of the third interview, the reporter is saying:
   ☐ I don't think it gets very hot in Cairo.
   ☐ I think it gets very hot in Cairo.

Grammar Presentation

NEGATIVE *YES / NO* QUESTIONS

WITH *BE* AS THE MAIN VERB

Questions
Be + Not + Subject
Aren't you from Rio de Janeiro?

Short Answers	
Affirmative	Negative
Yes, I **am**.	**No**, I'**m not**.

WITH ALL AUXILIARY VERBS EXCEPT *DO*

Questions
Auxiliary + *Not* + Subject + Verb
Aren't you moving?
Hasn't he been here before?
Can't they move tomorrow?

Short Answers			
Affirmative		Negative	
Yes,	I **am**.	**No**,	I'**m not**.
	he **has**.		he **hasn't**.
	they **can**.		they **can't**.

WITH *DO* AS THE AUXILIARY VERB

Questions
Do + Not + Subject + Verb
Doesn't he live here?
Didn't they move last year?

Short Answers			
Affirmative		Negative	
Yes,	he **does**.	**No**,	he **doesn't**.
	they **did**.		they **didn't**.

TAG QUESTIONS

WITH *BE* AS THE MAIN VERB

Affirmative Statement	Negative Tag
Subject + *Be*	*Be* + *Not* + Subject
You're from Rio,	**aren't you?**

Negative Statement	Affirmative Tag
Subject + *Be* + *Not*	*Be* + Subject
You're not from Rio,	**are you?**

WITH ALL AUXILIARY VERBS EXCEPT *DO*

Affirmative Statement	Negative Tag
Subject + Auxiliary	Auxiliary + *Not* + Subject
You're moving,	**aren't you?**
He's been here before,	**hasn't he?**
They can move tomorrow,	**can't they?**

Negative Statement	Affirmative Tag
Subject + Auxiliary + *Not*	Auxiliary + Subject
You're not moving,	**are you?**
He hasn't been here before,	**has he?**
They can't move tomorrow,	**can they?**

WITH *DO* AS AN AUXILIARY VERB

Affirmative Statement	Negative Tag
Subject + Verb	*Do* + *Not* + Subject
He lives here,	**doesn't he?**
They moved last year,	**didn't they?**

Negative Statement	Affirmative Tag
Subject + *Do* + *Not* + Verb	*Do* + Subject
He doesn't live here,	**does he?**
They didn't move,	**did they?**

GRAMMAR NOTES   **EXAMPLES**

1. Use **negative** *yes / no* **questions** and **tag questions** to:

a. check information you believe to be true

> NEGATIVE *YES / NO* QUESTION
> - **Doesn't Anton** live in Seoul?
>
> TAG QUESTION
> - Anton lives in Seoul, **doesn't he?**
>   *(In both sentences, the speaker believes that Anton lives in Seoul and wants to check this information.)*

b. comment on a situation

> NEGATIVE *YES / NO* QUESTION
> - **Isn't it** a nice day?
>
> TAG QUESTION
> - It's a nice day, **isn't it?**
>   *(In both sentences, the speaker is commenting on the weather.)*

2. Like affirmative *yes / no* questions, **negative *yes / no* questions** begin with a form of *be* or an auxiliary verb, such as *have, do, will, can,* or *should*.

> - **Aren't you** Paulo Lopes?
> - **Haven't I** seen you on TV?
> - **Don't you** like the weather here?
> - **Isn't it** beautiful?
> - **Didn't you** move here last year?
> - **Won't you** be sorry to leave?
> - **Can't you** stay longer?

USAGE NOTE: We almost always use contractions in negative questions.

> - **Shouldn't we** think about moving?
>   RARE ~~Should we not~~ think about moving?

► **BE CAREFUL!** Use *are* (not *am*) in negative questions with *I* and a contraction.

> - **Aren't I** right?
>   NOT ~~Am'nt~~ I right?

3. Form **tag questions** with **statement + tag**.

The statement expresses an **assumption**. The tag means *Right?* or *Isn't that true?*

statement	tag
• You're not from Rio,	**are you?**
• You're Paulo Lopes,	**aren't you?**

(*You're Paulo Lopes, right?*)

• You're not from Cairo, **are you?**
(*You're not from Cairo. Isn't that true?*)

a. If the statement verb is affirmative, the tag verb is negative.

affirmative	negative
• You **work** on Thursdays,	**don't** you?

b. If the statement verb is negative, the tag verb is affirmative.

negative	affirmative
• You **don't work** on Thursdays,	**do** you?

Form the tag with a form of *be* or an auxiliary verb, such as *have, do, will, can,* or *should*. Use the **same auxiliary** that is in the statement.

• It**'s** a nice day, **isn't** it?
• You**'ve** lived here a long time, **haven't** you?

If the statement does not use *be* or an auxiliary verb, use an appropriate form of ***do*** in the tag.

• You **come** from London, **don't** you?
• You**'ll** be here tomorrow, **won't** you?
• You **can** drive, **can't** you?

▶ **BE CAREFUL!** In the tag, only use pronouns.

• *Tom* works here, doesn't **he?**
NOT Tom works here, doesn't ~~Tom?~~

When the subject of the statement is *that*, the subject of the tag is *it*.

• *That's* a good idea, isn't **it?**
NOT That's a good idea, isn't ~~that?~~

---

4. Use **tag questions** in conversations when you expect the other person to agree with you. In this type of tag question, the <u>voice falls</u> on the tag.

A: It's getting warmer, **isn't it?**
B: Uh-huh. Seems more like spring than winter.

Use this type of tag question to:

a. **check** information you believe is correct. You expect the other person to answer (and agree).

A: It doesn't snow here, **does it?**
B: No, never. That's why I love it.

b. **comment** on a situation. This type of tag question is more like a statement than a question. The other person can just nod or say *uh-huh* to show that he or she is listening and agrees.

A: Beautiful day, **isn't it?**
B: Uh-huh. More like spring than winter.

(continued)

5. Tag questions can also be used to **get information**. This type of tag question is more like a *yes/no* question. You want to confirm your information because you are not sure it is correct. Like a *yes/no* question, the <u>voice rises</u> on the tag, and you usually get an answer.

A: You're not moving, **are you?**
(Are you moving?)

B: Yes. I'm returning to Berlin.

OR

No. I'm staying here.

6. Answer negative *yes/no* questions and tag questions the same way you answer affirmative *yes/no* questions. The answer is *yes* if the information is correct and *no* if the information is not correct.

A: **Don't you** work in Toronto?
B: **Yes, I do.** I work there.

A: You work in Toronto, **don't you?**
B: **No, I don't.** I work in Montreal.

Focused Practice

1 | DISCOVER THE GRAMMAR

🎧 *Read this conversation between Anton's mother, Petra, and a neighbor. Underline all the negative questions and circle all the tags.*

PETRA: Hi, Kurt. Nice day, (isn't it?)

KURT: Sure is. What are *you* doing home today? <u>Don't you usually work on Thursdays?</u>

PETRA: I took the day off to help my son. He just got back from Korea, and he's looking for an apartment. You don't know of any vacant apartments, do you?

KURT: Isn't he going to stay with you?

PETRA: Well, he just got a new job at an architecture firm downtown, and he wants a place of his own nearby. Do you know of anything?

KURT: As a matter of fact, I do. You know the Edwards family, don't you? They're moving back to Toronto next month.

PETRA: Are they? What kind of apartment do they have?

KURT: A one-bedroom.

PETRA: It's not furnished, is it? Anton really doesn't have any furniture.

KURT: Can't he rent some? I did that in my first apartment.

PETRA: I don't know. Isn't it less expensive to buy?

2 | GETTING READY TO MOVE   *Grammar Note 3*

Mr. and Mrs. Edwards are talking about their move to Toronto. Match the statements on the left with the tags on the right.

__*i*__ **1.** You've called the movers,	**a.** can we?
_____ **2.** They're coming tomorrow,	**b.** do we?
_____ **3.** This isn't going to be cheap,	**c.** is he?
_____ **4.** You haven't finished packing,	**d.** isn't it?
_____ **5.** We don't need any more boxes,	**e.** aren't they?
_____ **6.** Paul is going to help us,	**f.** have you?
_____ **7.** We can put some things in storage,	**g.** isn't he?
_____ **8.** Jack isn't buying our bookcases,	**h.** is it?
_____ **9.** We need to disconnect the phone,	**i.** haven't you?
_____ **10.** The movers aren't packing the books for us,	**j.** don't we?
_____ **11.** We can't turn off the electricity yet,	**k.** can't we?
_____ **12.** Moving is hard,	**l.** are they?

3 | A TV INTERVIEW   *Grammar Notes 3–5*

Complete this interview with Tessa Bradley. Use appropriate tags.

HOST: You've lived in Toronto for many years, ____*haven't you*____?
                                                        1.

BRADLEY: Since I came here to teach video arts. Seems like ages ago. Looking back now, I can't

believe I just packed one suitcase and got on a plane.

HOST: You didn't know anyone here either, _____?
                                                  2.

BRADLEY: No. And I didn't have a cent to my name. Just some ideas and a lot of hope. It sounds

crazy, _____?
            3.

HOST: Not when you look at all the TV shows you've done. Things have sure worked out for

you, _____? You've already worked on two big TV series, and you've
        4.

done some work for the movies as well. You're working on another movie now,

_____?
     5.

(continued)

BRADLEY: Yes. It's a comedy about some kids who become invisible.

HOST: Sounds like a good movie for the whole family. I know I'll certainly take my kids to see it. Speaking of kids, you have some of your own, _____?
6.

BRADLEY: Two boys and a girl—all very visible!

HOST: I know what you mean. Do you ever wish they were invisible?

BRADLEY: Hmmm. That's an interesting thought, _____?
7.

4 | ISN'T IT NICE?   *Grammar Notes 1–2, 6*

Anton is looking at an apartment. Complete these negative yes / no questions and short answers. Use the verbs that are in the sentences following the short answers.

1. OWNER: ____Isn't your name____ Andreas Hauswirth?

   ANTON: ____No, it isn't.____ My name is Anton Kada.

2. OWNER: You look familiar. _____ this apartment before?

   ANTON: _____ I've never seen it before. This is the first time.

3. ANTON: _____ an ad in the newspaper?

   OWNER: _____ I put an ad in yesterday's newspaper.

4. ANTON: The apartment feels hot. _____ an air-conditioner?

   OWNER: _____ It has a fan. That really keeps it cool enough.

5. ANTON: I notice that there are marks on the walls. _____ it?

   OWNER: _____ I'm going to paint it next week. I haven't had time yet.

6. OWNER: _____ a nice apartment?

   ANTON: _____ It's a very nice apartment. But I'm not sure I can take it.

7. OWNER: _____ big enough?

   ANTON: _____ It's big enough, but I can't afford it.

8. OWNER: _____ a roommate?

   ANTON: _____ I can find one, but I really want to live alone.

5 | MOVING AROUND

Grammar Notes 1–3, 6

Read this information about video artist Nam-Jun Paik. Imagine you are going to interview him, and you are not sure of the information in parentheses. Write negative yes / no questions or tag questions to check that information.

1. born July 1932 in Korea (in Seoul?)
2. at age 14, studied music (took piano lessons?)
3. family left Korea in 1950 (moved to Tokyo?)
4. moved to Germany in 1956 (studied music composition?)
5. began to compose electronic music (didn't write traditional music?)
6. during the 1960s created a new art form with TV screens and video (didn't paint on paper?)
7. moved to New York in 1964 (continued to miss Korea?)
8. produced a huge art installation for 1988 Seoul Olympics (used 1,003 TV monitors?)
9. after an illness in 1996 started painting on flat surfaces (doesn't do installations anymore?)
10. lives in New York (became a U.S. citizen?)

Nam-Jun Paik with his video art

1. *Weren't you born in Seoul?* OR *You were born in Seoul, weren't you?*

2. _____

3. _____

4. _____

5. _____

6. _____

7. _____

8. _____

9. _____

10. _____

6 | EDITING

Tessa Bradley is working on a new TV show. Read part of this TV script. There are nine mistakes in the use of negative questions, tag questions, and short answers. The first mistake is already corrected. Find and correct eight more.

BEN: It's been a long time, Joe, ~~haven't~~ *hasn't* it?

JOE: That depends on what you mean by a long time, doesn't that?

BEN: Are not you afraid to show your face around here?

JOE: I can take care of myself. I'm still alive, amn't I?

BEN: Until someone recognizes you. You're still wanted by the police, are you?

JOE: I'll be gone by morning. Look, I need a place to stay. Just for one night.

BEN: I have to think about my wife and kid. Don't you have any place else to go?

JOE: Yes, I do. There's no one to turn to but you. You have to help me.

BEN: I've already helped you plenty. I went to jail for you, haven't I? And didn't I kept my mouth shut the whole time?

JOE: Yeah, OK, Ben. Don't you remember what happened in Vegas, do you?

BEN: Don't ever think I'll forget that! OK, OK. I can make a call.

Communication Practice

7 | LISTENING

Listen to these people ask questions. Notice if their voices rise or fall at the end of each question. Listen again, and decide in each case if they are really asking a question (and expect an answer) or if they are just making a comment (and don't expect an answer). Check the correct column.

	Expect an answer	Don't expect an answer		Expect an answer	Don't expect an answer
1.	☐	☑	6.	☐	☐
2.	☐	☐	7.	☐	☐
3.	☐	☐	8.	☐	☐
4.	☐	☐	9.	☐	☐
5.	☐	☐	10.	☐	☐

8 | INFORMATION GAP: LONDON AND TORONTO

Work in pairs (A and B). Student B, look at the Information Gap on page 101 and follow the instructions there. Student A, look at the questions below. What do you know about London? Complete the questions by circling the correct words and writing the tags.

1. London (is) / isn't the largest city in the United Kingdom, _____isn't it_____?

2. It is / isn't the capital of the United Kingdom, _____?

3. London lies on a river / the ocean, _____?

4. It consists of two / thirty-two "boroughs," or parts, _____?

5. It has / doesn't have a lot of theaters, _____?

6. Many / Not many tourists visit London, _____?

7. It is / isn't a very safe city, _____?

Ask Student B the questions. Student B will read a paragraph about London and tell you if your information is correct or not.

Example: A: London is the largest city in the United Kingdom, isn't it?
B: That's right.

Now read about Toronto, and answer Student B's questions.

TORONTO

Although Toronto is not the capital of Canada, it is the country's largest city. It is also home to the CN Tower, the world's tallest structure. Lying on the northwest shore of Lake Ontario, Toronto is a busy port. It is also the business and financial center of the country, as well as the leading city for publishing and TV and movie production.

Toronto is a very international city. More than 100 different languages are spoken, and over one-third of Toronto residents speak a language other than English at home.
With all this diversity, it is interesting to note that Toronto is one of the safest cities in the world.

Example: B: Toronto is the largest city in Canada, isn't it?
A: Yes, it is.

9 | WHO KNOWS WHO BETTER?

How well do you know your classmates? Work with a partner. Complete the first ten questions with information about your partner that you think is correct. Add two questions of your own. Then ask the questions to check your information. Put a check next to each question that has correct information. Which one of you knows the other one better?

Examples: A: You're from Venezuela, aren't you?
B: That's right. OR No, I'm from Colombia.

A: Don't you play the guitar?
B: Yes. I play the guitar and the drums.

_____ 1. _____, aren't you?

_____ 2. Don't you _____?

_____ 3. _____, can you?

_____ 4. _____, haven't you?

_____ 5. _____, did you?

_____ 6. _____, do you?

_____ 7. Aren't you _____?

_____ 8. _____, will you?

_____ 9. Didn't you _____?

_____10. _____, can't you?

_____11. _____, _____?

_____12. _____?

10 | WRITING

You are going to interview a classmate about his or her city or school. Write eight questions. Use negative yes / no questions and tag questions. Ask your questions and write your classmate's answers.

Example: You're from Venezuela, aren't you?
Don't you speak French too?

11 | ON THE INTERNET

Work with a partner. Choose a city you both haven't been to. What do you know about the city? Write six tag questions with information you want to confirm. Then do a search and check your information. Take turns asking and answering questions.

Example: A: Rio isn't the capital of Brazil, is it?
B: No, it isn't. Brasília is.

INFORMATION GAP FOR STUDENT B

Student B, read about London and answer Student A's questions.

LONDON

London is the capital and largest city of the United Kingdom. It is also one of the oldest and largest cities in the world. Located in southeastern England, the city lies on the River Thames, which links it to shipping routes throughout the world. Because of its size, the city is divided into 32 "boroughs" or parts. With its many museums, palaces, parks, and theaters, tourism is a major industry. In fact, millions of tourists visit the city every year to take advantage of its many cultural and historical offerings. Unfortunately, like many great urban centers, London has problems such as traffic congestion, crime, and homelessness.

Example: A: London is the largest city in the United Kingdom, isn't it?
B: That's right.

Now look at the questions below. What do you know about Toronto? Circle the correct words and complete the tag questions.

1. Toronto (is)/ isn't the largest city in Canada, _____*isn't it*_____?

2. It is / isn't the capital of Canada, _____?

3. It has / doesn't have the tallest structure in the world, _____?

4. It lies on a lake / river, _____?

5. It has / doesn't have a lot of businesses, _____?

6. You can / can't hear many different languages there, _____?

7. It is / isn't a very safe place to live, _____?

Ask Student A the questions. Student A will read a paragraph about Toronto and tell you if your information is correct or not.

Example: B: Toronto is the largest city in Canada, isn't it?
A: Yes, it is.

So, Too, Neither, Not either, and *But*

Grammar in Context

BEFORE YOU READ

🎧 *Look at the photos of twins. What is different about them? What is the same? Read the article about identical twins.*

The TWIN Question: *Nature or Nurture?*

by Ruth Sanborn, *Family Life* Editor

MARK AND GERALD are identical twins. Mirror images of each other, they also share many similarities in lifestyle. Mark is a firefighter, and **so is Gerald**. Mark has never been married, and **neither has Gerald**. Mark likes hunting, fishing, and Chinese food. **Gerald does too**.

These similarities might not be unusual in identical twins, except for one fact: Mark and Gerald were separated when they were five days old. They grew up in different states with different families. Neither one knew that he had a twin until they found each other accidentally at age 31.

Average people are fascinated by twins, and **so are scientists**. Identical twins share the same genes. Therefore, they offer researchers the chance to study the effect of genetic inheritance on health and personality.

However, when identical twins grow up together, they also experience the same environment. How can researchers separate these environmental factors from genetic factors? By looking at identical twins who were separated at birth! Twins with completely different childhoods give researchers the chance to study the age-old question: Which has more effect on our lives, heredity (the genes we receive from our parents) or environment (the social influences in our childhood)?

MARK AND GERALD

The TWIN Question

JIM AND JIM

Some startling coincidences have turned up in these studies. One astonishing pair is the Springer and Lewis brothers, who were adopted by different families soon after birth. The Springer family named their adopted son Jim. **So did the Lewis family**. When the two Jims met for the first time as adults, they discovered more surprising similarities. Jim Lewis had worked as a gas station attendant and a law enforcement agent. **So had Jim Springer**. Both men had owned dogs. Lewis had named his Toy; **so had Springer**. And believe it or not, Lewis had married a woman named Linda, divorced her, and later married a woman named Betty. **So had Springer**.

Do our genes really determine our names, our spouses, our jobs, even our pets? The lives of other twins indicate that the question of nature or nurture is even more complicated than that.

Identical twins Andrea and Barbara, for example, were born in Germany and separated shortly after birth. Andrea stayed in Germany, **but Barbara didn't**. She moved to the United States with her adoptive American family. The twins grew up in different cultures, speaking different languages. Barbara didn't know she had a twin, **but Andrea did**, and she searched for her sister. When they met, they discovered amazing similarities. Each had a scar on her lip from an accident. Each had had a tonsillectomy—on the same day!

Nevertheless, there were important differences. Andrea is outgoing and expressive, **but Barbara isn't**, despite her identical genetic heritage. Both sisters got married and had two children. Andrea stayed married, but Barbara married and divorced several times.

Clearly, heredity doesn't completely govern our lives. **Our environment doesn't either**. The lives of twins separated at birth suggest that we have a lot to learn about the complex role these two powerful forces play in shaping human lives.

BARBARA AND ANDREA

This photograph was taken on the day Barbara and Andrea were reunited. The man standing between them, Thomas Gulotta, helped bring them together.

AFTER YOU READ

Write **T** *(true) or* **F** *(false).*

_____ **1.** Gerald is married.

_____ **2.** Gerald doesn't like hunting.

_____ **3.** Jim Springer once worked at a gas station.

_____ **4.** Jim Springer's wife was named Betty.

_____ **5.** Barbara stayed in Germany.

_____ **6.** Andrea knew she had a twin.

Grammar Presentation

SIMILARITY: *AND + SO, TOO, NEITHER, NOT EITHER*

WITH *BE* AS THE MAIN VERB

Affirmative	
Subject + *Be*	*And + So + Be* + Subject
Amy **is** a twin,	**and so is** Sue.

Negative	
Subject + *Be + Not*	*And + Neither + Be* + Subject
Amy **isn't** very tall,	**and neither is** Sue.

Affirmative	
Subject + *Be*	*And + Subject + Be + Too*
Amy **is** a twin,	**and** Sue **is too**.

Negative	
Subject + *Be + Not*	*And + Subject + Be + Not either*
Amy **isn't** very tall,	**and** Sue **isn't either**.

WITH ALL AUXILIARY VERBS EXCEPT *DO*

Affirmative	
Subject + Auxiliary	*And + So + Auxiliary* + Subject
Amy **has** had two sons,	**and so has** Sue.

Negative	
Subject + Auxiliary + *Not*	*And + Neither + Auxiliary* + Subject
Amy **can't** ski,	**and neither can** Sue.

Affirmative	
Subject + Auxiliary	*And + Subject + Auxiliary + Too*
Amy **has** had two sons,	**and** Sue **has too**.

Negative	
Subject + Auxiliary + *Not*	*And + Subject + Auxiliary + Not either*
Amy **can't** ski,	**and** Sue **can't either**.

WITH *DO* AS THE AUXILIARY VERB

Affirmative	
Subject + Verb	*And + So +* *Do + Subject*
Amy **likes** dogs,	**and so does** Sue.

Negative	
Subject + *Do + Not + Verb*	*And + Neither +* *Do + Subject*
Amy **doesn't** like cats,	**and neither does** Sue.

Affirmative	
Subject + Verb	*And + Subject +* *Do + Too*
Amy **likes** dogs,	**and** Sue **does too**.

Negative	
Subject + *Do + Not + Verb*	*And + Subject +* *Do + Not + Either*
Amy **doesn't** like cats,	**and** Sue **doesn't either**.

CONTRAST: *BUT*

WITH *BE* AS THE MAIN VERB

Affirmative	Negative
Subject + *Be*	*But + Subject + Be + Not*
Amy **is** outgoing,	**but** Sue **isn't**.

Negative	Affirmative
Subject + *Be + Not*	*But + Subject + Be*
Amy **isn't** quiet,	**but** Sue **is**.

WITH ALL AUXILIARY VERBS EXCEPT *DO*

Affirmative	Negative
Subject + Auxiliary	*But + Subject +* *Auxiliary + Not*
Amy **has** traveled,	**but** Sue **hasn't**.

Negative	Affirmative
Subject + Auxiliary + *Not*	*But + Subject +* *Auxiliary*
Amy **couldn't** swim,	**but** Sue **could**.

WITH *DO* AS THE AUXILIARY VERB

Affirmative	Negative
Subject + Verb	*But + Subject + Do + Not*
Amy **lives** here,	**but** Sue **doesn't**.

Negative	Affirmative
Subject + *Do + Not*	*But + Subject + Do*
Amy **doesn't** drive,	**but** Sue **does**.

GRAMMAR NOTES	EXAMPLES
1. Additions are clauses or short sentences that follow a statement. They express <u>similarity</u> to or <u>contrast</u> with the information in the statement. We use additions to avoid repeating information.	**SIMILARITY** • Lewis bites his fingernails, **and so does Springer**. *(Lewis bites his fingernails. Springer bites his fingernails.)* **CONTRAST** • Barbara's marriage ended, **but Andrea's didn't**. *(Barbara's marriage ended. Andrea's marriage didn't end.)*
2. Use *so*, *too*, *neither*, or *not either* to express **similarity**. Additions of similarity can either be clauses or separate sentences.	• Mark is a firefighter, **and *so* is Gerald**. OR • Mark is a firefighter, **and Gerald is *too***. *(Mark is a firefighter. Gerald is a firefighter.)* • Mark isn't married. ***Neither* is Gerald**. OR • Mark isn't married. **Gerald *isn't either***. *(Mark isn't married. Gerald isn't married.)*
3. Use *so* or *too* if the addition follows an <u>affirmative</u> statement. Use *neither* or *not either* if the addition follows a <u>negative</u> statement. ▶ **BE CAREFUL!** Notice the word order after *so* and *neither*. The verb comes before the subject.	• Mark **is** a firefighter, and *so* **is** Gerald. OR • Mark **is** a firefighter, and Gerald **is** *too*. • Mark **didn't** get married. ***Neither* did** Gerald. OR • Mark **didn't** get married. Gerald **did*n't* either**. • So **is Gerald**. NOT So ~~Gerald is~~. • Neither **did Gerald**. NOT Neither ~~Gerald did~~.

4. Use ***but*** in additions of **contrast**.

If the statement is affirmative, the addition is negative.

- Amy **lived** in Germany, ***but*** Sue **didn't**.

If the statement is negative, the addition is affirmative.

- Amy's family **didn't speak** English, ***but*** Sue's **did**.

---

5. Additions always use a form of *be*, an auxiliary verb, or a modal.

a. If the statement uses *be*, use ***be*** in the addition.

- I**'m** a twin, and so **is** my cousin.

b. If the statement uses an auxiliary verb (a form of *be*, *have*, *do*, or *will*), or a modal (for example, *can*, *could*, *should*, *would*) use the **same auxiliary verb or modal** in the addition.

- Jim Lewis **had** worked in a gas station, and so **had** Jim Springer.
- I **can't** drive, and neither **can** my twin.

c. If the statement doesn't use *be* or an auxiliary verb, use an appropriate form of ***do*** in the addition.

- Lewis **bought** a Chevrolet, and so **did** Springer.
- Lewis **owns** a dog, and so **does** Springer.

---

6. In conversation, you can use short **responses** with ***so***, ***too***, ***neither***, and ***not either*** to express **agreement** with another speaker.

A: I **have** a twin sister.
B: *So do I*. OR I do *too*.

A: I **don't have** any brothers or sisters.
B: *Neither* do I. OR I *don't either*.

USAGE NOTE: In informal speech, people say ***Me too*** to express agreement with an affirmative statement and ***Me neither*** to express agreement with a negative statement.

A: I **think** twin studies are fascinating.
B: *Me too*.

A: I**'ve never heard** of the Jim twins.
B: *Me neither*.

---

7. In conversation, use short **responses** with ***but*** to express **disagreement** with another speaker. You can often leave out *but*.

A: I **wouldn't like** to have a twin.
B: Oh, *(but)* **I would**.

Focused Practice

1 | DISCOVER THE GRAMMAR

🎧 *Read these short conversations between reunited twins. Decide if the statement that follows is true (**T**) or false (**F**).*

1. MARK: I like Chinese food.
    GERALD: So do I.
    __T__ Gerald likes Chinese food.

2. ANDREA: I don't want to go out tonight.
    BARBARA: Neither do I.
    _____ Barbara wants to go out tonight.

3. AMY: I didn't understand that article.
    KERRIE: Oh, I did.
    _____ Kerrie understood the article.

4. JEAN: I'm not hungry.
    JOAN: I'm not either.
    _____ Jean and Joan are hungry.

5. ANDREA: I was born in Germany.
    BARBARA: So was I.
    _____ Barbara and Andrea were both born in Germany.

6. AMY: I've always felt lonely.
    KERRIE: So have I.
    _____ Kerrie has felt lonely.

7. MARK: I'm ready to get married.
    GERALD: I'm not.
    _____ Gerald is ready to get married.

8. DAVE: I can meet at eight o'clock.
    PETE: I can too.
    _____ Pete can meet at eight o'clock.

9. JIM: I have a headache.
    JIM: So do I.
    _____ Both Jims have headaches.

10. DAVE: I'm not looking forward to the TV interview.
    PETE: I am.
    _____ Pete isn't looking forward to the TV interview.

2 | DOUBLE TROUBLE

Grammar Notes 1–5

Complete the paragraph about being a twin. Circle the correct words.

Sometimes being a twin can cause trouble. In high school, I was in Mr. Jacobs's history class.

Neither /(So) was Joe. One day we took a test. I got questions 18 and 20 wrong. Joe did so / too.
    1.   **2.**

I didn't spell *Constantinople* correctly, and either / neither did Joe. The teacher was sure we had
                                                     3.

cheated. As a result, I got an F on the test, and so did / got Joe. We tried to convince Mr. Jacobs
                                                       4.

of our innocence. After all, I had sat on the left side of the room, but Joe didn't / hadn't. As
                                                               5.

always, he sat on the right. But Mr. Jacobs just thought we had developed some elaborate way of

sharing answers across the room. Our parents believed we were honest, but Mr. Jacobs

didn't / weren't. The principal didn't either / too. We finally convinced them to give us another
    6.   **7.**

test. This time we were in separate rooms. I got questions 3 and 10 wrong. Guess what?

Neither / So did Joe. Our teacher was astounded, and / but we weren't. We were just amused.
    8.   **9.**

3 | WE HAVE SO MUCH IN COMMON

Grammar Note 6

🎧 *Two twins are talking. They agree on everything. Complete their conversation with short responses.*

MARTA: I'm so happy we finally found each other.

CARLA: So _____ am I _____. I always felt like something was missing from my life.
                1.

MARTA: So _____. I always knew I had a double somewhere out there.
           2.

CARLA: I can't believe how similar we are.

MARTA: Neither _____. It's like always seeing myself in the mirror.
                3.

CARLA: Not only do we look identical, we like and dislike all the same things.

MARTA: Right. I hate lettuce.

CARLA: I _____. And I detest liver.
            4.

MARTA: So _____. I love pizza, though.
            5.

CARLA: So _____. But only with tomato and cheese. I don't like pepperoni.
            6.

MARTA: Neither _____.
                7.

CARLA: This is amazing! I wonder if our husbands have so much in common.

MARTA: So _____!
            8.

4 | THE TWO BOBS

Look at this chart about the twins' husbands. Then complete the sentences about them. Add statements with **so**, **too**, **neither**, **not either**, *and* **but**.

	Bob Bowen	Bob Phillips
AGE	42	42
HEIGHT	6'2"	5'8"
WEIGHT	180 lb	180 lb
HAIR COLOR	blond	blond
EYE COLOR	blue	brown
HOBBIES	tennis	tennis
FAVORITE FOOD	steak	steak
MILITARY SERVICE	yes	no
EDUCATION	graduate degree	graduate degree
LANGUAGES	English, Spanish	English, French
JOB	lawyer	engineer
BROTHERS OR SISTERS	none	none

1. Bob Bowen is 42, _____ *and so is Bob Phillips.* OR *and Bob Phillips is too.* _____

2. Bob Bowen is 6'2", _____

3. Bob Bowen weighs 180 pounds, _____

4. Bob Bowen has blond hair, _____

5. Bob Bowen doesn't have green eyes, _____

6. Bob Bowen plays tennis, _____

7. Bob Bowen likes steak, _____

8. Bob Bowen served in the military, _____

9. Bob Bowen has attended graduate school, _____

10. Bob Bowen doesn't speak French, _____

11. Bob Bowen became a lawyer, _____

12. Bob Bowen doesn't have any brothers or sisters, _____

5 | EDITING

Read Ryan's composition. There are five mistakes in the use of sentence additions. The first mistake is already corrected. Find and correct four more.

My Brother and I

My brother is just a year older than I am. (I'm 18.) We have a lot of things in common.
                                                      is he
We look alike. I am 5'10", and so ~~he is~~. I have straight black hair and dark brown eyes,

and so does he. We share some of the same interests too. I love to play soccer, and he

too. Both of us swim every day, but I can't dive, and either can he.

   Although there are a lot of similarities between us, there are also many differences.

For example, he likes eating all kinds of food, but I don't. Give me hamburgers and fries

every day! My brother doesn't want to go to college, but I don't. I believe it's important

to get as much education as possible, but he wants to get real-life experience. Our

personalities are quite different. I am quiet and easygoing, but he not. He has lots of

energy and talks a lot. When I think about it, we really are more different than similar.

---

6 | BROTHERS   *Grammar Notes 2–5*

Look at Exercise 5. Complete the chart by putting a check in the correct column(s).

	Ryan	**Ryan's Brother**
1. is 18 years old	☑	☐
2. is 5'10" tall	☐	☐
3. has black hair	☐	☐
4. has dark brown eyes	☐	☐
5. loves soccer	☐	☐
6. swims	☐	☐
7. dives	☐	☐
8. prefers hamburgers and fries	☐	☐
9. wants to go to college	☐	☐
10. prefers real-life experience	☐	☐
11. is quiet	☐	☐
12. is easygoing	☐	☐

Communication Practice

7 | LISTENING

🎧 *A couple is out on a first date. Listen to their conversation. Then listen again, and check the correct column(s).*

	Man	Woman			Man	Woman
1. loves Italian food	☑	☑	6. enjoys fiction		☐	☐
2. cooks	☐	☐	7. plays sports		☐	☐
3. eats out a lot	☐	☐	8. watches sports on TV		☐	☐
4. enjoys old movies	☐	☐	9. watches news programs		☐	☐
5. reads biographies	☐	☐	10. wants to see the documentary		☐	☐

8 | LET'S EAT OUT

Work in pairs. Look at these two restaurant ads. What do the two restaurants have in common? In what ways are they different? Discuss these questions and agree upon the restaurant you want to go to.

Example: A: Luigi's serves Italian food.
B: So does Antonio's.

Luigi's
Italian Restaurant

Family-style eating since 1990

Open Tuesday–Sunday, 12:00–9:00

Early-Bird Special
(full dinner for $8.95 if ordered before 6:00)

No reservations necessary

No credit cards

875 Orange St.

Antonio's
Ristorante Italiano

Established in 1990

Relaxed dining in a romantic atmosphere

Open seven days a week—dinner only

Reservations suggested

All credit cards accepted

1273 Orange Street 453-3285

One free beverage with this ad

9 | A GOOD MATCH?

Work in pairs. Look at Exercise 7. Do you think that the man and woman are a good match? Discuss your reasons. How important is it for couples to have a lot in common?

Example: A: The man and woman have a lot in common.
B: He loves Italian food, and so does she.

10 | HOW COMPATIBLE ARE YOU?

Complete these statements. (For items 11 and 12, add your own statements.) Then read your statements to a classmate. He or she will give you a short response. Check the items the two of you have in common. Then do the same with another classmate.

Example: A: I like to walk in the rain.
B: So do I. OR Oh, I don't. I like to stay home and watch TV.

	I have these things in common with:	
	(Classmate 1)	**(Classmate 2)**
1. I like to _____	☐	☐
2. I never _____	☐	☐
3. I get angry when _____	☐	☐
4. I love _____ (name of food)	☐	☐
5. I can't _____	☐	☐
6. I would like to _____	☐	☐
7. I have never _____	☐	☐
8. When I was younger, I didn't _____	☐	☐
9. I will never _____	☐	☐
10. I have to _____	☐	☐
11. _____	☐	☐
12. _____	☐	☐

Count the number of checks for each of the two classmates. Which classmate do you have more in common with?

11 | MICHAEL AND MATTHEW

Work with a partner. Look at the pictures of these twins. How many things do they have in common? How many differences can you find? You have eight minutes to write your answers. Then compare your answers with those of another pair.

Michael

Matthew

Example: Michael has a mustache, and so does Matthew.

12 | NATURE OR NURTURE?

Reread the article beginning on page 102. Which is more important, nature or nurture? Have a class discussion. Give examples to support your views.

Example: In my opinion, nurture is more important than nature. For example, my brother and I grew up together, but we are very different. He could throw a ball when he was only three, but I couldn't. I hate sports . . .

13 | WRITING

Do you know any twins? If so, write two paragraphs about them. What do they have in common? What are their differences? If you don't know any twins, write about two people who are close (siblings, cousins, friends, spouses, etc.). Use **so, too**, **neither**, **not either**, *and* **but***. You can use Exercise 5 as a model.*

Example: My friends Marcia and Tricia are identical twins, but they work very hard to look different from each other. Marcia is 5'3" tall, and so is Tricia. Marcia has black hair and brown eyes, and Tricia does too. However, Marcia wears her hair very short and loves lots of jewelry. Tricia doesn't. She . . .

14 | ON THE INTERNET

Do a search on famous twins. Choose a pair you know about or one from the list. What kind of work do they do? Does being twins help them with their work? What do they have in common? What are their biggest differences? Discuss your information with a small group.

Alison Blackman Dunham and Jessica Blackman Freedman

Alvin and Calvin Harrison

Mark and Scott Kelly

Joel and Benji Madden

Ashley and Mary-Kate Olson

Larissa and Melanie Watson

Example: Alison Blackman Dunham and Jessica Blackman Freedman are both advice columnists. Alison has a master's degree and so does Jessica . . .

From **Grammar** to **Writing**
Avoiding Repetition with Sentence Additions

When you write, one way to avoid repetition is to use sentence additions.

Example: Brasília is a capital city. Washington, D.C. is a capital city. $\longrightarrow$
Brasília is a capital city, **and so is Washington, D.C.**

1 Read this student's essay comparing and contrasting Brasília and Washington, D.C.
Underline once all the additions that express similarity. Underline twice all the additions
that express contrast.

BRASÍLIA AND WASHINGTON, D.C.

Citizens of Brasília and citizens of Washington, D.C. live on
different continents, but their cities still have a lot in common.
Brasília is its nation's capital, and so is Washington. Brasília did
not exist before it was planned and built as the national capital.
Neither did Washington. Both cities were designed by a single
person, and both have a definite shape. However, twentieth-
century Brasília's shape is modern—that of an airplane—but
eighteenth-century Washington's isn't. Its streets form a wheel.

The cities reflect their differences in location and age. Brasília
is located in a dry area in the highlands, while Washington was
built on wet, swampy land. As a result, Brasília has moderate
temperatures all year, but Washington doesn't. Washington is
famous for its cold winters and hot, humid summers. Brasília
was built 600 miles from the Atlantic coast in order to attract
people to an unpopulated area. Washington, near the Atlantic
coast, includes old towns that had already existed. Brasília is
home to many famous theaters and museums, and so is
Washington. However, as a new city, Brasília has not yet become
its nation's real cultural center. Washington hasn't either.
Washington is its country's capital, but it is not its country's
most popular city. Neither is Brasília. Many people still prefer
the excitement of Rio and New York.

---

2 *Before writing the essay in Exercise 1, the student made a Venn diagram showing the things that Brasília and Washington, D.C. have in common, and the things that are different. Complete the student's diagram.*

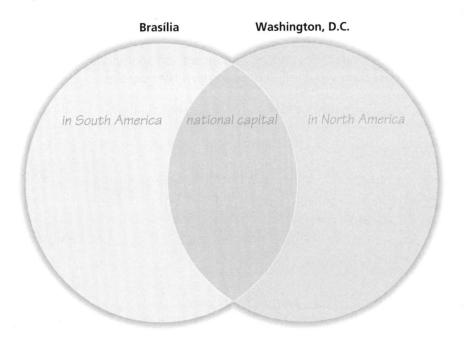

Brasília   Washington, D.C.

in South America   *national capital*   *in North America*

3 *Before you write . . .*

1. Work with a partner. Agree on a topic for an essay of comparison and contrast. For example, you can compare two places, two people, two types of food, or two TV programs.

2. Brainstorm ideas and complete a Venn diagram like the one in Exercise 2.

4 *Write an essay of comparison and contrast using your diagram in Exercise 3.*

5 *Exchange essays with a different partner. Underline once all the additions that show similarity. Underline twice the additions that show difference. Write a question mark (**?**) above the places where something seems wrong. Then answer the following questions.*

	Yes	**No**
1. Did the writer use the correct auxiliary verbs in the additions?	☐	☐
2. Did the writer use correct word order?	☐	☐
3. Do the examples show important similarities and differences?	☐	☐

4. What are some details you would like to know about the two things the writer compared?_____

_____

6 *Work with your partner. Discuss each other's editing questions from Exercise 5. Then rewrite your own paragraph and make any necessary corrections.*

Review Test

I Complete the tag questions and negative questions with an appropriate form of the verbs in parentheses. Some will be affirmative; some will be negative.

1. _____*Isn't*_____ the population of China over a billion?
   (be)

2. China _____ the largest Asian country, isn't it?
   (be)

3. _____ the Yangtze Delta usually _____ 25 percent of
   (produce)

   China's rice crop?

4. _____ the Chinese now _____ millions of trees
   (plant)

   to stop erosion?

5. China _____ a lot of fish, doesn't it?
   (export)

6. Beijing _____ always _____ the capital of China, has it?
   (be)

7. Marco Polo _____ Beijing, didn't he?
   (visit)

8. _____ Kublai Khan _____ Beijing *Dadu* a long time ago?
   (name)

9. The Chinese language _____ an alphabet, does it?
   (use)

10. _____ people _____ different dialects today in China?
    (speak)

II Complete these tag questions and negative questions.

1. Mr. Chen comes from China, _____*doesn't he*_____?

2. He's been staying with the Carsons, _____?

3. The Carsons haven't been to China yet, _____?

4. _____ they meet Mr. Chen for the first time in school?

5. They hadn't known him before then, _____?

6. The Carsons don't speak Chinese, _____?

7. _____ we having dinner with them next Saturday?

8. We should bring something, _____?

9. _____ we be staying there pretty late?

10. We'll have a lot of questions to ask, _____?

11. _____ it going to be an interesting evening?

III *Circle the letter of the correct response.*

1. John lives in L.A.   (**A**) **B C D**
   (**A**) So does Alice.   (**C**) But Alice does.
   (**B**) Neither does Alice.   (**D**) Alice doesn't either.

2. —Didn't he use to live in New York?   **A B C D**
   —_____ He lived in Boston.
   (**A**) No, he didn't.   (**C**) Neither did he.
   (**B**) Yes, he did.   (**D**) But he did.

3. Alice got married two years ago.   **A B C D**
   (**A**) Neither did John.   (**C**) So did John.
   (**B**) So does John.   (**D**) But John did.

4. —Alice is going to China, isn't she?   **A B C D**
   —_____ She's flying there on Friday.
   (**A**) No, she isn't.   (**C**) But she is.
   (**B**) Yes, she is.   (**D**) But she isn't.

5. Doesn't John work for A. Linden & Co.?   **A B C D**
   (**A**) He doesn't either.   (**C**) Yes, he is.
   (**B**) Neither does he.   (**D**) Yes, he does.

6. Alice has been working there for five years.   **A B C D**
   (**A**) But John hasn't.   (**C**) So does John.
   (**B**) John hasn't either.   (**D**) Neither has John.

7. Alice is looking for a new job.   **A B C D**
   (**A**) So is John.   (**C**) John does too.
   (**B**) But John doesn't.   (**D**) But John is.

8. John has an interview tomorrow, doesn't he?   **A B C D**
   (**A**) Yes, he will.   (**C**) So does he.
   (**B**) Yes, he does.   (**D**) Neither does he.

(continued)

9. John should look at the employment ads.   **A B C D**
   (**A**) But Alice should.   (**C**) Alice should too.
   (**B**) Alice shouldn't either. (**D**) Neither should Alice.

10. Wasn't Alice going to speak to her boss?   **A B C D**
    (**A**) No, she wasn't.   (**C**) No, she won't.
    (**B**) So is she.   (**D**) Neither does she.

IV *Complete these conversations with responses.*

1. **A:** I've never eaten here before.

   B: I _____ *haven't either* _____. But it's supposed to be very good.

2. **A:** I don't like cabbage.

   B: _____ my husband. He never eats the stuff. Maybe they have another vegetable.

3. **A:** My dish tastes very salty.

   B: _____ mine. We're going to be really thirsty later.

4. **A:** My mother often made this dish.

   B: My mother _____. It was always one of my favorites.

5. **A:** I was planning to invite Alice to join us.

   B: That's funny. I _____. I'm sorry we didn't.

6. **A:** I'd love some dessert.

   B: _____ I. The chocolate cake looks good.

7. **A:** I'm full.

   B: I _____. I can't eat another bite.

8. **A:** Luigi's doesn't accept credit cards.

   B: This restaurant _____. But don't worry. I have enough cash on me.

9. **A:** I shouldn't have any more coffee.

   B: _____ I. I won't be able to sleep.

10. **A:** I'm glad we did this.

    B: _____ I. It was a lot of fun.

V *Read this letter. There are seven mistakes in the use of negative questions, tag questions, and sentence additions. The first mistake is already corrected. Find and correct six more.*

Dear Stacy,

I'm a pretty bad letter writer, ~~amn't~~ *aren't* I? How are you? You didn't mention Marta in your last letter. Don't you roommates anymore? My new roommate's name is Rafaella. We have a lot in common. She's 18, and so I am. She lived in Chicago, and, of course, I did too. We have the same study habits too. She doesn't stay up late, and neither don't I.

Luckily, there are some important differences too. You remember what my room looked like at home, didn't you? Well, I'm not very neat, but Rafaella is. I can't cook, but she can too. So life is improving. You have a break soon, do you? Why don't you come for a visit? I know the three of us would have a good time.

Love,
Mona

▶ *To check your answers, go to the Answer Key on page RT-2.*

PART IV

Gerunds and Infinitives

9 Gerunds and Infinitives: Review and Expansion

Grammar in Context

BEFORE YOU READ

What do you think of fast-food restaurants like McDonald's? Read this article about the largest fast-food restaurant chain in the world.

McWORLD

"I'll have a Big Mac, a large fries, and a medium soda." The language may change, but you can **expect to hear** this order in more than 100 countries all over the world. Fast food has become almost synonymous with McDonald's™, the best known of all multinational fast-food restaurant chains. At the moment, Antarctica is the only continent that doesn't (yet!) have a McDonald's. And the numbers **keep growing**. In the United States alone, most McDonald's customers **need to travel** less than four minutes **to arrive** at the next pair of golden arches.

Dining on fast food has become a way of life for millions and millions of people from Illinois, U.S.A. (the first McDonald's location) to Colombo, Sri Lanka (a more recent opening). What is it **about eating** on the run that so many people find appealing? Of course, the most obvious answer is that, true

to its name, fast food is fast. In today's hectic society, people **don't want to waste** time. But apart from the speed **of ordering** and **getting** served, satisfied customers talk about convenience, price, and, yes, even good taste.

Many people also like the familiarity and reliability that fast-food chains provide. You can **count on getting** the same thing every time, every place. McDonald's **has started to introduce** some local variety, though. For example, in the New England region of the United States, you can get a lobster roll; in Japan, you can order a teriyaki McBurger; and in India, you can have a Maharaja Mac or a Vegetable Burger. And although most McDonald's restaurants resemble one another, some **try to adjust** to the surroundings. In Freiburg, Germany, one McDonald's is housed in an historic building more than 700 years old, and in Sweden, there's even a McSki lodge.

New Delhi, India

to other countries and **for underpaying** their workers. Then there is the issue of the environment. Those Big Macs and Quarter Pounders use a lot of disposable packaging and this, in turn, creates a lot of waste. It's a high **price to pay** for convenience.

But like it or not, it's **easy to see** that fast-food restaurants like McDonald's aren't going away. From Rovaniemi, Finland, in the north; Invercargill, New Zealand, in the south; Tokyo, Japan, in the east; and Vancouver, Canada, in the west, the sun never sets on the golden arches.

Not everyone is **in favor of** fast-food restaurants' **spreading** over the globe. In fact, a lot of people are **fed up with seeing** the same restaurants wherever they go. "**Walking** down the Champs Elysées just isn't as romantic as it used to be. When I see McDonald's or KFC (Kentucky Fried Chicken) everywhere I go, I feel that the world is shrinking too much," complained one traveler. But there are more serious objections.

Nutritionists point to the health consequences **of eating** fast foods since they are generally high in calories, fat, and salt, but low in fiber and nutrients. In a word, they're unhealthy. Sociologists complain that fast-food restaurants may **prevent** families **from spending** quality time together around the dinner table. Social critics **condemn** fast-food chains **for introducing** unhealthy foods

Tokyo, Japan

Fast Facts

- The average adult in the United States visits a fast-food restaurant six times a month.
- Hamburgers are the most popular fast food in the United States.
- Tacos are the second most popular fast-food choice in the United States, followed by pizza and chicken.
- Men are more **likely** than women **to order** a hamburger.
- Lunch is the most popular meal at a fast-food restaurant.

AFTER YOU READ

*Write **T** (true) or **F** (false).*

_____ 1. The number of McDonald's restaurants is increasing.

_____ 2. You can order exactly the same type of food at each McDonald's.

_____ 3. Everyone loves fast-food restaurants.

_____ 4. Fast-food restaurants don't pay their workers enough.

Grammar Presentation

GERUNDS AND INFINITIVES

Gerunds
Eating fast foods is convenient.
They **recommend reducing** fats in the food.
She **started buying** McBreakfast every day.
We're **tired of reading** calorie counts.
I **didn't like** *his* **ordering** fries.

Infinitives
It's convenient **to eat** fast foods.
They **plan to reduce** fats in the food.
She **started to buy** McBreakfast every day.
We were **surprised to read** the number of calories.
I **urged** *him* **to order** fries.
It's **time to eat**.

GRAMMAR NOTES

EXAMPLES

1. The **gerund** is often used as the <u>subject</u> of a sentence.	• **Eating** fast food can be fun. • **Not caring** about calories is a mistake.

2. The **gerund** is often used after certain verbs as the <u>object</u> of the verb. You can use a **possessive** (*Anne's, the boy's, your, his, her, its, our, their*) before the gerund. USAGE NOTE: In informal spoken English, many people use **object pronouns** instead of possessives before the gerund.	• I *dislike* eating fast food every day. • Julio *considered* **not eating** fast foods. • I dislike *Julio's* eating fast foods. • I dislike *his* eating fast foods. • I dislike *him* eating fast foods.

3. Some verbs can be followed by the **infinitive**. These verbs fall into three groups:

a. verb + infinitive

- They *hope* **to open** a new McDonald's.
- She *chose* **not to give up** meat.

b. verb + object + infinitive

- I *urge you* **to try** that new restaurant.
- She *convinced him* **not to order** fries.

c. verb + infinitive

OR

verb + object + infinitive

- I *want* **to try** that new restaurant.

- I *want her* **to try** it too.

USAGE NOTE: In formal written English, it is considered incorrect to "split" an infinitive by placing a word between *to* and the base form of the verb. However, many people do not follow this rule.

- We wanted **to order** quickly.
  NOT We ~~wanted to quickly order~~.

4. Some verbs can be followed by either the **gerund or the infinitive**. The <u>meanings are the same</u>.

- I *started* **bringing** my own lunch.

OR

- I *started* **to bring** my own lunch.

▶ BE CAREFUL! A few verbs (for example, *stop*, *remember*, and *forget*) can be followed by either the gerund or the infinitive, but the <u>meanings are very different</u>.

- She *stopped* **eating** pizza.
  (She doesn't eat pizza anymore.)
- She *stopped* **to eat** pizza.
  (She stopped another activity in order to eat pizza.)

- He *remembered* **meeting** her there.
  (First he met her. Then he remembered that he did it.)
- He *remembered* **to meet** her there.
  (First he remembered. Then he met her. He didn't forget.)

- I never *forgot* **eating** lunch at McDonald's.
  (I ate lunch at McDonald's and I didn't forget the experience.)
- I never *forgot* **to eat** lunch.
  (I always ate lunch.)

(continued)

5. The **gerund** is the only verb form that can <u>follow a preposition</u>.

There are many common **verb + preposition** and **adjective + preposition** combinations that must be followed by the gerund and not the infinitive.

▶ **BE CAREFUL!** *To* can be part of the infinitive or it can be a preposition. Use the <u>gerund after the preposition *to*</u>.

- I read an article ***about* counting** calories.
- I don't ***approve of* eating** fast food.
- We're ***interested in* trying** different types of food.
- We look forward ***to* having** dinner with you.
  NOT We look forward ~~to have~~ dinner with you.

6. The **infinitive** can often <u>follow an adjective</u>. Many of these adjectives express feelings or attitudes about the action in the infinitive.

- They were ***eager* to try** the new taco.
- She was ***glad* to hear** that it was low in calories.
- We're ***ready* to have** something different.

7. The **infinitive** can also <u>follow certain nouns</u>.

- It's ***time* to take** a break.
- I have the ***right* to eat** what I want.
- They made a ***decision* to lose** weight.
- It's a high ***price* to pay**.
- He has ***permission* to stay** out late.

8. Use the **infinitive** to explain the **purpose** of an action.

- Doug eats fast food **to save** time.

9. To make **general statements** you can use:

gerund as subject

OR

it + **infinitive**

- **Cooking** is fun.

OR

- *It's* fun **to cook**.

Reference Notes

For a list of **verbs that can be followed by the gerund**, see Appendix 3 on page A-2.
For lists of **verbs that can be followed by the infinitive**, see Appendices 4 and 5 on page A-3.
For a list of **verbs that can be followed by either the gerund or the infinitive**, see Appendix 6 on page A-3.
For lists of **verb + preposition** and **adjective + preposition combinations**, see Appendices 7 and 8 on page A-3.
For a list of **adjectives that can be followed by the infinitive**, see Appendix 9 on page A-4.

Focused Practice

1 | DISCOVER THE GRAMMAR

Read this questionnaire about fast-food restaurants. Underline the gerunds and circle the infinitives.

FAST-FOOD QUESTIONNAIRE

Please take a few minutes (to complete) this questionnaire about fast-food restaurants. Check (✓) all the answers that are appropriate for you.

1. In your opinion, eating fast food is
   ☐ convenient   ☐ fast   ☐ healthy   ☐ cheap   ☐ fun

2. Which meals are you used to eating at a fast-food restaurant?
   ☐ breakfast   ☐ lunch   ☐ dinner   ☐ snacks   ☐ none

3. Which types of fast food do you like to eat?
   ☐ hamburgers ☐ pizza   ☐ fried chicken ☐ tacos   ☐ sushi
   ☐ Other: _____   ☐ None

4. What is the most important issue to you in selecting a fast-food restaurant?
   ☐ choice of food   ☐ quality of food
   ☐ fast service   ☐ low prices
   ☐ Other: _____

5. How often are you likely to eat at a fast-food restaurant?
   ☐ 1–3 times a week   ☐ 4–6 times a week
   ☐ more than 6 times a week ☐ never

6. How much do you enjoy going to fast-food restaurants?
   ☐ I like it very much.   ☐ It's just OK.
   ☐ I don't enjoy it.   ☐ I never go.

7. How do you feel about seeing the same fast-food restaurants all over the world?
   ☐ I like it.   ☐ It doesn't bother me.   ☐ I don't like it.

8. Do you think the government should require fast-food restaurants to include healthy choices?
   ☐ Yes   ☐ No

2 | FOOD FOR THOUGHT

Grammar Notes 1–3, 5–6

Complete these statements with the correct form—gerund or infinitive—of the verbs in parentheses. Use the bar graph to find the number of calories.

Calorie Content of Fast-Food Favorites

1. _____*Ordering*_____ a Big Mac will "cost" you about _____*560*_____ calories.
   (Order)

2. _____ a Taco Bell taco is much less fattening. One taco has only about
   (Have)
   _____ calories.

3. If you want _____ weight, you should consider _____ a Subway
   (lose)   **(eat)**
   turkey sandwich. It contains around _____ calories.

4. You're likely _____ weight if you eat half of a medium pepperoni pizza. A single
   (gain)
   slice at Pizza Hut has about _____ calories.

5. Stop _____ so many french fries! An order at Wendy's contains about
   (eat)
   _____ calories.

6. Think about _____ an egg roll instead of fries. Leeann Chin's has just a little
   (choose)
   over _____ calories.

7. Nutritionists advise people _____ from fried chicken. A two-piece order at
   (stay away)
   KFC's contains about _____ calories.

3 | FOOD EXCHANGES
Grammar Notes 2–4

Complete each summary with the appropriate form of a verb from the box plus the gerund or infinitive form of the verb in parentheses.

| admit | deserve | ~~forget~~ | recommend | remember | stop | try | volunteer |

1. **CUSTOMER:** Uh, didn't I order a large fries too?

   SERVER: That's right, you did. I'll bring them right away.

   SUMMARY: The server _____*forgot to bring*_____ the fries.
   (bring)

2. **FATHER:** That Happy Meal isn't enough for you anymore. Have a Big Mac, OK?

   CHILD: OK, but I really wanted the toy in the Happy Meal.

   SUMMARY: The father _____ a Big Mac.
   (order)

3. **MOM:** This car is a mess! Somebody throw out all those fast-food containers!

   STAN: I'll do it, Mom.

   SUMMARY: Stan _____ the fast-food containers.
   (throw out)

4. **PAT:** Hi, Renee. Want to go to Pizza Hut with us?

   RENEE: Thanks, but I can't eat fast food now. I'm training for the swim team.

   SUMMARY: Renee _____ fast food.
   (eat)

5. **EMPLOYEE:** Thanks for the raise. I can really use it.

   MANAGER: You've earned it. You're our best drive-through server.

   SUMMARY: The employee _____ a raise.
   (receive)

6. **VIJAY:** I think you should quit that fast-food job. Your grades are suffering.

   CAROL: It's hard to decide. I need to save for college, but if my grades are bad . . .

   SUMMARY: Carol _____ whether to keep her job.
   (decide)

7. **MOM:** You're not eating dinner. You had some fast food today, didn't you?

   CHRIS: Well . . . Actually, I stopped at Arby's, but I only had a large fries.

   SUMMARY: Chris _____ at Arby's after school.
   (stop)

8. **TIM:** I used to stay in the McDonald's playground for hours when I was little.

   WANG: Yeah, me too. My mother couldn't get me to leave.

   SUMMARY: The boys _____ in the playground.
   (play)

4 | CHOICES

Use the correct forms of the words in parentheses to complete the letters to the editor of a school newspaper.

To the Editor,

Yesterday, my roommate Andre _____*persuaded me to have*_____ lunch with him in the
1.(persuade / I / have)

dining hall. I wondered about _____ there because last year he
2.(Andre / want / go)

_____ the dining hall completely. But when we went in, I
3.(stop / use)

understood. Instead of _____ greasy fries and mystery meat, I was
4.(find)

delighted _____ the colorful Taco Bell sombrero. In my opinion,
5.(see)

_____ to fast foods is the way _____. The
6.(switch)   7.(go)

administration made a great choice. I _____ fast food, and I
8.(support / they / offer)

_____ me to give campus food another try.
9.(appreciate / my friend / persuade)

M. Rodriguez

To the Editor,

I'm writing this letter _____ my anger and disappointment at
10.(express)

_____ fast-food chains in the dining halls. When a classmate and I
11.(have)

went to eat yesterday, I _____ the usual healthy choices of vegetables
12.(expect / we / find)

and salads. I _____ a fast-food court. In my opinion, it was
13.(not count on / see)

outrageous _____ fast food into the college dining hall. As a
14.(bring)

commuter, I _____ a healthy meal every evening before class, so I
15.(need / have)

_____ from fast foods. I _____ a salad bar
16.(attempt / stay away)   17.(urge / the administration / set up)

so that students like me can _____ meals on campus.
18.(keep on / buy)

B. Chen

5 | EDITING

Read these posts to an international online discussion group. There are fifteen mistakes in the use of the gerund and infinitive. The first mistake is already corrected. Find and correct fourteen more.

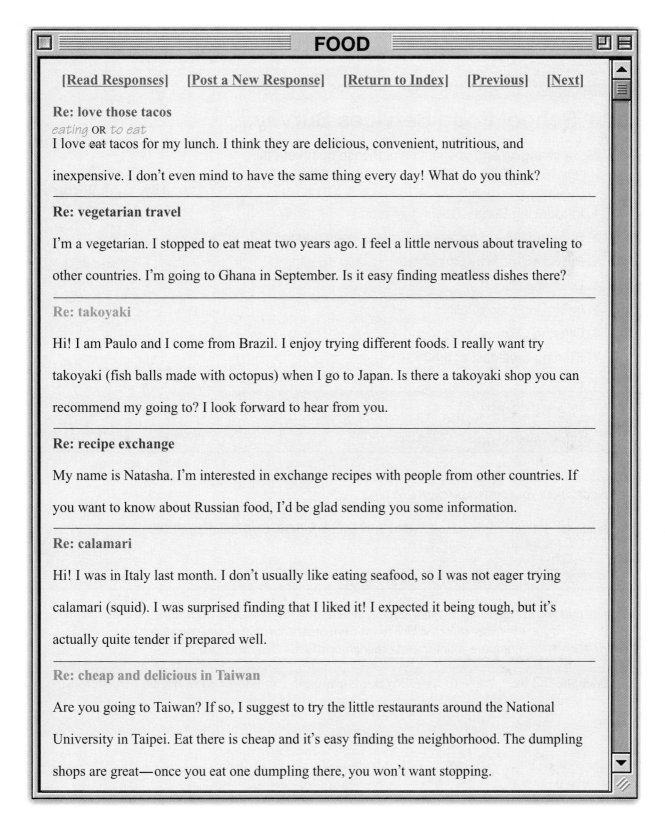

FOOD

[Read Responses]   [Post a New Response]   [Return to Index]   [Previous]   [Next]

Re: love those tacos

eating OR *to eat*
I love ~~eat~~ tacos for my lunch. I think they are delicious, convenient, nutritious, and inexpensive. I don't even mind to have the same thing every day! What do you think?

Re: vegetarian travel

I'm a vegetarian. I stopped to eat meat two years ago. I feel a little nervous about traveling to other countries. I'm going to Ghana in September. Is it easy finding meatless dishes there?

Re: takoyaki

Hi! I am Paulo and I come from Brazil. I enjoy trying different foods. I really want try takoyaki (fish balls made with octopus) when I go to Japan. Is there a takoyaki shop you can recommend my going to? I look forward to hear from you.

Re: recipe exchange

My name is Natasha. I'm interested in exchange recipes with people from other countries. If you want to know about Russian food, I'd be glad sending you some information.

Re: calamari

Hi! I was in Italy last month. I don't usually like eating seafood, so I was not eager trying calamari (squid). I was surprised finding that I liked it! I expected it being tough, but it's actually quite tender if prepared well.

Re: cheap and delicious in Taiwan

Are you going to Taiwan? If so, I suggest to try the little restaurants around the National University in Taipei. Eat there is cheap and it's easy finding the neighborhood. The dumpling shops are great—once you eat one dumpling there, you won't want stopping.

Communication Practice

6 | LISTENING

🎧 *Listen to two college students discuss their responses to a food services survey. Then listen again and check the suggestions that each student agrees with.*

School Food Services Survey

We're changing and you can help! Please complete the survey by checking (✓) the changes you want to see.

		Lily	Victor
1. Introducing Burger Queen fast foods	☐	☐	☑
2. Showing fat and calorie contents of each serving	☐	☐	☐
3. Providing more healthy choices	☐	☐	☐
4. Lowering prices	☐	☐	☐
5. Improving food quality	☐	☐	☐
6. Offering Chinese food	☐	☐	☐
7. Starting breakfast at 6:30 A.M.	☐	☐	☐

7 | QUESTIONNAIRE

Look again at the questionnaire on page 129. Answer the questions. Then have a class discussion about your answers. Tally the results.

Example: Fifteen students agree that eating fast food is convenient and cheap.

8 | FOODS FROM AROUND THE WORLD

Imagine that you are planning an international food festival. Which foods from your country would you like to see there? Which foods from other countries would you enjoy trying? Make a list. Compare your list with other groups' lists.

Example: I'd like people to try takoyaki. For myself, I'm interested in trying Turkish food.

9 | INFORMATION GAP: THE RIGHT JOB?

Work in pairs (A and B). Student B, go to page 137 and follow the instructions there.
Student A, ask Student B questions to complete the quiz below. Answer Student B's questions.

Example: A: What does Jennifer enjoy doing?
B: She enjoys working with others. What does Jennifer expect to do?
A: She expects to make a lot of money.

JOB / PERSONALITY QUIZ

Before you start looking at job ads, take this quiz to find out about your job preferences. Complete the statements with information about yourself.

Name: _____ Jennifer Johnson _____

1. I enjoy _____ *working with others* _____ .
2. I expect _____ *to make a lot of money* _____ .
3. I'm good at _____ .
4. I dislike _____ *working inside* _____ .
5. I don't mind _____ .
6. I'm willing _____ *to learn new skills* _____ .
7. I never complain about _____ .
8. I'm eager _____ *to meet new people* _____ .
9. I plan _____ next year.
10. I dream about _____ *owning my own business* _____ one day.
11. I can't stand _____ .
12. I expect people _____ *to be friendly* _____ .

JOB CENTER

Volunteering can lead to a high-paying job
Be a Park Volunteer!
Learn about plants and wildlife
Lead tours through the park

Word Processor
in busy 2-person office
~ 3 days/week
~ must type 60 wpm
~ must meet deadlines
~ $10/hr

Athletic
Department
Office Assistant
– answer phones
– assist students
during
registration
– file papers
– $6/hr

BURGER QUEEN
Server Wanted
evenings
$6/hr

When you are finished, compare quizzes. Are they the same? Look at the job notices to the right of the quiz. Which jobs do you think would be good for Jennifer? Which jobs wouldn't be good for her? Explain your choices.

10 | TROUBLESHOOTING

Work in small groups. For each of the social problems below, brainstorm as many solutions as you can in five minutes. (You can also add a problem not listed.) Then compare your answers with those of another group. You can use some of the following expressions.

I'm in favor of . . .	I'm opposed to . . .
I support . . .	I'm against . . .
I suggest . . .	What about . . .
I go along with . . .	We need . . .
I advise . . .	I recommend . . .
We should start / stop . . .	I urge . . .

1. In many countries, a lot of people are overweight. What can people do about this problem?

   Example: A: How about improving physical education programs in schools?
   B: I'm in favor of offering healthier meals in schools.
   C: We need to educate people about the role of exercise.

2. Heavy traffic is a big problem in both cities and suburbs. What can we do about it?

3. Many adults can't read or write well enough to function in society. What can be done about this problem?

4. There are millions of homeless people living in the streets and parks. How can we help solve this problem?

5. Another social problem: _____

11 | WRITING

Write a short editorial about a social problem. You can use one of the topics in Exercise 10 or choose your own. Express your opinions and give reasons for your ideas. Use gerunds and infinitives.

   Example: I'm in favor of requiring people to take a road test every time they renew their license. By polishing their skills every few years, people will become better drivers . . .

Exchange editorials with a classmate. After you read your classmate's editorial, write a letter to the editor explaining why you agree or disagree with your classmate's opinions.

   Example: To the Editor:
   I go along with requiring additional road tests for drivers. People's eyesight and reflexes can change a lot in five years . . .

12 | ON THE INTERNET

Do a search on a fast-food restaurant or an online restaurant menu. Using the information you find, complete the sentences. Use gerunds and infinitives. Share your opinions with a partner and decide which restaurant is the better choice.

Examples: At (name of restaurant), people can expect to find . . .
This restaurant seems . . .
Many people can / can't afford . . . because . . .
If you eat here, try to avoid . . .
I'd like / wouldn't like . . . because . . .
I recommend . . .

INFORMATION GAP FOR STUDENT B

Student B, answer Student A's questions. Then ask Student A questions to complete the quiz below.

Example: **A:** What does Jennifer enjoy doing?
B: She enjoys working with others. What does Jennifer expect to do?
A: She expects to make a lot of money.

JOB / PERSONALITY QUIZ

Before you start looking at job ads, take this quiz to find out about your job preferences. Complete the statements with information about yourself.

Name: ___Jennifer Johnson___

1. I enjoy ___working with others___.
2. I expect ___to make a lot of money___.
3. I'm good at ___talking to people___.
4. I dislike _____.
5. I don't mind ___working nights___.
6. I'm willing _____.
7. I never complain about ___following orders___.
8. I'm eager _____.
9. I plan ___to major in business___ next year.
10. I dream about _____ one day.
11. I can't stand ___rushing___.
12. I expect people _____.

JOB CENTER

Volunteering can lead to a high-paying job
Be a Park Volunteer!
*Learn about plants and wildlife
Lead tours through the park*

Word Processor
in busy 2-person office
~ 3 days/week
~ must type 60 wpm
~ must meet deadlines
~ $10/hr

BURGER QUEEN
Server Wanted
evenings
$6/hr

Athletic Department
Office Assistant
– answer phones
– assist students during registration
– file papers
– $6/hr

When you are finished, compare quizzes. Are they the same? Look at the job notices to the right of the quiz. Which jobs do you think would be good for Jennifer? Which jobs wouldn't be good for her? Explain your choices.

Grammar in Context

BEFORE YOU READ

🎧 *Look at the photos. How do you think these animals learned to perform like this? Do you think people should use animals for entertainment? Read this article about performance animals.*

That's Entertainment?

"Ooooh!" cries the audience as the orcas leap from the water in perfect formation. "Aaaah!" they shout as the trainer rides across the pool on the nose of one of the giants.

For years, dolphins, orcas, and other sea mammals have been **making** *audiences* **say** *ooooh* and *aaaah* at water parks like Sea World. But how do trainers **get** *nine-ton whales* **to do** acrobatic tricks with a human or **make** *them* **"dance"**?

It's not easy. Traditional animal trainers controlled animals with collars and leashes and **made** *them* **perform** by using cruel punishments. Then, in the 1940s, parks wanted to **have** *dolphins* **do tricks**. The first trainers faced big problems. You can't **get** *a dolphin* **to wear** a collar. And you can't punish a dolphin—it will just swim away from you! This challenge **made** *the trainers* **develop** a kinder, more humane method to teach animals.

This method, positive reinforcement, uses rewards rather than punishments for training. To begin teaching, a trainer **lets** *an animal* **act** freely. When the trainer sees the "correct" behavior, he or she immediately rewards the animal, usually with food. The animal quickly learns that a reward follows the behavior.

"Ooooh!"

That's Entertainment?

For complicated acts, the trainer breaks the act into many smaller parts and **has *the animal* learn** each part separately.

Positive reinforcement has revolutionized our treatment of animals in zoos. Elephants, for example, need a lot of physical care. However, traditional trainers used force to **make *elephants* "behave."** Elephants sometimes rebelled and hurt or even killed their keepers. Through positive reinforcement, elephants at modern zoos have learned to stand at the bars of their cage and **let *keepers* draw** blood for tests and **take care of** their feet. Trainers even **get *primates*** (monkeys and apes) **to bring** their own bedding to the keepers for washing. Gary Priest, a former orca trainer, **helped *the keepers* train** the elephants at the San Diego Zoo. Do the elephants like the new system? "They love it! They'll do anything we ask. They'd fly for us if they could," Priest said.

Unfortunately, not all trainers use positive reinforcement. Animal rights organizations have found abuses of animal actors by circuses and other entertainment companies. And the question remains: Even with kind treatment, should we keep animals captive and **have *them* perform** just for our entertainment? In the wild, orcas may travel 100 miles a day. Is it really kind to **make *them* live** in small pools of chemically treated water? Today, more and more people say the only real kindness is to **let *these animals* live** natural lives.

Elephant performing in circus

AFTER YOU READ

Read the first sentence of each item. Then circle the letter of the sentence that is closest in meaning.

1. You can't get a dolphin to wear a collar.
   a. Dolphins wear collars.
   b. Dolphins don't wear collars.

2. A trainer lets an animal act freely.
   a. The animal is allowed to do what it wants.
   b. The animal must behave well.

3. He helped the keepers train the elephants.
   a. He trained the elephants alone.
   b. He worked with the keepers.

Grammar Presentation

MAKE, HAVE, LET, HELP, AND GET

Make, Have, Let, Help				
Subject	Make / Have / Let / Help	Object	Base Form	
They	(don't) **make** **have** **let** **help***	them animals	**learn**	tricks.

* *Help* can also be followed by the infinitive.

Get				
Subject	Get	Object	Infinitive	
They	(don't) **get**	them animals	**to learn**	tricks.

GRAMMAR NOTES

EXAMPLES

1. Use *make*, *have*, and *let* + **object** + **base form** of the verb to talk about things that someone can **require**, **cause**, or **permit** another person (or an animal) to do.

You can also use *make* to mean *cause to*.

- They **make** *animals* **learn** tricks.
  (*They require animals to learn tricks.*)
- They **have** *them* **perform** for crowds.
  (*They cause them to perform for crowds.*)
- They **let** *them* **have** food as a reward.
  (*They permit them to have food as a reward.*)

- This will **make** *them* **learn** faster.
  (*This will cause them to learn faster.*)

2. *Help* can be followed by:

object + base form of the verb

OR

object + infinitive

The meaning is the same.

USAGE NOTE: *Help* + **base form** of the verb is more common.

- She **helped** *me* **do** the homework.

OR

- She **helped** *me* **to do** the homework.

3. *Get* has a similar meaning to *make* and *have*.

It is always followed by **object + infinitive**, not the base form of the verb.

- The teacher **got *us* to stay** a little later. (*After some effort, the teacher succeeded in persuading us to stay.*)
  NOT The teacher ~~got us stay~~ a little later.

Focused Practice

1 | DISCOVER THE GRAMMAR

Read the first sentence of each item. Then circle the letter of the sentence that is closest in meaning.

1. Ms. Bates got the principal to arrange a class trip to the zoo.
   a. Ms. Bates arranged a class trip.
   b. The principal arranged a class trip.

2. Mr. Goldberg had us do research about animals.
   a. Mr. Goldberg did research for us.
   b. We did research.

3. My teacher made me rewrite the report.
   a. I wrote the report again.
   b. I didn't write the report again.

4. She got me to add more information.
   a. I agreed to add more information.
   b. I didn't agree to add more information.

5. Ms. Lee let us use our dictionaries during the test.
   a. We were allowed to use our dictionaries.
   b. We had to use our dictionaries.

6. My mother didn't let me stay home from school.
   a. I stayed home from school.
   b. I went to school.

(continued)

7. Paulo helped Maria do her homework.

    a. Paulo did Maria's homework for her.

    b. Both Paulo and Maria worked on her homework.

8. Professor Washington let us choose our own topic for our term paper.

    a. We chose our own topic.

    b. We didn't choose our own topic.

2 | WHO'S THE BOSS?   *Grammar Notes 1–2*

Students in a conversation class are talking about their experiences with authority figures. Complete each sentence by circling the correct verb. Then match each situation on the left with the person in authority on the right and write the letter of the answer on the line.

_c_   **1.** The elephant was tired that day, so she didn't <u>help</u> /(have) it perform.   **a.** my teacher

_____   **2.** I didn't really want to work overtime this week, but she <u>made / let</u>   **b.** my doctor
me work late because some of my coworkers were sick.

_____   **3.** I forgot to turn on my headlights before I left the parking lot a few   **c.** the trainer
nights ago. She <u>made / let</u> me pull over to the side of the road and
asked to see my license.

_____   **4.** At first, we didn't really want to write in our journals. He explained   **d.** my father
that it would help us. Finally, he <u>had / got</u> us to try it.

_____   **5.** My check was delayed in the mail. I told him what had happened,   **e.** a police officer
and he <u>had / let</u> me pay the rent two weeks late.

_____   **6.** I needed to get a blood test for my school physical. He <u>got / had</u> me   **f.** the judge
roll up my sleeve and make a fist.

_____   **7.** We're a big family, and we all have our own chores. While she   **g.** my landlord
washed the dishes, she <u>helped / had</u> me dry. My brother swept.

_____   **8.** I'm an only child, and when I was young I felt lonely. He <u>let / got</u>   **h.** my boss
me sleep over at my friend's house.

_____   **9.** I wasn't paying attention, and I hit a parked car. He <u>let / made</u> me   **i.** my mother
tell the court what happened.

3 | IN CLASS

A *Complete each summary. Use the correct form of the verbs in parentheses. Some summaries will be affirmative; some will be negative.*

1.   **PABLO:** Ms. Allen, do I have to rewrite this composition on elephants?

   MS. ALLEN: Only if you want to.

       SUMMARY: Ms. Allen *didn't make Pablo rewrite* OR *didn't make him rewrite* his composition.
                                                 (make / rewrite)

2.   **ANA:** Could I work alone? I really don't like to work in a group.

   MS. ALLEN: You need to work in a group today.

       SUMMARY: She _____ in a group.
                                  (make / work)

3. **MS. ALLEN:** Fernando, could you do me a favor and clean the board before you leave?

   FERNANDO: Sure.

       SUMMARY: She _____ the board.
                                  (have / clean)

4. **MS. ALLEN:** Uri, please show Greta how to research orcas on the Internet.

   URI: Sure.

       SUMMARY: She _____ Greta how to do research on the
                                 (get / teach)

   Internet.

5.   **URI:** Google is a search engine. Just type *orca* in that space and hit "Return."

   GRETA: Wow! Look at all that information!

       SUMMARY: Uri _____ information about orcas.
                            (help / find)

6.   **HECTOR:** What does *positive reinforcement* mean?

   MS. ALLEN: Why don't you see if one of your classmates can explain it to you?

       SUMMARY: Ms. Allen _____ his classmates for help.
                           (have / ask)

   (continued)

B *Now complete the summaries with* **make**, **have**, **let**, **help**, *or* **get** *plus the correct form of the verbs in parentheses. Some summaries will be affirmative; some will be negative.*

1.   **MASAMI:** Can we use our dictionaries during the test?

   MS. ALLEN: No. You should be able to guess the meaning of the words from the context.

   SUMMARY: She _____*didn't let them use*_____ their dictionaries.
   (use)

2.   **MARÍA:** Mom, can I borrow the car?

   MOM: Only if you drive your sister to soccer practice.

   SUMMARY: María's mother _____ her sister to soccer practice.
   (drive)

3.   **JOHN:** Can I borrow your camera for our class trip to the zoo?

   DAD: Sure. I know you'll take good care of it.

   SUMMARY: John's father _____ his camera.
   (borrow)

4.   **JOHN:** Excuse me, could I take pictures in here?

   ZOO WORKER: Sure, but don't use the flash. Light bothers these animals.

   SUMMARY: The zoo worker _____ the flash on his camera.
   (use)

5.   **PAUL:** Ms. Allen, which movie on this list do you think we should rent?

   MS. ALLEN: You might like *Free Willy*. It's about a captive orca.

   SUMMARY: Ms. Allen _____ a movie to rent.
   (choose)

6.   **MARÍA:** John, the group wants you to read your report to the class.

   JOHN: No way! Sorry, but speaking in front of the class makes me nervous.

   SUMMARY: María _____ the report to the class.
   (read)

4 | EDITING

Read this e-mail petition about orcas. There are eight mistakes in the use of **make**, **have**, **let**, **help**, *and* **get**. *The first mistake is already corrected. Find and correct seven more.*

LET THEM GO!

LET THEM GO!

Orcas are beautiful and intelligent, so aquariums easily get audiences ~~buy~~ *to buy* tickets for orca shows. What does this mean for the orca? In the wild, an orca may swim up to 100 miles a day and dive hundreds of feet below the water. In captivity, we have this animal lives in a small pool where it may get sick and die of an infection. Some people argue that captive orcas have helped us learned about these animals. However, orcas cannot behave naturally in an aquarium. In captivity, trainers make them to perform embarrassing tricks for a "treat." In the wild, these animals have rich social lives in families. How can watching tricks help we learn about their lives? Orcas don't belong in aquariums!

Don't let these beautiful animals suffering in order to entertain us! First, help us stop aquarium shows. Stop going to these shows and get your friends and family stop also. Next, we must make aquariums stop buying orcas. Write to your mayor and tell him or her how you feel. Finally, aquariums must let others retrained these animals and release them to the wild.

Help us help the orcas! Sign this e-letter and send it to your friends.

Communication Practice

5 | LISTENING

Grammar Notes 1–3

🎧 *Listen to a student talk to his teacher about a writing assignment. Then listen again, and write **T** (true) or **F** (false) next to each statement.*

___T___ 1. Ms. Jacobson let Simon choose his own topic.

_____ 2. She let him change the topic of his essay.

_____ 3. She had him remove some details from his second paragraph.

_____ 4. She got him to talk about his uncle.

_____ 5. She helped him correct a grammar mistake.

_____ 6. Simon got Ms. Jacobson to correct the gerunds in his essay.

_____ 7. Ms. Jacobson made Simon look for the gerunds in his essay.

_____ 8. She let Simon make an appointment for another conference.

6 | TEXTBOOK SURVEY

Complete this survey. Then work in small groups. Compare answers. Do you and your classmates have the same opinion of your textbook?

Does this textbook . . .	Always	Often	Sometimes	Rarely	Never
1. make you think?	☐	☐	☐	☐	☐
2. help you learn?	☐	☐	☐	☐	☐
3. have you work in pairs and groups?	☐	☐	☐	☐	☐
4. get students to speak in class?	☐	☐	☐	☐	☐
5. get you to practice outside of class?	☐	☐	☐	☐	☐
6. let you find and correct mistakes?	☐	☐	☐	☐	☐
7. help you to speak accurately?	☐	☐	☐	☐	☐
8. make learning fun?	☐	☐	☐	☐	☐
9. let you test your own progress?	☐	☐	☐	☐	☐
10. let you choose your own topics for discussion?	☐	☐	☐	☐	☐

7 | BRINGING UP TEENAGERS

Look at this list. Check the things you think are important to make or let a teenager do.
Compare and discuss your list with a partner.

☐ stay out until midnight on weekends

☐ stay over at a friend's house

☐ travel alone to a foreign country

☐ get a part-time job

☐ dye his or her hair another color

☐ help with the housework

☐ play a musical instrument

☐ take care of younger children

☐ learn to drive

☐ study every day, including weekends

☐ exercise

☐ go to the dentist every year

☐ learn another language

☐ take care of a pet animal

> **Example:** **A:** I think it's important to make your kids come home before midnight—even on weekends.
>
> **B:** I'm not so sure. I think parents should let their children stay out late one night a week. It gives them a sense of responsibility . . .

8 | ROLE PLAY: HARD CHOICES

Work with a partner. Read about the following problems. Role-play your discussion about
*how to solve each one. Use **make**, **have**, **let**, **help**, and **get**.*

1. A parent and his or her 12-year-old daughter are discussing a school dance. The daughter wants permission to go to the dance with a boy her parent doesn't know. She wants to buy a new dress and wear makeup. Role-play the discussion between the parent and the daughter.

   > **Example:** **DAUGHTER:** All my friends are going. You never let me have any fun.
   > **PARENT:** You can go, but have the boy's parents call me before.

2. Two friends are spending the day at an amusement park. One wants to go to an aquarium show and would be very disappointed not to see it. The other feels it's wrong to keep wild animals in an aquarium and to make them perform. Role-play the discussion between the two friends.

9 | WRITING

Write a paragraph about someone who helped you learn something (for example, a parent, other relative, teacher, friend). What did the person get you to do that you never did before? How did this person help you? Did he or she let you make mistakes in order to learn? Use **make**, **have**, **let**, **help**, *and* **get**.

Example: My older brother was a big help to me when I was a teenager. He got me to try new things, and he even taught me to dance. He wasn't like a lot of my friends' older brothers. He never laughed at my mistakes or made me feel stupid . . .

10 | ON THE INTERNET

Do a search on a wild animal. Share your information with a small group. What is this animal's life like in the wild? What is it like in a zoo? Is it right to make this animal live in captivity? What are some arguments for and against?

Example: Pandas are very rare. I think zoos can help protect rare animals so they won't become extinct.

From **Grammar** to **Writing**
Using Parallel Forms: Gerunds and Infinitives

When you are writing a list using gerunds or infinitives, make sure the items are in parallel form. If a list starts with a gerund, all items in that list should be gerunds. If it starts with an infinitive, all items in the list should be infinitives.

Example: Homer loved hunting, fishing, and ~~to hike~~. ⟶
Homer loved **hunting, fishing,** and **hiking.**
OR
Homer loved **to hunt, fish,** and **hike.**

Note that in a list of infinitives it is not necessary to repeat *to*.

1 | *Read this movie summary. Correct any gerunds or infinitives that are not parallel.*

||||||||||||||||||||||||||||||||||| OCTOBER SKY |||||||||||||||||||||||||||||||||||||

Directed by Joe Johnston

It's October 1957, and the Soviet Union has just launched Sputnik. Homer, a

teenage boy (played by Jake Gyllenhaal), watches the satellite fly over his poor

coal-mining town in West Virginia and dreams of building and ~~to launch~~ *launching* his own

rocket. He teams up with three friends, and "The Rocket Boys" start to put

together and firing their homemade missiles. The boys' goal is to win the regional

science fair. First prize will bring college scholarships and a way out of Coalwood.

The school science teacher, Miss Riley, encourages him, but Homer's father

(played by Chris Cooper) is angry about the boys' project. He wants Homer to

follow in his footsteps and working at the mine. Nevertheless, the boys continue

launching rockets, failing in different ways, and to learn with each failure. People

begin changing their minds and to admire the Rocket Boys. Some even help them.

(continued)

However, success does not come easily in Coalwood. When a forest fire starts nearby, a rocket is blamed, and the boys must give up their project. Then Homer's father is injured, and Homer quits school to support his family as a miner. His father is proud of him, but Homer can't stand giving up his dream and to work in the mine. He uses mathematics to prove a rocket did not start the fire. Then he tells his father he plans to leave the mine and returning to school.

The Rocket Boys win first prize at the science fair, and all four of them receive scholarships. The whole town celebrates, and Homer wins another very valuable prize—his father attends the science fair and launches the rocket. It's clear that father and son will try to make peace and respecting each other.

2 | *Complete the story map with information from Exercise 1.*

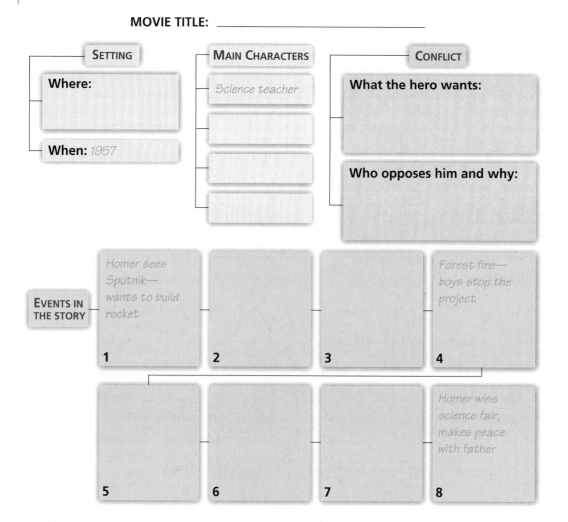

3 | *Before you write . . .*

1. Work with a partner. Choose a movie or TV show that you have both seen.

2. Create a story map like the one in Exercise 2.

4 | *Write about the movie or TV show you chose in Exercise 3. Use your story map for information. Remember to use gerunds and infinitives.*

5 | *Exchange your writing with a different partner. Underline all the gerunds once. Underline all the infinitives twice. Write a question mark (?) over anything that seems wrong in your partner's summary. Answer the following questions.*

	Yes	No
1. Did the writer use gerunds and infinitives?	☐	☐
2. Did the writer use gerunds and infinitives correctly?	☐	☐
3. Are gerunds and infinitives parallel when they are in a list?	☐	☐
4. Did you understand the story?	☐	☐

6 | *Work with your partner. Discuss each other's editing questions from Exercise 5. Then rewrite your own movie summary and make any necessary corrections.*

Review Test

I *Circle the letter of the correct word(s) to complete each sentence.*

1. Sue has always wanted _____ her own restaurant.

   (**A**) opening   (**C**) open

   (**B**) to open   (**D**) she opens

   A (B) C D

2. She took accounting courses _____ for her business.

   (**A**) prepare   (**C**) to prepare

   (**B**) prepared   (**D**) for preparing

   A B C D

3. Last year, she succeeded in _____ a loan from the bank.

   (**A**) getting   (**C**) her getting

   (**B**) got   (**D**) to get

   A B C D

4. We all celebrated _____ opening Sue's Kitchen.

   (**A**) she   (**C**) she was

   (**B**) hers   (**D**) her

   A B C D

5. When she first opened, she avoided _____ people to help her.

   (**A**) asked   (**C**) asking

   (**B**) to ask   (**D**) their asking

   A B C D

6. She was tired, but we couldn't _____ her accept our help.

   (**A**) made   (**C**) making

   (**B**) to make   (**D**) make

   A B C D

7. At first she was terrible at _____ the place.

   (**A**) she managed   (**C**) managed

   (**B**) managing   (**D**) to manage

   A B C D

8. _____ experience is important, so we all told her to keep trying.

   (**A**) Getting   (**C**) She's getting

   (**B**) To get   (**D**) She was getting

   A B C D

9. After a few weeks, she let _____ help her cook.

   (**A**) my   (**C**) I

   (**B**) mine   (**D**) me

   A B C D

10. I think she appreciated _____ giving her a hand.   **A B C D**
    (**A**) I was   (**C**) my
    (**B**) I am   (**D**) mine

11. Recently, she's been having me _____ entire meals.   **A B C D**
    (**A**) preparing   (**C**) to prepare
    (**B**) prepare   (**D**) prepared

12. Now she's finally thinking _____ hiring someone to help.   **A B C D**
    (**A**) on   (**C**) for
    (**B**) about   (**D**) to

13. A lot of people are afraid of _____ a business, but Sue isn't.   **A B C D**
    (**A**) they own   (**C**) owning
    (**B**) to own   (**D**) they're owning

14. We're proud of her for _____ such a big decision.   **A B C D**
    (**A**) made   (**C**) makes
    (**B**) to make   (**D**) making

15. Now we have to make _____ take a vacation.   **A B C D**
    (**A**) her   (**C**) hers
    (**B**) to   (**D**) she

II *Complete this letter to the editor of a newspaper. Use the correct form of the verbs in parentheses.*

Dear Editor:

Cars are essential in today's society. We need them _____*to get*_____ from place to place.
                                                        1. (get)

However, _____ is a privilege, not a right. I'm in favor of _____
              2. (drive)   **3. (suspend)**

licenses for serious moving violations. Furthermore, if someone has his or her license suspended

more than once, that person should not be permitted _____ at all.
                                                            4. (drive)

I learned _____ when I was sixteen. I remember _____ very
              5. (drive)   **6. (be)**

happy when I first got my license. In fact, my friends and family even helped celebrate my

_____ the road test. But my parents cautioned me _____ this new
      7. (pass)   **8. (not take)**

responsibility lightly. In order _____ me a sense of responsibility, they made me
                                      9. (give)

_____ my own car insurance from the start. They expected me _____
      10. (pay)   **11. (be)**

a cautious, courteous driver at all times. They insisted on my _____ all regulations.
                                                                    12. (obey)

(continued)

Some of my friends objected to _____ wear seatbelts. They couldn't stand
                                    13. (have to)

_____ "confined." Seatbelts save lives and help _____ serious
14. (feel)   15. (prevent)

injuries. It's completely irresponsible _____ them, and if my friends refused
                                          16. (not use)

_____, I didn't even let them _____ with me.
17. (buckle up)   18. (ride)

   I believe that too many people consider _____ a sport. Stricter laws, and the
                                            19. (drive)

enforcement of those laws, will make people _____ more carefully on the road, and
                                             20. (behave)

that, in turn, will result in _____ lives. It's time _____ our roads safer.
                              21. (save)   22. (make)

Sally McKay, Detroit

III *Each sentence has four underlined words or phrases. The four underlined parts of the*
sentences are marked A, B, C, or D. Circle the letter of the one underlined part that is
NOT CORRECT.

1. When I <u>was</u> sixteen, my parents <u>started</u> <u>to let</u> <u>I eat</u> whatever I wanted.   **A B C (D)**
          A   B   C   D

2. They stopped <u>to try</u> to <u>make</u> <u>me</u> <u>eat</u> healthy foods.   **A B C D**
                  A   B   C D

3. I <u>had begun</u> <u>working</u>, so I <u>could</u> afford <u>buying</u> fast food.   **A B C D**
       A   B   C   D

4. <u>Keeping</u> my weight down had never been a problem, so I <u>couldn't understand</u>   **A B C D**
      A

   I suddenly <u>gaining</u> fifteen pounds.
   C   D

5. <u>Jogging</u> and <u>ride my bike</u> didn't help <u>me lose</u> weight, so I asked <u>to see</u>   **A B C D**
      A   B   C   D

   my doctor.

6. The doctor had me <u>to write down</u> everything I <u>ate</u> for a week, and   **A B C D**
                           A   B

   she <u>made</u> me <u>calculate</u> the fat grams.
        C   D

7. I was amazed <u>to find out</u> how much fat fast food <u>contains</u>, and   **A B C D**
                 A   B

   I <u>couldn't stand</u> <u>eat</u> it anymore.
        C   D

8. By <u>they let</u> me <u>make</u> mistakes, my parents got <u>me to learn</u> a lesson.   **A B C D**
       A   B   C   D

IV *Complete these sentences with the correct form of the words in parentheses.*

1. My daughter's teacher _____*wants her to work*_____ harder.
(want / she / work)

2. She _____ questions when she doesn't understand.
(urge / Alicia / ask)

3. The teacher always _____ after class to ask questions.
(let / students / stay)

4. She _____ the class.
(not mind / my daughter / record)

5. Alicia _____ patient.
(appreciate / the teacher / be)

6. All the students _____ a lot from them.
(be used to / Ms. Allen / demand)

7. She _____ responsibility for their own learning.
(make / they / take)

8. She often _____ each other.
(get / they / help)

9. She really _____ well.
(want / they / do)

10. The students _____.
(be happy with / she / teach)

V *Read these conversations. Complete the summary statement using the correct form of the verbs in the box followed by the gerund or infinitive.*

afford	deny	invite	let	make
offer	persuade	~~postpone~~	quit	suggest

1. CARYN: It's raining. Maybe we shouldn't take the class on the trip today.

   JASON: You're right. Let's wait for a nicer day.

   SUMMARY: Caryn and Jason just _____*postponed taking the class on*_____ the trip.

2. CARYN: Can I use the new car tomorrow? I'm taking students on a trip, and my seatbelts aren't in good shape.

   DAN: OK. But please be sure to bring it back by five.

   SUMMARY: Dan _____ the new car tomorrow.

3. DAN: Why didn't you buy that van? I thought you liked it.

   CARYN: I like it very much. But it's too expensive. I don't have the money for it now.

   SUMMARY: Caryn can't _____ the van.

4.   JASON: You need a break. You're working too hard.

       CARYN: I really have to finish this report.

       JASON: You'll feel better if you take a break.

       CARYN: Oh, all right. I suppose you're right.

       SUMMARY: Jason _____ a break.

5.   DAN: Would you like to join us? We're going to Monticello, and it's supposed to be a beautiful day.

       JASON: Thanks. It would be nice to get out of the city.

       SUMMARY: Dan _____ them.

6.   JASON: Oh, no. I forgot to bring my lunch.

       CARYN: Why don't you share ours? We have fruit and some cheese sandwiches.

       JASON: Oh, thanks a lot. I'll just have some fruit. I don't eat cheese anymore. I'm trying to lower my fat intake.

       SUMMARY: Jason _____ cheese.

7.   CARYN: I can't lift the cooler into the van. Can you give me a hand?

       JASON: Sure. Just leave it. I'll do it.

       SUMMARY: Jason _____ the cooler.

8.   CARYN: It's hot in here.

       DAN: I know. Why don't we turn on the air conditioner?

       SUMMARY: Dan _____ the air conditioner.

9.   OFFICER: Show me your license, sir.

       DAN: Here it is, officer. What's the problem?

       SUMMARY: The officer _____ his license.

10.   CARYN: Did you call me last night at 11:00?

       JASON: No, I wouldn't call you that late. Besides, I was tired. I fell asleep at 8:00.

       SUMMARY: Jason _____ at eleven.

▶ *To check your answers, go to the Answer Key on page RT-3.*

Phrasal Verbs

Grammar in Context

BEFORE YOU READ

🎧 *Look at the photo and read the caption. What kind of advice do you think a feng shui consultant gives about people's homes? Do you think the furniture and colors in your home affect your life? Read this article about the ancient Chinese art of feng shui.*

☯ Wind and Water ☯

Ho Da-ming couldn't **figure out** why his restaurant was failing. He had **set it up** on a busy street. His chef was famous. He had paid a fortune for interior design. But customers rarely **came back**. Why? Mr. Ho **called in** a feng shui consultant to **find out**. Feng shui (meaning "wind and water" and pronounced FUNG SHWAY) is the ancient Chinese art of placing things in the environment. According to this art, the arrangement of furniture, doors, and windows affects our health, wealth, and happiness.

The consultant used a *loupan* (a feng shui compass) to **look into** the patterns of energy in the restaurant. He told Mr. Ho that the entrance was **letting** prosperity **out**. The desperate owner **tore down** the old entrance and **put up** a new one. His action **paid off**. Soon business **picked up**, and Mr. Ho became rich.

Feng shui has **caught on** with modern architects and homeowners everywhere. Although the complex charts of feng shui are hard to **work out**, the theory is simple: We are part of nature, and we must adjust to its natural energies. To be healthy and prosperous, we must **lay out** our homes and workplaces to allow *chi* (good energy) to circulate gently and to **cut off** *sha* (harmful energy).

Try this activity **out** in your home, dorm room, or office. First **sit down** and think about how you feel in this room. Now look around. Try to **pick out** the things that make you feel good or bad. To **find out** more, go to your library or bookstore and **pick up** a book on basic feng shui. And of course, you can always **look up** the topic online. You'll be surprised at what you learn.

A feng shui consultant on the job with his *loupan*

AFTER YOU READ

Find a phrasal verb from the article that means:

1. returned   _____

2. improved   _____

3. stop   _____

4. choose   _____

Grammar Presentation

PHRASAL VERBS: REVIEW

TRANSITIVE PHRASAL VERBS

Not Separated			
Subject	**Verb**	**Particle**	**Direct Object**
She He	**called**	**in**	a consultant.
	figured	**out**	the problem.

Separated			
Subject	**Verb**	**Direct Object**	**Particle**
She He	**called**	a consultant him	**in**.
	figured	the problem it	**out**.

INTRANSITIVE PHRASAL VERBS

Not Separated			
Subject	**Verb**	**Particle**	
They It	**came**	**back**	quickly.
	caught	**on**	everywhere.

GRAMMAR NOTES   **EXAMPLES**

1. A **phrasal verb** (also called a *two-word verb*) has two parts: a main verb and a particle.

   Verb + Particle = Phrasal Verb

   Particles and prepositions look the same, but they act differently.

   Prepositions <u>do not change the meaning</u> of the main verb.

   Particles often <u>change the meaning</u> of the main verb.

verb + particle
• Let's **figure out** this problem now.
verb + particle
• Ho **called in** a consultant.

verb + preposition
• He **looked into** the room.
   *(He was outside the room and **looked** in.)*
verb + particle
• He **looked into** the problem.
   *(He **researched** the problem.)*

---

2. The verb and particle are usually common words, but their separate meanings are often very different from the **meaning of the phrasal verb**.

PHRASAL VERB	MEANING
come back	return
figure out	understand
look into	research
pick up	improve
put up	erect

   USAGE NOTE: Phrasal verbs are very common in everyday speech.

   ▶ BE CAREFUL! Like other verbs, phrasal verbs often have more than one meaning.

• Customers didn't **come back**.
• We had to **figure out** the problem.
• We **looked into** feng shui.
• Business has **picked up**.
• He **put up** a new entrance.

• We're **putting up** signs for our business.
   (We're erecting signs for our business.)

• Please **turn down** the radio. The music is too loud.
   (Please lower the volume.)
• Bill didn't get the restaurant job. They **turned down** his application.
   (They rejected his application.)

3. Many phrasal verbs are **transitive**. They take objects.

PHRASAL VERB	MEANING
call off something	cancel
pick out something	choose
take away something	remove
think up something	invent
work out something	solve

phrasal verb + object
- **Let's call off** *the meeting*.
- **Pick out** *the chair* you like best.
- **Take away** *the dishes*.
- He **thought up** *good answers*.
- He **worked out** *the problem*.

4. Most transitive phrasal verbs are **separable**. This means that **noun objects** can go:

- <u>after</u> the particle

  OR

- <u>between</u> the verb and the particle.

▶ **BE CAREFUL!** If the direct object is a **pronoun**, it must go <u>between</u> the verb and the particle.

USAGE NOTE: When the noun object is part of a <u>long phrase</u>, we usually <u>do not separate</u> the phrasal verb.

verb + particle + object
- They **tore down** *the entrance*.

  OR

verb + object + particle
- They **tore** *the entrance* **down**.

- I didn't understand the word, so I **looked** *it* **up** in the dictionary. NOT I ~~looked up it~~.
- Ho **tried out** the many complex theories of feng shui. NOT Ho ~~tried the many complex theories of feng shui out~~.

5. Some phrasal verbs are **intransitive**. They do not take an object. They are always inseparable.

PHRASAL VERB	MEANING
catch on	become popular
get ahead	make progress
show up	appear
sit down	take a seat

- Feng shui has **caught on** all over.
- Tina is **getting ahead** in her career.
- The consultant **showed up** early.
- **Sit down** over there.

Reference Notes

For a list of **transitive phrasal verbs**, see Appendix 17 on pages A-6–A-7.
For information about **transitive verbs that are inseparable**, see Unit 12.
For a list of **intransitive phrasal verbs**, see Appendix 18 on page A-8.

Focused Practice

1 | DISCOVER THE GRAMMAR

A *Read this article about feng shui. Underline all the phrasal verbs and circle the direct objects of the transitive phrasal verbs.*

Everyday Feng Shui

Have you noticed that some spaces cheer you up and give you energy, while others bring you down? This feng shui diagram uses mythological animals to explain why. Look it over, and then imagine yourself in the center. A phoenix takes off in front of you and gives you inspiration. Behind you, a tortoise guards you from things you cannot see. On your left and right, a dragon and a tiger balance each other. The dragon floats above the floor and helps you take in the big picture, not just small details. The tiger's energy gives you courage.

These symbols can be important in setting up a work environment. Dana, for example, needed ideas and energy in order to get ahead. Unfortunately, her undecorated, windowless cubicle took away most of her powers. After she hung up a scenic poster in the phoenix area in front of her desk, she began to feel more inspired. She gave her tiger some power by picking out plants to put on the file cabinet to her right. For her dragon, she hung a cheerful mobile from the top of the left wall of her cubicle. Try these ideas out in your own work area and see what happens!

B *Now read these statements and write* **T** *(true) or* **F** *(false).*

__T__ **1.** Your environment can bring about changes in your mood.

_____ **2.** The phoenix remains sitting in the space ahead of you.

_____ **3.** The dragon's energy helps you understand an overall plan.

_____ **4.** Dana wanted a promotion.

_____ **5.** From the beginning, Dana's work area inspired her.

_____ **6.** She removed a poster from the area in front of her desk.

_____ **7.** There were no plants in her cubicle at first.

2 | FENG SHUI Q AND A
Grammar Notes 1–2

Circle the correct particles to complete these questions and answers from an online feng shui message board.

Q: I've been having a lot of trouble sleeping. My bed faces north. Is that OK?

A: No. Turn it (around) / up so that your head is to the north and your feet to the south.
    1.

Q: Our building owner has cut down / up all the trees in our garden. Now he's going to put on / up
    2.   **3.**

   a tall building there! This will block away / out all our light. What can we do?
    4.

A: I don't know if you can work this problem off / out. You may need to think about moving.
    5.

Q: I am opening a new restaurant in Los Angeles. I would like to have a feng shui consultant look

   it over / up to see if the energy is positive. Could you recommend someone?
    6.

A: We don't give out / up names online. E-mail me, and I will put together / off a list for you.
    7.   **8.**

Q: I hung up / out a beautiful mirror on my bedroom wall. Then I read that mirrors bring too
    9.

   much energy into a bedroom. I don't want to take it out / down! What can I do?
    10.

A: Before you go to sleep, put a scarf over the mirror. That will keep on / out the "bad energy."
    11.

Q: I don't know much about feng shui. How can I find after / out more about it?
    12.

A: There are hundreds of books about feng shui. Go to your local library and take some out / up.
    13.

   Or look after / up feng shui on an online bookstore website to get a list of titles.
    14.

3 | I. M. PEI

Read about one of the most famous modern architects. Complete the information with the correct forms of the phrasal verbs in the boxes.

~~grow up~~	put up	settle on	turn out

Born in 1917, Ieoh Ming Pei (better known as I. M. Pei) _____*grew up*_____ in Canton, China. As a child, he
　　　　　　　　　　1.
watched workers _____ large new
　　　　　　　　　　　　2.
buildings. When he was 17, he went to the United States to learn about building. He considered becoming an engineer or an architect. In fact, he didn't

_____ his career until after he enrolled in
　　3.
college. As it _____, Pei became one of the most famous modern architects in
　　　　　　　　4.
the world.

I. M. Pei in front of the Louvre pyramid

figure out	go up	let in	put on	tear down

Pei is famous for his strong geometric forms made of steel, glass, concrete, and stone. One of his most controversial projects was his glass pyramid at the Louvre in Paris. The old museum was dark, confusing, and crowded. No one wanted to _____ the old
　　　　　　　　　　　　　　　　　　　　　　　　　5.
structure, so Pei had to _____ a solution to the Louvre's problems and still be
　　　　　　　　　　6.
sensitive to the famous old building and its surroundings. When he proposed his 71-foot-high glass pyramid as a new entrance to the museum, many Parisians were shocked and they

_____ buttons asking "Why the pyramid?" However, the glass pyramid
　　7.

_____ anyway, blending with the environment, reflecting the sky, and
　　8.

_____ the sunlight. Today, many people say that it is a good example of the
　　9.
principles of feng shui.

give up	go back	keep on	set up

In spite of harsh criticism, Pei _____
10.

building structures that reflected their environment—

from the 70-story Bank of China skyscraper in Hong

Kong to the Rock 'n' Roll Hall of Fame in Cleveland,

Ohio. He has received many prizes. He used some of the

prize money to _____ a scholarship fund
11.

for Chinese students to study architecture in the United

Inside the Louvre pyramid

States and then to _____ to China to work as architects.
12.

Pei is both creative and perfectionistic. He is also persistent. Throughout his career he

has faced a lot of opposition to his work, but Pei strongly believes that "you have to identify

the important things and press for them and not _____."
13.

4 | IN THE DORM

Grammar Notes 3–4

*Complete the conversations with the correct form of the phrasal verb used in the first line of
each conversation and a pronoun object.*

1. **A:** Could I borrow your truck? I need to pick up some chairs this week.

   B: Sure. When are you _____ *going to pick them up* _____?

2. **A:** Hey! Who took down my feng shui posters?

   B: Sorry. I _____. I thought you didn't like them anymore.

3. **A:** I need to cheer up my roommate. He just flunked a big test.

   B: Why don't you straighten up the room? That will _____.

4. **A:** This room is depressing. Let's try out some of these feng shui ideas.

   B: I agree. Let's _____ this weekend.

5. **A:** We need something to light up that corner. It's awfully dark.

   B: I have an extra lamp. This will _____ nicely.

6. **A:** Can someone touch up the paint in my dorm room? It's cracked in several places.

   B: Sure. We'll send someone to _____ next week.

5 | EDITING

Read this student's journal entry. There are ten mistakes in the use of phrasal verbs. The first mistake is already corrected. Find and correct nine more.

>   *down*
>   I just read an article about feng shui. The author suggests sitting ~~up~~ in your home and
>
> thinking about how your environment makes you feel. I tried out it.
>
>   My apartment is bright and sunny. This cheers me out. At night, it's very dark, but
>
> I've figured up what to do. I'm going to buy another lamp to light the apartment at
>
> night up. I'll leave it on when I go out at night, so I can see light as soon as I come in. I
>
> also like the light green walls in my bedroom, but the chipped paint has been bringing
>
> down me. I'm going to touch it over soon.
>
>   My apartment is too small, but I can't tear up the walls. I think it will look more
>
> spacious if I just straighten it up. I'll try to put books back after I take them off the
>
> shelves and hang away my clothes at night. With just a few small changes, I'll end up
>
> feeling happier in my home. It's worth trying on.

Communication Practice

6 | LISTENING

🎧 *Listen to the short conversations. Complete them with the words that you hear. Then listen again and check your answers.*

1. AMY: How's the temperature in here?

   BEN: It's a little too cold for me. Do you mind if I turn the air-conditioner ___*down*___?

1.

2. AMY: What did you think about that information on feng shui?

   BEN: I haven't had the chance to look it _____ yet.

2.

3. AMY: Have you finished redecorating your office?

   BEN: Almost. I'm going to IKEA today to pick _____ a new couch.

3.

4. AMY: The living room is a mess. Your books are all over the place.

    BEN: Don't worry. I'll put them _____ as soon as I'm done with my homework.

                                      4.

5. AMY: I really don't like those new curtains.

    BEN: Neither do I. I'm going to take them _____ tomorrow.

                                        5.

6. AMY: This mattress isn't as comfortable as it used to be.

    BEN: I know. I think we need to turn it _____.

                                        6.

7. AMY: What color should we paint the kitchen?

    BEN: I don't know. Let's discuss it when we get _____.

                                        7.

Now look at the completed sentences. Decide if the statements below are true (T) or false (F).

  F   **1.** Ben doesn't want to have any air-conditioning on.

_____ **2.** He is going to look in a book for information about feng shui.

_____ **3.** He hasn't selected a couch yet.

_____ **4.** He is going to return the books to their original place.

_____ **5.** He is going to return the curtains to the store tomorrow.

_____ **6.** He thinks they should change the position of the mattress so the underside is now on top.

_____ **7.** Amy and Ben are going somewhere.

7 | REDECORATING

Work in small groups. How would you like to change your classroom or your school? What would you like to remain the same? Use some of these phrasal verbs in your discussion.

cover up	do over	hang up	leave on
light up	make up	move around	pick out
put away	put up	straighten up	tear down
throw away	touch up	turn around	turn on / off

    Example: **A:** I think we should hang up some posters.

                      B: It would be nice to hang some photographs up too.

8 | WHAT'S DIFFERENT?

Work with a partner. Look at the Before *and* After *pictures of Amy's room for two minutes. Write down all the differences you can find. Then compare your list with another pair's list.*

Before

After

> **Example:** She took the curtains down.

9 | WRITING

Write about how you feel in your home, office, or classroom. What makes you feel good? What makes you feel bad? What would you like to change? Use phrasal verbs. You can use the journal entry in Exercise 5 as a model.

> **Example:** My dorm room is bright and sunny. The room always cheers me up when I get back from a hard day at school. My roommate and I picked out the curtains together. We also put up some new posters on the walls . . .

10 | ON THE INTERNET

Do a search on **home makeover**. *Look for* Before *and* After *photos. Choose two photos to write about and print them out. How did the room look before? How did it make you feel? How does it look now? What were some of the changes? How does the room make you feel now? Discuss your answers with a partner.*

> **Example:** The room looked too dark and crowded before. They moved some furniture around. They also took down those dark curtains. Now it looks more comfortable.

Phrasal Verbs: Separable and Inseparable

Grammar in Context

BEFORE YOU READ

🎧 *Look at the cartoon. Who do you think is calling the man? How does the man feel about the call? Read this magazine article about telemarketers.*

WELCOME HOME!

"I just got home. Can you call back tomorrow when I'm still at work?"

You just **got back** from a long, hard day at the office. You're exhausted. All you want to do is **take off** your jacket, **put down** your briefcase, and relax over a great dinner. Then, just as you're about to **sit down** at the table, the phone rings. You hesitate to **pick** it **up**. It's probably just another telemarketer trying to **talk** you **into** buying something you really

don't need. But, what if it's not? It could be important. Maybe there's a family emergency. You have to **find out**!

"Hello?" you answer nervously.

"Hello, is this Mr. Groaner?" a strange voice asks. You know right away it's a telemarketer. Your name is Groden. "We have great news for you! You've been chosen to receive an all-expense-paid trip to the Bahamas! It's an offer you can't afford to **turn down**!"

Telemarketing—the practice of selling products and services by phone—is rapidly spreading throughout the world as the number of household phones **goes up** and phone rates **come down**. To most people it is about as welcome as a bad case of the flu.

What can be done about this invasion of privacy? Here are several tactics you can **try out**:

☎ **Sign up** to have your phone number placed on "Do Not Call" lists. Many countries are **setting up** lists of people who do not want to be called by telemarketers. These lists actually make it against the law for telemarketers to call you. If you still receive calls, **write down** the date and time of the call. **Find out** the name of the organization calling you. You can then report the illegal call to the proper authorities.

(continued)

WELCOME HOME!

☎ Use Caller ID (a service that identifies the phone number of the caller) to help identify telemarketers. If an unfamiliar number **shows up** on your ID screen, don't **pick up** the phone.

☎ If you *have* answered the phone, say (firmly but politely!): "I'm **hanging up** now," and **get off** the phone.

☎ Ask the individual telemarketing company to **take** you **off** their list. But don't **count on** this happening immediately. You may have to ask several times before it takes effect.

None of these measures will eliminate *all* unwanted telephone solicitations, but they should **cut down** the number of calls you receive.

Telemarketing, however, is just part of the larger problem. We are constantly being flooded with unwanted offers and requests. "Junk mail" **fills up** our mailboxes (and later our trash cans when we **throw** it **out**). And the invasion is, of course, not limited to paper. When you **turn on** your computer to check your e-mail, you are greeted by dozens of commercial messages. Known as *spam*, it's the electronic equivalent of junk mail.

What's the solution? Leave home? Move to a desert island? Maybe not. They'll probably **get to** you there too!

AFTER YOU READ

Find a phrasal verb from the article that means:

1. returned _____

2. convince _____

3. reject _____

4. register _____

5. appears _____

6. remove _____

Grammar Presentation

PHRASAL VERBS: SEPARABLE AND INSEPARABLE

Separable Transitive			
Subject	Verb	Particle	Direct Object
She	**picked**	**up**	the phone.

Separable Transitive			
Subject	Verb	Direct Object	Particle
She	**picked**	the phone it	**up**.

Inseparable Transitive			
Subject	Verb	Particle	Direct Object
He	**counts**	**on**	your calls. them.

Intransitive		
Subject	Verb	Particle
They	**sat**	**down**.

GRAMMAR NOTES

1. As you learned in Unit 11, most transitive phrasal verbs are **separable**. This means that **noun objects** can go <u>after</u> the particle <u>or between</u> the verb and the particle.

▶ **BE CAREFUL!** If the direct object is a **pronoun**, it must go <u>between</u> the verb and the particle.

USAGE NOTE: When the noun object is part of a long phrase, we usually do not separate the phrasal verb.

2. Some transitive phrasal verbs are **inseparable**. This means that both noun and pronoun objects always go <u>after</u> the particle. You cannot separate the verb from its particle.

EXAMPLES

verb + particle + object
- I just **took off** *my coat*.

OR

verb + object + particle
- I just **took** *my coat* **off**.

- I **wrote** *it* **down**.
  NOT I wrote ~~down it~~.

- I **filled out** the form from the Do Not Call service.
  NOT I ~~filled the form from the Do Not Call service out~~.

- I **ran into** *Karim* at work.
  NOT I ~~ran Karim into~~ at work.
- I **ran into** *him* at work.
  NOT I ~~ran him into~~.

(continued)

3. A small group of transitive phrasal verbs **must be separated**.

PHRASAL VERB	MEANING
keep something **on**	not remove
talk someone **into**	persuade

- **Keep** *your coat* **on**.
  Not Keep ~~on your coat~~.
- She **talked** *them* **into** a vacation.
  Not She talked ~~into them~~ a vacation.

4. Some transitive phrasal verbs are used in combination with certain prepositions.

A **phrasal verb + preposition** combination (also called a *three-word verb)* is usually **inseparable**.

PHRASAL VERB	MEANING
come up *with* something	invent
drop out *of* something	quit
keep up *with* something OR someone	go as fast as

- She **came up** *with* a plan to stop junk mail.
- I **dropped out** *of* school and got a job.
- He couldn't **keep up** *with* his e-mail. There was too much to read.

5. As you learned in Unit 11, some phrasal verbs are **intransitive**. This means that they do not take an object.

- He's been away and just **got back**.
- They don't **give up**. They keep calling.

Reference Notes
For a list of **separable phrasal verbs**, see Appendix 17 on pages A-6–A-7.
For a list of **inseparable transitive phrasal verbs**, see Appendix 17 on pages A-6–A-7.
For a list of **phrasal verbs that must be separated**, see Appendix 17 on pages A-6–A-7.
For a list of **phrasal verb + preposition combinations**, see Appendix 7 on page A-3.
For a list of **intransitive phrasal verbs**, see Appendix 18 on page A-8.

Focused Practice

1 | DISCOVER THE GRAMMAR

A *Underline the phrasal verbs in this article about dealing with telemarketers.*

HOLD ON, PLEASE! Your phone number is on the Do Not Call list, but you keep on receiving some telemarketing calls. Why not have some fun with them? Here are some strategies:

- When the telemarketer asks, "How are you today?"—tell her! Don't leave anything out. Say, "I have a headache you wouldn't believe, and my back is acting up again. Now I can't figure out the instructions for my DVD player . . ."
- When a telemarketer calls during dinner, ask for his home telephone number so you can call him back. When he refuses, ask him to hold on. Put the phone down and continue eating until you hear the dial tone.
- Ask the telemarketer to spell her first and last name and the name of the company. Tell her to speak slowly—you're writing it all down. Ask questions until she hangs up.
- To credit card offers, say, "Thanks a lot! My company just laid me off, and I really need the money!"

B *Now write down each phrasal verb from the article next to its meaning.*

1. _____ causing problems

2. _____ continue

3. _____ ends a phone call

4. _____ fired from a job

5. ____hold on____ not end a phone call

6. _____ omit

7. _____ return a call

8. _____ stop holding

9. _____ understand after thinking about

10. _____ putting on paper in order to remember

2 | SCAM ALERT!   *Grammar Notes 1–5*

A scam *is a dishonest plan, usually with the goal of getting money. Read about how to avoid some common scams. Complete the information with the correct forms of the phrasal verbs in the boxes.*

end up with	hang up	let down	~~throw out~~

I just ____*threw out*____ my first issue of *Motorcycle Mama*. I'm nobody's mama and I don't
         1.

own a motorcycle, so how did I _____ this subscription? Well, my neighbor's son was
              2.

raising money for his soccer team, and I didn't want to _____ him _____. It's
                       3.

easy to _____ on telemarketers, but it's hard to say *no* to your friends and neighbors.
   4.

fall for	get to	help out	watch out for

The magazine company _____ me through a friendship. It's one of the ways
         5.

"persuasion professionals" get us to say *yes*. Of course it's OK to _____ the local soccer
          6.

team. But a lot of people _____ scams because of similar techniques. _____
      7.   **8.**

these common scams.

find out	give back	go along with	lay out	turn down

When someone gives you something, you want to _____ something _____.
         9.

This desire to return a favor can cost you money when a telemarketer announces you've won a

vacation or a new car. These offers aren't free. When people _____ them, they always
        10.

_____ that there's a tax or a fee to collect the "free" prize. Since they've accepted the
 11.

offer, they feel obligated to pay. You should _____ these offers _____. These are
            12.

scams—all too often people _____ money and receive nothing.
     13.

count on	fill out	pick out	put on	turn up

A TV actor will _____ a doctor's white jacket and talk about cough medicine. In a
                        14.

magazine ad, a woman in a business suit will help you _____ the best investment firm.
                                                                      15.

Ads with fake "authority figures" are easy to spot, but there's a new Internet scam that's harder to

recognize. The scammer sends e-mails that seem to be from well-known banks. They tell you that

a problem with your account has _____. Then they send you to an Internet site to
                                            16.

_____ forms with your account information and password. The site seems to have
        17.

authority—it looks like the real thing. But a real bank will **never** ask for your information over the

Internet. You can _____ that!
                              18.

3 | PHONE TALK
Grammar Note 1

Complete the conversations. Use phrasal verbs and pronouns.

1. **A:** Tell Ana not to pick the phone up. It's probably a telemarketer.

   B: Too late. She's already _____ *picked it up* _____.

2. **A:** You can't turn down this great offer for cat food!

   B: I'm afraid I have to _____. I don't have a cat.

3. **A:** Did you fill out the online Do Not Call form?

   B: I _____ yesterday. Thanks for telling me about it.

4. **A:** I left out my office phone and fax numbers on that form.

   B: Why did you _____?

5. **A:** Remember to call your mother back.

   B: I _____ last night.

6. **A:** Did you write down the dates of the calls?

   B: I _____, but then I lost the piece of paper.

7. **A:** Can you take my mother's name off your calling list?

   B: Sure. We'll _____ right away.

8. **A:** Let's turn the phone off and have dinner.

   B: I can't _____. I'm expecting an important call.

4 | SPAM!

Complete the ads. Use the correct forms of the phrasal verbs and objects in parentheses.
Place the object between the verb and the particle when possible.

LOSE WEIGHT!

Lose Weight!

Take those extra pounds off fast! Love bread and cake? Don't _____.
1. (Take off / those extra pounds)   **2.** (give up / them)

No diet! No pills! No exercise! Our delicious drinks will _____ while you
                                                    3. (fill up / you)

lose weight. _____ at no cost. It's FREE for one month!
            4. (Try out / our plan)

Our weight loss secrets can be yours today. _____ as soon as you
                                           5. (Find out / them)

_____. Want to know more? Click <u>here</u> for our information request form.
6. (sign up for / our plan)

_____ to get our brochure. Just _____, and watch
7. (Fill out / it)   **8.** (stick to / our plan)

those pounds come off! If you do not want to receive e-mail from us, we will

_____ our list.
9. (take off / you)

MAKE $$$$$

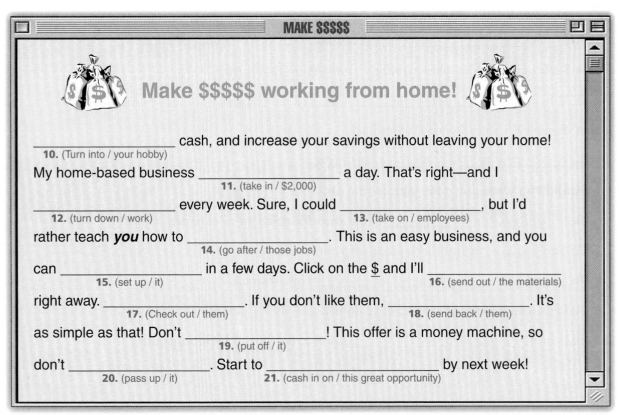

Make $$$$$ working from home!

_____ cash, and increase your savings without leaving your home!
10. (Turn into / your hobby)

My home-based business _____ a day. That's right—and I
                       11. (take in / $2,000)

_____ every week. Sure, I could _____, but I'd
12. (turn down / work)   **13.** (take on / employees)

rather teach **you** how to _____. This is an easy business, and you
                           14. (go after / those jobs)

can _____ in a few days. Click on the <u>$</u> and I'll _____
    15. (set up / it)   **16.** (send out / the materials)

right away. _____. If you don't like them, _____. It's
           17. (Check out / them)   **18.** (send back / them)

as simple as that! Don't _____! This offer is a money machine, so
                        19. (put off / it)

don't _____. Start to _____ by next week!
      20. (pass up / it)   **21.** (cash in on / this great opportunity)

5 | EDITING

Read this transcript of a phone call between a telemarketer (TM) and Janis Linder (JL).
There are fourteen mistakes in the use of phrasal verbs. The first mistake is already
corrected. Find and correct thirteen more.

TM: Hello, Ms. Linder?

JL: Yes. Who's this?

TM: This is Bob Watson from *Motorcycle Mama*. I'm calling to offer you a 12-month

subscription for the low price of just $15 a year. Can I sign ~~up you~~ *you up*?

JL: No thanks. I'm not interested in signing in for any more magazine subscriptions.

Besides, I just sat up for dinner.

TM: Why don't you at least try out it for six months? Don't pass this great opportunity

down! It's a once in a lifetime chance.

JL: Sorry, I'm really not interested. I don't even have a motorcycle.

TM: Well then, this is a great opportunity to find all about them out! We'll send you a

free copy and you can look over it.

JL: You're not going to talk me in it! In fact, I'm going to hang the phone down right

now. And please take my name out your list.

TM: No, hold out! Don't go away! Don't turn this great offer down! You'll be sorry if

you do. Chances like this don't come around every day! Don't miss it out on!

JL: OK. I have an idea. Why don't you give me your phone number, and I'll call back

you during YOUR dinner?

[click as the telemarketer hangs the phone.]

JL: Hello? Hello?

Communication Practice

6 | LISTENING

⌒ *Listen to this telemarketing call. Then listen again and complete Mr. Chen's notes.*

> ### *Get Together Program*
>
> • Just ____5 cents____ a minute on all long-distance calls.
>   **1.**
> • Cell phone service included.
> • $ _____ monthly fee.
>   **2.**
> • $20 fee to _____ new plan.
>   **3.**
> • (Fee will _____ on first bill.)
>   **4.**
> • _____ activation fee (to _____ the phone _____).
>   **5.**   **6.**   **7.**
> • New cell phone usually costs _____.
>   **8.**
> • If I _____ right now, they'll _____ me _____ $20.
>   **9.**   **10.**   **11.**
> • Offer good for only _____.
>   **12.**

*Now look at the notes and read these statements. Decide if the statements are true (**T**) or false (**F**).*

__F__ **1.** With the new service, Mr. Chen's long-distance phone bill will go down.

_____ **2.** The phone bill will include both long-distance and cell phone calls.

_____ **3.** It costs $30 to set up the new plan.

_____ **4.** There's no charge to turn the cell phone service on.

_____ **5.** With the rebate, the cost of the new cell phone comes to $30.

_____ **6.** The telemarketer is going to give Mr. Chen some time to think over the plan.

_____ **7.** Mr. Chen is going to sign up for the service.

7 | FOR OR AGAINST?

Work in groups. Talk about these questions.

- What do you think of telemarketing? Does it offer consumers anything positive?

- Do you go along with the idea of Do Not Call lists? Should certain organizations be allowed to keep on calling you? If yes, what kind?

- Do you get a lot of calls from telemarketers? How do you handle them? Do you think people should just hang up? Or should they put them off with a polite excuse, such as, "Thanks. I'll think it over."?

Example: Telemarketing is a terrible idea. I've never gotten anything useful out of a telemarketing call.

8 | ROLE PLAY: YOU MAKE THE CALL

Work with a partner. Role-play these situations. Choose one role play to perform for your class or a group.

- You have come home from a very rough day at work. Just as you sit down to dinner, the phone rings. A telemarketer wants to give away an all-expense-paid vacation. You don't hang up because you really need a vacation. You go along with the conversation until you hear about the "tax" you must pay.

- Your neighbor asks you over. He or she has also invited other neighbors. This neighbor often gives parties to sell scented candles and other gift items. You'd like to get together with your neighbors, but not at a sales event. You try to find out more about the party. Your neighbor doesn't want to give much information.

- You are a telemarketer. You must make at least one sale tonight or you will lose your job. One person sounds very interested in your product at first. But the person wants to write everything down. He or she keeps on asking you to talk more slowly. You can't give up because you really need this sale!

Example: A: Hello?
          B: Mr. Regal? Congratulations! Wonderland Cruises is giving away two all-expense-paid vacations, and you're a winner!

9 | SAVVY CONSUMERS

Bring in an ad from a magazine, a piece of junk mail, spam, or an offer from the Internet. Discuss these ads in a group. Talk about these questions.

- What group of people might want this product or service (children, teenagers, older people, men, women)?

- How does the ad try to get people to want this product or service?

- Is this an honest offer or a scam? What makes you think so?

Example: I think this ad is trying to get to teenagers. It shows a group of teens fooling around and having a good time while they're drinking soda.

10 | WRITING

Write a paragraph about an experience you have had on the phone. It could be a conversation with a friend, a wrong number, or a telemarketing call. Use some of these phrasal verbs:

call back	come up	end up	figure out	find out	give up
go on	go over	hang up	hold on	keep on	pick up
sign up	talk into	think over	turn down	turn out	wake up

Example: When I first got to this country, I had difficulty understanding English speakers on the phone. I often couldn't figure out what people were saying to me. I kept on asking the person to repeat. Sometimes I had to give up, say "Sorry," and hang up.

11 | ON THE INTERNET

*Do a search on the phrase **do not call**. Find out the following information. Discuss your findings with your classmates.*

- How can people sign up?
- What type of form do they have to fill out?
- What can they do if telemarketers keep on calling them?
- How can people find out more information?

Example: It's easy to sign up. You just . . .

From **Grammar** to **Writing**
Using the Appropriate Degree of Formality

Phrasal verbs are more common in informal writing than their one-word synonyms.

Example: What time do you **board** the bus? *(more formal)*
What time do you **get on** the bus? *(less formal)*

1 | *Read this letter to a friend. Make it less formal by using phrasal verbs for the words in parentheses. Use Appendices 17 and 18, pages A-6–A-8 if you need help.*

Dear Van,

Sorry I haven't written sooner, but I've been really busy. I just moved

into a new apartment. Here's what a typical day looks like for me:

I _____*get up*_____ early, usually at 6:30. After running two miles,
    1. (arise)

showering, and having breakfast, I _____ the bus and go to my
                                        2. (board)

9:00 English class. In addition to English, I'm taking statistics this semester.

I'm finding it really hard, but I'm going to _____ it. I'll need it
                                             3. (persevere)

later for business school.

After classes I have just enough time for a quick lunch with some friends

before getting to McDonald's at 1:00 for my four-hour shift. On the way home,

I've been _____ some things for my apartment. This evening,
          4. (purchasing)

for example, I bought a new computer workstation, which I'm going to

_____ this weekend. (By the way, thanks for telling me about
5. (assemble)

feng shui! I've been using it to _____ my apartment.)
                                 6. (redecorate)

(continued)

When I get home, I prepare a quick dinner, and then spend several hours on my homework. I'm also writing a report for my statistics class. I can't believe how much paper (and time) this project is _____! It's
        7. (consuming)
interesting, but I'll be glad when it's over. Then at least I'll be able to

_____ on the couch that I just bought and watch some TV
   8. (recline)
before going to bed. These days I go straight to bed as soon as I finish my

homework. By the time I _____ the lights, it's 11:00 P.M. and
       9. (extinguish)
I'm absolutely exhausted.

    Well, that's enough about me and my life. I really don't think that I've

_____ anything important. How are you? What have you
   10. (omitted)
been doing? I'd love to see you. The weekend of the 12th I'll be going to visit

Tania, but I'm sure it would be OK for you to _____ with me.
       11. (accompany)
Let me know!

   Looking forward to hearing from you,

          Marta

   P.S. I think I _____ Victor's e-mail address before copying it
      12. (discarded)
into my address book. Do you have it?

2 | *Use information from the letter in Exercise 1 to complete Marta's schedule.*

Time	To Do
6:30 A.M.	get up
6:45	run two miles
7:30	
7:45	breakfast
8:15	
	English class
11:00	statistics class

Time	To Do
12:00 noon	
P.M.	McDonald's
5:30–6:00	
6:30	dinner
7:00–10:30	
	go to bed

3 | *Before you write . . .*

Make a schedule like the one in Exercise 2 of a typical day in your life.

4 | *Write an informal letter to a friend or relative about some of the things you've been doing lately. Use information from your schedule in Exercise 3. Remember to use phrasal verbs.*

5 | *Exchange letters with a partner. Underline the phrasal verbs in your partner's letter. Write a question mark (?) where something seems wrong or missing. Then answer the following questions.*

	Yes	No
1. Did the writer use phrasal verbs correctly?	☐	☐
2. Are there other places where the writer could use phrasal verbs?	☐	☐
3. If there are phrasal verbs with pronouns, are the pronouns in the right place?	☐	☐

6 | *Discuss your editing suggestions with your partner. Then rewrite your own paragraph. Make any necessary corrections.*

Review Test

I   *Circle the best words to complete these classroom guidelines.*

1. Fill (out)/ up the school questionnaire completely.

2. Answer all the questions. Don't leave anything off / <u>out</u>.

3. Clear <u>away</u> / up any problems you have about your homework assignment before you begin.

4. If you make a lot of mistakes, do the assignment <u>over</u> / up.

5. Look <u>over</u> / up your homework before submitting it.

6. Please hand out / <u>in</u> all your homework on time.

7. You must come up <u>with</u> / to an idea for your science project by March 2.

8. Next week, I will pass <u>out</u> / up a list of suggested topics for your project.

9. Pick <u>out</u> / up one of the suggested topics or choose one of your own.

10. If you have an idea for a topic, please talk it into / <u>over</u> with me.

11. If you are having trouble with your project, don't give <u>up</u> / away. Come speak to me.

12. If I turn <u>down</u> / off your project topic, I will help you think back on / <u>up</u> another one.

13. If you don't know how to spell a word, look it over / <u>up</u> in the dictionary. Spelling counts!

14. All projects must be turned <u>in</u> / up on time. There will be no extensions!

15. If you are having trouble keeping away from / <u>up with</u> the class, let me know. Additional help can be arranged for you.

16. There are extra handouts in the back of the room. Supplies are limited. Please take one before they run <u>out</u> / over.

17. All tests will be graded and given <u>back</u> / up on the next day of class.

18. The final exam is scheduled for May 15 and cannot be put away / <u>off</u>.

19. If you get over / <u>through with</u> the exam early, you may leave.

20. Please put <u>away</u> / off all test tubes and chemicals after class.

21. Please shut away / <u>off</u> all lights and equipment before leaving the room.

22. Straighten over / <u>up</u> your desks before the break so we have a neat room to come off / <u>back</u> to.

II *Circle the letter of the words closest in meaning to the underlined words.*

1. Do you think feng shui will ever <u>become popular</u> here? A B (C) D
   - (**A**) straighten up
   - (**B**) touch up
   - (**C**) catch on
   - (**D**) try out

2. My computer is <u>causing problems</u>. Can you help me? A B C D
   - (**A**) setting up
   - (**B**) going up
   - (**C**) acting up
   - (**D**) keeping up

3. I'm not a telemarketer. Please don't <u>end this call</u>! A B C D
   - (**A**) drop out
   - (**B**) call back
   - (**C**) end up
   - (**D**) hang up

4. The Do Not Call List is a great idea! Who <u>invented it</u>? A B C D
   - (**A**) thought it up
   - (**B**) charged it up
   - (**C**) let it in
   - (**D**) let it out

5. This paint is scratched. Let's <u>improve it</u> a little. A B C D
   - (**A**) fill it up
   - (**B**) touch it up
   - (**C**) make it up
   - (**D**) bring it up

6. Mark works so hard that he's sure to <u>succeed</u>. A B C D
   - (**A**) give up
   - (**B**) work off
   - (**C**) turn over
   - (**D**) get ahead

7. When did the company <u>hire them</u>? A B C D
   - (**A**) take them off
   - (**B**) take them on
   - (**C**) work them out
   - (**D**) bring them up

8. My student days were great. I <u>remember them</u> often. A B C D
   - (**A**) leave them on
   - (**B**) see them through
   - (**C**) think back on them
   - (**D**) look them up

9. Don't <u>believe</u> that offer. It's probably a scam. A B C D
   - (**A**) run into
   - (**B**) lay out
   - (**C**) fall for
   - (**D**) get along

10. A lamp will <u>illuminate</u> this corner nicely. A B C D
    - (**A**) turn on
    - (**B**) blow up
    - (**C**) put up
    - (**D**) light up

(continued)

11. Instead of arguing about the problem, let's <u>discuss it</u>.　　　　　　**A　B　C　D**

    (**A**) look it over　　　　　　　(**C**) take it away

    (**B**) charge it up　　　　　　　(**D**) talk it over

12. Carla <u>got</u> some interesting ideas from the Internet.　　　　　　**A　B　C　D**

    (**A**) picked out　　　　　　　(**C**) picked up

    (**B**) pointed out　　　　　　　(**D**) called up

13. Jason wanted to be an artist, but he <u>unexpectedly went</u> to medical school.　　**A　B　C　D**

    (**A**) ended up going　　　　　　(**C**) figured out going

    (**B**) dreamt up going　　　　　　(**D**) brought about going

14. Be careful with those chemicals. They could <u>explode</u>.　　　　　　**A　B　C　D**

    (**A**) break down　　　　　　　(**C**) come off

    (**B**) blow up　　　　　　　　(**D**) take down

15. Why did our cell phone charges <u>increase</u>?　　　　　　**A　B　C　D**

    (**A**) fill up　　　　　　　　(**C**) keep up

    (**B**) go up　　　　　　　　(**D**) bring up

III　*Complete these conversations with phrasal verbs and pronouns.*

1. **A:** I'm thinking over a possible topic for my project.

   B: Well, don't _____ *think it over* _____ too long. It's due soon.

2. **A:** I heard that they called off the last class.

   B: Really? Why did they _____?

3. **A:** Today we're going to carry out an experiment.

   B: What materials do we need to _____?

4. **A:** Could you switch on the light?

   B: I've already _____.

5. **A:** Do you get along with John?

   B: Sure. I _____. Why do you ask?

6. **A:** Keep away from those chemicals! They're dangerous.

   B: Don't worry! I'll _____.

7. **A:** Could you put back that book when you're done?

   B: Sure. I'll _____.

8. **A:** You can take off your safety goggles now.

   B: We've already _____.

9. **A:** Will someone please wake up Alice? She's fallen asleep again.

   B: I'll _____.

10. **A:** We have three problems to work out before our next class.

    B: When are you going to _____?

IV *Each sentence has four underlined words or phrases. The four underlined parts of the sentences are marked A, B, C, or D. Circle the letter of the one underlined part that is NOT CORRECT.*

1. You <u>ought to</u> <u>look over</u> your notes for the test, so don't <u>throw</u> <u>away them</u>.   **A   B   C (D)**
   A   B   C   D

2. The teacher <u>turned off</u> my idea, so I <u>have to</u> <u>think</u> <u>up</u> a new one.   **A   B   C   D**
   A   B   C   D

3. We've <u>looked</u> <u>up</u> a lot of information, and now we're <u>trying</u> to draw   **A   B   C   D**
   A   B   C

   <u>together it</u> for our report.
   D

4. Put <u>the new white lab coat I bought you on</u> before <u>you</u> <u>set up</u> <u>the experiment</u>.   **A   B   C   D**
   A   B   C   D

5. You really <u>let me down</u> when you stopped <u>handing</u> <u>up</u> your homework.   **A   B   C   D**
   A   B   C   D

6. I couldn't <u>work</u> <u>out</u> the charts in Chapter 6, and I just <u>gave</u> <u>down</u>.   **A   B   C   D**
   A   B   C   D

7. Please <u>call off</u> <u>for an appointment</u>. Don't just <u>show</u> <u>up</u> without one.   **A   B   C   D**
   A   B   C   D

8. <u>Go after</u> your goals aggressively, and you'll <u>be sure</u> to <u>get</u> <u>over</u>.   **A   B   C   D**
   A   B   C   D

9. Today I have to <u>pick</u> <u>up Nilda</u> at school and <u>drop</u> <u>off her</u> at the library.   **A   B   C   D**
   A   B   C   D

10. We <u>came up</u> <u>the answer with</u> while we were <u>fooling</u> <u>around</u> on the computer.   **A   B   C   D**
    A   B   C   D

11. The school <u>laid</u> <u>out a fortune</u> for the new microscope. Have you tried <u>it</u> <u>on</u> yet?   **A   B   C   D**
    A   B   C   D

12. I <u>turned</u> <u>down</u> the telemarketer's offer, and then I <u>hung</u> <u>down</u> the phone.   **A   B   C   D**
    A   B   C   D

V *Rewrite the sentences that have underlined words. Use the correct form of the appropriate phrasal verbs in the box to replace the underlined words.*

blow up	~~come up~~	give up	leave out	let down
point out	show up	throw away	turn down	turn in

1. A question <u>arose</u> about the science project.

    A question came up about the science project.

2. Keep all your old notes. Please don't <u>discard</u> them.

    _____

3. The teacher <u>rejected</u> my topic proposal.

    _____

4. All forms must be <u>submitted</u> by April 8.

    _____

5. Be very careful when working with these chemicals. They could <u>explode</u>.

    _____

6. Don't <u>abandon</u> hope. Keep trying.

    _____

7. What happened to the last problem? You <u>omitted</u> it.

    _____

8. The test grades were very high. The students didn't <u>disappoint</u> me.

    _____

9. There's something wrong with that equation. Can someone <u>indicate</u> what the mistake is?

    _____

10. Please make an appointment to see me. Don't just <u>appear</u> without one.

    _____

▶ *To check your answers, go to the Answer Key on page RT-3.*

Adjective Clauses

13 Adjective Clauses with Subject Relative Pronouns

Grammar in Context

BEFORE YOU READ

🎧 *Look at the photos. How do you think the people feel about each other? What is your definition of a friend? Read this article about friendship.*

Section 5 • October 2005   Lifestyles • Page 15

A Word with Many Meanings

Almost everyone has friends, but ideas about friendship differ from person to person. For some, a friend can be a person **who chats with you on the Internet**. For others, a friend is someone **who has known you all your life**. What one person defines as a friend, another calls an acquaintance, and vice versa.

As you see, definitions of friendship can vary a lot within a single culture. Imagine the differences between cultures. In Russia, for example, friendship is a relationship **that emphasizes sharing your innermost feelings**—friends are people **who know each other "behind the soul."** In Mexico, it is a lifelong commitment, and a friend is someone **who becomes part of your family** and **who helps you in all areas of life**. Anthropologist Margaret Mead compared notions of friendship in some Western countries. She says:

"For the French, friendship is a one-to-one relationship **that demands keen awareness of the other person's intellect, temperament, and particular interests**. A friend is someone **who brings out your own best qualities**." For French friends, **who enjoy arguing about intellectual issues**, disagreement is "the breath of life." However, Mead notes, ". . . for Germans, **whose friendships are based on mutuality of feeling**, deep disagreement on any subject **that matters to both is** . . . a tragedy."

A Word with Many Meanings

Germans form friendships early in life, and, like Mexican friends, German friends usually become part of each other's family life. As a result, Mead reports, young Germans **who come to the United States** often have difficulty making friends with Americans, **whose friendships are less permanent**. American friendships fade "as people move, change their jobs, marry, or discover new interests."

Mead describes a different pattern in British friendships, **which usually stay outside the family**. These relationships are based on shared activity. Although British friends may not be as deeply attached to each other as German friends, their relationships can survive a long separation. For the British, friends **who meet after a long separation** are like a couple **who begin to dance again** when the orchestra starts playing after a pause.

Studies of American friendships indicate that, like the French and British, people in the United States often form friendships around interests. They have friends **who enjoy sports**, friends **who go shopping with them**, friends **who share a hobby**. And, like the Germans and Russians, some also form long-lasting friendships **which are based on feelings**. In fact, the variety of relationships **that come under Americans' definition of friendship** can confuse people from other cultures, especially when Americans say things like, "I just made a new friend yesterday."

Nevertheless, the term does not seem to confuse Americans, **who know very well the difference between friends and acquaintances**. According to a survey in *Psychology Today*, those **who answered the survey** "find it easy to distinguish between close and casual friends and reported they have more close friends than casual ones."

Although different people and cultures emphasize different aspects of friendship, there is one element **which is always present**, and that is the element of choice. We may not be able to select our families, our co-workers, or even the people **that ride the bus with us**, but we can pick our friends. As Mead puts it, "a friend is someone **who chooses and is chosen**." It is this freedom of choice **that makes friendship such a special and unique relationship**.

AFTER YOU READ

Match the cultures with their descriptions of friendship from the article.

_____ **1.** Friends like to argue about ideas.

_____ **2.** Friends tell each other their deepest feelings.

_____ **3.** Friends are like family members.

_____ **4.** Friends like the same activities.

a. German and Mexican

b. British

c. French

d. Russian

Grammar Presentation

ADJECTIVE CLAUSES WITH SUBJECT RELATIVE PRONOUNS

ADJECTIVE CLAUSES AFTER THE MAIN CLAUSE

Main Clause			Adjective Clause		
Subject	Verb	Predicate Noun/ Pronoun	Subject Relative Pronoun	Verb	
I	read	a book	*that*	discusses	friends.
A friend	is	someone	*who*	knows	you well.

			Whose + Noun		
I	have	a friend	*whose* home	is	in Boston.

ADJECTIVE CLAUSES INSIDE THE MAIN CLAUSE

Main Clause	Adjective Clause			Main Clause (cont.)	
Subject Noun/ Pronoun	Subject Relative Pronoun	Verb		Verb	
The book	*that*	discusses	friends	is	by Ruben.
Someone	*who*	knows	you	can give	you advice.

	Whose + Noun				
My friend	*whose* sister	writes	books	lives	in Boston.

GRAMMAR NOTES

EXAMPLES

1. Use **adjective clauses** to **identify** or give **additional information** about nouns (people, places, or things).

- I know the woman **who lives across the street**.
  (The clause who lives across the street *identifies the woman.)*

- Hamburg, **which is my hometown**, is still my favorite city.
  (The clause which is my hometown *gives additional information about Hamburg.)*

Adjective clauses can also identify or describe indefinite pronouns such as *one*, *someone*, *somebody*, *something*, *another*, and *other(s)*.

- I'd like to meet *someone* **who speaks Spanish**.

In most cases the adjective clause <u>directly follows the noun</u> (or pronoun) it is identifying or describing.

2. **Sentences with adjective clauses** can be seen as a <u>combination of two sentences</u>.

I have a friend. + She loves to shop. =
- I have a friend **who loves to shop**.

Pietro calls often. + He lives in Rome. =
- Pietro, **who lives in Rome**, calls often.

Lea has a son. + His name is Max. =
- Lea has a son **whose name is Max**.

(continued)

3. Adjective clauses begin with **relative pronouns**. Relative pronouns that can be the **subject** of the clause are *who*, *that*, *which*, and *whose*.

   a. Use *who* or *that* to refer to **people**.

- I have a **friend** *who* lives in Mexico.

OR

- I have a **friend** *that* lives in Mexico.

   b. Use *which* or *that* to refer to **places** or **things**.

- New York is a **city** *which* attracts a lot of tourists.

OR

- New York is a **city** *that* attracts a lot of tourists.

USAGE NOTE: *That* is less formal than *who* and *which* and more frequently used in conversation.

   c. Use *whose* + **noun** to show **possession** or **relationship**.

- She's the neighbor *whose* **house** is for sale.

▶ **BE CAREFUL!** Do not use a subject pronoun (*I, you, he, she, it, we, they*) and a subject relative pronoun in the same adjective clause.

- Scott is someone *who* **never forgets** a friend's birthday.
NOT Scott is someone who ~~he~~ never forgets a friend's birthday.

---

4. Relative pronouns have the <u>same form</u> whether they refer to singular or plural nouns, or to males or females.

- That's the **man** *who* lives next door.
- That's the **woman** *who* lives next door.
- Those are the **people** *who* live next door.

---

5. The **verb in the adjective clause** is singular if the subject relative pronoun refers to a singular noun. It is plural if it refers to a plural noun.

- Ben is my **friend who** *lives* in Boston.
- Al and Ed are my **friends who** *live* in Boston.

▶ **BE CAREFUL!** When *whose* + **noun** is the subject of an adjective clause, the verb agrees with the subject of the adjective clause.

- Maria is a person **whose friends** *are* important to her.
NOT Maria is a person whose friends ~~is~~ important to her.

6. There are two kinds of adjective clauses,
identifying and **nonidentifying** (sometimes
called *restrictive* and *nonrestrictive*).

  a. Use an **identifying** adjective clause to
identify <u>which member of a group</u> the
sentence talks about. Do not use commas
with this kind of adjective clause.

- I have a lot of good friends. My friend
who lives in Chicago visits me often.
*(The adjective clause is necessary to
identify which friend.)*

  b. Use a **nonidentifying** adjective clause to give
<u>additional information</u> about the noun it
refers to. The information is not necessary to
identify the noun. Use a comma before and
after the adjective clause.

- I have a lot of good friends. My best
friend, **who lives in Chicago,** visits me
often.
*(The friend has already been identified as
the speaker's best friend. The adjective
clause gives additional information, but it
isn't needed to identify the friend.)*

▶ **BE CAREFUL!** Do not use *that* to introduce
nonidentifying adjective clauses. Use *who* for
people and *which* for places and things.

- **Marielle,** *who* introduced us at the
party, called me last night.
NOT Marielle, ~~that~~ introduced us at the
party, called me last night.

- **Miami,** *which* reminds me of home, is
my favorite vacation spot.
NOT Miami, ~~that~~ reminds me of home, is
my favorite vacation spot.

---

7. In **writing**, a nonidentifying adjective clause is
separated from the rest of the sentence by
commas.

nonidentifying adjective clause
- My sister, **who lives in Seattle,** came to
visit me this year.

In **speaking**, a nonidentifying adjective clause is
separated from the rest of the sentence by brief
pauses.

- My sister *(pause)* **who lives in Seattle**
(pause) came to visit me this year.
*(I have only one sister. She lives in
Seattle.)*

Without commas or pauses the same sentence
has a very <u>different meaning</u>.

identifying adjective clause
- My sister **who lives in Seattle** came to
visit me this year.
*(I have several sisters. This one lives in
Seattle.)*

Focused Practice

1 | DISCOVER THE GRAMMAR

Read this article about different types of friends. First circle the relative pronouns and underline the adjective clauses. Then draw an arrow from the relative pronoun to the noun or pronoun that it refers to.

Wellness Today   September–October 2005   47

Not Just Friends
BY BUD E. FREUND

Most of us have very few "best friends" throughout our lives. These are friends who are loyal to us through good times and bad. They are people who accept us completely (warts and all) and who know our most secret thoughts. But we have contact with many others whose relationships with us may be less deep but are still important. What would our lives be without these acquaintances, buddies, and dear old friends?

ACQUAINTANCES. These are people whose paths often cross ours. We attend the same school committee meetings or share a car pool with them. Acquaintances may exchange favors easily. The neighbor who borrows your chairs for a big party or the colleague who waters your plants while you're on vacation fits this category. But we usually don't get too intimate with them. One woman commented, "Our next-door neighbor, who carpools with us, is very nice. But we don't have anything in common. We never get together for anything but car pool."

BUDDIES. A lot of people have a friend who shares a particular activity or interest. These usually aren't close relationships, but they're important ones that keep us connected to our interests and hobbies. Because they're based on activities rather than feelings, it's relatively easy to make a new buddy. One foreign-exchange student reported, "For the first two months I was here, I didn't have any real friends. My table-tennis partner, who's from Beijing, was my only social contact. We couldn't communicate in English very well, but we had a good time anyway. Without him, I would have been completely isolated."

OLD FRIENDS. "Delores knew me when I worked in the mailroom," recalls an advertising executive. "I'll never forget this day. The vice president who promoted me called me for an interview. I didn't have the right clothes, and Delores was the one who came with me to buy my first business suit." We all have old friends who knew us "back when." They keep us in touch with parts of ourselves which are easy to lose as we move through life. "Whenever I go home, I always visit Delores," recalls the executive. "We look through old photo albums and talk about experiences that have helped form us. She always reminds me how shy I used to be. I agree with George Herbert, who said that the best mirror is an old friend."

2 | DEFINITIONS

A *Match the words on the left with the descriptions on the right.*

_e_	1. acquaintance	**a.** This person is married to you.
____	2. album	**b.** This event brings people together after a long separation.
____	3. soul mate	**c.** This relationship exists between friends.
____	4. colleague	**d.** This person is your husband's or wife's relative.
____	5. confidant	**e.** This person knows you but is not a close friend.
____	6. empathy	**f.** This feeling lets you experience another person's feelings.
____	7. friendship	**g.** This person is very similar to you in thought and feeling.
____	8. in-law	**h.** This book has pages for saving photos.
____	9. reunion	**i.** This person listens to your private feelings and thoughts.
____	10. spouse	**j.** This person has the same job or profession as you.

B *Now write definitions for the words on the left. Use the correct description on the right and appropriate relative pronouns.*

1. _An acquaintance is a person who knows you but is not a close friend._ _____

2. _____

3. _____

4. _____

5. _____

6. _____

7. _____

8. _____

9. _____

10. _____

3 | SURVEY RESULTS

A U.S. magazine, Psychology Today, *conducted a national survey on friendship. Below are some of the results and opinions about them. Complete each sentence with an appropriate relative pronoun and the correct form of the verbs in parentheses.*

1. A person ____who____ ____has____ lived in the same place has more casual friends than someone
   (have)

   _____ _____ moved around.
   (have)

2. People _____ _____ moved a lot have fewer casual friends.
   (have)

3. The qualities _____ _____ most important in a friend are loyalty, warmth, and the
   (be)

   ability to keep secrets.

4. People _____ _____ a crisis turn first to their friends for help, not to their families.
   (face)

5. Betrayal is the reason _____ _____ most often given for ending a friendship.
   (be)

   Most people cannot forgive this break in trust.

6. Most people can maintain friendships with friends _____ _____ become more
   (have)

   successful than they are.

7. Many people have friends _____ social or religious backgrounds _____ different from
   (be)

   theirs. These differences don't seem to affect their friendships.

8. Most people _____ friends _____ members of the opposite sex say that these
   (include)

   relationships are different from relationships with the same sex.

9. This survey, _____ _____ in a past issue of *Psychology Today*, was completed by
   (appear)

   typical readers of this magazine.

10. Someone _____ _____ *Psychology Today* might have different ideas about friendship.
    (not read)

11. For some, friends must be people _____ _____ the same social or religious beliefs.
    (share)

12. Today a close friend can be someone _____ _____ in touch online. You may rarely see
    (stay)

    your online friends.

4 | BETWEEN FRIENDS

Grammar Notes 2, 6–7

Read the conversations. Then use the first sentence in each conversation to help you write a summary. Use adjective clauses. Remember to use commas where necessary.

1.   **A:** This article is really interesting.

      B: What's it about?

      A: It discusses the different types of friendship.

   SUMMARY: *This article, which discusses the different types of friendship, is really interesting.*

2.   **A:** They'll meet us at the restaurant, OK?

      B: Which restaurant?

      A: You know the one. It's across the street from the library.

   SUMMARY: _____

3.   **A:** The navy blue suit looked the best.

      B: Which navy blue suit?

      A: The one on sale.

   SUMMARY: _____

4.   **A:** Bill and Sue aren't close friends with the Swabodas.

      B: No. The Swabodas' interests are very different from theirs.

   SUMMARY: _____

5.   **A:** I loaned some chairs to the new neighbors.

      B: Why did they need chairs?

      A: They're having a party tonight.

   SUMMARY: _____

6.   **A:** I was just laughing at an old picture of Jason.

      B: Which one? You have hundreds.

      A: You know the one—it shows him holding hands with Amy.

   SUMMARY: _____

7.   **A:** My boyfriend left me a lot of plants to water.

      B: How come?

      A: He went to Venezuela for two weeks.

   SUMMARY: _____

5 | EDITING

Read this student's essay about a friend. There are ten mistakes in the use of adjective clauses and their punctuation. Each incorrectly punctuated clause counts as one mistake. (For example, "My mother who is my best friend just turned 50" needs two commas, but it counts as one mistake.) The first mistake is already corrected. Find and correct nine more.

Good Friends

A writer once said that friends are born, not made. I think he meant that friendship is like love at first sight—we become friends immediately with people who ~~they~~ are compatible with us. I don't agree with this writer. Last summer I made friends with some people who's completely different from me.

In July, I went to Mexico City to study Spanish for a month. In our group, there were five adults, which were all language teachers from our school. Two teachers stayed with friends in Mexico City, and we only saw those teachers during the day. But we saw the teachers, who stayed with us in the dormitory, both day and night. They were the ones who they helped us when we had problems. Bob Taylor who is much older than I am became a really good friend. In my first week, I had a problem that was getting me down. Mexico City, that is a very exciting place, was too distracting. I went out all the time, and I stopped going to my classes. Bob, who have studied abroad a lot, helped me get back into my studies. After the trip I kept writing to Bob, who's letters are always interesting and encouraging. Next summer, he's leading another trip what sounds interesting. It's a three-week trip to Spain, which is a place he knows a lot about. I hope I can go.

Communication Practice

6 | LISTENING

🎧 *Some friends are at a high school reunion. They haven't seen one another for 25 years. Look at the picture and listen to the friends talk about the people at the table. Then listen again and write the correct name next to each person.*

Ann	Asha	~~Bob~~	Kado	Pat	Pete

7 | A FRIEND IS SOMEONE WHO . . .

Complete the questionnaire. Check all the items that you believe are true.

A friend is someone who . . .

☐ **1.** always tells you the truth.

☐ **2.** has known you for a very long time.

☐ **3.** cries with you.

☐ **4.** lends you money.

☐ **5.** talks to you every day.

☐ **6.** helps you when you are in trouble.

☐ **7.** listens to your problems.

☐ **8.** does things with you.

☐ **9.** respects you.

☐ **10.** accepts you the way you are.

☐ **11.** understands you.

☐ **12.** gives you advice.

☐ **13.** keeps your secrets.

☐ **14.** cares about you.

Other: _____

Now compare questionnaires with a partner. Discuss the reasons for your choices.

> **Example:** **A:** I think a friend is someone who always tells you the truth.
> **B:** I don't agree. Sometimes the truth can hurt you.

After your discussion, tally the results of the whole class. Discuss the results.

8 | WHAT'S THE DIFFERENCE?

Work in small groups. Discuss the differences between these terms.

a friend and an acquaintance

a friend and a colleague

a friend and a best friend

a friend and a buddy

Now discuss these questions:

- What is the word for *friend* in your first language? Is it used the same way in English?
- Can men and women be friends? What about people of different ages?
- Can people from different religious, social, or economic backgrounds be friends?

9 | QUOTABLE QUOTES

Work in a small group. Choose five of these quotations and talk about what they mean.
Give examples from your own experience to support your ideas.

Chance makes our relatives, but choice makes our friends.

—*Jacques Delille (French poet, 1738–1813)*

> **Example:** **A:** I think this means that we can't choose our families, but we can choose our friends.
>
> **B:** I agree. When I was in high school my best friend was someone who was completely different from my family . . .

The best mirror is an old friend.
—*George Herbert (English poet and novelist, 1593–1633)*

Friendship is a plant which we must often water.
—*German proverb*

A good man finds all the world friendly.
—*Hindustan proverb*

He is wise who can make a friend of a foe.
—*Scottish proverb*

Show me a friend who will weep with me; those who will laugh with me I can find myself.
—*Slavic proverb*

A friend in need is a friend indeed.
—*English proverb*

Very few people can congratulate without envy a friend who has succeeded.
—*Aeschylus (Greek playwright, 525–456 B.C.)*

[A friend is] another I.
—*Zeno (Greek philosopher, 335–263 B.C.)*

Wherever you are it is your own friends who make your world.
—*Ralph Barton Perry (U.S. philosopher, 1876–1957)*

Have no friends not equal to yourself.
—*Confucius (Chinese philosopher, 551–479 B.C.)*

A true friend is somebody who can make us do what we can.
—*Ralph Waldo Emerson (U.S. writer, 1803–1882)*

10 | WRITING

Write an essay of two paragraphs about a friend. You may want to begin your essay with one of the quotations from Exercise 9. Use adjective clauses with subject relative pronouns. You can use the essay in Exercise 5 as a model.

Example: Do friends have to be people who have the same interests or personality? I don't think so. My best friend Richie is someone whose personality is completely different from mine. He can walk into a room that is full of strangers, and in an hour, they'll all be new friends. I'm very shy . . .

11 | ON THE INTERNET

People have many different ideas about friendship. Do a search on the phrase **"a friend is someone who."** *Use quotation marks. Write down some of the definitions that you find. Discuss them with a group. Which ones do you agree with? Which ones do you disagree with? Give reasons for your opinions.*

Example: One definition that I found is, "A friend is someone who is concerned with everything you do." I don't agree. Friends don't have to be involved with every part of each other's lives.

Adjective Clauses with Object Relative Pronouns or *When* and *Where*

Grammar in Context

BEFORE YOU READ

🎧 *What is an autobiography? Look at the title of the book reviews below. What do you think the two autobiographies are about? Read these reviews.*

TORN BETWEEN TWO WORLDS

"I'm filled to the brim with what I'm about to lose—images of Cracow, **which I loved as one loves a person**, of the sun-baked villages **where we had taken summer vacations**, of the hours **I spent poring over passages of music with my music teacher**, of conversations and escapades with friends."

These sad words were written by Eva Hoffman, author of *Lost in Translation: A Life in a New Language* (New York: Penguin, 1989). Hoffman, who spent her early childhood in Cracow, Poland, moved with her family to Vancouver, Canada, when she was 13. Her autobiography describes her experiences as she leaves her beloved Cracow and struggles to find herself in a new place and a new language.

In spite of her family's poverty and small, crowded apartment, Ewa Wydra (Hoffman's Polish name) loved her native Cracow. It was a place **where life was lived intensely**. She visited the city's cafés with

(continued)

TORN BETWEEN TWO WORLDS

her father, **who she watched in lively conversations with his friends**. Hoffman remembers neighbors, "People **between whose apartments there's constant movement with kids, sugar, eggs, and teatime visits**." As she grew up, her friendship with Marek, **whose apartment she visited almost daily**, deepened, and the two always believed that they would be married.

Madame Witeszczak, Ewa's piano teacher, was the last person **Ewa said goodbye to** before she left Poland. "What do you think you'll miss most?" her teacher asked. "Everything. Cracow. The school . . . you. Everything . . ."

At her new school in Vancouver, Ewa is given her English name, Eva, **which her teachers find easier to pronounce**. Ewa, however, feels no connection to the name. In fact, she feels no connection to the English name of anything **that she feels is important**. All her memories and feelings are still in her first language, Polish. The story of Eva as she grows up and comes to terms with her new identity and language is fascinating and moving.

Also recommended is *The Rice Room*, by Ben Fong-Torres (New York: Hyperion, 1994). Unlike Hoffman, Fong-Torres was born in the United States. However, his parents had emigrated from China, and many of the problems **that he describes** are, like Hoffman's, connected to language. Fong-Torres struggles to bring together his family's culture and his new culture. He lacks the language **he needs to do this** because he only has the Chinese **that he**

had learned as a child. A successful radio announcer and journalist in English, Fong-Torres cannot really talk to his parents, **for whom English is still a foreign language**.

"When we talk, it sounds like baby talk—at least my half of it. . . . I don't know half the words **I need**; I either never learned them, or I heard but forgot them." The language barrier separated Fong-Torres and his parents ". . . through countless moments **when we needed to talk with each other**, about the things **parents and children usually discuss**: jobs and careers; marriage and divorce; health and finances; history, the present, and the future. This is one of the great sadnesses of my life. . . . I'm a journalist and a broadcaster—my job is to communicate—and I can't with the two people **with whom I want to most**."

Whether first- or second-generation immigrant—the issues are the same. These two books describe the lives of people trying to connect the worlds **that they left behind** and the worlds **that they now call home**.

AFTER YOU READ

Check the correct person.

	Hoffman	Fong-Torres
1. Who studied music?	☐	☐
2. Who was born in the United States?	☐	☐
3. Who went to cafés with a parent?	☐	☐
4. Who had a name change?	☐	☐
5. Who has difficulty communicating with family?	☐	☐

Grammar Presentation

ADJECTIVE CLAUSES WITH OBJECT RELATIVE PRONOUNS OR *WHEN* AND *WHERE*

ADJECTIVE CLAUSES AFTER THE MAIN CLAUSE

Main Clause			Adjective Clause		
Subject	Verb	Predicate Noun / Pronoun	(Object Relative Pronoun)	Subject	Verb
He	read	the book	(*that*)	she	**wrote.**
She	is	someone	(*who[m]*)	I	**respect.**

			Whose + Noun		
That	is	the author	*whose* **book**	I	**read.**

			Where / (When)		
She	loves	the city	*where*	she	**grew up.**
They	cried	the day	(*when*)	they	**left.**

(continued)

ADJECTIVE CLAUSES INSIDE THE MAIN CLAUSE

Main Clause	Adjective Clause			Main Clause (cont.)	
Subject	(Object Relative Pronoun)	Subject	Verb	Verb	
The book	*(that)*	**I**	**read**	is	great.
Someone	*(who[m])*	**you**	**know**	was	there.

	Whose + Noun				
	Whose + Noun				
The man	*whose* **sister**	**you**	**know**	writes	books.

Main Clause	Adjective Clause			Main Clause (cont.)	
Subject	*Where / (When)*	Subject	Verb	Verb	
The library	*where*	**I**	**work**	has	videos.
The summer	*(when)*	**she**	**left**	passed	slowly.

GRAMMAR NOTES

EXAMPLES

1. In Unit 13, you learned about adjective clauses in which the **relative pronoun** was the **subject** of the clause.

Relative pronouns can also be the **object** of an adjective clause. Notice that:

a. The **object relative pronoun** comes at the <u>beginning</u> of the adjective clause.

b. Relative pronouns (subject or object) have the <u>same form</u> whether they refer to singular or plural nouns, or to males or females.

c. The **verb** in the adjective clause <u>agrees with the subject</u> of the adjective clause. It does not agree with the relative pronoun or the noun that the relative pronoun refers to.

▶ **BE CAREFUL!** Do not use an object pronoun (*me, you, him, her, it, us, them*) together with an object relative pronoun in an adjective clause.

subj.
Eva is a writer. + ***She*** *was born in Poland.* =
subj.
• Eva, *who* **was born in Poland**, is a writer.

obj.
Eva is a writer. + *I saw* ***her*** *on TV.* =

obj.
• Eva, *who(m)* **I saw on TV**, is a writer.
• That's the **man** *who(m)* I met.

• That's the **woman** *who(m)* I met.
• Those are the **people** *who(m)* I met.

subj.　verb
• I like the **columns which he** *writes*.
• I like the **column which they** *write*.

• She is the writer *who* **I saw on TV**.
  NOT She is the writer who I saw ~~her~~ on TV.

2. REMEMBER: There are two kinds of adjective clauses, **identifying** and **nonidentifying**.

IDENTIFYING

- I read a lot of books. The book **which I just finished** is by Eva Hoffman.
  (The adjective clause is necessary to identify which book I mean.)

NONIDENTIFYING

- I read a lot of books. This book, **which I just finished**, is by Eva Hoffman.
  (I'm pointing to the book, so the adjective clause isn't needed to identify it. The clause gives additional information.)

You can often leave out an **object** relative pronoun in an **identifying adjective clause**. (You cannot leave out subject relative pronouns.)

- He's the author **that I talked to**.
  OR
- He's the author **I talked to**.

---

3. Relative pronouns that can be the **object** of the adjective clause are **who(m)**, **that**, **which**, and **whose**.

Formality
More

a. Use **whom**, **who**, or **that** to refer to **people**. Note that in this case, you can also leave out the relative pronoun.

USAGE NOTE: **Whom** is very formal. Most people do not use *whom* in everyday speech. **That** is less formal than **who**. In everyday speech, most people use no relative pronoun.

- She's the writer **whom** I met.
  OR
- She's the writer **who** I met.
  OR
- She's the writer **that** I met.
  OR
- She's the writer **I met**.

Less

More

b. Use **which** or **that** to refer to **things**. You can also leave out the relative pronoun.

USAGE NOTE: Again, **that** is less formal than **which**. In everyday speech, most people use no relative pronoun.

- I read a book **which** she wrote.
  OR
- I read a book *that* she wrote.
  OR
- I read a book **she wrote**.

Less

c. Use **whose** to show **possession** or **relationship**. You cannot leave out *whose*.

- That's the author **whose** book I read.
  NOT That's the author ~~book I read~~.

▶ **BE CAREFUL!** You can only leave out relative pronouns in identifying adjective clauses. You <u>must use the relative pronoun in a nonidentifying</u> adjective clause. You cannot leave it out.

- She remembers Marek, **who she visited often**.
  NOT She remembers Marek ~~she visited often~~.

(continued)

4. The relative pronouns *who(m)*, *that*, *which*, and *whose* can be the **object of a preposition**.

He's the writer. + *I work for him.* =

Formality
More

- He's the writer **whom** I work **for**.
  OR
- He's the writer **who** I work **for**.
  OR
- He's the writer **that** I work **for**.
  OR
- He's the writer I work **for**.

Less

He's the writer. + I work for his wife. =

Note that you can leave out *who(m)*, *that*, and *which*, but not *whose*.

- He's the writer **whose** wife I work **for**.

USAGE NOTES

In **everyday spoken English** and in **informal writing**, we put the preposition at the end of the clause.

- He's the writer **who** I work **for**.
- That's the book **that** he spoke **about**.

In **formal English**, we put the preposition at the beginning of the clause. When the preposition is at the beginning, we use only *whom* (not *who* or *that*) for people, and *which* (not *that*) for things.

- He's the writer **for whom** I work.
- That's the book **about which** he spoke.

---

5. *When* and *where* can also be used to begin adjective clauses.

a. *Where* refers to a **place**.

That's the library. + She works there. =

- That's the library **where she works**.

b. *When* or *that* refers to a **time**.

I remember the day. + I met him then. =

- I remember the day **when** I met him.
  OR
- I remember the day **that** I met him.
  OR

Note that you can leave out *when* and *that* in identifying adjective clauses.

- I remember the day **I met him**.

Reference Note

For additional information about **identifying and nonidentifying adjective clauses**, see Unit 13, page 195.

Focused Practice

1 | DISCOVER THE GRAMMAR

The excerpt below comes from Eva Hoffman's book, Lost in Translation. *It describes Hoffman's home in Cracow, Poland. First circle all the words that introduce adjective clauses (relative pronouns,* **when***, and* **where***) and underline the adjective clauses. Then draw an arrow from the relative pronoun to the noun or pronoun that it refers to.*

The kitchen is usually steamy with large pots of soup cooking on the wood stove for hours, or laundry being boiled in vats for greater whiteness; behind the kitchen, there's a tiny balcony, barely big enough to hold two people, on which we sometimes go out to exchange neighborly gossip with people peeling vegetables, beating carpets, or just standing around on adjoining balconies. Looking down, you see a paved courtyard, in which I spend many hours bouncing a ball against the wall with other kids, and a bit of garden, where I go to smell the few violets that come up each spring and climb the apple tree, and where my sister gathers the snails that live under the boysenberry bushes, to bring them proudly into the house by the bucketful. . . .

Across the hall from us are the Twardowskis, who come to our apartment regularly. . . . I particularly like the Twardowskis' daughter, Basia, who is several years older than I and who has the prettiest long braids, which she sometimes coils around her head. . . .

Now read this excerpt about Hoffman's music school. There are four adjective clauses in which the relative pronouns have been left out. The first one is already underlined. Find and underline three more.

Pani Konek teaches at the Cracow Music School, which I've been attending for two years—ever since it has been decided that I should be trained as a professional pianist. I've always liked going to school. At the beginning of the year, I like buying smooth navy blue fabric from which our dressmaker will make my school uniform—an anonymous overdress we are required to wear over our regular clothes in order to erase economic and class distinctions; I like the feel of the crisp, untouched notebook . . . and dipping my pen into the deep inkwell in my desk, and learning how to make oblique letters. It's fun to make up stories about the eccentric characters I know, or about the shapes icicles make on the winter windows, and try to outwit the teacher when I don't know something, and to give dramatic recitations of poems we've memorized. . . .

2 | FIRST IMPRESSIONS

*Complete this interview from a school newspaper. Use a relative pronoun, **when** or **where**, and the correct forms of the verbs in parentheses.*

The Grover   September 18, 2006   **page 3**

Meet Your Classmates

Maniya, _____who_____ a lot of our readers already _____know_____,
                                                    1. (know)
has been at Grover High for three years now. We interviewed Maniya about her

experiences coming to the United States.

INTERVIEWER: How did your family choose Atlanta, Maniya?

MANIYA: My cousin, _____ we _____ with at
                                            2. (stay)
first, lives here.

INTERVIEWER: What were your first impressions?

MANIYA: At first it was fun. We got here in the summer, _____ there

_____ no school, so I didn't feel much pressure to speak English.
3. (be)

INTERVIEWER: What was the most difficult thing about going to school?

MANIYA: Of course, the class in _____ I _____ the biggest problems at
                                                    4. (have)
first was English. It was so hard for me to write compositions or to say the things

_____ I _____ to say. Now it's much easier.
                        5. (want)

INTERVIEWER: What was the biggest change for you when you got here?

MANIYA: We used to live in a big house, _____ there _____ always a lot
                                                            6. (be)
of people. Here I live with my parents and sister, _____ I _____
                                                                    7. (take care of)
after school.

INTERVIEWER: How did you learn English so quickly?

MANIYA: At night, I write words and idioms on a piece of paper _____ I

_____ in my shirt pocket. Then I study them at school whenever I have a chance.
8. (put)

INTERVIEWER: Is there anything _____ you still _____ trouble with?
                                                    9. (have)

MANIYA: One thing _____ I still _____ hard to do is make jokes in English.
                                            10. (find)
Some things are funny in Tagalog but not in English.

3 | MEMORIES

Combine the pairs of sentences. Make the second sentence in each pair an adjective clause. Make any other necessary changes.

1. That's the house. I grew up in the house.

   That's the house that I grew up in.

2. I lived with my parents and my siblings. You've met them.

   _____

3. I had two sisters and an older brother. I got along well with my sisters.

   _____

4. My sisters and I shared a room. We spent nights talking there.

   _____

5. My brother slept on the living room couch. I hardly ever saw him.

   _____

6. It was a large old couch. My father had made the couch himself.

   _____

7. My best friend lived across the hall. I saw her every day.

   _____

8. We went to the same school. We both studied English there.

   _____

9. Mr. Robinson was our English teacher. Everyone was a little afraid of Mr. Robinson.

   _____

10. After school I worked in a bakery. My aunt and uncle owned it.

    _____

11. They sold delicious bread and cake. People stood in line for hours to buy the bread and cake.

    _____

12. I took piano lessons from a woman. The woman's sister worked in the bakery.

    _____

13. I remember one summer. The whole family went to the lake then.

    _____

(continued)

14. It was a great summer. I'll never forget that summer.

_____

15. My brother and sisters live far away now. I miss them.

_____

16. When we get together we like to talk about the old days. We all lived at home then.

_____

4 | EDITING

Read this student's essay. First put commas where necessary. (Remember: Nonidentifying adjective clauses need commas.) Then delete the relative pronouns where possible.

Tai Dong, where I grew up, is a small city on the southeast coast of Taiwan. My family moved there from Taipei the summer ~~when~~ I was born. I don't remember our first house which we rented from a relative, but when I was two, we moved to the house that I grew up in. This house where my parents still live is on a main street in Tai Dong. To me, this was the best place in the world. My mother had a food stand in our front courtyard where she sold omelettes early in the morning. All her customers whom I always chatted with were very friendly to me. On the first floor, my father conducted his tea business in the front room. After school, I always went straight to the corner where he sat drinking tea with his customers. In the back was our huge kitchen with its stone floor and brick oven. I loved dinnertime because the kitchen was always full of relatives and the customers that my father had invited to dinner. It was a fun and noisy place to be. Next to the kitchen, there was one small bedroom. My oldest cousin whose father wanted him to learn the tea business slept there. Our living room and bedrooms were upstairs. My two sisters slept in one bedroom, and my older brother and I slept in the other. My younger sister shared a room with my grandmother who took care of her a lot of the time.

Communication Practice

5 | LISTENING

🎧 *Listen to this woman describe her old room. Then listen again and choose the correct picture.*

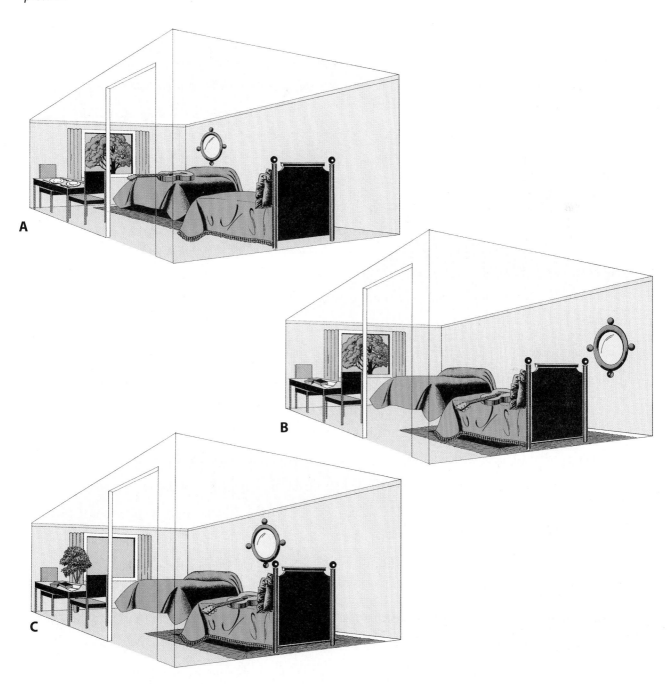

A

B

C

Listen again and check the correct box.

This description is in _____ English.

☐ formal

☐ informal

6 | INFORMATION GAP: BIOGRAPHY

Work in pairs (A and B). Student B, go to page 218 and follow the instructions there. Student A, read the biography of Ben Fong-Torres below. Then ask Student B questions about him in order to fill in the missing information. Answer Student B's questions.

Example: **A:** When was the Exclusion Act still in effect?
B: In 1929. Where did his father obtain a birth certificate?
A: In the Philippines.

Ben Fong-Torres was born in Alameda, California, in 1945. He was the son of first-generation Chinese parents. His father had immigrated to the United States _____*in 1929*_____, when the Exclusion Act, which limited the number of Chinese entering the country, was still in effect. To avoid this obstacle, his father first went to the Philippines, where he obtained a birth certificate and added *Torres* to his name. Ben's mother came to the United States _____, when their marriage was arranged by relatives.

Ben, along with his brother and sister, grew up in Oakland, California, where there was a large Chinese community. His family owned _____, where all the children worked when they were not in school. Ben's parents, whose views were quite traditional, were a little surprised and concerned about their children's love for U.S. culture. Ben was an enthusiastic reader of cartoons and a fan of popular music, which he heard on the radio.

At the age of twelve, Ben went with his father to _____, where they opened another Chinese restaurant. It was a difficult time for Ben because he was among people who had had no previous contact with Asians. Back in Oakland, after the failure of the Texas restaurant, Ben got jobs writing for various magazines and newspapers. After graduation from college in 1966, he wrote for *Rolling Stone* magazine, which covered stories about contemporary U.S. political and cultural life. His interviews with hundreds of famous musicians included the Beatles, the Rolling Stones, Grace Slick, and an interview with _____, for which he won an award for music journalism. Fong-Torres was also a DJ for San Francisco radio station KSAN, which plays rock music, and in 1976 he won an award for broadcasting excellence. Fong-Torres and Diane Sweet, who he married in 1976, still live in San Francisco. He hosts many events for the Chinese community in that city, and continues to write about music for the e-zine (Internet magazine) *Asia Currents* and other publications.

When you are finished, compare biographies with your partner. Are they the same?

7 | PEOPLE AND PLACES

Bring in some family photos to share with your classmates. Work in small groups. Describe the people and places in your photos.

> **Example:** A: This is the street where we lived before we moved here.
> B: Is that the house you grew up in?
> A: Yes, it is. I lived there until I was 10.

8 | QUOTABLE QUOTES

Work in small groups. Choose three of these quotations and talk about what they mean. Give examples from your own experience to support your ideas.

Where we love is home,
Home that our feet may leave, but not our hearts.
   —*Oliver Wendell Holmes, Sr. (U.S. doctor and author, 1809–1894)*

Home is not where you live but where they understand you.
   —*Christian Morgenstern (German poet, 1871–1914)*

You can't go home again.
   —*Thomas Wolfe (U.S. novelist, 1900–1938)*

Home is the place where, when you have to go there, they have to take you in.
   —*Robert Frost (U.S. poet, 1874–1963)*

'Mid pleasures and palaces though we may roam,
Be it ever so humble, there's no place like home.
   —*John Howard Payne (U.S. actor, 1791–1852)*

9 | WRITING

*Write a paragraph about a place you remember from your childhood. Use adjective clauses with object relative pronouns or **when** and **where** to help you explain where things were and why they were important. You can use the essay in Exercise 4 as a model.*

> **Example:** The town where I grew up was a small farming village. Living there was like living in an earlier century. We didn't lock our doors, and my friends, who lived across the street, could visit whenever they wanted to . . .

10 | ON THE INTERNET

*Do a search on **Cracow** or **Taipei**. Make a list of some of the sights and describe them using adjective clauses.*

> **Example:** In Cracow, you can walk around the square, where there are a lot of cafés.

INFORMATION GAP FOR STUDENT B

Student B, read the biography of Ben Fong-Torres below. Then ask Student A questions about him in order to fill in the missing information. Answer Student A's questions.

Example **A:** When was the Exclusion Act still in effect?
B: In 1929. Where did his father obtain a birth certificate?
A: In the Philippines.

Ben Fong-Torres was born in Alameda, California, in 1945. He was the son of first-generation Chinese parents. His father had immigrated to the United States in 1929, when the Exclusion Act, which limited the number of Chinese entering the country, was still in effect. To avoid this obstacle, his father first went to _____ *the Philippines* _____, where he obtained a birth certificate and added *Torres* to his name. Ben's mother came to the United States ten years later, when their marriage was arranged by relatives.

Ben, along with his brother and sister, grew up in _____, where there was a large Chinese community. His family owned a Chinese restaurant, where all the children worked when they were not in school. Ben's parents, whose views were quite traditional, were a little surprised and concerned about their children's love for U.S. culture. Ben was an enthusiastic reader of cartoons and a fan of _____, which he heard on the radio.

At the age of twelve, Ben went with his father to Texas, where they opened another Chinese restaurant. It was a difficult time for Ben because he was among people who had had no previous contact with Asians. Back in Oakland, after the failure of the Texas restaurant, Ben got jobs writing for various magazines and newspapers. After graduation from college in 1966, he wrote for _____, which covered stories about contemporary U.S. political and cultural life. His interviews with hundreds of famous musicians included the Beatles, the Rolling Stones, Grace Slick, and an interview with Ray Charles, for which he won an award for music journalism. Fong-Torres was also a DJ for San Francisco radio station KSAN, which plays rock music, and in 1976 he won an award for broadcasting excellence. Fong-Torres and _____, who he married in 1976, still live in San Francisco. He hosts many events for the Chinese community in that city, and he continues to write about music for the e-zine (Internet magazine) *Asia Currents* and other publications.

When you are finished, compare biographies with your partner. Are they the same?

From **Grammar** to **Writing**
Adding Details with Adjective Clauses

Details help to explain what you are writing about. One way to add details is with adjective clauses that give more information about *Who, What, Which, Whose, Where,* and *When.*

Example: She was born in Chile. ⟶
She was born in Chile, ***where*** her parents had emigrated after the Spanish Civil War.

1 | *Read this student's essay about a famous person. Underline the adjective clauses.*

Octavio Paz is considered one of the greatest writers that the Spanish-speaking world has produced. He was born in Mexico in 1914. As a child, he was exposed to writing by his grandfather and father. His childhood was hard because of his father's political activities, which forced his family into exile and poverty.

Paz began writing when he was very young. He published his first poem at age 16. He attended law school in Mexico City, where he joined a Marxist student group. Around the same time, he married his first wife, Elena Garro. Paz's literary career received a boost in his early twenties, when he sent a manuscript to the Chilean poet Pablo Neruda. Neruda was impressed, and he encouraged Paz to go to Spain to attend a writing conference. Paz remained there and joined the forces that were fighting against General Franco in the Spanish Civil War. Later, he went on to become a diplomat, representing his country in France, Japan, the United States, and India.

Paz wrote both poetry and prose. He is most famous for *The Labyrinth of Solitude*, a collection of essays that deal with the character of the Mexican people. He also founded *Vuelta*. In 1990 he received the Nobel Prize for Literature. He died eight years later.

2 | *The student added details in a second draft. Read the student's notes below. Then find places in the essay to add the information. Rewrite the sentences with adjective clauses. Remember to use commas when necessary.*

> ### Additional Information
> - Both his grandfather and father were political journalists.
> - Elena Garro was also a writer.
> - Pablo Neruda was already famous in Spain and Latin America.
> - <u>Vuelta</u> was one of Latin America's most famous literary magazines.

1. *As a child, he was exposed to writing by his grandfather and father, who were both political journalists.*

2. _____

3. _____

4. _____

3 | *Before you write . . .*

1. Choose a famous person to write about. Do some research in the library or on the Internet. Take notes about the main events in this person's life.

2. Exchange notes with a partner. Write a question mark (**?**) next to items you would like your partner to add more details about.

4 | *Write your essay. Answer your partner's questions using adjective clauses to add details.*

5 | *Exchange essays with a different partner. Underline the adjective clauses. Write a question mark (**?**) where you would like more information. Then answer the following questions.*

	Yes	No
1. Did the writer use adjective clauses?	☐	☐
2. Did the writer use the correct relative pronoun for each adjective clause?	☐	☐
3. Did the writer punctuate the adjective clauses correctly?	☐	☐
4. Did the writer give enough details?	☐	☐

6 | *Work with your partner. Discuss each other's editing questions from Exercise 5. Then rewrite your essay and make any necessary corrections.*

Review Test

I *Complete these sentences by circling the correct words.*

1. The neighborhood (that)/ who I grew up in was very friendly.

2. There were a lot of people <u>who / which</u> liked to do things together.

3. Mrs. Morris, <u>that / who</u> lived across the street, was one of my mother's closest friends.

4. She lived in a big old house, <u>where / which</u> I spent many happy hours.

5. I played there every day with her daughter, <u>which / whose</u> name was Katy.

6. Katy had a little dog to <u>which / that</u> I was very attached.

7. We took the dog for walks in the park <u>where / which</u> was down the block.

8. There we met other children <u>who / whose</u> we knew from school.

9. The classmate <u>that / which</u> I remember best was Rosa.

10. She had beautiful long hair, <u>that / which</u> she wore in braids.

11. I remember the summer <u>when / which</u> the whole community had a big picnic in the park.

12. I like to think back on the "good old days" <u>when / which</u> people seemed to have more time for one another.

II *Combine these pairs of sentences using adjective clauses. Use a relative pronoun,* **when**, *or* **where**. *Make any other necessary changes.*

1. That's my neighbor. I water her plants.

   That's my neighbor whose plants I water.

2. She lives in the house. The house is across the street.

   _____

3. This is the time of the year. She always goes away at this time.

   _____

4. She travels with her older sister. Her sister lives in Connecticut.

   _____

(continued)

5. This year they're taking a trip with the car. She just bought the car.

_____

6. They're going to Miami. They grew up there.

_____

7. They have a lot of relatives in Florida. They haven't seen them in years.

_____

8. The family is going to have a reunion. They've been planning the reunion all year.

_____

9. They'll be staying with their Aunt Sonya. Her house is right on a canal.

_____

10. They really need this vacation. They've been looking forward to it all year.

_____

III *Each sentence has four underlined words or phrases. The four underlined parts of the sentences are marked A, B, C, or D. Circle the letter of the <u>one</u> underlined part that is NOT CORRECT.*

1. After a week, <u>we</u> finally got to <u>Miami,</u> <u>where</u> my aunt <u>live</u>.
            A   B   C   D   **A** **B** **C** (**D**)

2. My aunt's new <u>house</u> is next to a beautiful <u>canal</u> <u>in where</u> we <u>go</u> swimming every day.
                 A   B   C   D   **A** **B** **C** **D**

3. Our cousins, <u>who</u> <u>are</u> five and <u>seven</u> <u>are</u> great.
                A B   C   D   **A** **B** **C** **D**

4. <u>They</u> love the <u>T-shirts</u> <u>what</u> you <u>helped me</u> pick out.
     A   B   C   D   **A** **B** **C** **D**

5. The <u>hotel</u> <u>at that</u> the family reunion <u>is taking</u> place <u>is</u> gorgeous.
        A   B   C   D   **A** **B** **C** **D**

6. The hotel is right on the <u>beach</u> where I used to play <u>on</u> <u>when</u> I <u>was</u> a kid.
                   A   B C   D   **A** **B** **C** **D**

7. My favorite uncle, <u>which</u> <u>lives</u> in <u>Texas,</u> <u>arrived</u> last night.
               A   B   C   D   **A** **B** **C** **D**

8. I'll never forget <u>the day</u> <u>where</u> he <u>took</u> <u>me</u> horseback riding.
                 A   B   C D   **A** **B** **C** **D**

9. The horse <u>that</u> he let me ride <u>was</u> the most beautiful animal <u>who</u> I <u>had ever seen</u>.
            A   B   C   **A** **B** **C** **D**
       D

10. My <u>niece</u> and nephew, <u>who</u> <u>lives</u> in England, <u>are arriving</u> tomorrow.   **A B C D**

      A   B C   D

11. Please remember to water my <u>plants</u>, especially the one <u>that</u> <u>have</u>   **A B C D**

                                A   B C

    the purple <u>flowers</u>.

                   D

IV   *Circle the letter of the correct word(s) to complete each sentence. Choose (—) when no word is necessary.*

1. Bring in the roll of film _____ Uncle Pete took at the reunion.   **A B Ⓒ D**
   (**A**) what   (**C**) —
   (**B**) with which   (**D**) whom

2. Send some copies to the reporter who _____ to write an article.   **A B C D**
   (**A**) want   (**C**) will
   (**B**) —   (**D**) wants

3. Pay all the bills _____ are due this week.   **A B C D**
   (**A**) —   (**C**) when
   (**B**) that   (**D**) they

4. Call the women _____ I met at lunch.   **A B C D**
   (**A**) which   (**C**) —
   (**B**) whose   (**D**) those

5. Please write to Mr. Coppel, _____ I met at the pool.   **A B C D**
   (**A**) that   (**C**) —
   (**B**) who   (**D**) where

6. I'm looking for the books Mr. Jay _____.   **A B C D**
   (**A**) recommend   (**C**) recommends
   (**B**) recommends them (**D**) recommend them

7. The neighbor _____ children watered our plants lives across the street.   **A B C D**
   (**A**) their   (**C**) —
   (**B**) whom   (**D**) whose

8. Annie found the souvenirs that _____ wanted at the gift shop.   **A B C D**
   (**A**) —   (**C**) she
   (**B**) where   (**D**) which

(continued)

9. Have you sent thank-you notes to the relatives from _____ you received   **A B C D**
   gifts?
   (**A**) which   (**C**) them
   (**B**) whom   (**D**) that

10. Let's try to agree on a time _____ we can all get together.   **A B C D**
    (**A**) which   (**C**) —
    (**B**) where   (**D**) at

V *Read this student's essay. There are seven mistakes in the use of adjective clauses. The first mistake is already corrected. Find and correct six more. (In some cases, you can also correct the sentence by leaving out the relative pronoun.)*

which OR *that**

There is an old German proverb that says "Friendship is a plant ~~who~~ we must often water." This means that we have to nurture our relationships to make them grow and flourish. A relationship that you neglect will wilt and die.

When I was ten, my family moved from Germany to the United States. There I had a "friend" (whom I will call Jack) who he never invited me to do things with him. Jack lived in a house where I never got to see even though it was just a few blocks away from mine. He had family and friends whom I never met. Of course, today I realize that Jack really wasn't a friend at all. He was what people in Germany call a *Bekannter*—someone who you knows— an acquaintance. And for an acquaintance, his behavior was fine. I got confused on the day where Jack referred to me as his friend.

"Friend" is a word that has a different set of expectations for me. In Germany, that word is reserved for people with that one is really close. I learned through the experience with Jack that although you can translate a word from one language to another, the meaning can still be different. Today I have friends from many countries. I also have many acquaintances who friendships I have learned to value too.

*In this sentence, you can also leave out the relative pronoun.

▶ *To check your answers, go to the Answer Key on page RT-3.*

Modals:
Review and Expansion

Grammar in Context

BEFORE YOU READ

🎧 *Do you like to watch reality TV? Which shows do you enjoy? Can you learn something from these shows or are they just entertaining? Read this article about reality TV.*

Josh Souza

REALITY TV

"*Everyone Should Have an Audience*"
—*Josh Souza, contestant,* Big Brother 2, *USA*

"*I know reality TV is not really reality.*"
—*Ikaika Kaho'ano, contestant,* Making the Band, *United States*

The situations in reality TV **may** not always **be** realistic, but those contestants on the screen are really laughing, crying, and plotting against each other. Viewers continue to be fascinated.

Although some **might think** a show is cruel or embarrassing and they **ought to stop** watching, they simply **can't change** the channel. With everyone at school or work talking about last night's episode, a lot of people **may watch** reality TV just to keep up with the conversations. But the secret thrill of many viewers **has got to be** the thought, "The next celebrity **could be** me!"

"*Reality is the best business model for TV.*"
—*Shuman Ghosemajumder, media expert, www.shumans.com*

Reality TV started in Europe at a time when local TV networks **weren't able to afford** to buy foreign shows. And because writers and actors were expensive, they also **couldn't develop** shows of their own. Then Bob Geldof of the British television company Planet 24 had the bright idea of filming ordinary people in out-of-the-ordinary situations. Geldof knew that people love seeing themselves on TV, so he thought there **had to be** a lot of people willing to try it. Why **should** producers **pay** for actors and writers when they **could use** real people with real emotions?

"I didn't know we actually had to survive."
—*Martin Melin, first winner,* Expedition Robinson, *Sweden*

Expedition Robinson was Geldof's brainchild. A group of contestants and a television crew go to a desert island. The contestants **have to figure out** how to survive, and the television audience **can watch** their struggle. Geldof **couldn't sell** his idea in England, but an adventurous Swedish producer bought it. It just **might work**, she thought. Filming started in 1997.

Everyone struggled that first season. The contestants and the crew were on a tropical island, and technicians thought the equipment **might not work** in the heat. The winner, Martin Melin, was shocked that his group **had to find** their own food. The TV crew was equally shocked when the group wanted to explore the island. "You **can't go** into the jungle!" they yelled. But the group went—and the crew **was able to follow** with cameras. To everyone's surprise, it all worked, and the show was a smash hit. Now known as *Survivor*, it has become popular all over the world.

Tribes compete on Survivor Africa

"I can't act, I can't sing, I can't dance—but people don't care."
—*Brian Dowling, winner,* Big Brother 2, *UK*

Big Brother, first produced in the Netherlands in 1999, was another surprise hit. In this show, a group of strangers **had to stay** in a house for 100 days. They **couldn't go out** or **talk** to anyone outside the group. Intense feelings developed in this situation, and cameras and microphones recorded everything that happened. Viewers were glued to their television screens, and the show's website got 100 million hits during that first season. Today, *Big Brother* is the most successful reality show in the world, with versions in North and South America, Europe, and Africa.

Contestants on Big Brother 4 *react to new housemates*

". . . viewers often prefer homegrown shows that better reflect local tastes, cultures, and historical events."
—*Suzanne Kapner,* New York Times, *January 2, 2003*

Reality shows around the world reflect different cultural values. Japanese viewers, for example, love to watch contestants who **are able to face** difficulty and not complain. Italian audiences, on the other hand, enjoy seeing big emotional reactions. Some cultures don't like fierce competition between individuals. On one Chinese show, for example, relatives win prizes for each other, reflecting the idea that people **should win** for their families, not only themselves. In Europe, contestants **might not have** perfect teeth or figures, but in the United States, even the losers **have got to be** gorgeous.

Reality shows come in different flavors for different audiences, but in one way, they're all the same. All over the world, it's clear that ordinary people like to be on TV—and viewers love to watch them. That **must be** why they are tuning in by the millions!

AFTER YOU READ

*Write **T** (true) or **F** (false).*

_____ **1.** Some people believe that it's wrong to watch cruel reality shows.

_____ **2.** Bob Geldof believed there were many people willing to be on reality shows.

_____ **3.** In the first *Expedition Robinson*, the crew was required to find food for everyone.

_____ **4.** The first *Big Brother* contestants were allowed to call their families.

_____ **5.** Some contestants on European shows are not beautiful or handsome.

Grammar Presentation

MODALS AND SIMILAR EXPRESSIONS: REVIEW

Ability: *Can* and *Could*			
Subject	Modal	Base Form of Verb	
She	can (not)	act.	
	could (not)	act	last year.

Ability: *Be able to**				
Subject	*Be able to*		Base Form of Verb	
She	is (not)	able to	act.	
	was (not)		act	last year.

Advice: *Should, Ought to, Had better*			
Subject	Modal	Base Form of Verb	
You	should (not) ought to had better (not)	watch	this TV show.

Necessity: *Must* and *Can't*			
Subject	Modal	Base Form of Verb	
You	must (not) can't	go.	

Necessity: *Have (got) to**			
Subject	*Have (got) to*	Base Form of Verb	
They	(don't) have to	go.	
He	has (got) to		

*Unlike modals, which have one form, *be* in *be able to* and *have* in *have (got) to* change for different subjects.

Assumptions: *May, Might, Could, Must, Can't*			
Subject	Modal	Base Form of Verb	
They	**may (not)** **might (not)** **could (not)** **must (not)** **can't**	**be**	actors.

Assumptions: *Have (got) to**			
Subject	*Have (got) to*	Base Form of Verb	
They	**have (got) to**	**be**	actors.
He	**has (got) to**		an actor.

*Unlike modals, which have one form, *have* in *have (got) to* changes for different subjects.

Future Possibility: *May, Might, Could*			
Subject	Modal	Base Form of Verb	
It	**may (not)** **might (not)** **could**	**start**	at 8:00.

GRAMMAR NOTES

EXAMPLES

1. Modals are auxiliary ("helping") verbs. They express:

   a. social functions such as giving advice.

   b. logical possibilities such as making assumptions.

REMEMBER: Modals have only one form. They do not have *-s* in the third person singular. Always use **modal + base form** of the verb.

- You **should watch** this program.
- It **could be** the best of the season.

- She **might record** it.
  NOT She ~~mights~~ record it.
  NOT She might ~~to record~~ it.

2. Use *can* or *be able to* to describe **present ability**.

USAGE NOTE: *Can* is more common than *be able to* in the present.

Use *could* or *was / were able to* for **past ability**.

REMEMBER: Use the correct form of *be able to* for all other verb forms.

- She **can sing**, but she **can't dance**.
- We **aren't able to get** Channel 11.

- Before she took lessons, she **could sing**, but she **wasn't able to dance** very well.

- Since her lessons, she **has been able to get** good roles on TV.

(continued)

3. Use *should* and *ought to* to give **advice**.

USAGE NOTE: *Should* is more formal than *ought to*.

Use *had better* for **urgent advice**—when you believe that something bad will happen if the person does not follow the advice.

Use *should* to **ask for advice**.

Use *shouldn't* and *had better not* for negative statements.

- You **should watch** *Survivor* tonight.
- Terri **ought to watch** it too.

- You**'d better stop** watching so much TV or your grades will suffer.

- **Should I buy** a new TV set?
- You **shouldn't get** your old TV repaired.
- You**'d better not stay up** too late.

---

4. Use *have to*, *have got to*, and *must* to express **necessity**.

USAGE NOTES

a. We usually use *have to* in conversation and informal writing.

b. We also use *have got to* in conversation and informal writing to express a strong feeling.

c. *Must* expresses necessity in <u>writing</u>, including official forms, signs, and manuals.

When *must* is used in <u>spoken</u> English, the speaker

- is usually in a position of power.

- is expressing urgent necessity.

Use *must* and *have got to* for the present or future.

REMEMBER: Use the correct form of *have to* for all other verb forms.

▶ BE CAREFUL! The meanings of *must not* and *don't have to* are very different.

Use *must not* to express **prohibition**.

Use *don't have to* to express that something is **not necessary**.

USAGE NOTE: We often use *can't* to express prohibition in spoken English.

- You **have to press** *Start* to begin recording.

- You**'ve got to see** this! It's really funny!

- You **must put** it on Channel 3 to record. *(VCR instruction manual)*

- You **must go** to bed right now, Tommy! *(mother talking to her young son)*
- You **must see** a doctor about that cough. *(friend talking to a friend)*

- You **must go** to bed now.
- You**'ve got to get up** early tomorrow.

- He **had to go** to bed early last night.
- She **has had to miss** her favorite program since she enrolled in that class.

- They **must not leave** the house. *(They are not allowed to leave.)*
- They **don't have to leave** the house. *(It isn't necessary for them to leave.)*

- He **can't leave**.

5. Use modals to make **assumptions** ("best guesses"). These modals show how certain we are about something.

100% certain

AFFIRMATIVE	**NEGATIVE**
must	can't, couldn't
have (got) to	must not
may	may not
might, could	might not

0% certain

a. Use *must*, *have to*, and *have got to* when you are almost **100% certain** that something is true.

- It **must be** 10:00. *Mystery Time* just came on.
- This **has to be** a rerun. I'm sure I've seen it before.

Use *may*, *might*, and *could* when you are **less certain**.

- He **may be** the murderer. He looks guilty.
- He **could be** home now. The lights are on.

b. Use *can't* and *couldn't* when you are almost 100% certain that something is **impossible**.

- They **can't be** guilty. They weren't even in the city when the crime occurred.
- They **couldn't own** a gun. They hate violence.

Use *must not* when you are **slightly less certain**.

- You **must not know** them very well. You've only met them twice.

Use *may not* and *might not* when you are **even less certain**.

- We **may not have** enough evidence. No one saw the suspect.

---

6. Use *may*, *might*, and *could* to talk about **future possibility**.

- The show **may start** at 10:00. I'm not sure.
- It **might be** very good.
- Josh **could win** the contest tonight.

Use *may not* and *might not* to say that something **possibly will not happen**.

- It **may not make** people laugh.
- It **might not be** good.

▶ **BE CAREFUL!** *Couldn't* means that something is **impossible**.

- It **couldn't start** at 10:00. *Mystery Time* is on then.

USAGE NOTE: We usually do not begin questions about possibility with *may*, *might*, or *could*. Instead we use *will* or *be going to* and phrases such as *Do you think . . . ?* or *Is it possible that . . . ?*

A: *Do you think* Midge *will find* the murderer?

B: She **might**. She's a good detective.

However, we often use *may*, *might*, or *could* in **short answers** to these questions.

A: *Is* she *going to be* in the show next year?

B: She **may**. She hasn't decided yet.

Focused Practice

1 DISCOVER THE GRAMMAR

A *Read the FAQ (Frequently Asked Questions) from a reality TV website. Underline the modals and similar expressions. Also underline the verbs that follow.*

FAQ

1. I'd like to be on your show! How do I apply?

You have to submit an online application.

2. I applied last year and was not accepted. I might apply again this year. Should I submit a new application, or will you be able to use my old one?

We could use your old application, but you really ought to send us a new one. Update your information and make a new video, and you might have a better shot at getting on the show.

3. You must get thousands of videos! What's the secret to getting your attention?

We really just want you to be yourself! This is reality TV, remember? Be real!

4. What type of video do I have to send?

It must be VHS format, and it can't last more than three minutes. You should tell us about your life and why you want to be on our show.

5. Do you let people know when you receive their applications and videos?

Sorry. We get thousands of applications, so we can't send receipts.

6. *Survival 5* had to be the most difficult show in the series. Where's the next show?

It could take place in a jungle, or on a desert island, or anywhere in the world!

7. The competitions are very hard. Contestants must need a lot of athletic ability. Are only super athletes eligible?

No! But you have to be in excellent shape—physically and mentally.

B *Write the underlined verbs next to the correct categories.*

Ability: _____

Advice: _____

Necessity: _*have to submit*_____

Future Possibility: _____

Assumptions: _____

2 | **A NIGHT OF TV**

Circle the correct words to complete these conversations.

1. **A:** What do you feel like watching?

   B: It's 8:00. We (could)/ shouldn't watch *Survivor*. It's just starting now.

2. **A:** Do you think Josh is still the most unpopular guy on the island?

   B: He <u>can't / must</u> be. He's been lying to everybody, and now they know it.

3. **A:** This show is really exciting, but I <u>may / 've got to</u> leave now, or I'll be late.

   B: No problem. I <u>can / should</u> tape the rest of the show for you.

4. **A:** There's a two-hour mystery on at 9:00.

   B: If we watch that, we won't <u>be able to / have to</u> watch *Big Brother* at 9:00.

   A: That's what VCRs are for. We <u>could / 'd better not</u> watch one show and tape the other.

5. **A:** This mystery is good! I think the law clerk is the killer.

   B: The clerk <u>doesn't have to / couldn't</u> be the killer. She was on a plane to Barbados at the time.

6. **A:** Is it OK if I turn the volume up? I <u>shouldn't / can't</u> hear what they're saying.

   B: Sure. But you <u>'re not able to / 'd better not</u> make it too loud, or you'll wake the baby.

7. **A:** What's the matter with Chet on *Fear Factor*? He's acting kind of strange.

   B: He <u>must / 'd better</u> be sick. He <u>had to / should</u> eat that disgusting food, remember?

8. **A:** I'm going to see what's on Channel 13. I love their nature shows.

   B: Look at that cheetah run! They <u>have got to / ought to</u> be the fastest animals in the world!

9. **A:** Do you think Tara's team <u>can / has to</u> win the race tonight?

   B: Oh, they <u>might / couldn't</u> win. They're too far behind.

10. **A:** Poor Rob is leaving *Big Brother*. It <u>must / might</u> be awful to get kicked out of the house.

    B: Don't worry. He's famous now. I'm sure he <u>might / 'll be able to</u> find a job on TV.

11. **A:** How <u>can / should</u> you watch those horror movies? They give me the creeps.

    B: You <u>'ve got to / don't have to</u> remember that it's all special effects.

12. **A:** I just heard the weather forecast. It's going to clear up this afternoon.

    B: Oh, good. That means I <u>don't have to / must not</u> take my umbrella.

3 | THAT COULD BE ME! *Grammar Notes 1–6*

Complete this Entertainment Today *interview with reality-show producer Chris Barrett.*
Rewrite the phrases in parentheses. Use modals.

ENTERTAINMENT TODAY

ET: People _____ *can't stop* _____ talking about reality TV. Why is it so popular?
  1. (do not have the ability to stop)

CB: I _____ you why TV producers love it. They
  2. (have the ability to tell)

  _____ writers or actors. That means they
  3. (it isn't necessary that they hire)

  _____ reality shows very cheaply.
  4. (have the ability to make)

ET: That _____ the reason for the huge audiences, though.
  5. (I'm almost 100% certain that isn't)

CB: We _____ all the reasons, but viewers
  6. (it's possible we will never know)

  _____ watching ordinary people like themselves. They
  7. (almost certainly love)

  _____ at a winner and think, "That
  8. (it's possible that they look)

  _____ me someday!"
  9. (it's possible that will be)

ET: But we _____ all the contestants on these shows, do we?
  10. (it's not necessary for us to love)

CB: No, but we _____ strongly about the contestants—love *or*
  11. (it's urgent that we feel)

  hate them.

ET: It _____ hard to find the right contestants. What do you
  12. (I'm certain that it is)

  look for?

CB: They _____ problems talking about personal stuff.
  13. (it's advisable that they not have)

  We like it when they _____ in front of a camera.
  14. (have the ability to cry)

ET: Maybe we _____ about what's next for you.
  15. (it's advisable that we talk)

CB: Next season, I _____ a drama about 12 people shipwrecked
  16. (it's possible that I will do)

  on an island.

ET: No more reality TV? You _____ looking for writers and actors!
  17. (it's urgent that you start)

4 | EDITING

Read these posts to a reality TV message board. There are thirteen mistakes in the use of modals. The first mistake is already corrected. Find and correct twelve more.

REALITY TV MESSAGE BOARD

[Follow-Ups] [Post a Reply] [Message Board Index]

Did anyone watch "Pop Idols" last night? I couldn't ~~to~~ believe Jennifer Tasco didn't win! She have to be the best singer on the show.

Tonight on "Get a Job," Ronald Trunk interviewed Lateesha and Sam. Trunk can only keep one of them. Who should he fires? I think he mights get rid of Lateesha, but I really believe Sam ought to go. Last week, he said he didn't able to work because he had a headache. Ha! He's just lazy.

Everybody knows that Sam was really sick last week. He had to go to the doctor! If you don't know that, then you don't have to know very much about the show. That's my guess.

I just read an interesting article about "Be Afraid." Watching this show should be dangerous for people with an extreme fear of things like snakes or insects. So if you have that problem, you ought to watch "Be Afraid."

"Amazing Journey" will start next summer. That's great, because I won't be in school, so I won't having to worry about missing classes to watch. They will go to Vietnam this year, but it's not certain yet.

I cried after "Housemates" on Monday. I can't even sleep that night. They were so mean to Sharifa! I not might watch this show anymore. It depends on what happens next week.

I just watched "Lose to Win." All these people are competing to lose the most weight. This doesn't have to be healthy! I think they exercise too hard and they have too much stress. Some people might not lose weight in a week even when they don't cheat. That's normal.

Communication Practice

5 | LISTENING

🎧 *Listen to these two contestants in a reality TV show. Then listen again and complete their conversation with the modals that you hear. Listen a third time to check your answers.*

JOSH: We _'ve got to_ climb the hill today. I _____ go first.
           1.   **2.**

TARA: OK, Josh, but you _____ mess up this time.
                                  3.

JOSH: Why is everybody so mad at me? They _____ know I'm really a nice guy.
                                                4.

TARA: Very funny. Well, we _____ work together today, and they know it.
                                    5.

JOSH: Are you worried? That hill _____ be very hard to climb.
                                                6.

TARA: We have to go down the other side. It's almost straight down to the water. Pete

_____ be able to do it.
           7.

JOSH: You _____ help him climb down.
                   8.

TARA: Oh, really? You _____ know what he's been saying about me.
                                 9.

JOSH: I know, but let's face it—Pete _____ help us in the next challenge.
                                         10.

TARA: Hmmm. We _____ find our team's flag in the water near the rocks.
                               11.

JOSH: It _____ very deep out there.
             12.

TARA: So I _____ let Pete know that *I* know that he's been plotting against me?
          13.

JOSH: You know you _____ do it. And tonight I'll get him voted off the island.
                          14.

TARA: I don't know about that. He _____ be the most popular guy here.
                               15.

JOSH: And everybody hates me. Never mind. I _____ make it happen.
                                          16.

*Now read the statements and decide if they are true (**T**) or false (**F**).*

__T__ 1. Josh thinks it's a good idea for him to go first.

_____ 2. Josh thinks it will be hard to climb the hill.

_____ 3. Tara believes it's possible that Pete won't be able to climb down the hill.

_____ 4. Pete can't help them find the flag.

_____ 5. Josh isn't sure he can get Pete voted off the island.

6 | SPECULATING SPECTATORS

Work with a partner. Look at the TV listings. Discuss the types of programs you think they are.

	8:00	8:30	9:00	9:30	10:00	10:30	11:00	11:30
SATURDAY 8 P.M.–MIDNIGHT								
Channel 1	Around the World in 18 Days		The Dark Glove ('98) Roy Collins				Live at 11	Johnny!
2	Great Performances: Vivaldi, Mozart, Stravinsky					Garden World		Nighttime
3	To Mars and Back		King of the Jungle		The Joke's on You	How to Boil Water	The Hulk vs. Bad Boy	Pet Heroes
4	Judge Jim	Detective Ramsey	The Long Goodbye ('96) Vera Garcia, Antonio Serrano				Top Ten	Volcano
5	Argentina vs. Spain				The Week that Was		The Civil War	
6	Elvis Presley: A Portrait of a Singer's Life		Recipes for Life	Ask Dr. Anne	Shadows in the Sand ('99) Crystal Powers (Part 2)			
7	Rita's World	You Guessed It!	Money Week	October Sky ('99) Laura Dern, Jake Gyllenhaal			A Laugh a Minute	

Example: A: *Around the World in 18 Days*. What type of show do you think that is?
B: It could be a travel show.
A: Or it might be a news show with international reports.
C: With a name like that, it's got to be a reality show.

7 | INTERNATIONAL TV

As a class, talk about TV in a country that you know. Discuss these questions:

- How many channels can you watch?
- How late can you watch?
- What programs do you recommend? What programs don't you recommend?
- Which reality shows can you watch?
- Do you have to pay a tax or government fee for using a TV?
- Do you have to have any special equipment, such as a satellite dish?
- Can you watch programs from other countries?
- Should foreign shows have subtitles, or should they be dubbed?

8 | DESERT ISLAND

Work in small groups. You are going to be on a reality TV show called Desert Island. *Your group will be on the island for five weeks and can take only three of the following items. As a group, decide on the three items. Compare your choices with the choices of the other groups.*

matches	a battery-operated CD player	a knife
a solar-powered computer	a book (your choice)	a flashlight
a toothbrush	a pen and paper	chocolate

Example: **A:** We have to take matches. With matches we can start a fire . . .
B: I agree. And with a fire, we could cook.

Now add one more item (not from the list) to take with you.

Example: **A:** I think we should take a blanket.

9 | WRITING

Write a transcript of a conversation between two reality show contestants. They have to choose three things to bring with them to a desert island. Use modals and similar expressions. You can use Exercise 5 and Exercise 8 for ideas.

Example: **DINO:** I've got to have some chocolate.
TRISH: Be real! You can't make a fire with chocolate.

10 | ON THE INTERNET

Do a search on **Survivor**, **Big Brother**, *or another reality show that you like. What do you have to do to be on the show? Check their websites for "eligibility requirements" or "application." Make a list. Then work in a group and compare information about different shows.*

Example: **A:** For *Big Brother* you have to send a video of yourself, but it can't be more than two minutes long.
B: You have to send a video for *Survivor* too. But it doesn't have to be only two minutes. It can be three minutes.

Advisability in the Past

Grammar in Context

BEFORE YOU READ

What are some examples of typical regrets that people have? Why do you think the article is called "Useless Regrets"? Read this article from a popular psychology magazine.

Useless Regrets ▶▶▶▶▶▶▶▶▶▶▶▶

"It **might have been**." These are not only the saddest words, but perhaps the most destructive. According to recent ideas in psychology, our feelings are mainly the result of the way we *think* about reality, not reality itself.

According to Nathan S. Kline, M.D., it's not unusual to feel deep regret about things in the past that you think you **should have done** and did not do—or the opposite, about things you did and feel you **should not have done**. In fact, we learn by thinking about past mistakes. For example, a student who fails a test learns that he or she **should have studied** more and can improve on the next test.

However, thinking too much about past mistakes and missed opportunities can create such bad feelings that people be-come paralyzed and can't move on with their lives. Arthur Freeman, Ph.D., and Rose DeWolf have labeled this process "woulda/coulda/shoulda thinking," and they have written an entire book about this type of disorder.

(continued)

For all sad words of tongue or pen
*The saddest are these: "It **might have been**."*
—John Greenleaf Whittier

I **should have been** rich and famous by now.

I **ought to have applied** to college.

I **could have become** a doctor.

My parents **shouldn't have discouraged** me.

Useless Regrets ▶▶▶▶▶▶▶▶▶▶▶▶▶▶▶▶▶▶▶▶▶▶▶

In *Woulda/Coulda/Shoulda: Overcoming Regrets, Mistakes, and Missed Opportunities*, Freeman and DeWolf suggest challenging regrets with specifics. "Instead of saying, 'I **should have done** better,'" they suggest, "Write down an example of a way in which you **might have done** better. Exactly what **should** you **have done** to produce the desired result? Did you have the skills, money, experience, etc. at the time?" In the case of the student who **should have studied** more, perhaps on that occasion it was not really possible.

When people examine their feelings of regret about the past, they often find that many of them are simply not based in fact. A mother regrets missing a football game in which her son's leg was injured. She blames herself and the officials. "I **should have gone**," she keeps telling herself. "I **could have prevented** the injury. They **might** at least **have telephoned** me as soon as it happened." Did she *really* have the power to prevent her son's injury? **Should** the officials **have called** her *before* looking at the injury? Probably not.

Once people realize how unrealistic their feelings of regret are, they are more ready to let go of them. Cognitive psychologist David Burns, M.D., suggests specific strategies for dealing with useless feelings of regret and getting on with the present. One amusing technique is to spend 10 minutes a day writing down all the things you regret. Then say them all aloud (better yet, record them), and listen to yourself.

After you recognize how foolish most feelings of regret sound, the next step is to let go of them and to start dealing with the problems you face right now.

I **shouldn't have told** that joke in the office. My career is ruined.

I **ought to have cleaned** the house instead of going out this weekend. My mother's right. I'm just lazy.

My boyfriend **could have told** me he was going out of town this weekend. He's an inconsiderate jerk. I **should** never **have started** going out with him.

AFTER YOU READ

Look at the photo on page 239. Then read the following statements. Write **T** *(true) or* **F** *(false).*

_____ 1. The woman is rich and famous.

_____ 2. She is a doctor.

_____ 3. She applied to college.

_____ 4. Her parents didn't encourage her.

Grammar Presentation

ADVISABILITY IN THE PAST:
SHOULD HAVE, OUGHT TO HAVE, COULD HAVE, MIGHT HAVE

Statements				
Subject	**Modal***	*Have*	**Past Participle**	
He	**should (not)** **ought (not) to** **could** **might**	**have**	**told**	her.

Contractions		
should have	=	**should've**
could have	=	**could've**
might have	=	**might've**
should not have	=	**shouldn't have**

**Should, ought to, could,* and *might* are modals. Modals have only one form.
They do not have *-s* in the third person singular.

Yes / No Questions				
Should	**Subject**	*Have*	**Past Participle**	
Should	he	**have**	**told**	her?

Short Answers					
Affirmative			**Negative**		
Yes,	he	**should have.**	**No,**	he	**shouldn't have.**

Wh- Questions					
Wh- Word	*Should*	**Subject**	*Have*	**Past Participle**	
When	**should**	he	**have**	**told**	her?

(continued)

GRAMMAR NOTES	EXAMPLES
1. Use the modals *should have*, *ought to have*, *could have*, and *might have* to talk about actions and states that were **advisable** (good ideas) in the past, **but did not happen**. These modals often communicate a sense of regret or blame.	• I **should've applied** to college. *(I didn't apply to college, and now I'm sorry.)* • I **ought to have taken** that job. *(I didn't take the job. That was a big mistake.)* • She **could've gone** to a much better school. *(She didn't go to a better school. Now she regrets her choice.)* • You **might've told** me. *(You didn't tell me. That was wrong.)*
2. USAGE NOTE: *Should not have* and *ought not to have* are the only forms used in **negative** statements about advisability in the past. *Should not have* is more common. *Should have* is the most common form used in **questions**.	• He **shouldn't have missed** the math exam. • He **ought not to have missed** the math exam. • **Should** he **have called** the teacher?
3. PRONUNCIATION NOTES: **a.** In informal speech, *have* in modal phrases is often pronounced like the word *of*. ▶ **BE CAREFUL!** Do not write *of* instead of *have* with past modals. **b.** In informal speech, *to* in *ought to* is pronounced like the word *a*. ▶ **BE CAREFUL!** Do not write *a* instead of *to* with *ought*.	• **could have** ("could of") • I **should** *have* **gone**. NOT I ~~should of~~ gone. • **ought to** ("oughta") • I **ought** *to* **have gone**. NOT I ~~ought a~~ have gone.

Reference Note
For information about *could have* and *might have* to express **speculations about the past,** see Unit 17, pages 252–253.

Focused Practice

1 | DISCOVER THE GRAMMAR

Read the first sentence in each item. Circle the letter of the sentence that is closest in meaning.

1. I shouldn't have called him.
  (a.) I called him.
  b. I didn't call him.

2. My parents ought to have moved away from that neighborhood.
  a. They're going to move, but they're not sure when.
  b. Moving was a good idea, but they didn't do it.

3. I should have told them what I thought.
  a. I didn't tell them, and now I regret it.
  b. I told them, and that was a big mistake.

4. He might have warned us about the traffic.
  a. He didn't know, so he couldn't tell us.
  b. He knew, but he didn't tell us.

5. Felicia could have been a vice president by now.
  a. Felicia didn't become a vice president.
  b. Felicia is a vice president.

6. They shouldn't have lent him their car.
  a. They refused to lend him their car.
  b. They lent him their car.

7. I ought not to have bought that sweater.
  a. I bought the sweater.
  b. I didn't buy the sweater.

2 | ETHICS DISCUSSION
Grammar Notes 1–3

A class is discussing an ethical problem. Complete the discussion with the correct form of the verbs in parentheses or with short answers. Choose between affirmative and negative.

PROBLEM: Greg, a college student, worked successfully for a clothing store for a year. He spent most of his salary on books and tuition. One week he wanted some extra money to buy a sweater to wear to a party. He asked for a raise but his boss refused. The same week, Greg discovered an extra sweater in a shipment he was unpacking. It was very stylish and just his size. Greg "borrowed" it for the weekend and then brought it back. His boss found out and fired him.

(continued)

TEACHER: _____*Should*_____ Greg's boss _____*have given*_____ him a raise?
1. (Should / give)

STUDENT A: Yes, he _____*should have*_____. After all, Greg had worked there for a whole
2.

year. His boss _____*shouldn't have refused*_____ at that point.
3. (should / refuse)

STUDENT B: But maybe his boss couldn't afford a raise. Anyway, Greg still

_____ the sweater. It wasn't his.
4. (should / take)

TEACHER: What _____ he _____ instead?
5. (should / do)

STUDENT C: He _____ his boss to sell him the sweater. Then he
6. (might / ask)

_____ for it slowly, out of his salary.
7. (could / pay)

STUDENT A: He _____ his old clothes to the party. A new sweater just
8. (ought to / wear)
wasn't worth all this trouble.

TEACHER: Well, _____ Greg's boss _____ him?
9. (should / fire)

STUDENT B: No, he _____. Greg had been a good employee for a year.
10.
And he brought the sweater back.

TEACHER: How _____ his boss _____ the situation?
11. (should / handle)

STUDENT C: He _____ him. He _____ just
12. (ought to / warn)

_____ him without any warning.
13. (should / fire)

3 | GRETA REGRETS

Grammar Notes 1–3

Complete Greta's regrets or complaints about the past using the modals in parentheses.
Choose between affirmative and negative.

1. I didn't go to college. Now I'm unhappy with my job.

(should) __*I should have gone to college.*_____

2. My brother quit a good job, and now he's sorry. I knew it was a mistake, but I didn't warn

him. How inconsiderate of me.

(might) _____

3. I feel sick. I ate all the chocolate.

(should) _____

4. Christina didn't come over. She didn't even call.

(might)_____

5. I didn't have enough money to buy the shirt. Why didn't Ed offer to lend me some?

(could)_____

6. I jogged five miles yesterday, and now I'm exhausted.

(should)_____

7. The supermarket charged me for the plastic bag. They used to be free.

(should)_____

8. I didn't do the laundry yesterday, so I don't have any clean socks. Everyone else gets their laundry done on time. Why can't I?

(ought to)_____

9. I didn't invite Cynthia to the party. Now she's angry at me.

(should)_____

10. Yesterday was my birthday, and my brother didn't send me a card. I'm hurt.

(might)_____

4 | EDITING

Read this journal entry. There are six mistakes in the use of modals. The first mistake is already corrected. Find and correct five more.

December 15

About a week ago, Jennifer was late for work again, and Doug, our boss, told me he wanted to fire her. I was really upset. Of course, Jennifer shouldn't ~~had~~ *have* been late so often, but he might has talked to her about the problem before he decided to let her go. Then he told me to make her job difficult for her so that she would quit. I just pretended I didn't hear him. What a mistake! I ought a have confronted him right away. Or I could at least have warned Jennifer. Anyway, Jennifer is still here, but now I'm worried about my own job. Should I of told Doug's boss? I wonder. Maybe I should handle things differently last week. The company should never has hired this guy.

Communication Practice

5 | LISTENING

🎧 *Jennifer is taking Dr. David Burns's advice by recording all the things she regrets at the end of the day. Listen to her recording. Then listen again and check the things she did.*

TO DO

- ☐ Homework
- ☑ Walk to work
- ☐ Make $100 bank deposit
- ☐ Buy coat

- ☐ Call Aunt Rose
- ☐ Call Ron
- ☐ Go to supermarket
- ☐ Finish David Burns's book

---

6 | WHAT A MESS!

Work with a partner. Look at the picture of Jennifer's apartment. What should she have done? What shouldn't she have done? Write as many sentences as you can in five minutes. When you are done, compare your answers with those of your classmates.

Example: She should have paid the electric bill.

7 | S.O.S.

A sense of obligation is a feeling that you should do or should have done something. How strong is your sense of obligation? Take this test and find out.

Sense of Obligation Survey (S.O.S.)

INSTRUCTIONS: Read each situation. Circle the letter of your most likely response.

1. You want to lose 10 pounds, but you just ate a large dish of ice cream.
   a. I shouldn't have eaten the ice cream. I have no willpower.
   b. I deserve to enjoy things once in a while. I'll do better tomorrow.

2. Your friend quit her job. Now she's unemployed.
   a. Maybe she was really unhappy at work. It's better that she left.
   b. She shouldn't have quit until she found another job.

3. You had an appointment with your doctor. You arrived on time but had to wait more than an hour.
   a. My doctor should have scheduled better. My time is valuable too.
   b. Maybe there was an emergency. I'm sure it's not my doctor's fault.

4. You bought a coat for $140. A day later you saw it at another store for just $100.
   a. That was really bad luck.
   b. I should have looked around before I bought the coat.

5. Your brother didn't send you a birthday card.
   a. He could have at least called. He only cares about himself.
   b. Maybe he forgot. He's really been busy lately.

6. You just got back an English test. Your grade was 60 percent.
   a. That was a really difficult test.
   b. I should have studied harder.

7. You just found out that an electrician overcharged you.
   a. I should have known that was too much money.
   b. How could I have known? I'm not an expert.

8. You forgot to do some household chores that you had promised to do. Now the person you live with is angry.
   a. I shouldn't have forgotten. I'm irresponsible.
   b. I'm only human. I make mistakes.

9. You got a ticket for driving five miles per hour above the speed limit.
   a. I ought to have obeyed the speed limit.
   b. The police officer could've overlooked it and not given me the ticket. It was only five miles over the speed limit.

10. You went to the movies but couldn't get a ticket because it was sold out.
    a. I should've gone earlier.
    b. Wow! This movie is really popular!

SCORING
Give yourself one point for each of these answers:

1. a	6. b
2. b	7. a
3. a	8. a
4. b	9. a
5. a	10. a

The higher your score, the stronger your sense of obligation.

Now compare your survey results with those of a classmate.

Example: A: What was your answer to Question 1?
   B: I said I shouldn't have eaten the ice cream. What about you?

8 | DILEMMAS

Work with a group. Read and discuss each case. Did the people act properly or should they have done things differently?

Case 1: Sheila was in her last year of college when she decided to run for student council president. During her campaign, a school newspaper reporter asked her about something he had discovered about her past. In high school, Sheila had once been caught cheating on a test. She had admitted her mistake and repeated the course. She never cheated again. Sheila felt that the incident was over, and she refused to answer the reporter's questions. The reporter wrote the story without telling Sheila's side, and Sheila lost the election.

> **Example:** **A:** Should Sheila have refused to answer questions about her past?
> **B:** I don't think so. She should've told her side of the story.

Case 2: Mustafa is a social worker who cares deeply about his clients. Recently, there was a fire in his office building. After the fire, the fire department declared the building unsafe and wouldn't allow anyone to go back in. Mustafa worried because all his clients' records were in the building. He needed their names, telephone numbers, and other information in order to help them. He decided to take the risk, and he entered the building to get the records. His supervisor found out and fired him.

Case 3: Pierre's wife has been sick for a long time. One day, the doctor told Pierre about a new medicine that might save her life. He warned Pierre that the medicine was still experimental, so Pierre's insurance would not pay for it. At the pharmacy, Pierre discovered that the medicine was so expensive that he didn't have enough money to pay for it. The pharmacist refused to let Pierre pay for it later. Pierre took extra work on nights and weekends to pay for the medicine. Now he can't take care of his wife as well as he had before.

9 | WRITING

Write about a dilemma that you have faced. Discuss what you and others should have, might have, or could have done in the situation. Use Exercise 4 as a model. When you finish writing, exchange paragraphs with another student and discuss your ideas.

10 | ON THE INTERNET

ⓒ *It's important to avoid blunders (unnecessary mistakes) in an interview. Do a search on* **interview blunders** *for a list of mistakes. With a partner, role-play an interview in which the person interviewed makes some of these blunders. Then act it out for a group. Discuss the mistakes with your group.*

> **Example:** **A:** He shouldn't have talked so much. He should have let the interviewer ask more questions.
> **B:** She shouldn't have said bad things about her previous employer. She might have just said, "I'm ready to take on more responsibility now."

Speculations and Conclusions About the Past

Grammar in Context

BEFORE YOU READ

🎧 *The great achievements of ancient cultures fascinate modern people. Look at the photo below. What do you think the design represents? Who do you think made it? When? Read one writer's theories.*

CLOSE ENCOUNTERS

In 1927, Toribio Mexta Xesspe of Peru **must have been** very surprised to see lines in the shapes of huge animals and geometric forms on the ground below his airplane. Created by the ancient Nazca culture, these beautiful forms (over 13,000 of them) are too big to recognize from the ground. However, from about 600 feet in the air, the giant forms take shape. Xesspe **may have been** the first human in almost a thousand years to recognize the designs.

Since their discovery, many people have speculated about the Nazca lines. Without airplanes, how **could** an ancient culture **have made** these amazing pictures? What purpose **could** they **have had**?

One writer, Erich von Däniken, has a theory as amazing as the Nazca lines themselves. According to von Däniken, visitors from other planets brought their civilization to the Earth thousands of years ago. When these astronauts visited ancient cultures here on Earth, the people of those cultures **must have believed** that the visitors were gods. Since the Nazcans **could have**

(*continued*)

Nazca lines

CLOSE ENCOUNTERS

built the lines according to instructions from an aircraft, von Däniken concludes that the drawings **might have marked** a landing strip for the spacecraft of the ancient astronauts. Von Däniken writes, "The builders of the geometrical figures **may have had** no idea what they were doing. But perhaps they knew perfectly well what the 'gods' needed in order to land."

In his book *Chariots of the Gods?* von Däniken offers many other "proofs" that ancient cultures had contact with visitors from other planets. Giant statues on Easter Island provide von Däniken with strong evidence of the astronauts' presence. Von Däniken estimates that the island **could** only **have supported** a very small population. After examining the simple tools that the islanders probably used, he concludes that even 2,000 men working day and night **could not have been** enough to carve the figures out of hard stone. In addition, he says that at least part of the population **must have worked** in the fields, gone fishing, and **woven** cloth. "Two thousand men alone **could not have made** the gigantic statues." Von Däniken's conclusion: Space visitors **had to have built** them.

Scientists, among others, are skeptical and prefer to look for answers closer to home. However, von Däniken's theories continue to fascinate people, both believers and nonbelievers. And even nonbelievers must admit that space visitors **might have contributed** to human culture. After all, no one can prove that they didn't.

Easter Island: Statues of space visitors?

AFTER YOU READ

Read the statements about von Däniken's ideas. Look at the text again. How certain was he? Check the correct column for each statement.

	Certain	Possible	Impossible
1. The Nazca lines marked a landing strip for ancient astronauts.	☐	☐	☐
2. The Nazca people believed that the visitors were gods.	☐	☐	☐
3. There were enough people on Easter Island to carve the huge statues.	☐	☐	☐

Grammar Presentation

SPECULATIONS AND CONCLUSIONS ABOUT THE PAST:
MAY HAVE, MIGHT HAVE, COULD HAVE, MUST HAVE, HAD TO HAVE

Statements				
Subject	Modal* / Had to	Have	Past Participle	
They	**may (not)** **might (not)** **could (not)** **must (not)** **had to**	**have**	**seen**	the statues.

Contractions		
may have	=	**may've**
might have	=	**might've**
could have	=	**could've**
must have	=	**must've**
could not	=	**couldn't**

NOTE: We usually do not contract *may not have*, *might not have*, and *must not have*.

May, *might*, *could*, and *must* are modals. Modals have only one form. They do not have *-s* in the third person singular.

Questions			
Do / Be	Subject	Verb	
Did	they	**carve**	these statues?
Were			aliens?

Short Answers			
Subject	Modal / Had to	Have	Been
They	**may (not)** **might (not)** **could (not)**	**have.**	
	must (not) **had to**	**have**	**been.**

Yes / No Questions: *Could*				
Could	Subject	*Have*	Past Participle	
Could	he	**have**	**seen**	aliens?
			been	an alien?

Short Answers			
Subject	Modal / Had to	Have	Been
He	**may (not)** **might (not)** **could (not)**	**have.**	
	must (not) **had to**	**have**	**been.**

Wh- Questions				
Wh- Word	*Could*	*Have*	Past Participle	
Who	**could**	**have**	**built**	the statues?
What			**happened**	to these people?

GRAMMAR NOTES	EXAMPLES
1. Use *may have*, *might have*, and *could have* to express **speculations**, or possibilities, about a past situation. These speculations are usually based on facts that we have.	**FACT** Archaeologists found pictures of creatures with wings. **SPECULATIONS** • Space beings **may have visited** that civilization. • The pictures **might have marked** a landing strip for a spacecraft. • The pictures **could have shown** mythological creatures.

2. Use *must have* and *had to have* when you are almost certain about your **conclusions**. Do not use *had to have* in negative statements to draw conclusions.	**FACT** The Easter Island statues are made of stone. **CONCLUSIONS** • The islanders **must have had** very sharp tools. • The stone **must not have been** too hard for their tools. **FACT** The statues are very big. **CONCLUSIONS** • They **had to have been** very difficult to move. • They **must not have been** very easy to move. NOT They ~~didn't have to have been~~ easy to move.

3. *Couldn't have* often expresses a feeling of disbelief or **impossibility**.	• He **couldn't have believed** space visitors helped them! It doesn't make any sense.

4. Use *could have* in questions about possibility. Do not use *may have* or *might have*.	• **Could** the Nazca people **have drawn** those lines?

5. Use *been* in short answers to questions that include a form of *be*. Use only the **modal + *have*** in short answers to questions with other verbs.	**A: Could** Erich von Däniken **have been** wrong? **B:** He certainly **could have *been*.** There are other explanations. **A:** *Was* Xesspe surprised when he saw the Nazca lines? **B:** He **must have *been*.** No one knew about them at that time. **A: Did** archaeologists **measure** the drawings? **B:** They *must have*. They studied them for years.

6. Pronunciation note: In informal speech, *have* in modal phrases is often pronounced like the word *of*. ▶ **Be careful!** Do not write *of* instead of *have* with these past modals.	• **could have** ("could of") • They **must *have*** been very skillful. Not They ~~must of~~ been very skillful.

Reference Note
For information about *could have* and *might have* to express **past advisability**, see Unit 16, page 242.

Focused Practice

1 | DISCOVER THE GRAMMAR

Match the facts with the speculations and conclusions.

Facts

<u> e </u> 1. The original title of *Chariots of the Gods?* was *Erinnerungen an die Zukunft.*

_____ 2. Von Däniken visited every place he described in his book.

_____ 3. In 1973, he wrote *In Search of Ancient Gods.*

_____ 4. He doesn't have a degree in archaeology.

_____ 5. *Chariots of the Gods?* was published the same year as the Apollo moon landing.

_____ 6. In the 1900s, writer Annie Besant said beings from Venus helped develop culture on Earth.

_____ 7. Von Däniken's books sold millions of copies.

_____ 8. As soon as von Däniken published his book, scientists attacked his theories.

Speculations and Conclusions

a. He must have made a lot of money.

b. He may have known about her ideas.

c. He could have learned about the subject on his own.

d. He must have traveled a lot.

e. He must have written it in German.

f. This great event had to have increased sales of the book.

g. They must not have believed his theories.

h. He might have written other books too.

2 | ON THEIR OWN?

Grammar Notes 1–4

Circle the correct words to complete the review of von Däniken's book, Chariots of the Gods?

Who could have <u>make / made</u> the Nazca lines?
1.
Who could have <u>carve / carved</u> the Easter Island
2.
statues? According to Erich von Däniken, ancient

achievements like these are mysteries because our

ancestors could not <u>have / had</u> created these things on
3.
their own. His solution: They <u>must / couldn't</u> have gotten
4.
help from space visitors.

Von Däniken's readers may not realize that

"Here comes another one."

experiments have helped explain some of these "mysteries." Von Däniken asks: How <u>may / could</u>
5.

the Nazcans have planned the lines from the ground? Archaeologists now believe that this

civilization might <u>have / has</u> developed flight. They think ancient Nazcans may <u>draw / have drawn</u>

      6.   7.

pictures of hot-air balloons on pottery. To test the theory, archaeologists built a similar balloon

with Nazcan materials. The balloon soared high enough to view the Nazca lines, showing that

Nazcans themselves <u>could / couldn't</u> have designed the pictures from the air.

                        8.

    But what about the Easter Island statues? <u>Did / Could</u> islanders have carved the huge statues

                                         9.

from hard rock with primitive tools? And how could only 2,000 people <u>had / have</u> moved them?

                                                                      10.

3 | WHY NOT?   *Grammar Notes 1–4*

Now complete the rest of the review from Exercise 2. Use the verbs in parentheses.

    Von Däniken and early explorers thought the island's ancient culture _____ *must have been* _____

                                                              1. (must / be)

simple. They assumed that Easter Island _____ many natural resources,

                                           2. (must not / have)

so it _____ a civilization. They were wrong. Studies have shown that a

          3. (couldn't / support)

large population and a complex culture _____ on the island. Large

                                   4. (could / develop)

palm trees once grew there. Islanders _____ large boats from the

                                   5. (must / make)

trees and _____ in deep water because ancient garbage dumps are full

          6. (must / fish)

of the bones of deep sea fish. Ancient islanders _____ very well, and

                                   7. (must / eat)

as many as 15,000 people _____ on the island. From trees, they

                              8. (may / live)

_____ ropes to pull their statues. In 1994, DNA tests proved that the

      9. (could / make)

islanders _____ from Polynesia, where there is a tradition of ancestor

          10. (had to / come)

worship. But doubts remained—in the language of Rapa Nui (Easter Island), the statues are called

the living faces of our ancestors. How _____ the Nazca people

_____ these lifeless images "living faces"? Then Sergio Rapu, a Rapa

      11. (could / call)

Nui archaeologist, realized that the statues _____ coral eyes. Pieces of

                                   12. (must / have)

coral he had found fit one of the statues perfectly, and its face seemed to come to life. Scientists

are still experimenting with ways islanders _____ the huge images.

                                   13. (might / move)

However, now no one says, "The people of Rapa Nui _____ these

                                   14. (couldn't / create)

statues."

4 | NATURE PUZZLES

Read about these puzzling events. Then rewrite the answers to the questions about their causes. Substitute a modal phrase for the underlined words.

Dinosaurs existed on the Earth for about 135 million years. Then, about 65 million years ago, these giant reptiles all died in a short period of time. What could have caused the dinosaurs to become extinct?

1. It's likely that the Earth became colder. (must)

   The Earth must have become colder.

2. <u>Probably</u>, dinosaurs didn't survive the cold. (must not)

   _____

3. It's been suggested that a huge meteor hit the Earth. (might)

   _____

In 1924, Albert Ostman went camping alone in Canada. Later, he reported that a Bigfoot (a large, hairy creature that looks human) had kidnapped him and taken him home, where the Bigfoot family treated him like a pet. Ostman escaped after several days. What do you think happened? Could a Bigfoot really have kidnapped Ostman?

4. A Bigfoot didn't kidnap Ostman—<u>that's impossible</u>. (couldn't)

   _____

5. Ostman <u>probably</u> saw a bear. (must)

   _____

6. <u>It's possible that</u> Ostman dreamed about a Bigfoot. (could)

   _____

In 1932, a man was taking a walk around Scotland's beautiful Loch Ness. Suddenly, a couple hundred feet from shore, the water bubbled up and a huge monster appeared. The man took a photo. When it was developed, the picture showed something with a long neck and a small head. Since then, many people have reported similar sightings. What do you think? Did the man really see the Loch Ness monster?

7. <u>Most likely</u> the man changed the photo. (have to)

   _____

8. <u>Perhaps</u> the man saw a large fish. (might)

   _____

9. <u>It's possible that</u> the man saw a dead tree trunk. (may)

   _____

10. <u>It's very unlikely that</u> a dinosaur was in the lake. (couldn't)

    _____

5 | **ARCHAEOLOGY 101**   *Grammar Note 5*

Some archaeology students are asking questions in class. Use the modals in parentheses to write short answers.

1. **A:** Were the Nazcans really able to fly?

   B: _____*They might have been*_____. There's some evidence that they had hot-air
   <u>(might)</u>
   balloons made of cloth.

2. **A:** Is it possible that the Nazcan lines were ancient streets?

   B: _____. Some of them just lead to the tops of mountains
   <u>(could not)</u>
   and then end abruptly.

3. **A:** Do you think the Nazcans used them during

   religious ceremonies?

   B: _____. But
   <u>(might)</u>
   we have no proof.

4. **A:** Do you think the people on Rapa Nui built the

   giant statues themselves?

   B: _____. They
   <u>(could)</u>
   had the knowledge and the tools.

5. **A:** Did the original settlers of Rapa Nui come from Polynesia?

   B: _____. There's a lot of scientific evidence to support this.
   <u>(must)</u>

6. **A:** Von Däniken says that many ancient artifacts show pictures of astronauts. Could these

   pictures have illustrated anything closer to Earth?

   B: _____. It's possible that the pictures show people dressed
   <u>(may)</u>
   in local costumes.

7. **A:** Was von Däniken upset by all the criticism he received?

   B: _____. After all, it created more interest in his books.
   <u>(might not)</u>

8. **A:** Do you think von Däniken helped increase general interest in archaeology?

   B: _____. Just look at how many of you are taking
   <u>(must)</u>
   this class!

6 | EDITING

Read this student's essay about Easter Island. There are ten mistakes in the use of modals.
The first mistake is already corrected. Find and correct nine more.

Rapa Nui (Easter Island) is a tiny island in the middle of
the Pacific. To get there, the first settlers had to ~~had~~ *have*
traveled more than 1,000 miles in open boats. Some scientists
believed only the Polynesians of the Pacific islands could
have make the journey. Others thought that Polynesians
couldn't have carved the huge stone statues on Rapa Nui. They
believed Mayans or Egyptians maybe have traveled there. (Some
people even said that space aliens might helped!) Finally, a
University of Oslo scientist was able to study the DNA from
ancient skeletons. Professor Erika Halberg announced, "These
people has to have been the descendants of Polynesians."

We now know that the islanders built the statues, but we
have also learned that they must had solved even more
difficult problems. The first settlers came some time between
A.D. 400 and 700. At first, Rapa Nui must be a paradise with
its fishing, forests, and good soil. Their society may have
grown too fast for the small island, however. Botanical
studies show that by the 1600s they had cut down the last
tree. The soil must not have washed away, so they couldn't
farm. And with no wood for boats, they couldn't have able to
fish. For a period of time, people starved and fought
violently, but when the Dutch discovered Rapa Nui in 1722,
they found a peaceful, healthy population growing fields of
vegetables. How the islanders could have learned in this short
period of time to live peacefully with so few resources? For
our troubled world today, this might be the most important
"mystery of Easter Island."

Communication Practice

7 | LISTENING

🎧 *Some archaeology students are discussing artifacts they have found at various sites. Look at the pictures. Then listen to the students speculate and draw conclusions about what each item is. Listen again and match the pictures with the correct conversation.*

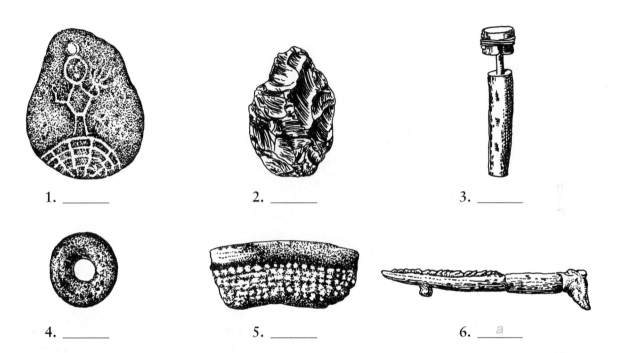

1. _____

2. _____

3. _____

4. _____

5. _____

6. _*a*_____

8 | USEFUL OBJECTS

Work in small groups. Look at the objects that archaeologists have found in different places. Speculate on what they are and how people might have used them. After your discussion, share your ideas with the rest of the class.

1. Archaeologists found this object in the sleeping area of an ancient Chinese house. It's about the same size as a basketball.

   Example: I think people might have used this as a footstool. The floor must have been cold at night, and people could have rested their feet on it.

(continued)

2. Archaeologists have found objects like these with men's and women's clothing. This one is about the size of a cordless telephone.

3. These artifacts were used by ancient Egyptians. The handles are each about the length of a toothbrush.

4. People in the Arctic started using these around 2,000 years ago. They used them when they were hunting or traveling. They are small enough to put in your pocket.

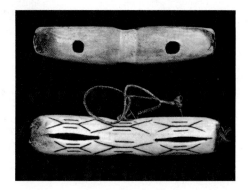

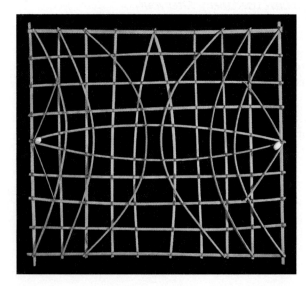

5. Polynesian people used these when they traveled. They made them with sticks, coconut fiber, and seashells. This one is about 1 foot (30.5 centimeters) wide and 1 foot long.

9 | CHARIOTS OF THE GODS?

Reread the article that begins on page 249. Then discuss your opinion about Erich von Däniken's theory with a partner. Afterward, have a class discussion. How many students think space creatures might have visited the Earth? How many think space creatures couldn't have affected human culture?

10 | ON THE INTERNET

Do a search on one of these unsolved mysteries. Find several explanations. Which explanations seem more likely? Compare your information and ideas in groups.

1. The ancient Maya once inhabited the Yucatán Peninsula in what today is Mexico and Guatemala. They had a very advanced civilization. In about A.D. 900, for no known reason, the Maya suddenly left their large and well-built cities. The jungle soon covered the entire area. Why did the Maya abandon their cities? Why did they never return?

   Example: A: The climate could have gotten drier. They might not have had enough water.
   B: Or they may have moved out of the cities for religious reasons.

2. On October 23, 1947, at about 7:30 A.M. in Marksville, Louisiana, a small town in the United States, it suddenly started raining fish. The town's bank director reported that hundreds of fish had fallen into his yard, and townspeople were hit by the falling fish as they walked to work. The fish were only the kinds found in local rivers and lakes, and they were all very fresh. Nothing else—no frogs, turtles, or water plants—fell that morning, only fish. How could this have happened?

3. In 1991 hikers in the Italian Alps discovered a body in some melting ice. The body, which had been in the ice for more than 5,000 years, was in almost perfect condition. The "Ice Man" had several broken ribs. He had been wearing warm winter clothing, and had been carrying a knife, an ax, dried meat, and medicines. He had been making a bow and arrows, but he had not finished them. What could have happened to him?

11 | WRITING

Write a paragraph about one of the unsolved mysteries in Exercise 10. Use modals to speculate about what caused the event. Which explanation do you think is the most likely, and why?

   Example: The Ice Man might have brought his animals into the mountains to feed. People from his time and culture often did that. Someone from another tribe could have attacked him.

From **Grammar** to **Writing**
Organizing Ideas from Freewriting

Freewriting is a way to develop ideas about a topic. To freewrite, write for a specified length of time without stopping. Don't worry about mistakes. Then organize the ideas in your freewriting.

Example: Can't stop thinking about M's wedding in Quito last year. *(freewriting)*
I can't stop thinking about Miguel's wedding in Quito last year. *(formal writing)*

1 | *Read Clara's freewriting about a problem she had with her cousin Miguel. Underline her ideas about Miguel's reasons for what he did. Bracket (**[ ]**) her ideas about the appropriateness of Miguel's and her own behavior.*

Can't stop thinking about Miguel's wedding in Quito last year. Still feeling hurt and confused. Why didn't he invite me? Or even tell me about it? [This was a family reunion and he should have sent everyone an invitation.] He knows I'm a student, and he must have thought I couldn't afford the airfare to Ecuador. He could've sent me an invitation and let me decide for myself. On the other hand, I should have called him to discuss it. He might have even decided that I couldn't afford to send a gift. He shouldn't have decided for me. He couldn't have been angry with me! I've got to let him know how I feel. I should write a letter.

2 | *Clara decided to write a letter to Miguel. Read her outline in Exercise 3.*
Write the paragraph number where Clara decides to do each of the following:

1. discuss the appropriateness of Miguel's and her own behavior ___3___

2. introduce the problem _____

3. suggest resolving the problem _____

4. speculate on reasons for Miguel's behavior _____

3 | *Complete Clara's letter with ideas from Exercise 1.*

> Dear Miguel,
>
> I'm sorry that I haven't written for some time, but I'm still feeling hurt and confused. Miguel, why didn't you invite me to your wedding last year? You didn't even tell me about it!
>
> Maybe your reasons for not inviting me were actually thoughtful. You know I'm a student, and ___you must have thought I couldn't afford the airfare.___
>
> _____
>
> _____
>
> However, I believe you should have handled the situation in a different way. This was a family reunion, and you should have sent everyone an invitation.
>
> _____
>
> _____
>
> _____
>
> We ought to solve this as soon as possible. I miss you. Please write as soon as you get this letter.
>
> Love,
>
> Clara

4 *Before you write . . .*

1. Think of a problem you had with a friend or relative. Freewrite about the problem: the reasons it might have happened and what you and other people could have done differently.

2. Choose ideas and organize them.

5 *Write a letter to the friend or relative who you had the problem with. Include ideas from your freewriting in Exercise 4. Use past modals to speculate about reasons for your problem and to express regrets and obligations.*

6 *Exchange letters with a partner. Write a question mark (?) over anything in the letter that seems wrong. Then answer the following questions.*

	Yes	No
1. Did the writer correctly use past modals to speculate about reasons?	☐	☐
2. Did the writer correctly use past modals to express appropriateness?	☐	☐
3. Did the writer express his or her feelings and ideas clearly?	☐	☐

7 *Work with your partner. Discuss each other's editing questions from Exercise 6. Then rewrite your letter and make any necessary corrections.*

Review Test

I *Complete this conversation by circling the correct modals.*

A: You <u>should have</u> / (<u>must have</u>) been up late last night. You look tired.
           1.

B: I <u>couldn't</u> / <u>didn't have to</u> sleep. My boss gave Joe a raise instead of me.
     2.

    He <u>could have</u> / <u>couldn't have</u> given me one. I've been there a whole year.
         3.

A: I <u>can't</u> / <u>don't have to</u> believe he did that! Well, the company <u>could</u> / <u>must not</u> have the
     4.   **5.**

    money right now.

B: Wrong. Ann got a raise and a promotion. And she<u>'s got to</u> / <u>should</u> be the worst
                                       6.

    employee there. By the way, your friend Amy also got a promotion.

A: Really? She <u>has to</u> / <u>may</u> be pleased about that. But, getting back to you—you
           7.

    <u>should</u> / <u>shouldn't</u> call me when you get upset. I <u>must have</u> / <u>might have</u> been able to
       8.   **9.**

    help last night.

B: I called you at 8:00. You <u>must have</u> / <u>might not have</u> been out.
                         10.

A: I wasn't out. I <u>could not have</u> / <u>must not have</u> heard the phone.
              11.

    I <u>could have</u> / <u>ought to have</u> been in the shower.
       12.

B: Well, I ended up calling Sam. What a mistake. I <u>should</u> / <u>shouldn't have</u> called him.
                                     13.

    He repeated everything to Ann.

A: That's terrible! He <u>shouldn't have</u> / <u>must not have</u> done that. I'm going to talk with him
               14.

    about it.

B: You <u>couldn't</u> / <u>'d better not</u>. He'll just repeat that conversation too.
    15.

II Complete this conversation with past modals. Use the correct form of the verbs in parentheses. Choose between affirmative and negative.

A: I got a C on my math test. I ____*should have done*____ better than that.
   1. (should / do)

B: Don't be so hard on yourself. It _____ your fault. It just
   2. (may / be)

_____ a more difficult test than usual.
   3. (could / be)

A: No, it _____ that difficult. The rest of the class did pretty well.
   4. (could / be)

I _____ harder.
   5. (should / study)

B: What _____ you _____ differently?
   6. (could / do)

A: Well, for one thing, I _____ that day of class.
   7. (should / miss)

B: You missed a day? Did you get the notes?

A: No. I _____ them. Some of the problems which I got wrong
   8. (ought to / copy)

_____ from that day.
   9. (must / come)

III Summarize these sentences. Use the past form of the modals in parentheses. Choose between affirmative and negative.

1. It was a mistake to stay up so late.

   (should) *I shouldn't have stayed up so late.*

2. I regret not watching the show about Easter Island.

   (should) _____

3. I'm sure it was very interesting.

   (must) _____

4. I was surprised that the local library never bought books about Easter Island.

   (ought to) _____

5. I'm annoyed at Sara for not reminding me about it.

   (should) _____

6. I wish that John had told me about it.

   (could) _____

7. I'm sure he didn't remember our conversation about it.

   (must) _____

8. I feel bad that my roommate didn't invite me to the party.

   (might) _____

9. It's possible that John didn't get an invitation.

   (might) _____

10. I'm sure he didn't forget our date.

   (could) _____

IV   *Circle the letter of the correct word(s) to complete each sentence.*

1. There are no clean socks. I should _____ the laundry yesterday.   **A B (C) D**
   - (**A**) did   (**C**) have done
   - (**B**) do   (**D**) not have done

2. Kai wants better grades next semester. He _____ harder.   **A B C D**
   - (**A**) must have studied   (**C**) must not study
   - (**B**) will have to study   (**D**) shouldn't study

3. Dana didn't buy her brother a birthday card. She must _____.   **A B C D**
   - (**A**) have forgotten   (**C**) forget
   - (**B**) not have forgotten   (**D**) forgets

4. My wallet is missing. I _____ dropped it in the store.   **A B C D**
   - (**A**) ought to have   (**C**) could have
   - (**B**) might   (**D**) must

5. He's going for a walk in a few minutes. He may _____ at Molly's on the way.   **A B C D**
   - (**A**) have stopped   (**C**) stops
   - (**B**) stopping   (**D**) stop

6. You're not coming tonight? It's already seven o'clock! You _____ let me know sooner.   **A B C D**
   - (**A**) may   (**C**) can't
   - (**B**) might have   (**D**) must have

7. You should _____ *Fear Factor* tomorrow night. I hear that it's going to be a really exciting show.   **A B C D**
   - (**A**) have missed   (**C**) not miss
   - (**B**) not have missed   (**D**) miss

(continued)

8. Mayan buildings are beautiful. The Mayans must _____ an advanced   **A B C D**

   civilization.

   (**A**) have   (**C**) had

   (**B**) have had   (**D**) had had

9. I don't understand this show. Clio was in Tampa on Thursday, so   **A B C D**

   she couldn't _____ the money from a Boston bank that day.

   (**A**) steal   (**C**) have stolen

   (**B**) had stolen   (**D**) stole

10. I'm sorry, but I _____ able to meet you for lunch tomorrow.   **A B C D**

    (**A**) won't be   (**C**) can't be

    (**B**) haven't been   (**D**) don't be

V *Read this journal entry. There are nine mistakes in the use of modals. The first mistake is already corrected. Find and correct eight more.*

Friday, October 25

    What a day! I guess I'd ~~not better~~ *better not* stay up so late anymore. This morning I should of gotten up much earlier. When I got to the post office, the lines were already long. I must have wait at least half an hour. My boss was furious that I was late. He might fires me for lateness—even though I couldn't have worked during that time anyway. The computers were down again! We must had lost four hours because of that. While the system was down, some of us were able go out to lunch. Later, we all felt sick. It had to has been the food—we all ate the same thing. On the way home, I got stuck in traffic. A trip that should taken twenty minutes took forty-five. Tomorrow's Saturday. I just might sleeping until noon.

▶ *To check your answers, go to the Answer Key on page RT-4.*

PART VIII

The Passive

18 The Passive: Overview

Grammar in Context

BEFORE YOU READ

🎧 *Look at the title of the article. What is geography? Have you ever studied geography in school? Did you enjoy studying geography? Is it an important subject? Why or why not? Read this article about* National Geographic, *a famous magazine.*

GEOGRAPHY
The Best Subject on Earth

Geography is the study of the Earth and its people. It sounds exciting, doesn't it? Yet for decades, students yawned just hearing the word. They **were forced** to memorize the names of capital cities, important rivers and mountains, and natural resources. They **were taught** where places were and what **was produced** there. But they **weren't shown** how our world looks and feels.

Then came *National Geographic* magazine. From the Amazon rain forests to the Sahara Desert, and from Kuala Lumpur to Great Zimbabwe—the natural and human-made wonders of our world **have been brought** to life **by** fascinating reporting and beautiful photographs, such as this one of a Russian couple, which **was taken by** Reza Deghati.

The National Geographic Society **was formed** in Washington, D.C., in 1888 **by** a group of professionals including geographers, explorers, teachers, and mapmakers. Nine months later, the first *National Geographic* magazine **was published** so that the Society could fulfill its mission—to spread the knowledge of and respect for the world, its resources, and its inhabitants.

GEOGRAPHY The Best Subject on Earth

In 1995, the first foreign-language edition of *National Geographic* magazine **was published** in Japan. Today, the magazine **is printed** in more than 20 languages and **sold** all over the world. *National Geographic* also puts out a number of special publications. *National Geographic Explorer*, for example, **has been created** for classrooms. Other publications feature travel and adventure. *National Geographic* TV programs **are watched** in over 160 million homes in 145 countries.

The study of geography has come a long way since 1888. The Society's mission **has been fulfilled**. In fact, it **has** even **been extended** to include worlds beyond Earth. From the deep seas to deep space, geography has never been more exciting!

AFTER YOU READ

Answer these questions.

1. Who memorized names of capital cities? _____

2. Who took the photo of the Russian couple? _____

3. Who formed the National Geographic Society? _____

4. Who watches *National Geographic* TV? _____

Grammar Presentation

THE PASSIVE

Active	Passive
Millions of people **buy** it.	It **is bought** by millions of people.
Someone **published** it in 1888.	It **was published** in 1888.
They **have reached** their goal.	Their goal **has been reached**.

Passive Statements

Subject	Be (not)	Past Participle	(By + Object)	
It	**is (not)**	**bought**	**by** millions of people.	
It	**was (not)**	**published**		in 1888.
Their goal	**has (not) been**	**reached**.		

(continued)

Yes / No Questions			
Be / Have	Subject	*(Been +)* Past Participle	
Is Was	it	sold	in Japan?
Has		been sold	

Short Answers					
Affirmative			Negative		
Yes,	it	is. was. has (been).	No,	it	isn't. wasn't. hasn't (been).

Wh- Questions			
Wh- Word	*Be / Have*	Subject	*(Been +)* Past Participle
Where	is was	it	sold?
	has		been sold?

GRAMMAR NOTES

EXAMPLES

1. Active and **passive** sentences often have similar meanings, but a **different focus**.

Active sentences focus on the **agent** (the person or thing doing the action).

Passive sentences focus on the **object** (the person or thing receiving the action).

ACTIVE
- Millions of **people read** the magazine.
  (The focus is on people.)

PASSIVE
- The **magazine is read** by millions of people.
  (The focus is on the magazine.)

2. Form the **passive** with a form of *be* + past participle.

▶ **BE CAREFUL!** Only **transitive verbs** (verbs that can have objects) have passive forms.

- It *is* **written** in more than 20 different languages.
- It *was* first **published** in 1888.
- It *has been* **sold** all over the world.

    transitive verb   object
- Ed Bly **wrote** *that article*.
- That article **was written** by Ed Bly.
  (passive form)

   intransitive verb
- It **seems** interesting.
  NOT It ~~was~~ seemed interesting.
  (no passive form)

3. Use the **passive** in the following situations:

a. When the **agent** (the person or thing doing the action) is <u>unknown or not important</u>.

- The magazine **was started** in 1888. *(I don't know who started it.)*
- The magazine **is sold** at newsstands. *(It is not important who sells it.)*

b. When you want to <u>avoid mentioning</u> the agent.

- Some mistakes **were made** in that article on Bolivia. *(I know who made the mistakes, but I don't want to blame the person.)*

4. Use the passive with *by* if you mention the **agent**. Only mention the agent when it is important to know who it is.

- The photographs in this article are wonderful. They were **taken** *by a famous photojournalist*.
- One of the first cameras **was invented** *by Daguerre*.

▶ **BE CAREFUL!** In most cases, you do not need to mention an agent in passive sentences. Do not include an agent unnecessarily.

- Ed Bly took a really great photo. It **was taken** last February, but it won't appear until May. NOT It was taken last February ~~by him~~ . . .

Focused Practice

1 | DISCOVER THE GRAMMAR

Read the sentences and decide if they are active **(A)** *or passive* **(P)**.

_P_ **1.** The first *National Geographic* magazine was published in October 1888.

_____ **2.** Today, millions of people read it.

_____ **3.** The magazine is translated into many other languages.

_____ **4.** My cousin reads it in Russian.

_____ **5.** Most of the articles are translated from English.

_____ **6.** Some of them are written by famous writers.

_____ **7.** Many expeditions have been sponsored by the National Geographic Society.

(continued)

_____ 8. The results are reported in the magazine.

_____ 9. It is known for its wonderful photography.

_____ 10. The first underwater color photographs were taken by a *National Geographic* photographer.

_____ 11. Photographers are sent all over the world.

_____ 12. They take pictures of people and nature.

_____ 13. *National Geographic* is sold at newsstands.

_____ 14. It is published once a month.

_____ 15. The *National Geographic* cable television channel has become very popular.

2 | MANY TONGUES
Grammar Notes 1–3

Look at the chart. Then complete the sentences. Some sentences will be active; some will be passive.

Language	Number of Speakers*
Arabic	197
Chinese (Cantonese and Mandarin)	1,070
English	443
Japanese	125
Korean	71
Russian	293
Spanish	341
Turkish	46

*in millions

1. Japanese _is spoken by 125 million people_____.

2. Almost 300 million people _____.

3. _____ by 71 million people.

4. Spanish _____.

5. _____ Chinese.

6. _____ 197 million people.

7. More than 400 million people _____.

8. _____ 46 million people.

3 | AN INTERVIEW

🎧 *Jill Jones is interviewing a Bolivian cultural attaché for an article she's writing.*
Complete her interview with the passive form of the verbs in parentheses and short answers.

JONES: Thanks for giving me some time today. Here is my first question:

_____*Was*_____ the area first _____*inhabited*_____ by the Inca?
                                        1.(inhabit)

ATTACHÉ: _____. Long before the Inca, a great civilization _____
              2.   **3.(create)**

around Lake Titicaca by the Aymara. The Aymara still live in Bolivia.

JONES: Fascinating. Let's talk about agriculture. I know potatoes are an important crop in the

mountains of the Andes. _____ corn _____ there as well?
                                                              4.(grow)

ATTACHÉ: _____. The climate is too cold. But quinoa grows well there.
              5.

JONES: Quinoa? How _____ that _____? With a *k*?
                                                      6.(spell)

ATTACHÉ: No. With a *q*—q-u-i-n-o-a. It's a traditional grain. It _____ by the
                                                                        7.(eat)

people of the Andes for 5,000 years.

JONES: Everyone associates llamas with Bolivia. How _____ they

_____?
      8.(use)

ATTACHÉ: In many ways—fur, meat, transportation. But they only do well in the Andes. They

_____ in the lowlands of the Oriente, the eastern part of the country.
      9.(not raise)

JONES: I see. I know that tin is important. Where _____ it _____?
                                                                          10.(mine)

ATTACHÉ: The richest deposits _____ in the Andes.
                                  11.(find)

JONES: How about the Oriente? What _____ there?
                                        12.(produce)

ATTACHÉ: Oil. Petroleum _____ there. Rice and cattle are important there too.
                            13.(find)

JONES: What other languages _____ besides Spanish?
                                14.(speak)

ATTACHÉ: Actually, more people speak Native American

languages than Spanish.

JONES: Naturalists love Bolivia. _____ jaguars

still _____ there?
        15.(see)

ATTACHÉ: _____. And so are condors and river
              16.

dolphins—many, many species.

Jaguar

4 | FREQUENTLY ASKED QUESTIONS

Grammar Note 3

Complete the FAQ (Frequently Asked Questions) about how photographers send their film
to National Geographic (NG). *Use the correct forms of the verbs in the boxes.*

number	put	~~receive~~	send	shoot	use

National Geographic photographers on expedition have to make sure their work

_____*is received*_____ by NG safely and in good condition. How do they do it? Read the
      1.

FAQ to find out.

Q: How _____ film usually _____ to NG headquarters?
                          2.

A: The film _____ into its original film can. Then very secure packaging
            3.

_____ to protect the film during shipment.
    4.

Q: How do the photographers and editors know what is on each roll of film?

A: Each roll _____ in the order that it _____.
       5.   **6.**

damage	divide	lose	pack	save

Q: _____ shipments ever _____ or _____ in the mail?
                        7.   **8.**

A: Yes, they have been, but we've learned what to do. Now big shipments _____

usually _____ into two. The even-numbered rolls _____ in one
        9.   **10.**

shipment, and the odd in another. That way, half the rolls _____ if there's a
                              11.

problem with one shipment.

find	notify	ship	start	take	trace

Q: What other precautions _____ usually _____?
                                 12.

A: The NG office _____ by the photographer when film _____.
          13.   **14.**

If the film does not arrive on time, it _____ immediately. Lost shipments
                         15.

_____ more easily when this process _____ right away.
    16.   **17.**

5 | **CHECKING FACTS**

Read Jill Jones's article. Her editor found and circled nine factual mistakes.

A Land of Contrasts

by Jill Jones

Visitors to Bolivia are amazed by the contrasts and charmed by the beauty of this South American country's landscapes—from the breathtaking Andes in the west to the tropical lowlands in the east.

Two-thirds of Bolivia's 5 million people are concentrated in the cool western highlands, or *altiplano*. Today, as in centuries past, (corn)? and (kuinoa)*spelling?* are grown in the mountains. Llamas are raised only for (transportation).? And tin, Bolivia's richest natural resource, is mined in the high Andes.

The Oriente, another name for the eastern lowlands, is mostly tropical. Rice is the major food crop, and (llamas)? are raised for meat in the lowlands. (Rubber)? is also found in this region.

Bolivia is home to many fascinating forms of wildlife. The colorful (parrot)? is seen in the highest mountains. Boa constrictors, jaguars, and many other animals are found in the rain forests.

Hundreds of years before the Inca flourished, a great civilization was created on the shores of (the Pacific),? probably by ancestors of Bolivia's Aymara people. Their descendants still speak the Aymara language. Today, Native American languages are still widely spoken in Bolivia. Although (Portuguese)? is spoken in the government, Quechua and Aymara are used more widely by the people. Traditional textiles are woven by (machine.)? Music is played on reed pipes whose tone resembles the sound of the wind blowing over high plains in the Andes.

(continued)

Now rewrite the incorrect sentences with information from Exercise 3.

1. _Corn isn't grown in the mountains. Potatoes are grown in the mountains._

2. _____

3. _____

4. _____

5. _____

6. _____

7. _____

8. _____

9. _____

6 | DID YOU KNOW?   *Grammar Notes 3–4*

Read Ed Bly's soccer trivia column. Complete the information with the correct form of the verbs in the first set of parentheses. If the agent (in the second set of parentheses) is necessary, include it in your answer. If not, cross it out.

⚽ Soccer is the most popular sport in the world. It ____ *is played by more than 20 million people* ____.
   1. (play) (more than 20 million people)

⚽ It ____ *is called* ____ football _____ in 144 countries.
   2. (call)   ~~(people)~~

⚽ Except for the goalie, players _____ to use their hands. Instead, the
   3. (not allow) (the rules)

   ball _____.
   4. (control) (the feet, the head, and the body)

⚽ Soccer _____ in the United States very much until 20 years
   5. (not play) (people)

   ago. Since then, the game _____.
   6. (make popular) (Pelé, Beckham, and other international stars)

⚽ Forms of soccer _____ for thousands of years. A form of
   7. (play) (different cultures)

   soccer _____ in China 2,000 years ago.
   8. (enjoy) (Chinese people)

⚽ It _____ in 1365—his archers spent
   9. (ban) (King Edward III of England)

   too much time playing, and too little time practicing archery.

⚽ Medieval games _____ for entire days, over miles of
   10. (play) (players)

   territory.

⚽ Today, the World Cup games _____ every four years.
   11. (hold) (The World Cup Association)

   The best teams in the world compete.

Read this short biography of an internationally famous photographer whose photos have appeared in National Geographic. *(He took the photo on page 270.) There are seven mistakes in the use of the passive. The first mistake is already corrected. Find and correct six more.*

Seeing the World
by Diana Brodylo

Reza Deghati ~~is~~ ^{was} born in Tabriz, Iran, in 1952. When he was only 14 years old, he began teaching himself photography. At first, he took pictures of his own country—its people and its architecture. When he was 25, he was decided to become a professional photographer. During a demonstration he was asked by a French news agency to take photos. He only shot one and a half rolls of film (instead of the usual 20 to 40), but his photos was published in *Paris Match* (France), *Stern* (Germany), and *Newsweek* (U.S.A).

Reza, as he is knew professionally, has covered several wars, and he has be wounded on assignment. Among all his assignments, the project dearest to his heart is photographing children, who he calls "the real victims of war." He has donated these photos to humanitarian organizations.

When he was interviewed by an interviewer, he was asked to give advice to wannabe* photojournalists. Reza replied, "There is a curtain between the photographer and the subject unless the photographer is able to break through it. . . . Open your heart to them so they know you care."

Today Reza Deghati lives in Paris. His photos is widely distributed in more than 50 countries around the world, and his work is published in *National Geographic* as well as many other internationally famous magazines and newspapers.

*wannabe = want-to-be

Communication Practice

8 | LISTENING

🎧 *Listen to the conversations between editors at* Modern Reader. *Then listen again to each conversation and circle the letter of the sentence you hear.*

1. **a.** Jill hired Bob.
   b. Jill was hired by Bob.

2. **a.** I trained Minna.
   b. I was trained by Minna.

3. **a.** It's published just six times a year.
   b. It was published just six times a year.

4. **a.** Tony fired Jill.
   b. Tony was fired by Jill.

5. **a.** She interviewed Jay.
   b. She was interviewed by Jay.

6. **a.** He was laid off.
   b. Was he laid off?

9 | SAID AROUND THE WORLD

Read these proverbs from around the world. What do you think they mean? Discuss them in small groups. Are there proverbs from other cultures that mean the same thing?

- Rome wasn't built in a day. (*English*)

  Example: **A:** I think this means that big projects aren't finished quickly.
  B: Yes. They take a lot of time and you have to be patient.
  C: There's a proverb in French that means the same thing: "Paris wasn't built in a day."

- He who was bitten by a snake avoids tall grass. (*Chinese*)

- He ran away from the rain and was caught in a hailstorm. (*Turkish*)

- Silence was never written down. (*Italian*)

- Never promise a fish until it's caught. (*Irish*)

- Stars are not seen by sunshine. (*Spanish*)

- Write the bad things that are done to you in sand, but write the good things that happen to you on a piece of marble. (*Arab*)

- Skillful sailors weren't made by smooth seas. (*Ethiopian*)

- A good year is known by its spring. (*Portuguese*)

- Knowledge is like a garden: if it is not cultivated, it cannot be harvested. (*Guinean*)

- Great trees are envied by the wind. (*Japanese*)

- The night is dark, but the apples have been counted. (*Afghan*)

10 | INFORMATION GAP: THE PHILIPPINES

The Philippines consist of many islands. The two largest are Luzon in the north and Mindanao in the south.

Work in pairs (A and B). Student B, go to page 284 and follow the instructions there.

Student A

1. Look at the map of Luzon below. Complete the chart for Luzon. Write *Y* for yes and *N* for no.

2. Student B has the map of Mindanao. Ask Student B questions about Mindanao and complete the chart for Mindanao.

   Example: **A:** Is tobacco grown in Mindanao?
   B: No, it isn't.

3. Student B doesn't have the map of Luzon. Answer Student B's questions about Luzon.

   Example: **B:** Is tobacco grown in Luzon?
   A: Yes, it is. It's grown in the northern and central part of the island.

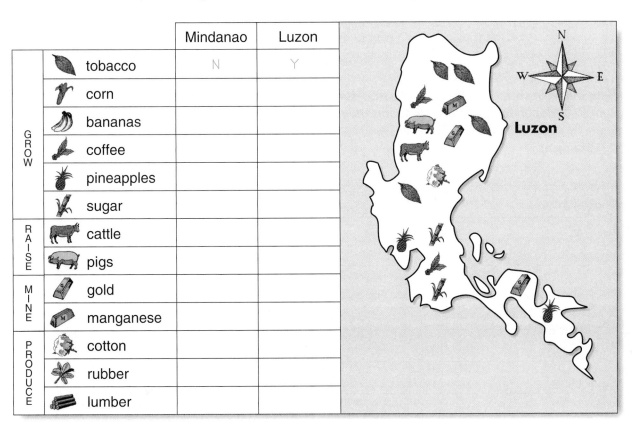

			Mindanao	Luzon
G R O W	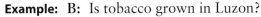	tobacco	N	Y
		corn		
		bananas		
		coffee		
		pineapples		
		sugar		
R A I S E		cattle		
		pigs		
M I N E		gold		
		manganese		
P R O D U C E		cotton		
		rubber		
		lumber		

When you are done, compare charts. Are they the same?

11 | TRIVIA QUIZ

National Geographic Explorer often has games and puzzles. Work in pairs. Complete this quiz. Then compare answers with your classmates. The answers are on page 284.

Do you know . . . ?

1. Urdu is spoken in _____.

a. Ethiopia   **b.** Pakistan   **c.** Uruguay

2. Air-conditioning was invented in _____.

a. 1902   **b.** 1950   **c.** 1980

3. The X-ray was discovered by _____.

a. Thomas Edison   **b.** Wilhelm Roentgen   **c.** Marie Curie

4. The Petronas Towers in Kuala Lumpur were designed by _____.

a. Minoru Yamasaki   **b.** Cesar Pelli   **c.** I. M. Pei

5. The 2004 Olympics were held in _____.

a. Greece   **b.** Japan   **c.** Korea

6. A baby _____ is called a cub.

a. cat   **b.** dog   **c.** lion

Now, with your partner, make up your own questions with the words in parentheses. For item 10, add your own question. Ask another pair to answer your questions.

Example:

_____ Guernica _____   _____ was painted _____ by __b__ .
                               (paint)

a. _____ Monet _____   **b.** _____ Picasso _____   **c.** _____ El Greco _____

7. _____ _____ by ____.
                                 (invent)

a. _____   **b.** _____   **c.** _____

8. _____ _____ by ____.
                               (compose)

a. _____   **b.** _____   **c.** _____

9. _____ _____ by ____.
                               (write)

a. _____   **b.** _____   **c.** _____

10. _____ _____ by ____.

a. _____   **b.** _____   **c.** _____

12 | WRITING

Complete the table with information about a country that you know well. Then write an essay about the country with the information you have gathered. Use the passive. You can use the article in Exercise 5 as a model.

Example: Turkey is both a European and an Asian country. European Turkey is separated from Asian Turkey by the Sea of Marmara. Citrus fruits and tobacco are grown in . . .

Name of country	
Geographical areas	
Crops grown in each area	
Animals raised in each area	
Natural resources found in each area	
Wildlife found in each area	
Languages spoken	
Art, handicrafts, or music created	

13 | ON THE INTERNET

National Geographic is famous for its photographs. Go to its website at www.nationalgeographic.com and search the photo archives. Find a photo that interests you. When and where was it taken? Who was it taken by? What does it show? What do you like about the photo? Print the photo and discuss it with your classmates.

Example: This photo was taken in Afghanistan in 1933 by Maynard Owen Williams. It shows . . .

INFORMATION GAP FOR STUDENT B

1. Look at the map of Mindanao below. Complete the chart for Mindanao. Write *Y* for yes and *N* for no.

2. Student A doesn't have the map of Mindanao. Answer Student A's questions about Mindanao.

   Example: **A:** Is tobacco grown in Mindanao?
   B: No, it isn't.

3. Student A has the map of Luzon. Ask Student A questions about Luzon and complete the chart for Luzon.

   Example: **B:** Is tobacco grown in Luzon?
   A: Yes, it is. It's grown in the northern and central part of the island.

		Mindanao	Luzon
GROW	tobacco	N	Y
	corn		
	bananas		
	coffee		
	pineapples		
	sugar		
RAISE	cattle		
	pigs		
MINE	gold		
	manganese		
PRODUCE	cotton		
	rubber		
	lumber		

Mindanao

When you are done, compare charts. Are they the same?

The Passive with Modals and Similar Expressions

Grammar in Context

BEFORE YOU READ

🎧 *What does the title of the article mean? What are some problems that can occur when people from different cultures must live and work together? Read this article about an international space project.*

CLOSE QUARTERS

Japanese astronauts fear that decisions **will be made** too fast, while Americans worry that in an emergency, they **might not be made** quickly enough. The French and Dutch worry that dinner **won't be taken** seriously, and Italians suspect that their privacy **may not be respected**.

The focus of all this apprehension is the International Space Station (ISS), a major international project that was launched in 1998. The finished station **will be operated** by a crew of astronauts from sixteen countries, including Brazil, Canada, Japan, Russia, and the United States, and members of the European Union. Parts of the project **have had to be delayed**, but large sections of the station have already been assembled. A crew of two or three astronauts can stay aboard for six months at a time. In addition, international scientists and even space tourists **can be transported** there for short stays. The ISS **will be completed** in 2010. The stay on the completed station **could be lengthened** to prepare for a two-year trip to Mars.

How **can** an international group of astronauts **be expected** to get along during long periods in this "trapped environment"? To find out, anthropologist Mary Lozano and engineer Clifford Wong

(*continued*)

Astronauts in Space Station

CLOSE QUARTERS

asked astronauts from around the world about their concerns. The two scientists are hopeful that many cross-cultural problems **will be avoided** by what they have learned.

Besides the concerns already mentioned, all the astronauts worry about language. English will be the official language of the station, and, of course, a great deal of technical language **must be mastered** by everyone. However, on a social level, some members of the ISS team fear that they **might be treated** like outsiders because they won't know American slang. Another concern is food. What time **should** meals **be served**? How **should** preparation and cleanup **be handled**? **Can** religious dietary restrictions **be observed** on board?

To deal with cross-cultural differences like these, Lozano and Wong feel strongly that astronauts **should be taught** interpersonal skills as well as **given** technical and survival know-how. They have interviewed participants in each country, and they hope that what they learn from them **will be applied** in training. In the long run, they believe, cross-cultural training will not only save money but also reduce errors caused by misunderstandings, ranging from misreading a facial expression to incorrectly interpreting data.

Often qualities like sensitivity and tolerance **can't be taught** from a textbook; they **have to be observed** and **experienced**. Lozano and Wong say that the necessary model for space station harmony **can be found** in the TV series *Star Trek.* The multicultural *Enterprise* crew has been getting along in space for eons now, and the scientists suggest that watching the show might be helpful for future astronauts. Since cross-cultural harmony **could be imagined** by the *Star Trek* creators, it **can be achieved** by the crew of the ISS. This might turn out to be the project's greatest achievement.

—LISA DOBRUS

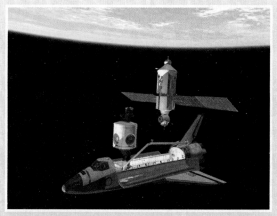

The International Space Station in space

AFTER YOU READ

Write **T** *(true),* **F** *(false), or* **?** *(the information isn't in the article).*

_____ **1.** Astronauts from 16 countries will operate the ISS.

_____ **2.** Scientists had to delay the project.

_____ **3.** The astronauts have to master technical language.

_____ **4.** Robots will serve the meals.

_____ **5.** A textbook can teach sensitivity and tolerance.

Grammar Presentation

THE PASSIVE WITH MODALS AND SIMILAR EXPRESSIONS

Statements				
Subject	**Modal***	***Be***	**Past Participle**	
The crew	**will (not)** **should (not)** **must (not)** **can (not)** **had better (not)**	**be**	**replaced**	next month.

*Modals have only one form. They do not have -*s* in the third person singular.

Statements				
Subject	***Have (got) to /*** ***Be going to****	***Be***	**Past Participle**	
The crew	**has (got) to** **doesn't have to** **is (not) going to**	**be**	**replaced**	next month.

**Unlike modals, *have* in *have (got) to* and *be* in *be going to* change for different subjects. Questions and negatives with *have (got) to* need a form of *do*.

Yes / No Questions			
Modal	**Subject**	***Be***	**Past Participle**
Will	it	**be**	**replaced?**
Should			
Must			
Can			

Short Answers					
Affirmative			**Negative**		
Yes,	it	**will.**	**No,**	it	**won't.**
		should.			**shouldn't.**
		must.			**doesn't have to be.**
		can.			**can't.**

Yes / No Questions				
Auxiliary Verb	**Subject**	***Have to /*** ***Going to***	***Be***	**Past Participle**
Does	it	**have to**	**be**	**replaced?**
Is		**going to**		

Short Answers					
Affirmative			**Negative**		
Yes,	it	**does.**	**No,**	it	**doesn't.**
		is.			**isn't.**

GRAMMAR NOTES	EXAMPLES
1. After a modal, form the passive with: *be* + **past participle**	• The shuttle *will* **be used** to complete the space station. • The crew *won't* **be replaced** this month. • The new menu *must* **be planned** very carefully. • Decisions *shouldn't* **be made** too quickly.
2. Use *will* or *be going to* with the passive to talk about the **future**.	• The project *will* **be completed** in five years. OR • The project *is going to* **be completed** in five years.
3. Use *can* with the passive to express **present ability**. Use *could* with the passive to express **past ability**.	• The space station *can* **be seen** from Earth. • It *could* **be seen** very clearly last year too.
4. Use *could*, *may*, *might*, and *can't* with the passive to express **future possibility** or **impossibility**.	• It *could* **be completed** very soon. • Tourists *may* **be invited**. • Plants *might* **be grown** on board. • The job *can't* **be done** by just one person.
5. Use *have (got) to*, *had better*, *should*, *ought to*, and *must* with the passive to express: **a. obligation** **b. advisability** **c. necessity**	 • Privacy *had better* **be respected**. • The crew *should* **be prepared** to deal with cultural differences. • Crew members *ought to* **be given** cross-cultural training. • Everyone *must* **be consulted**. • Free time *has (got) to* **be provided**.

Reference Note
For a review of **modals and similar expressions**, see Unit 15.

Focused Practice

1 | DISCOVER THE GRAMMAR

🎧 *Read this interview with scientist Dr. Bernard Kay (BK) by* Comet Magazine *(CM).*
Underline all the examples of the passive with modals and similar expressions.

CM: The International Space Station <u>has had to be delayed</u>. When will it be completed?

BK: It could be finished by 2010. With the shuttle* running again, work might be speeded up.

CM: What still has to be done?

BK: The new habitation module, where the astronauts eat and sleep, must be completed. When it's finished, there'll be more living space and the crew can be increased.

CM: At that point, will a separate sleeping cabin be provided for each crew member?

BK: Definitely. We feel strongly that each crew member should be given some private space.

CM: I've heard that looking out the window is the astronauts' favorite leisure activity. Maybe windows ought to be added to the cabins.

BK: Oh, they will be. A window is going to be placed in each cabin.

CM: What kind of experiments will be done on the ISS?

BK: Many kinds. But most important of all, human interactions have got to be understood better. An international crew from 16 different countries makes the ISS a wonderful laboratory for cross-cultural understanding.

CM: I guess we don't know what might be discovered, right?

BK: Right. That's what makes it so exciting.

*The space shuttle is a space vehicle. Like an airplane, it is flown by pilots and it can be used many times. The space shuttle has been used to bring crews, equipment, and supplies back and forth to the ISS.

2 | ZERO-G

Grammar Notes 1–5

Complete this article about zero-G (zero gravity or weightlessness) with the correct form of the words in parentheses.

Juggling oranges—it's easy in zero-G

Some tasks _____*can be accomplished*_____
1. (can / accomplish)

more easily in zero-G. Inside the station, astronauts

_____ from the
2. (can / protect)

deadly conditions of space—but life in almost zero-G

still _____ normal.
3. (can't / consider)

What's it like to live on the ISS?

(continued)

*G*etting Rest: Sleeping _____ to floating in water. It's
4. (can / compare)

relaxing, but sleeping bags _____ to the walls of the cabins.
5. (must / attach)

Otherwise, astronauts will drift around as they sleep.

*K*eeping Clean: Showers _____ because in zero-G, water from
6. (can't / use)

a shower flies in all directions, and sensitive equipment _____.
7. (might / damage)

Instead, astronauts take sponge baths. Used bath water _____
8. (have to / suck)

into a container by a vacuum machine. Clothes _____ by putting them
9. (could / wash)

into a bag with water and soap, but astronauts really _____ with laundry.
10. (not have to / concern)

They usually put dirty clothes into a trash container which _____ back
11. (can / send)

toward Earth and _____ in Earth's atmosphere.
12. (burn up)

*D*ining: From the beginning, ISS planners have known that food _____
13. (should / take)

very seriously. Unlike meals on early space missions, food on the ISS _____
14. (not have to / squeeze)

out of tubes. Frozen and dehydrated meals _____ in a kitchen
15. (can / prepare)

and _____ at a table. Regular utensils are used, but meals are
16. (eat)

packed into containers that _____ to a tray so they don't float
17. (must / attach)

away.

*T*aking It Easy: Not surprisingly, a stressed astronaut is a grouchy astronaut. Free time

_____. Now crew members _____
18. (have got to / provide)   19. (be going to / give)

pocket computers. They _____ for listening to music, looking
20. (will / use)

at photos from home, and reading e-books. Time also _____
21. (must / allow)

for exercise. In low-gravity environments, muscle and bone _____
22. (could / lose)

quickly without exercise.

3 | AFTER THE SIMULATION

Some scientists who are going to join the space station have just completed a simulation of life on the station. Complete their conversations using the modals in parentheses and correct verbs from the boxes.

accept	keep	make	require	simulate	~~solve~~

CESAR: This simulation was great, but there are still some problems. I hope they

_____ *can be solved* _____ before our mission.
1. (can)

GINA: I agree. It was too warm in there. I think the temperature _____
2. (should)

at 68°.

CESAR: For me, that's still warm. Our clothing _____ of lighter material.
3. (ought to)

GINA: A space tourist _____ to join our mission. I heard they're
4. (might)

considering her application now.

CESAR: I heard that too. She _____ to take part in a simulation before she
5. (had better)

goes.

LYLE: You know, they can simulate daily life, but space walks _____
6. (can't)

very realistically.

approve	change	do	send	surprise

HANS: Did you fill in your food preference forms? They _____ to the
7. (should)

Food Systems Lab today.

HISA: I did. I'm glad the new dishes _____ by everyone. I really liked
8. (have to)

some of the Japanese and Russian meals.

HANS: Well, choose carefully. When we get to the station, the menu _____!
9. (can't)

LUIS: Shaving in zero-G is weird. The whisker dust from my beard and mustache kept flying

back into my face. I wonder if something _____ about that.
10. (could)

HANS: I have a feeling we _____ by a lot of unexpected problems.
11. (be going to)

4 | EDITING

Read an astronaut's journal notes. There are eight mistakes in the use of the passive with modals and similar expressions. The first mistake is already corrected. Find and correct seven more.

October 4

October 4

6:15 A.M. I used the sleeping restraints last night, so my feet and hands didn't float around as much. I slept a lot better. I'm going to suggest some changes in the restraints, though—I think they ought to be *made* ~~make~~ more comfortable. I felt really trapped. And maybe these sleeping quarters could designed differently. They're too small.

10:45 A.M. My face is all puffy, and my eyes are red. Exercise helps a little—I'd better be gotten on the exercise bike right away. I can be misunderstanding very easily when I look like this. Sometimes people think I've been crying. And yesterday Max thought I was angry when he turned on *Star Trek*. Actually, I love that show.

1:00 P.M. Lunch was pretty good. Chicken teriyaki. It's nice and spicy, and the sauce can actually been tasted, even at zero gravity. They'd better fly in some more of it for us pretty soon. It's the most popular dish in the freezer.

4:40 P.M. I'm worried about my daughter. Just before I left on this mission, she said she was planning to quit school at the end of the semester. That's only a month away. I want to call her and discuss it. But I worry that I might get angry and yell. I might overheard by the others. They really should figure out some way to give us more privacy.

10:30 P.M. The view of Earth is unbelievably breathtaking! My favorite time is spent looking out the window—watching Earth pass below. At night a halo of light surrounds the horizon. It's so bright that the tops of the clouds can see. It can't be described. It simply have to be experienced.

Communication Practice

5 | LISTENING

🎧 *Some crew members aboard the space station are watching television. Listen and read the script below. Then listen again and circle the underlined words you hear.*

PICARRO: Spaceship *Endeavor* calling Earth . . . This is Captain Picarro speaking. We've been hit by a meteorite.

EARTH: Is anyone hurt?

PICARRO: No, everyone is safe.

EARTH: You'd better start repairing the damage immediately.

PICARRO: It <u>can / can't</u> be repaired out here.
　　　　　　1.

★　★　★　★　★　★　★　★　★

PICARRO: We'll be approaching Planet CX5 of the Delta solar system in a few hours. Is their language on our computer, Dr. Sock?

SOCK: I'm checking now. . . . We don't have a language for CX5 on the computer, but we have one for CX4. Shall we try it?

PICARRO: We'd better be very careful. Our messages <u>could / should</u> be misunderstood.
　　　　　　　　　　　　　　　　　　　　　　2.

★　★　★　★　★　★　★　★　★

LON: OK. I'm ready. Let's go.

RAY: What about oxygen?

LON: Isn't the atmosphere on CX5 just like Earth's?

RAY: I think you've been in space too long. Read your manual: Oxygen <u>must / must not</u> be used on other planets.　　　　　　　　　　　　　　　　　3.

★　★　★　★　★　★　★　★　★

PICARRO: I've lost contact with Lon and Ray. I hope their equipment works on CX5.

SOCK: Don't worry. They'll <u>pick up / be picked up by</u> the radar.
　　　　　　　　　　　　　　　4.

★　★　★　★　★　★　★　★　★

LON: Look at those plants. I want to take some back to the ship.

RAY: They <u>can / can't</u> be grown in space. We've already tried.
　　　　　　5.

LON: That's right. I forgot.

★　★　★　★　★　★　★　★　★

CX5: What do you want to ask us, Earthlings?

RAY: Our vehicle was hit by a meteorite. We request permission to land on your planet.

CX5: Permission granted. Our engineers will be ready for you.

RAY: Thank you. As you know, we <u>have to help / have to be helped</u> with the repairs.
　　　　　　　　　　　　　　　　　6.

6 | CLOSE QUARTERS

Work in small groups. Imagine that in preparation for a space mission, your group is going to spend a week together in a one-room apartment. Make a list of rules. Use the passive with modals and similar expressions. Compare your list with that of another group.

Some Issues to Consider

Food	Cleanliness
Clothes	Privacy
Room temperature	Language
Noise	Entertainment
Neatness	Other: _____

Example: Dinner will be served at 6:00 P.M.
The dishes must be washed after each meal.

7 | WHAT SHOULD BE DONE?

Work in groups. Look at the picture of a student lounge. You are responsible for getting it in order, but you have limited time and money. Agree on five things that should be done.

Example: **A:** The window has to be replaced.
B: No. That'll cost too much. It can just be taped.
C: That'll look terrible. It should be replaced.
D: OK. What else should be done?

8 | MONEY FOR SPACE

Sending people to the International Space Station costs millions of dollars. Should money be spent for these space projects, or could it be spent better on Earth? If so, how should it be spent? Discuss these questions with your classmates.

Example: A: I think space projects are useful. A lot of new products are going to be developed in space.

B: I don't agree. Some of that money should be spent on public housing.

9 | WRITING

Write two paragraphs about your neighborhood, your school, or your place of work. In your first paragraph, write about what might be done to improve it. In your second paragraph, write about what shouldn't be changed. Use the passive with modals and similar expressions.

Example: I enjoy attending this school, but I believe some things could be improved. First, I think that more software ought to be purchased for the language lab . . .

10 | ON THE INTERNET

 Do a search on **International Space Station***. Answer some of the questions below. Compare your information in a small group.*

1. What parts of the station are going to be assembled next?

2. How will they be used?

3. How many tourists will be permitted to travel with the crew?

4. How much money will be spent?

5. What experiments are going to be carried out?

6. When will the next mission be completed?

7. Do any problems have to be solved before the next mission?

BEFORE YOU READ

🎧 *Look at the photos. Which forms of body art do you think are attractive? Read this article from a fashion magazine.*

Body Art

E ach culture has a different ideal of beauty, and throughout the ages, men and women have done amazing things to achieve the ideal. They have **had** *their hair* **shaved, cut, colored, straightened**, and **curled**; and they have **had** *their bodies* **decorated** with painting and tattoos. Here are some of today's many options:

HAIR

Getting *your hair* **done** is the easiest way to change your appearance. Today, both men and women **have** *their hair* **permed**. This chemical procedure can curl hair or just give it more body. If your hair is long, you can, of course, **get** *it* **cut**. But did you know that you can also **have** *short hair* **lengthened** with hair extensions? Of course you can **have** *your hair* **colored** and become a blonde, brunette, or redhead. But you can also **have** *it* **bleached** white or **get** *it* **dyed** blue, green, or orange!

Body Art

TATTOOS

This form of body art was created thousands of years ago. Today, tattoos have again become popular. More and more people are **having** *them* **done**. However, caution is necessary. Although you can now **get** *a tattoo* **removed** with less pain and scarring than before, **having** *one* **applied** is still a big decision.

BODY PAINT

If a tattoo is not for you, you can **have** *ornaments* **painted** on your skin instead. Some people **have** *necklaces and bracelets* **painted** on their neck and arms or **get** *a butterfly mask* **applied** to their face for a special party. Unlike a tattoo, these decorations can be washed off.

PIERCING

Pierced ears are an old favorite, but lately the practice of piercing has expanded. Many people now **are getting** *their noses, lips, or other parts of the body* **pierced** for jewelry. Piercing requires even more caution than tattooing, and aftercare is very important.

COSMETIC SURGERY

You can **get** *your nose* **shortened**, or **have** *your chin* **lengthened**. You can even **have** *the shape of your body* **changed**. There is always some risk involved, so the decision to have cosmetic surgery requires thought.

Some ways of changing your appearance may be cheap and temporary. However, others are expensive and permanent. So, think before you act, and don't let today's choice become tomorrow's regret.

—*By Debra Santana*

AFTER YOU READ

Check the correct answers.

This article discusses changes people can make to their:

☐ **1.** hair length   ☐ **5.** teeth

☐ **2.** hair color   ☐ **6.** clothing

☐ **3.** eyes   ☐ **7.** nose

☐ **4.** skin   ☐ **8.** body shape

Grammar Presentation

THE PASSIVE CAUSATIVE

Statements					
Subject	*Have / Get*	Object	Past Participle	(*By* + Agent)	
She	**has**	*her hair*	**cut**	*by André*	every month.
He	**has had**	*his beard*	**trimmed**		before.
I	**get**	*my nails*	**done**		at André's.
They	**are going to get**	*their ears*	**pierced.**		

Yes / No Questions					
Auxiliary Verb	Subject	*Have / Get*	Object	Past Participle	(*By* + Agent)	
Does	she	**have**	*her hair*	**cut**	*by André*	every month?
Has	he	**had**	*his beard*	**trimmed**		before?
Do	you	**get**	*your nails*	**done**		at André's?
Are	they	**going to get**	*their ears*	**pierced?**		

Wh- Questions						
Wh- Word	Auxiliary Verb	Subject	*Have / Get*	Object	Past Participle	(*By* + Agent)	
How often	**does**	she	**have**	*her hair*	**cut**	*by André?*	
Where	**did**	he	**get**	*his beard*	**trimmed**		before?
When	**do**	you	**get**	*your nails*	**done**		at André's?
Why	**are**	they	**going to get**	*their ears*	**pierced?**		

GRAMMAR NOTES	EXAMPLES

1. Form the **passive causative** with the appropriate form of *have* or *get* + **object** + **past participle**. *Have* and *get* have the same meaning.
 	
The passive causative can be used with:
  a. all verb forms
  b. modals
  c. gerunds
  d. infinitives
	• I **get** *my hair* **cut** by André.
	      OR
	• I **have** *my hair* **cut** by André.
	
	• I'll **have** *the car* **washed** tomorrow.
	• You **should get** *the oil* **changed**.
	• I love **having** *my hair* **done**.
	• I want **to get** *it* **colored**.

2. Use the passive causative to talk about **services** that you arrange for someone to do for you.
 	
▶ **BE CAREFUL!** Do not confuse the passive causative with *had* with the past perfect.
	• I used to color my own hair, but now I **have** *it* **colored**.
	• André is going to **get** *his hair salon* **remodeled** by a local architect.
	
	PASSIVE CAUSATIVE WITH *HAD*
	• I **had** *it* **colored** last week.
	  (Someone did it for me.)
	
	PAST PERFECT
	• I **had colored** it before.
	  (I did it myself.)

3. Use *by* when it is necessary to mention the **agent** (the person doing the service). Do not use *by* when it is clear who is doing the service.	• This week Lynne **is getting her hair done** *by a new stylist*. NOT: Where does Lynne get her hair done ~~by a hair stylist~~?

Reference Note
For information on when to include the **agent**, see Unit 18, page 273.

Focused Practice

1 | DISCOVER THE GRAMMAR

*Read the conversations. Decide if the statement that follows each conversation is true (**T**) or false (**F**).*

1. JAKE: Have you finished writing your article on body art?

    DEBRA: Yes. I'm going to get it copied and then take it to the post office.

    ___F___ Debra is going to copy the article herself.

2. DEBRA: I'm glad that's done. Now I can start planning for our party.

    JAKE: Me too. I'm going to get my hair cut tomorrow after work.

    _____ Jake cuts his own hair.

3. DEBRA: Speaking about hair—Amber, *your* hair's getting awfully long.

    AMBER: I know, Mom. I'm cutting it tomorrow.

    _____ Amber cuts her own hair.

4. AMBER: Mom, why didn't you get your nails done last time you went to the hairdresser?

    DEBRA: Because I did them just before my appointment.

    _____ Debra did her own nails.

5. AMBER: I was thinking of painting a butterfly on my forehead for the party.

    DEBRA: A butterfly! Well, OK. As long as it washes off.

    _____ Someone is going to paint a butterfly on Amber's forehead for her.

6. DEBRA: Jake, do you think we should get the floors waxed before the party?

    JAKE: I think they look OK. We'll get them done afterward.

    _____ Debra and Jake are going to hire someone to wax their floors after the party.

7. DEBRA: I'm going to watch some TV and then go to bed. What's on the agenda for tomorrow?

    JAKE: I have to get up early. I'm getting the car washed before work.

    _____ Jake is going to wash the car himself.

8. DEBRA: You know, I think it's time to change the oil too.

    JAKE: You're right. I'll do it this weekend.

    _____ Jake is going to change the oil himself.

2 | **ESSENTIAL SERVICES** *Grammar Notes 1–2*

It's February 15. Look at the Santanas' calendar and write sentences about when they **had things done**, *and when they are* **going to have things done**.

FEBRUARY

SUNDAY	MONDAY	TUESDAY	WEDNESDAY	THURSDAY	FRIDAY	SATURDAY
1	2	3	4	5	6	7 Deb– hairdresser
8	9	10	11	12 Jake– barber	13 carpets	14 dog groomer
15 TODAY'S DATE	16 windows	17	18	19	20 food and drinks	21 party!! family pictures
22	23	24	25 Amber– ears pierced	26	27	28

1. The Santanas / have / family pictures / take

   The Santanas are going to have family pictures taken on the 21st.

2. Debra / get / her hair / perm

   _____

3. Amber / have / the dog / groom

   _____

4. They / get / the windows / wash

   _____

5. They / have / the carpets / clean

   _____

6. Amber / have / her ears / pierce

   _____

7. Jake / get / his hair / cut

   _____

8. They / have / food and drinks / deliver

   _____

3 | GETTING THINGS DONE

Debra and Jake are going to have a party. Complete the conversations with the passive causative of the appropriate verbs in the box.

color	cut	develop	dry clean
paint	repair	~~shorten~~	wash

1. AMBER: I bought a new dress for the party, Mom. What do you think?

   DEBRA: It's pretty, but it's a little long. Why don't you _____*get it shortened*_____?

   AMBER: OK. They do alterations at the cleaners. I'll take it in tomorrow.

2. AMBER: By the way, what are *you* planning to wear?

   DEBRA: My blue silk dress. I'm glad you reminded me. I'd better _____.

   AMBER: I can drop it off at the cleaners with my dress.

3. JAKE: The house is ready, except for the windows. They look pretty dirty.

   DEBRA: Don't worry. We _____ tomorrow.

4. DEBRA: Amber, your hair is getting really long. I thought you were going to cut it.

   AMBER: I decided not to do it myself this time. I _____ by André.

5. DEBRA: My hair's getting a lot of gray in it. Should I _____?

   JAKE: It looks fine to me, but it's up to you.

6. AMBER: Mom, someone's at the door and it's only twelve o'clock!

   DEBRA: No, it's not. The clock stopped again.

   JAKE: Oh no, not again. I don't believe it! I _____ already

   _____ twice this year, and it's only February!

7. GUEST: The house looks beautiful, Jake. I love the color. _____

   you _____?

   JAKE: No, actually we did it ourselves last summer.

8. DEBRA: I have one shot left in the camera. Come on, everyone! Say "cheese"!

   GUESTS: Cheese!

   DEBRA: Great. We took three rolls of pictures today. Maybe we can _____

   before Mom and Dad go back to Florida.

4 | EDITING

Read Amber's diary entry. There are seven mistakes in the use of the passive causative. The first mistake is already corrected. Find and correct six more.

> *cleaned*
>
> February 21: The party was tonight. It went really well! The house looked great. Mom and Dad had the floors waxed and all the windows ~~clean~~ professionally so everything sparkled. And of course we had the whole house painted ourselves last summer. (I'll never forget *that*. It took us two weeks!) I wore my new black dress that I have shortened by Bo, and I got cut my hair by André. He did a great job. There were a lot of guests at the party. We had almost 50 people invited, and they almost all showed up! The food was great too. Mom made most of the main dishes herself, but she had the rest of the food prepare by a caterer. Mom and Dad hired a professional photographer, so at the end of the party we took our pictures. I can't wait to see them!

Communication Practice

5 | LISTENING

🎧 Amber has just gone to college. Listen to her conversation with Jake. Then listen again and check the correct column.

	Amber did the job herself	Amber hired someone to do the job
1. Change the oil in her car	☐	☑
2. Change the locks	☐	☐
3. Paint the apartment	☐	☐
4. Put up bookshelves	☐	☐
5. Bring new furniture to the apartment	☐	☐
6. Paint her hands	☐	☐
7. Cut her hair	☐	☐
8. Color her hair	☐	☐

6 | MAKING PLANS

Work in groups. Imagine that you are taking a car trip together to another country. You'll be gone for several weeks. Decide where you're going. Then make a list of things you have to do and arrange before the trip. Use the ideas below and ideas of your own.

Passport and visa

Car (oil, gas, tires, brake fluid)

Home (pets, plants, mail, newspaper delivery)

Personal (clothing, hair)

Medical (teeth, eyes, prescriptions)

Other: _____

Example: **A:** I have to get my passport renewed.
B: Me too. And we should apply for visas right away.

Now compare your list with that of another group. Did you forget anything?

7 | TOTAL MAKEOVER

Work in pairs. Look at the Before *and* After *pictures of a fashion model. You have five minutes to find and write down all the things she had done to change her appearance.*

Before

After

Example: She had her nose shortened.

When the five minutes are up, compare your list with that of another pair. Then look at the pictures again to check your answers.

8 | WHAT DO YOU THINK?

Work in pairs. Look at the Before *and* After *pictures in Exercise 7. Do you think the woman looks better? Why or why not?*

Example: A: I don't know why she had her nose fixed.
B: Neither do I. I think it looked fine before.

9 | BEAUTY TALK

Work in small groups. Think about other cultures. Discuss the types of things people get done in order to change their appearance. Report back to your class.

Example: In India, women get their hands painted for special occasions. I think it looks nice.

10 | WRITING

Write a short letter to someone you know. Describe your activities. Include things that you have recently done or have had done. Also talk about things you are going to do or are going to have done. Use the passive causative.

Example: Dear Sara,
I've just moved into a new apartment. I've already had it painted, but there are still so many things that I have to get done! . . .

11 | ON THE INTERNET

 Do a search on a TV show or magazine that features makeovers. Use the phrase **Before and After + Beauty Makeover**. *Print out some* Before *and* After *photos and discuss them with your classmates. What did the people have done? How do you feel about the results?*

Example: A: Mike had his hair colored.
B: I think he looks great as a blond. What about you?

From **Grammar** to **Writing**
Changing the Focus with the Passive

In a report, you often focus on the results of an action rather than the people who performed the action. Use the passive to focus on the results.

> **Example:** Artists **carved** many wooden statues for the temple. *(active)*
> Many wooden statues **were carved** for the temple. *(passive)*

1 | *Read this report about a famous building in Korea. Underline the passive forms.*

Two Buddhist monks built Haeinsa Temple in 802 A.D. The king gave them the money to build the temple after the two monks saved his queen's life. Haeinsa burned down in 1817, but the Main Hall was rebuilt in 1818 on its original foundations. Today, Haeinsa is composed of several large, beautiful buildings. It contains many paintings and statues. Someone carved three of the statues from a single ancient tree. Behind the Main Hall is a steep flight of stone stairs that leads to the Storage Buildings. These buildings, which escaped the fire, were constructed in 1488 in order to store wooden printing blocks of Buddhist texts. It was believed that these printing blocks could protect the country against invaders. Monks carved the 81,258 wooden blocks in the 13th century. A century later, nuns carried them to Haeinsa for safekeeping. Architects designed the Storage Buildings to preserve the wooden blocks. For more than five hundred years, the blocks have been kept in perfect condition because of the design of these buildings. Haeinsa, which means *reflection on a smooth sea*, is also known as the Temple of Teaching because it houses the ancient printing blocks.

2 | *Find five sentences in Exercise 1 that would be better expressed in the passive. Rewrite them.*

1. *Haeinsa Temple was built by two Buddhist monks in A.D. 802.* _____

2. _____

3. _____

4. _____

5. _____

3 | *Answer these questions about Haeinsa Temple.*

1. When was it built?

   _____

2. Who built it?

   _____

3. Why was it built?

   _____

4. What are some of its features?

   _____

5. What is it famous for?

   _____

4 | *Before you write . . .*

   1. Choose a famous building to write about. Do some research in the library or on the Internet. Answer the questions in Exercise 3.

   2. Work with a partner. Ask and answer questions about your topic.

5 | *Write a research report about the building you researched. Use the passive where appropriate. If possible, include a photograph or drawing of the building.*

6 | *Exchange paragraphs with a different partner. Answer the following questions.*

   1. Did the writer answer all the questions in Exercise 3? _____

   2. What interested you the most about the building? _____

   3. What would you like to know more about? _____

   4. Did the writer use the passive appropriately? _____

   5. Are the past participles correct? _____

VIII

Review Test

I *Complete these conversations by circling the active or passive form of the verbs.*

LINDSAY: This is Lindsay Boyle from AL Metals. I (didn't receive) / wasn't received my airline tickets
1.
today, and I <u>leave / 'm left</u> for Jamaica in two days.
2.

AGENT: Let me check. Hmmm. That's strange. The tickets <u>mailed / were mailed</u> a week ago.
3.
You should <u>be had / have</u> them by now.
4.

LINDSAY: How about my hotel reservations?

AGENT: Those <u>made / were made</u> for you last week. They <u>confirmed / were confirmed</u> by the
5. **6.**
Hotel Mariel today. Will you <u>need / be needed</u> a car when you arrive?
7.

LINDSAY: Not right away. I'll <u>be met / meet</u> at the airport by my client. I'll probably <u>rent / be rented</u>
8. **9.**
a car later on. Oh, the receptionist <u>was just handed / just handed</u> me a note. The tickets
10.
are here. They <u>were sent / sent</u> to the wrong floor.
11.

AGENT: Sorry about that.

LINDSAY: Never mind. We have them now, so no harm <u>did / was done</u>.
12.

II *Complete these conversations with the modal and the passive form of the verbs in parentheses.*

LINDSAY: _____*Will*_____ the reports _____*be printed*_____ by the end of next week?
1. (Will / print)

TED: Sure. In fact they _____ to the office by Tuesday.
2. (might / deliver)

LINDSAY: Good. I hope they turn out well. They _____ by a lot of people.
3. (will / read)

TED: Don't worry. This company always does nice work. I'm sure you _____
4. (will / satisfy)
when you see them.

LINDSAY: Oh, by the way, those reports _____ for shipment as soon as they
5. (have to / pack)
arrive. I'm taking them with me to Jamaica.

TED: I didn't know you planned to bring them. I _____ things like

6. (ought to / tell)

that. So how long are you staying?

LINDSAY: About a week. But my stay _____. It depends on how things go.

7. (could / extend)

TED: You know, your office _____ while you're gone. And your

8. (should / paint)

computer _____. So maybe you should stay another week.

9. (have to / service)

LINDSAY: I think that _____. I hear it's a pretty nice place.

10. (can / arrange)

III *Circle the letter of the correct word(s) to complete each sentence.*

1. Reggae music is _____ at Jamaica's Sunsplash Festival.   **A B Ⓒ D**
   - (**A**) perform   (**C**) performed
   - (**B**) performing   (**D**) performs

2. This wonderful festival _____ be missed.   **A B C D**
   - (**A**) isn't   (**C**) shouldn't
   - (**B**) wasn't   (**D**) hasn't

3. Music lovers from all over the world can _____ found at the festival.   **A B C D**
   - (**A**) be   (**C**) been
   - (**B**) have   (**D**) were

4. Swimmers and divers _____ Jamaica's beautiful beaches.   **A B C D**
   - (**A**) are enjoyed   (**C**) enjoys
   - (**B**) enjoy   (**D**) are enjoyed by

5. Go deep-sea fishing, and get your picture _____ with your catch.   **A B C D**
   - (**A**) taken   (**C**) took
   - (**B**) taking   (**D**) be taken

6. Jamaica _____ avoided in the fall because of dangerous storms.   **A B C D**
   - (**A**) ought to   (**C**) should have
   - (**B**) should   (**D**) ought to be

7. Jamaica was settled _____ people from Africa and Europe.   **A B C D**
   - (**A**) at   (**C**) from
   - (**B**) by   (**D**) of

(continued)

8. In the early days, many languages could _____ in Jamaica. **A B C D**
   (**A**) be heard (**C**) heard
   (**B**) were heard (**D**) hear

9. Today Creole, a mixture of languages, _____ spoken widely. **A B C D**
   (**A**) was (**C**) is
   (**B**) were (**D**) are

10. Tickets _____ from any travel agent or directly from the airline. **A B C D**
    (**A**) may be purchased (**C**) purchase
    (**B**) may purchase (**D**) purchased

11. The last time, I _____ my ticket sent directly to my office. **A B C D**
    (**A**) have (**C**) was
    (**B**) get (**D**) had

IV *Complete this memo with the correct forms of **have** or **get** and the verbs in parentheses.*

DATE: February 17

TO: Trish

FROM: Lindsay

I'd like to ____*have*____ some work ____*done*____ in my office, and this seems like
                                    1. (do)
a good time for it. Please _____ my carpet _____ while I'm gone. And
                                                        2. (clean)
while you're at it, could you _____ my computer and printer _____? It's
                                                                      3. (look at)
been quite a while since they've been serviced. Ted wants to _____ my office
_____ while I'm gone. Please tell him any color is fine except pink.
4. (paint)
    Last week, I _____ some new brochures _____. Please call the
                                                    5. (design)
printer and _____ them _____ directly to the sales reps. And could you
                                6. (deliver)
_____ more business cards _____ too? We're almost out.
                                    7. (make up)
    When I get back, it will be time to plan the holiday party. I think that we should
_____ it _____ this year. While I'm gone, why don't you call around and
              8. (cater)
get some estimates from caterers? _____ the estimates _____ to Ted. See
                                                                  9. (send)
you in two weeks!

V *Complete these facts about Jamaica with the passive form of the verbs in the box. Include the agent in parentheses only where necessary.*

~~discover~~	employ	export	grow	listen to	popularize	strike

1. Jamaica _____*was discovered by Europeans*_____ on May 4, 1494, during
   (Europeans)

   Columbus's second voyage.

2. Some of the best coffee in the world _____
   (coffee growers)

   on the slopes of Jamaica's Blue Mountains.

3. About 50,000 people _____.
   (the sugar industry)

4. Sugar _____ to many countries.
   (sugar exporters)

5. The island _____ about once every
   (hurricanes)

   eight years, and some have caused severe damage.

6. Reggae music originated in Jamaica. It _____
   (Bob Marley)

   in the 1970s.

7. Now it _____ everywhere.
   (people)

VI *Each sentence has four underlined words or phrases. The four underlined parts of the sentences are marked A, B, C, or D. Circle the letter of the <u>one</u> underlined part that is NOT CORRECT.*

1. The reports <u>were</u> <u>arrived</u> late, so I <u>had</u> <u>them sent</u> to you this morning.
      A   B   C   D
      (A) B   C   D

2. Some mistakes <u>were</u> <u>made</u> in the brochure, but they might <u>corrected</u>
             A   B   C
      A   B   C   D

   before you <u>get</u> back.
             D

3. You<u>'ll</u> <u>see</u> a copy before they<u>'re</u> <u>printed</u> <u>by the printer</u>.
     A   B   C   D
      A   B   C   D

   (continued)

4. A funny thing <u>was</u> happened when your <u>office</u> <u>was</u> <u>redecorated</u> yesterday.
          A   B   C   D   **A B C D**

5. Your office <u>was</u> almost <u>painted</u> pink, but we <u>had</u> the painters <u>used</u>   **A B C D**
               A   B   C   D

white instead.

6. An estimate from the party caterer <u>were</u> <u>left</u> on my desk, but we've   **A B C D**
                                        A   B

<u>got</u> <u>to wait</u> for your decision.
 C   D

7. <u>Has</u> your stay <u>been</u> <u>extended</u>, or will you <u>be returned</u> next week?   **A B C D**
    A   B   C   D

▶ *To check your answers, go to the Answer Key on page RT-5.*

PART

IX

Conditionals

Grammar in Context

BEFORE YOU READ

🎧 *What is a cyber mall? Have you ever purchased something online? What are some steps people should take to shop safely online? Read this article about cyber malls.*

Pick and Click Shopping@Home
By E. Buyer

Where is the largest mall in the world? **If you think it's in Alberta, Canada, you're wrong!** It's in cyberspace! And you can get there from home on your very own computer.

Cyber shopping is fast, convenient, and often less expensive. **It doesn't matter if it's a book or a diamond necklace**—with just a click of your mouse, you can buy anything without getting up from your chair. **If you're looking for the best price, you can easily compare prices and read other buyers' reviews of products.** Shopping online can save you time and money—but you need to surf and shop safely. Here are some tips to make your trip to the cyber mall a good one:

🔒 **You are less likely to have a problem if you shop with well-known companies.**

🔒 **If you don't know the company, ask them to send you information.** What is their address? Their phone number?

🔒 **Always pay by credit card if you can. If you are unhappy with the product (or if you don't receive it), then you can dispute the charge.**

🔒 Only enter your credit card information on a secure site. **If you see a closed lock (🔒) or complete key (🔑) symbol at the bottom of your screen, the site is secure.** Also, the web address will change from http://www to https://www. This means that your credit card number will be encrypted (changed so that others can't read it). **If the site isn't secure, don't enter your credit card information.**

Pick and Click Shopping@Home

🔒 **If you have kids, don't let them give out personal information.**

🔒 **If you have any doubts about a site's security, contact the store by phone or e-mail.**

🔒 Find out the return policy. **What happens if you don't like the product?**

🔒 Print out and save a record of your purchase. **If there is a problem, the receipt gives you proof of purchase.**

🔒 **If you change your mind about an order, contact the company immediately.**

As you can see, many of these steps are similar to the ones you follow in a "store with doors." Use common sense. **If you take some basic precautions, you shouldn't have any problems.**

Internet shopping has literally brought a world of opportunity to consumers. Today we can shop 24 hours a day, 7 days a week in stores that are halfway around the globe without ever having to leave home or stand in line. As with many things in life, there are some risks. Just remember that online or off—**if an offer seems too good to be true, it probably is**. Happy cyber shopping!

"Now think long and hard Samantha. What else exactly did you purchase online with Daddy's credit card details?"

AFTER YOU READ

Write **T** *(true) or* **F** *(false).*

_____ **1.** The largest mall in the world is in Canada.

_____ **2.** You can buy a diamond necklace online.

_____ **3.** It's best to use a credit card when shopping online.

_____ **4.** The author of the article thinks cyber shopping is very dangerous.

_____ **5.** You can't trust all online offers.

Grammar Presentation

PRESENT REAL CONDITIONALS

Statements	
If Clause	Result Clause
If I **shop** online,	I **save** time.
If the mall **is** closed,	I **can shop** online.

Statements	
Result Clause	*If* Clause
I **save** time	**if** I **shop** online.
I **can shop** online	**if** the mall **is** closed.

Yes / No Questions	
Result Clause	*If* Clause
Do you **save** time	**if** you **shop** online?
Can you **shop** online	**if** the mall **is** closed?

Short Answers			
Affirmative		Negative	
Yes,	I **do**.	No,	I **don't**.
	I **can**.		I **can't**.

Wh- Questions	
Result Clause	*If* Clause
What **happens**	**if** I **don't like** it?

GRAMMAR NOTES

EXAMPLES

1. Use **present real conditional** sentences for **general truths**.

The *if* clause talks about the condition, and the result clause talks about what happens if the condition occurs.

Use the simple present in both clauses.

USAGE NOTE: We often use *even if* when the result is surprising.

- *if* clause   result clause
  If it**'s** a holiday, the store **is** closed.
- *if* clause   result clause
  If you **use** a credit card, it**'s** faster.

- ***Even if*** it's a holiday, this store stays open.

2. You can also use **real conditional** sentences for **habits** and things that happen again and again.

Use the simple present or present progressive in the *if* clause. Use the simple present in the result clause.

You can often use ***when*** instead of ***if***. This is especially true when you talk about general truths, habits, and things that happen again and again.

- **If** Bill **shops** online, he **uses** a credit card.

- **If** I**'m surfing** the Web, I **use** Google.

- ***When*** Bill **shops** online, he **uses** a credit card.
- ***When*** I**'m surfing** the Web, I **use** Google.

3. You can use **modals** (*can, should, might, must . . .*) in the result clause.

- If you don't like the product, you *can* **return** it.
- If you have children, you *shouldn't* **let** them shop online.

---

4. Use the **imperative** in the result clause to give **instructions**, **commands**, and **invitations** that depend on a certain condition.

Usage note: We sometimes use *then* to emphasize the result in real conditional sentences with imperatives or modals.

- If you change your mind, **call** the company.
- If a site isn't secure, **don't enter** your credit card information.

- If you change your mind, *then* **call** the company.
- If a site isn't secure, *then* **don't enter** your credit card information.

---

5. You can begin conditional sentences with the *if* clause or the result clause. The meaning is the same.

▶ Be careful! Use a comma between the two clauses only when the *if* clause comes first.

- **If I shop online,** I save time.
    OR
- I save time **if I shop online**.

Focused Practice

1 | DISCOVER THE GRAMMAR

Read these shopping tips. In each real conditional sentence, underline the result clause once. Underline the clause that expresses the condition twice.

KNOW BEFORE YOU GO

   You're shopping in a foreign city. Should you pay full price, or should you bargain? If you don't know the answer, you can pay too much or miss a fun experience. Bargaining is one of the greatest shopping pleasures if you know how to do it. The strategies are different in different places. Check out these tips before you go.

Hong Kong

   Hong Kong is one of the world's greatest shopping cities. If you like to bargain, you can do it anywhere except the larger department stores. The trick is not to look too interested. If you see something you want, pick it up along with some other items and ask the prices. Then make an offer below what you are willing to pay. If the seller's offer is close to the price you want, then you should be able to reach an agreement quickly.

(continued)

Italy

Bargaining in Italy is appropriate at outdoor markets and with street vendors. In stores, you can politely ask for a discount if you want to bargain. Take your time. Make conversation if you speak Italian. Show your admiration for the object by picking it up and pointing out its wonderful features. When you hear the price, look sad. Make your own offer. End the bargaining politely if you can't agree.

Mexico

In Mexico, people truly enjoy bargaining. There are some clear rules, though. You should bargain only if you really are interested in buying the object. If the vendor's price is far more than you want to pay, then politely stop the negotiation. If you know your price is reasonable, walking away will often bring a lower offer.

Remember, bargaining is always a social interaction, not an argument. And it can still be fun even if you don't get the item you want at the price you want to pay.

---

2 | IF YOU'RE SHOPPING IN . . . Grammar Notes 1–4

Read this online forum about shopping around the world. Write conditional sentences to summarize the advice.

1. Hong Kong

Q: I want to buy some traditional crafts. Any ideas?

A: You ought to visit the Western District on Hong Kong Island. It's famous for its crafts.

If you want to buy some traditional crafts, you ought to visit the Western District on Hong Kong Island.

2. Barcelona

Q: I'd like to buy some nice but inexpensive clothes. Where can I go?

A: Take the train to open air markets in towns *outside* of the city. They have great stuff.

_____

3. Rome

Q: I'm looking for a shopping mall. Are there any in Rome?

A: You need to go away from the city center. But I think the small shops are nicer.

_____

4. Istanbul

Q: I want to go shopping in the Grand Bazaar. Is it open on Sunday?

A: You have to go during the week. It's closed on Sunday.

_____

5. New York

> Q: I want to buy some unusual gifts. Any suggestions?
>
> A: Shop in Soho. The neighborhood has lots of very interesting stores.

---

6. Bangkok

> Q: My son wants to buy computer games. Where should he go?
>
> A: He should try the Panthip Plaza. The selection is huge.

---

7. Mexico City

> Q: I plan to buy some silver jewelry in Mexico. Any tips?
>
> A: You should be able to get something nice at a very good price. Try bargaining.

---

8. London

> Q: I'd like to find some nice secondhand clothing shops. Can you help me?
>
> A: Try the Portobello market on the weekend. Happy shopping!

---

3 | FREQUENT BUYER
Grammar Notes 1–2, 5

Complete the interview with Claudia Leggett, a fashion buyer. Combine the two sentences in parentheses to make a real conditional sentence. Keep the same order and decide which clause begins with **if**. *Make necessary changes in capitalization and punctuation.*

INTERVIEWER: Is understanding fashion the most important thing for a career as a buyer?

LEGGETT: It is. *If you don't understand fashion, you don't belong in this field.*
1. (You don't understand fashion. You don't belong in this field.)

But buyers need other skills too.

INTERVIEWER: Such as?

LEGGETT: _____
2. (You can make better decisions. You have good business skills.)

INTERVIEWER: "People skills" must be important too.

LEGGETT: True. _____
3. (A buyer needs great interpersonal skills. She's negotiating prices.)

(continued)

INTERVIEWER: Do you travel in your business?

LEGGETT: A lot! _____
4. (There's a big international fashion fair. I'm usually there.)

INTERVIEWER: Why fashion fairs?

LEGGETT: Thousands of professionals attend. _____
5. (I go to a fair. I can see hundreds of products in a few days.)

_____

INTERVIEWER: You just got back from the Leipzig fair, didn't you?

LEGGETT: Yes, and I went to Paris and Madrid too. _____
6. (I usually stay two weeks. I travel to Europe.)

_____

INTERVIEWER: Does your family ever go with you?

LEGGETT: Often. _____
7. (My husband can come. He and our son, Pietro, do things together.)

_____
8. (Pietro comes to the fair with me. My husband can't get away.)
Next week, we're all going to Hong Kong.

INTERVIEWER: What do you do when you're not at a fashion fair?

LEGGETT: _____
9. (I always go shopping. I have free time.)

4 | WHEN IT'S NOON IN MONTREAL . . . *Grammar Note 2*

Look at the chart. Write sentences about the cities with clocks. Use the words in parentheses and **when**.
Note: The light clocks show daylight hours; the shaded clocks show evening or nighttime hours.

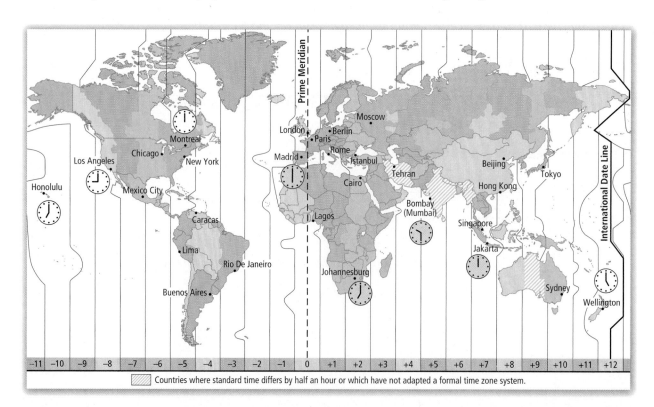

1. <u>When it's noon in Montreal, it's midnight in Jakarta.</u>
   (be noon / be midnight)

2. <u>When stores are opening in Los Angeles, they're closing in Johannesburg.</u>
   (stores open / stores close)

3. _____
   (people watch the sun rise / people watch the sun set)

4. _____
   (be midnight / be 6:00 P.M.)

5. _____
   (people eat lunch / people eat dinner)

6. _____
   (people get up / people go to bed)

7. _____
   (be 7:00 A.M. / be 7:00 P.M.)

8. _____
   (be 5:00 A.M. / be 9:00 A.M.)

5 | EDITING

Read Claudia's e-mail message. There are eight mistakes in the use of present real conditionals. The first mistake is already corrected. Find and correct seven more. Don't forget to check punctuation.

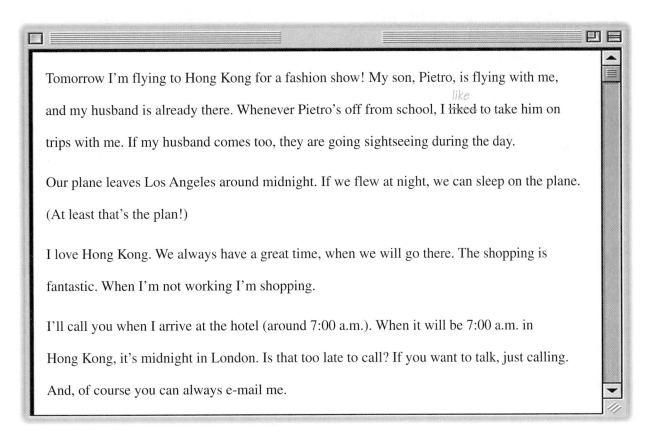

Tomorrow I'm flying to Hong Kong for a fashion show! My son, Pietro, is flying with me,

and my husband is already there. Whenever Pietro's off from school, I ~~liked~~ *like* to take him on

trips with me. If my husband comes too, they are going sightseeing during the day.

Our plane leaves Los Angeles around midnight. If we flew at night, we can sleep on the plane.

(At least that's the plan!)

I love Hong Kong. We always have a great time, when we will go there. The shopping is

fantastic. When I'm not working I'm shopping.

I'll call you when I arrive at the hotel (around 7:00 a.m.). When it will be 7:00 a.m. in

Hong Kong, it's midnight in London. Is that too late to call? If you want to talk, just calling.

And, of course you can always e-mail me.

Communication Practice

6 | LISTENING

🎧 *Claudia and her ten-year-old son, Pietro, are flying from Los Angeles to Hong Kong by way of Taipei. First, read the situations below. Then listen to the announcements. Listen again and check the correct box.*

	True	False
1. Claudia has two pieces of carry-on luggage and Pietro has one. They can take them on the plane.	☑	☐

2. These are their boarding passes:

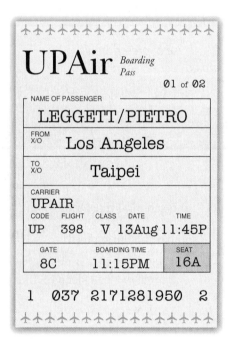

They can board now.	☐	☐
3. Look at their boarding passes again. They can board now.	☐	☐
4. Pietro is a child. Claudia should put his oxygen mask on first.	☐	☐
5. Claudia is sitting in a left-hand window seat. She can see the lights of Tokyo.	☐	☐
6. Claudia needs information about their connecting flight. She can get this information on the plane.	☐	☐

7 | TRAVELING IN COMFORT

Work in small groups. Discuss what you do to stay comfortable when you travel. Talk about traveling by car, bus, train, and plane.

Example: A: When I travel by car, I stop every three hours.
B: I always dress comfortably when I travel by car.

8 | INFORMATION GAP: IF YOU GO . . .

Work in pairs (A and B). Student B, go to page 325 and follow the instructions there. Student A, ask Student B questions to complete the chart below. Answer Student B's questions.

	Best Time to Go	Currency	Time: When it's noon in New York . . .
Caracas, Venezuela	*December–April*	bolívar	
Istanbul, Turkey			8:00 P.M.
Rio de Janeiro, Brazil	April–October		2:00 P.M.
Seoul, South Korea		won	2:00 A.M.*
Vancouver, Canada	July–September		9:00 A.M.
Moscow, Russia		ruble	

*the next day

Example: A: If you travel to Caracas, what's the best time to go?
B: December through April.
What kind of currency do you need if you go there?
A: The bolívar.
When it's noon in New York, what time is it in Caracas?

When you are finished, compare charts. Are they the same?

9 | SHOPPING TIPS

Work in small groups. Discuss what you do when you want to make an important purchase (a gift, a camera, a car).

> **Example:** **A:** If I want to buy a camera, I check prices online.
> **B:** When I buy a camera, I always ask friends for recommendations.

10 | PROS AND CONS

Work in a small group. Look at the cartoon. What are some of the differences between shopping in a "store with doors" and shopping online? What are the advantages and disadvantages of each?

> **Example:** **A:** If you shop for clothes in a store, you can try them on first.
> **B:** But you have a lot more choices if you shop online.

11 | WRITING

Work in pairs. Imagine that you are preparing an information sheet for tourists about your city or town. Write a list of tips for visitors. Use present real conditional sentences. Compare your list with another pair's.

> **Example:** If you like to shop, Caterville has the biggest mall in this part of the country.
> If you enjoy swimming or boating, you should visit Ocean Park.

12 | ON THE INTERNET

Work in pairs. Decide on something you'd both like to buy (a pair of jeans, a camera, a car). Then check prices for the item at different online stores. Compare your information with your partner's.

> **Example:** **A:** If you buy the camera from Digital World, it costs $280. It's cheaper if you buy it from Gizmos.
> **B:** But you have to pay shipping if you buy it from Gizmos.

INFORMATION GAP FOR STUDENT B

Student B, answer Student A's questions. Then ask Student A questions to complete the chart below.

	Best Time to Go	Currency	Time: When it's noon in New York . . .
Caracas, Venezuela	December–April	*bolívar*	1:00 P.M.
Istanbul, Turkey	April–October	Turkish lira	
Rio de Janeiro, Brazil		real	
Seoul, South Korea	October–March		
Vancouver, Canada		Canadian dollar	
Moscow, Russia	May–September		8:00 P.M.

Example: **A:** If you travel to Caracas, what's the best time to go?
B: December through April.
What kind of currency do you need if you go there?
A: The bolívar.
When it's noon in New York, what time is it in Caracas?

When you are finished, compare charts. Are they the same?

22 Future Real Conditionals

Grammar in Context

BEFORE YOU READ

Look at the pictures. What is a superstition? Can you give an example of one? Do you believe in any superstitions? Do you wear or carry things that make you feel lucky? Read this magazine article about superstitions.

KNOCK ON WOOD!

If you knock on wood, you'll keep bad luck away.

You'll get a good grade on the test if you wear your shirt inside out.

You'll get a bad grade unless you use your lucky pen.

Superstitions sound silly, but millions of people all over the world believe in their power to bring good luck or prevent bad luck. Many cultures share similar superstitions:

> ♣ If you break a mirror, you'll have seven years of bad luck.
> ♣ If the palm of your hand itches, you're going to get some money.
> ♣ If it rains when you move to a new house, you'll get rich.

All superstitions are based on a cause and effect relationship: **If X happens, then Y will also happen.** However, in superstitions, the cause is magical and unrelated to the effect. In our scientific age, why are these beliefs so powerful and widespread? The Luck Project, an online survey of superstitious behaviors, gives us some fascinating insight. Here are some of the findings:

❧ Emotions can influence superstitions, especially in uncertain situations where people do not have control. **People will react more superstitiously if they are worried. They will feel less superstitious if they aren't feeling a strong need for control**.

❧ We make our own luck. **If you believe you're lucky, you will carry out superstitions that make you feel good** (crossing your fingers for luck, for example). You probably won't fear bad luck superstitions. In contrast, **you will expect the worst if you think you're unlucky**.

❧ More people than you might think believe in superstitions. Of the 4,000 people surveyed, 84 percent knocked on wood for good luck. Almost half feared walking under a ladder. And 15 percent of the people who studied or worked in the sciences feared the number 13.

Clearly, education doesn't "cure" superstition—college students are among the most superstitious people. Other superstitious groups are performers, athletes, gamblers, and stock traders. People in these groups often have personal good luck rituals.

Deanna McBrearty, a New York City Ballet member, has lucky hair bands. **"If I have a good performance when I'm wearing one, I'll keep wearing it,"** she says. Brett Gallagher, a stock trader, believes **he'll be more successful if he owns pet fish**. "I had fish for a while, and after they died the market didn't do so well," he points out.

Will you do better on the test if you use your lucky pen? Maybe. **If the pen makes you feel more confident, you might improve your score**. So go ahead and use it. But don't forget—**your lucky pen will be powerless unless you study**. The harder you work, the luckier you'll get.

AFTER YOU READ

Match the two parts of each sentence. Use information from the article.

_____ **1.** If you are worrying about something,   **a.** you'll have more good luck superstitions.

_____ **2.** If you feel you're lucky,   **b.** you might act more superstitious.

_____ **3.** If you study science,   **c.** your good luck pen won't work.

_____ **4.** If you don't study,   **d.** you could still be superstitious.

Grammar Presentation

FUTURE REAL CONDITIONALS

Statements	
If Clause: Present	Result Clause: Future
If she **studies**,	she **won't fail** the test. she**'s going to pass** the test.
If she **doesn't study**,	she**'ll fail** the test. she **isn't going to pass** the test.

Yes / No Questions	
Result Clause: Future	*If* Clause: Present
Will she **pass** the test **Is** she **going to pass** the test	**if** she **studies**?

Short Answers			
Affirmative		Negative	
Yes,	she **will**. she **is**.	**No,**	she **won't**. she **isn't**.

Wh- Questions	
Result Clause: Future	*If* Clause: Present
What **will** she **do** What **is** she **going to do**	**if** she **passes** the test?

GRAMMAR NOTES

EXAMPLES

1. Use **future real conditional** sentences to talk about what will happen under certain conditions. The *if* clause gives the condition. The result clause gives the probable or certain result.

   Use the simple present in the *if* clause.

   Use the future with ***will*** or ***be going to*** in the result clause.

   if clause   result clause
   - **If** I **use** this pen, **I'll pass** the test.
     (It's a real possibility that I will use this pen.)
   - **If** you **feel** lucky, you**'ll expect** good things.
   - **If** you **feel** unlucky, you**'ll expect** the worst.

2. You can use **modals** (*can, should, might, must . . .*) in the result clause.

   ▶ **BE CAREFUL!** Even though the *if* clause refers to the future, use the simple present.

   - If she studies hard, she ***might get*** an A on her test.

   - **If** she **gets** an A on her test, she will stop worrying.
     NOT If she ~~will get~~ an A on her test, she will stop worrying.

3. You can begin conditional sentences with the *if* clause or the result clause. The meaning is the same.

▶ **BE CAREFUL!** Use a comma between the two clauses only when the *if* clause comes first.

- ***If she uses that pen,*** she'll feel lucky.

OR

- She'll feel lucky ***if she uses that pen***.

4. You can use ***if*** and ***unless*** in conditional sentences, but their meanings are very different.

Use ***unless*** to state a **negative condition**.

Unless often has the same meaning as ***if . . . not***.

- ***If*** he studies, he will pass the test.

- ***Unless*** he studies, he will fail the test. *(If he doesn't study, he will fail the test.)*

- ***Unless*** you're superstitious, you won't be afraid of black cats.

OR

- ***If*** you are***n't*** superstitious, you won't be afraid of black cats.

Focused Practice

1 | DISCOVER THE GRAMMAR

Match the conditions with the results.

Condition

_d_ **1.** If I lend someone my baseball bat,

____ **2.** If it rains,

____ **3.** If I give my boyfriend a new pair of shoes,

____ **4.** If the palm of your hand itches,

____ **5.** If I use my lucky pen,

____ **6.** If you wear your sweater backwards,

Result

a. you could have an allergy.

b. people might laugh at you.

c. I'll get a good grade on the test.

d. I won't hit a home run.

e. I'm going to get wet.

f. he'll walk out of the relationship.

Now write the sentences that are superstitions.

1. _If I lend someone my baseball bat, I won't hit a home run._

2. _____

3. _____

2 | SUPERSTITIOUS STUDENTS

Grammar Note 4

*Two students are talking about a test. Complete their conversations with **if** or **unless**.*

1. YUKI: It's midnight. __Unless__ we get some sleep, we won't do well tomorrow.

   EVA: But I won't be able to sleep _____ I stop worrying about the test.

   YUKI: Here's my rabbit foot. _____ you put it in your pocket, you'll do fine!

2. EVA: I found my blue shirt! _____ I wear my blue shirt today, I know I'll pass!

   YUKI: Great. Now _____ we just clean up the room, we can leave for school.

   EVA: We can't clean up! There's a Russian superstition that says: _____ you clean your

   room, you'll get a bad test grade!

3. YUKI: _____ we finish the test by noon, we can go to the job fair.

   EVA: I want to get a job, but nobody is going to hire me _____ I pass this test.

4. EVA: I'm looking for my lucky pen. _____ I find it, I won't pass the test!

   YUKI: Don't worry. _____ you use the same pen that you used to study with, you'll do

   great! The pen will remember the answers.

5. EVA: I was so nervous without my lucky pen. It'll be a miracle _____ I pass.

   YUKI: I don't believe in miracles! _____ you study, you'll do well. It's that simple.

6. EVA: Do you think Eastward will offer me a job _____ I fill out an application?

   YUKI: Only _____ you use your lucky pen. I'm kidding! You won't know

   _____ you try!

3 | A WORLD OF SUPERSTITIONS

Grammar Note 1

Complete the superstitions. Use the correct form of the verbs in parentheses.

- If you _____*spill*_____ salt at the breakfast table, you _____*'ll have*_____ an
        1. (spill)   2. (have)

  argument. *(Russia)*

- If a cat _____ behind its ears, it _____. *(England)*
                 3. (wash)   4. (rain)

- If you _____ under a ladder, you _____ bad
                 5. (walk)   6. (have)

  luck. *(North America)*

- If you _____ the dirt and dust out of your house through the front door, you
  7. (sweep)

  _____ away your family's good luck.   *(China)*
  8. (sweep)

- If your right hand _____ itchy, you _____ money.
  9. (be)   10. (get)

  If your left hand _____, you _____ money.   *(Greece)*
  11. (itch)   12. (give)

- If somebody _____ away a dead mouse, the wind _____ to blow
  13. (throw)   14. (start)

  from that direction.   *(Iceland)*

- If you _____ at the corner of the table, you _____
  15. (sit)   16. (not get)

  married.   *(Slovakia)*

- If you _____ red beans at a newly married couple, they _____ good
  17. (throw)   18. (have)

  luck.   *(Mexico)*

4 | YOU'LL BE SORRY
Grammar Notes 1 and 3

*Eva is thinking of working for Eastward. Her friend Don, who used to work there, thinks it's
a terrible idea. Write his responses. Use the words in parentheses and future real
conditional sentences.*

1. EVA: If I work for Eastward, I'm going to be happy. I'm sure of it.

   DON: *If you work for Eastward, you're not going to be happy. You're going to be miserable.*
   (miserable)

2. EVA: You're such a pessimist! I'll have the chance to travel a lot if I take this job.

   DON: Not true. _____
   (never leave the office)

3. EVA: But I'll get a raise every year if I stay at Eastward.

   DON: _____
   (every two years)

4. EVA: Well, if I join Eastward, I'm going to have wonderful health care benefits.

   DON: Stay healthy! _____
   (terrible health care benefits)

5. EVA: If I go to Eastward, I'll have helpful co-workers.

   DON: _____
   (uncooperative)

6. EVA: I don't believe you! If I accept Eastward's offer, it will be the best career move of my life.

   DON: Believe me, _____
   (the worst)

5 | WHAT IF . . .

Yuki Tamari is not sure whether to go to law school. She made a decision tree to help her decide. In the tree, arrows connect the conditions and the results. Write future real conditional sentences about her decision. Use **may**, **might**, *or* **could** *if the result is uncertain.*

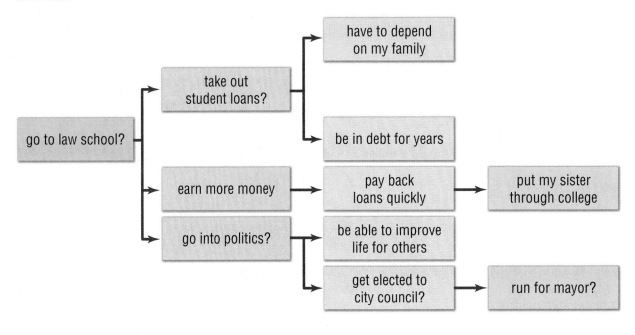

1. *If I go to law school, I might take out student loans.*

2. *I'll be in debt for years if I take out student loans.*

3. _____

4. _____

5. _____

6. _____

7. _____

8. _____

9. _____

10. _____

6 | EDITING

Read Yuki's journal entry. There are seven mistakes in the use of future real conditionals. The first mistake is already corrected. Find and correct six more. Don't forget to check punctuation.

October 1

    Should I campaign for student council president? I'll have to decide soon if I ~~wanted~~ want to run. If I'll be busy campaigning, I won't have much time to study. That's a problem because I'm not going to get into law school if I get good grades this year. On the other hand, there's so much to do in this school, and nothing is getting done if Todd Laker becomes president again. A lot of people know that. But will I know what to do if I'll get the job? Never mind. I'll deal with that problem, if I win. If I become president, I cut my hair. That always brings me good luck.

Communication Practice

7 | LISTENING

Yuki is talking about her campaign platform. Listen to the interview. Then read the list of issues. Listen again and check the things that Yuki promises to work for if she is elected.

☑ **1.** have contact with a lot of students

☐ **2.** improve the student council's newsletter

☐ **3.** publish teacher evaluations on the student council's website

☐ **4.** get the college to provide a bus service from the airport

☐ **5.** get the college to offer a major in environmental science

☐ **6.** reduce tuition costs

8 | SOLUTIONS

*Work in pairs. Read these problems and discuss possible solutions. Use **if**, **if . . . not**, or* **unless**.

1. Your neighbors are always playing music so loudly that you can't fall asleep.

   Example: If they don't stop, I'll call the police.
   Unless they stop, I'll call the landlord.
   I'll consider moving if they continue to bother me.

2. You've had a headache every day for a week. You can't concentrate.

3. You keep phoning your parents, but there is no answer. It's now midnight.

4. You like your job, but you just found out that other workers are making much more money than you are.

5. You live in an apartment building. It's winter and the building hasn't had any heat for a week. You're freezing.

6. You're 10 pounds overweight. You've been trying for months to lose weight, but so far you haven't lost a single pound.

7. You bought a radio at a local store. It doesn't work, but when you tried to return it, the salesperson refused to take it back.

8. Your roommates don't clean up after they cook. You've already reminded them several times, but they always "forget."

9. You paid for a parking space near school or work. For the past week the same car has taken your space.

9 | GOOD LUCK / BAD LUCK

Here are some superstitions about luck. Work in small groups and discuss similar superstitions that you know about.

- If you cross your fingers, you'll have good luck.

  Example: In Germany, people believe that if you press your thumbs together, you will have good luck.

- If you touch blue, your dreams will come true.

- If you break a mirror, you will have seven years of bad luck.

- If you put a piece of clothing on inside out, you will have good luck.

- If your palm itches, you're going to find some money soon.

10 | WRITING

Imagine you are running for class or school president. Write a short speech. Include five campaign promises. Use future real conditionals. In small groups, give your speeches and elect a candidate. Then hold a general class election.

Example: If I become school president, I will ask for 10 new computers . . .

11 | ON THE INTERNET

Do a search for information about superstitions in different cultures. Share your information with a group. Do different cultures have any similar superstitions?

Example: **A:** In Canada, some people believe that if a black cat walks across your path, you'll have bad luck.
B: That's a common superstition in Turkey too.

Grammar in Context

BEFORE YOU READ

🎧 *Read the first sentence of the story and look at the picture. Is this a true story? How do fairy tales begin in your culture? Read this version of a famous fairy tale.*

The Fisherman and His Wife

Once upon a time there was a poor fisherman and his wife who lived in a pigpen near the sea. Every day the man went to fish. One day, after waiting a very long time, he caught a very big fish. To his surprise, the fish spoke and said, "Please let me live. I'm not a regular fish. **If you knew my real identity, you wouldn't kill me**. I'm an enchanted prince."

"Don't worry. I won't kill you," said the kind-hearted fisherman. With these words, he threw the fish back into the clear water, and went home to his wife.

"Husband," said the wife, "didn't you catch anything today?"

"I caught a fish, but it said it was an enchanted prince, so I let it go."

"You mean you didn't wish for anything?" asked the wife.

"No," said the fisherman. "What do I need to wish for?"

"Just look around you," said the wife. "We live in a pigpen. **I wish we had a nice little cottage. If we had a cottage, I would be a lot happier**. You saved the prince's life. Go back and ask him for it."

"I'm not going to ask for a cottage! **If I asked for a cottage, the fish might get angry**." But in the end, the fisherman was more afraid of his wife's anger.

When he got to the sea, it was all green and yellow. "**My wife wishes we had a cottage**," said the fisherman. "Just go on back," said the fish. "She already has it."

When he returned home, the fisherman found his wife sitting outside a lovely little cottage. The kitchen was filled with food and all types of cooking utensils. Outside was a little garden with vegetables, fruit trees, hens, and ducks.

Things were fine for a week or two. Then the wife said, "This cottage is much too crowded. **I wish we lived in a bigger house. If we lived in a big stone castle, I would be much happier**. Go and ask the fish for it."

The fisherman didn't want to go, but he did. When he got to the sea, it was dark blue and gray. "**My wife wishes we lived in a big stone castle**," he said to the fish.

"Just go on back. She's standing in front of the door," said the fish.

When he returned home, the fisherman found his wife on the steps of a great big stone castle. The inside was filled with beautiful gold furniture, chandeliers, and carpets. There were servants everywhere.

The next morning the wife woke up and said, "**I wish I were King of all this land**."

"**What would you do if you were King?**" asked her husband. "**If I were King, I would own all this land**. Go on back and ask the fish for it."

This time, the sea was all blackish gray, and the water was rough and smelled terrible. "What does she want now?" asked the fish.

"She wants to be King," said the embarrassed fisherman.

"Just go on back. She already is."

When the fisherman returned home, he found an enormous palace. Everything inside was made of marble and pure gold,

and it was surrounded by soldiers with drums and trumpets. His wife was seated on a throne, and he said to her, "How nice for you that you are King. Now we won't need to wish for anything else."

But his wife was not satisfied. "I'm only King of *this* country," she said. "**I wish I were Emperor of the whole world. If I were Emperor, I would be the most powerful ruler on Earth**."

"Wife, now be satisfied," said the fisherman. "You're King. You can't be anything more."

The wife, however, wasn't convinced. She kept thinking and thinking about what more she could be. "**If I were Emperor, I could have anything—and you wouldn't have to ask the fish for anything more**. Go right now and tell the fish that I want to be Emperor of the world."

"Oh, no," said the fisherman. "The fish can't do that. **If I were you, I wouldn't ask for anything else**." But his wife got so furious that the poor fisherman ran back to the fish. There was a terrible storm, and the sea was pitch black with waves as high as mountains. "Well, what does she want now?" asked the fish.

"**She wishes she were Emperor of the whole world**," said the fisherman.

"Just go on back. She's sitting in the pigpen again."

And they are still sitting there today.

AFTER YOU READ

*Write **T** (true) or **F** (false).*

_____ 1. Before the man caught the fish, he and his wife lived in a nice little cottage.

_____ 2. At first, the fish believed that the man was going to kill him.

_____ 3. The man didn't want to ask for the first wish because he didn't want to make the fish angry.

_____ 4. The wife was satisfied with the stone castle.

_____ 5. The man advised his wife not to ask to be Emperor of the whole world.

Grammar Presentation

PRESENT AND FUTURE UNREAL CONDITIONALS

Statements	
If Clause: Simple Past	Result Clause: *Would* (*not*) + Base Form
If Mia **had** money, **If** she **were*** rich,	she **would live** in a palace. she **wouldn't live** in a cottage.
If Mia **didn't have** money, **If** she **weren't** rich,	she **wouldn't live** in a palace. she **would live** in a cottage.

*With the verb *be*, use *were* for all subjects.

Contractions		
I would	=	**I'd**
you would	=	**you'd**
he would	=	**he'd**
she would	=	**she'd**
we would	=	**we'd**
they would	=	**they'd**
would not	=	**wouldn't**

Yes / No Questions	
Result Clause	*If* Clause
Would she **live** here	**if** she **had** money? **if** she **were** rich?

Short Answers	
Affirmative	Negative
Yes, she **would**.	**No**, she **wouldn't**.

Wh- Questions	
Result Clause	*If* Clause
What **would** she **do**	**if** she **had** money? **if** she **were** rich?

GRAMMAR NOTES

EXAMPLES

---

1. Use **present and future unreal conditional** sentences to talk about unreal conditions and their results. A condition and its result may be untrue, imagined, or impossible.

The sentence can be about:

a. the **present**

OR

b. the **future**

The *if* clause gives the unreal condition, and the result clause gives the unreal result of that condition.

if clause   result clause
- **If** I **had** more time, I **would read** fairy tales to my children.
  (But I don't have time, so I don't read fairy tales to my children.)

if clause   result clause
- If I **lived** in a palace *now*, I **would give** parties all the time.
  (But I don't live in a palace now, so I don't give parties all the time.)

if clause   result clause
- If I **moved** *next month*, I **would buy** new furniture.
  (But I'm not going to move next month, so I won't buy new furniture.)

---

2. Use the **simple past** in the *if* clause.

Use *would*, *might*, or *could* + **base form** of the verb in the result clause.

▶ **BE CAREFUL!**

a. The *if* clause uses the simple past, but the meaning is not past.

b. Don't use *would* in the *if* clause.

c. Use *were* for all subjects when the verb in the *if* clause is a form of *be*.

USAGE NOTE: Some people use *was* with *I*, *he*, *she*, and *it*. However, many people think this is incorrect.

- **If** they **had** a nice house, they **wouldn't want** to move.

- **If** I **had** more money *now*, I would take a trip around the world.

- **If** she **knew** the answer, she would tell you.
  NOT If she ~~would know~~ the answer . . .

- **If** I **were** King, I would make you Prime Minister.
  NOT If I ~~was~~ King . . .

(continued)

3. Use *would* in the result clause if the result is <u>certain</u>. Do not use *will* in unreal conditional sentences.

- They love to travel. If they had time, they *would* take a trip next summer.

Use *might* or *could* in the result clause if the result is <u>not certain</u>. Do not use *may* and *can*.

- They've never been to Asia. If they took a trip, they *might* go to Japan.

  OR

- If they took a trip, they *could* go to Japan.

You can also use *could* in the result clause to express <u>ability</u>.

- You don't know Japanese. If you knew Japanese, you *could* translate this article for them.

---

4. You can begin conditional sentences with the *if* clause or the result clause. The meaning is the same.

- **If I had more money,** I would move.

  OR

- I would move **if I had more money.**

▶ **BE CAREFUL!** Use a comma between the two clauses only when the *if* clause comes first.

---

5. Use *If I were you*, . . . to give **advice**.

- **If I were you**, I wouldn't ask the fish for anything else. He could get angry.

---

6. Use *wish* + **simple past** to talk about things that you want to be true now, but that are not true.

- I **wish** I **lived** in a castle.
  (*I don't live in a castle now, but I want to live in one.*)
- I **wish** we **had** a yacht.
  (*We don't have a yacht now, but I want one.*)

Use *were* instead of *was* after *wish*.

- I **wish** I *were* a child again.
  NOT I wish I ~~was~~ a child again.

Use *could* or *would* after *wish*. Don't use *can* or *will*.

- I **wish** I *could* **buy** a car.
  NOT I wish I ~~can~~ buy a car.
- I **wish** she *would* **call** tomorrow.
  NOT I wish she ~~will~~ call tomorrow.

Focused Practice

1 | DISCOVER THE GRAMMAR

*Read the numbered statements. Decide if the sentences that follow are true (**T**) or false (**F**).*

1. If I had time, I would read fairy tales in English.

    __F__ **a.** I have time.

    __F__ **b.** I'm going to read fairy tales in English.

2. If it weren't so cold, I would go fishing.

    _____ **a.** It's cold.

    _____ **b.** I'm going fishing.

3. If I caught an enchanted fish, I would make three wishes.

    _____ **a.** I believe I'm going to catch an enchanted fish.

    _____ **b.** I'm going to make three wishes.

4. If I had three wishes, I wouldn't ask for a palace.

    _____ **a.** I have three wishes.

    _____ **b.** I don't want a palace.

5. If my house were too small, I would try to find a bigger one.

    _____ **a.** My house is big enough.

    _____ **b.** I'm not looking for a bigger house right now.

6. If I got a raise, I could buy a new car.

    _____ **a.** I recently got a raise.

    _____ **b.** I want a new car.

7. If we didn't earn enough money, I might train for a better job.

    _____ **a.** We don't earn enough money.

    _____ **b.** I'm training for a better job.

8. Your friend tells you, "If I were you, I wouldn't change jobs."

    _____ **a.** Your friend is giving you advice.

    _____ **b.** Your friend thinks you shouldn't change jobs.

9. I wish I were a princess.

    _____ **a.** I'm a princess.

    _____ **b.** I want to be a princess.

10. I wish I lived in a big house.

    _____ **a.** I want to live in a big house.

    _____ **b.** I don't live in a big house.

2 | ABRACADABRA?

Complete this article from a popular psychology magazine. Use the correct form of the verbs.

Marty Hijab has always wanted to invite his whole family over for the

holidays, but his apartment is small, and his family is very large.

"If I _____*invited*_____ them all for dinner, there
    1. (invite)

_____ enough room for everyone to sit down," he
    2. (not be)

told a friend. If Marty _____ a complainer, he
                        3. (be)

_____ about the size of his apartment and spend the
    4. (moan)

holiday at his parents' house. But Marty is a problem solver. This

year he is hosting an open house. People can drop in at different

times during the day, and there will be room for everyone.

"If life _____ a fairy tale, we
             5. (be)

_____ problems away," noted therapist Joel Grimes.
    6. (can / wish)

"What complainers are really saying is, 'If I _____ a magical solution, I
                                                7. (have)

_____ with this myself.' I wish it _____ that easy," says Grimes. He
    8. (not have to deal)   **9. (be)**

gives an example of a very wealthy client who complains about his limited time for his family.

"He's waiting for a miracle to give him the time he needs. But if he _____ about the
                                                                       10. (think)

problem creatively, he _____ the time," says Grimes.
                        11. (can / find)

Even the rich have limited time, money, and space. If complainers _____ this,
                                                                    12. (realize)

then they _____ that there will always be problems. They could then stop
          13. (understand)

complaining and look for solutions. Marty is a student. If he _____ on a bigger
                                                               14. (insist)

apartment for his party, he _____ for years before inviting his family over. Instead,
                             15. (may / have to wait)

he is creatively solving his problems right now.

There's an old saying: "If wishes _____ horses, then beggars
                                    16. (be)

_____." But wishes aren't horses. We have to learn to create our own good fortune
    17. (can / ride)

and not wait for a genie with three wishes to come along and solve our problems.

3 | MAKING EXCUSES

In his practice, psychologist Joel Grimes hears all types of excuses from his clients. Rewrite these excuses using the present unreal conditional.

1. I'm so busy. That's why I don't read bedtime stories to my little girl.

   If I weren't so busy, I would read bedtime stories to my little girl.

2. My husband's not ambitious. That's why he doesn't ask for a raise.

   _____

3. I'm not in shape. That's why I don't play sports.

   _____

4. I don't have enough time. That's why I'm not planning to study for the exam.

   _____

5. I'm too old. That's why I'm not going back to school.

   _____

6. My boss doesn't explain things properly. That's why I can't do my job.

   _____

7. I'm not good at math. That's why I don't balance my checkbook.

   _____

8. I feel nervous all the time. That's why I can't stop smoking.

   _____

9. I'm so tired. That's why I get up so late.

   _____

4 | THE FISH'S WISHES

Remember the fish from the fairy tale on pages 336–337? Read the things the fish would like to change. Then write sentences with **wish**.

1. I'm a fish. *I wish I weren't a fish.* _____

2. I'm not a handsome prince. _____

3. I live in the sea. _____

4. I don't live in a castle. _____

5. I have to swim all day long. _____

6. I am not married to a princess. _____

(continued)

7. The fisherman comes here every day._____

8. His wife always wants more. _____

9. She isn't satisfied. _____

10. They don't leave me alone. _____

5 | WHAT IF?   *Grammar Notes 1–4*

Marty is having his open house holiday party. His nieces and nephews are playing a fantasy question game. Write questions using the present unreal conditional.

1. What / you / do / if / you / be a millionaire?

    What would you do if you were a millionaire?

2. What / you / do / if / you / be the leader of this country?

    _____

3. How / you / feel / if / you / never need to sleep?

    _____

4. What / you / do / if / you / have more free time?

    _____

5. What / you / ask for / if / you / have three wishes?

    _____

6. What / you / do / if / you / not have to work?

    _____

7. Where / you / travel / if / you / have a ticket for anywhere in the world?

    _____

8. If / you / can build anything / what / it / be?

    _____

9. If / you / can meet a famous person / who / you / want to meet?

    _____

10. Who / you / have dinner with / if / you can invite three famous people?

    _____

6 | EDITING

Read part of a book report that Marty's niece wrote. There are eight mistakes in the use of the present unreal conditional. The first mistake is already corrected. Find and correct seven more.

NAME: Laila Hijab   CLASS: English 4

The Disappearance

                                                                    disappeared
What would happen to the women if all the men in the world ~~would disappear~~?
What would happen to the men when there were no women? Philip Wiley's 1951
science-fiction novel, *The Disappearance*, addresses these intriguing questions.
The answers show us how society has changed since the 1950s.

According to Wiley, if men and women live in different worlds, the results would
be catastrophic. In Wiley's vision, men are too aggressive to survive on their
own, and women are too helpless. If women didn't control them, men will start
more wars. If men aren't there to pump gas and run the businesses, women
wouldn't be able to manage.

If Wiley is alive today, would he write the same novel? Today, a lot of men take
care of their children, and a lot of women run businesses. If Wiley were here to
see these changes, he learns that men are not more warlike than women, and
women are not more helpless than men.

I think if all people, both men and women, learned to cooperate more, the world
will be a much better place.

Communication Practice

7 | LISTENING

🎧 *You are going to listen to a modern fairy tale about Cindy, a clever young girl, and a toad. Read the statements and listen to the story. Then listen again and write **T** (true) or **F** (false).*

___F___ **1.** Cindy wishes she had a new soccer ball.

_____ **2.** The toad wishes Cindy would marry him.

_____ **3.** If Cindy married the toad, he would become a prince.

_____ **4.** Cindy wishes she could become a beautiful princess.

_____ **5.** If Cindy became a princess, she'd have plenty of time to study science.

_____ **6.** The toad doesn't know how to use his powers to help himself.

_____ **7.** Cindy wants to become a scientist and help the prince.

_____ **8.** Cindy and the prince get married and live happily ever after.

8 | JUST IMAGINE

Work in small groups. Answer the questions in Exercise 5. Discuss your answers with your classmates.

> **Example:** **A:** What would you do if you were a millionaire?
> **B:** If I were a millionaire, I would donate half my money to charity.

9 | IF I WERE YOU . . .

Work in a group. One person describes a problem. Group members give advice with **If I were you, I would / wouldn't** . . . *Use the problems below and write three more.*

1. You need $500 to pay this month's rent. You only have $300.

> **Example:** **A:** I don't know what to do! I can't pay the rent this month. I only have $300, and I need $500.
> **B:** If I were you, I'd try to borrow the money.
> **C:** If I were you, I'd call the landlord right away.

2. You are lonely. You work at home and never meet new people.

3. You never have an opportunity to practice English outside of class.

4. You have been invited to dinner. You know that the main dish is going to be shrimp. You hate shrimp.

5. _____

6. _____

7. _____

10 | JUST THREE WISHES

In fairy tales, people are often given three wishes. Imagine that you had just three wishes. What would they be? Write them down. Discuss them with a classmate.

Example: 1. I wish I were famous.

2. I wish I spoke perfect English.

3. I wish I knew how to fly a plane.

There is an old saying: "Be careful what you wish for; it may come true." Look at your wishes again. Discuss negative results that might happen if they came true.

Example: If I were famous, I would have no free time. I wouldn't have a private life . . .

11 | WRITING

Reread the book report on page 345. Does Philip Wiley believe men and women should live in separate worlds? What are his arguments? Do you agree with him? Write two paragraphs that support your opinion. Use the present and future unreal conditional.

Example: I don't think men and women should live in separate societies, but sometimes I think that boys and girls would learn better if they went to separate schools. For example, when I was in middle school, boys and girls were embarrassed to make mistakes in front of each other . . .

12 | ON THE INTERNET

Imagine that you have just won $10,000. How would you use the money? Do a search for information about things you would do or buy. Share your information with a group.

Example: If I won $10,000, I would take my parents on a trip to Korea. If we flew Korean Airlines, the tickets would cost about $1,000 each. My brother is in college. He could come too if we went during summer vacation.

Grammar in Context

BEFORE YOU READ

 Look at the photo and the information next to it. What do you think the movie is about? What does the reviewer think of the movie? Read this online movie review.

DVD Movie Guide

It's A Wonderful Life (1946)

Rating: ★★★★ out of ★★★★
Director: Frank Capra
Producer: Frank Capra
Screenplay: Frank Capra, Frances Goodrich, Albert Hacket, and Jo Swerling
Stars: James Stewart, Donna Reed, Lionel Barrymore, Thomas Mitchell, and Henry Travers
Running Time: 129 minutes
Parental Guidelines: suitable for the whole family

Buy this DVD

What would have happened if you had never been born? George Bailey learns the answer in Frank Capra's great movie classic, *It's a Wonderful Life*.

When the movie opens, George is standing on a bridge thinking about suicide. Throughout his life, he has sacrificed his dreams in order to help other people. **He could have gone to college if the family business hadn't needed him. He would have traveled around the world** instead of remaining in his hometown of Bedford Falls. Now, facing a failed business and a possible jail sentence, George decides to end his life by jumping into the river. Enter Clarence, an angel sent to help him. Clarence jumps into the water first, certain that, as always, George will put aside his own problems in order to rescue someone else.

DVD Movie Guide

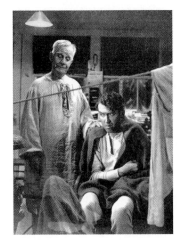

Safely back on land, **George wishes he had never been born**. "I suppose **it would have been better if I had never been born at all**," he tells Clarence. "You've got your wish: You've never been born," responds his guardian angel.

Clarence then teaches George a hard lesson. In a series of painful episodes, he shows him what **life would have been like in Bedford Falls without George Bailey**. George goes back to the site of his mother's home. He finds, instead, an old, depressing boardinghouse. **If George had not supported his mother, she would have become a miserable, overworked boardinghouse owner**. George's own home is a ruin, and his wife, Mary, is living a sad and lonely life. Each scene is more disturbing than the last, until finally we end in a graveyard. We see the grave of George's little brother, Harry. **If George hadn't been alive, he couldn't have saved Harry's life. Harry would have never grown up to be a war hero**, saving the lives of hundreds of soldiers. "Harry wasn't there to save them because you weren't there to save Harry," explains Clarence. "You see, George, you really had a wonderful life."

The ending of the movie delivers a heartwarming holiday message. *It's a Wonderful Life* shows us the importance of each person's life and how each of our lives touches those of others. We see through George's eyes how **the lives of those around him would have been different if he hadn't known them**.

This movie is highly recommended for the whole family.

Buy this DVD

AFTER YOU READ

Check the things that George Bailey did.

- ☐ **1.** helped other people
- ☐ **2.** went to college
- ☐ **3.** traveled around the world
- ☐ **4.** jumped into the river
- ☐ **5.** supported his mother
- ☐ **6.** got married
- ☐ **7.** saved his younger brother's life
- ☐ **8.** became a war hero

George is reunited with his family

Grammar Presentation

PAST UNREAL CONDITIONALS

Statements	
If Clause: Past Perfect	Result Clause: *Would (not) have* + Past Participle
If George **had had** money,	he **would have moved** away. he **wouldn't have stayed** home.
If he **had not stayed** home,	his father's business **would have failed**. he **wouldn't have married** Mary.

Yes / No Questions	
Result Clause	*If* Clause
Would he **have left**	**if** he **had had** money?

Short Answers	
Affirmative	Negative
Yes, he **would have**.	**No**, he **wouldn't have**.

Wh- Questions	
Result Clause	*If* Clause
What **would** he **have done**	**if** he **had had** money?

Contractions		
would have	=	**would've**
would not have	=	**wouldn't have**

GRAMMAR NOTES

1. Use **past unreal conditional** sentences to talk about past unreal conditions and their results. A condition and its result may be untrue, imagined, or impossible.

The *if* clause gives the unreal condition, and the result clause gives the unreal result of that condition.

2. Use the **past perfect** in the *if* clause. Use *would have*, *might have*, or *could have* + past participle in the result clause.

USAGE NOTE: Sometimes speakers use *would have* in the *if* clause. However, many people think this is not correct.

EXAMPLES

if clause   result clause
- **If** he **had died** young, he **wouldn't have had** children.
  (But he didn't die young, so he had children.)
- **If** George **hadn't been born**, many people's lives **would have been** worse.
  (But George was born, so people's lives were better.)

- **If** the film **had won** an Academy Award, it **would have become** famous right away.

- **If** I **had owned** a DVD player, I would have watched the movie. NOT If I ~~would have~~ owned . . .

3. Use **would have** in the result clause if the result is <u>certain</u>. Do not use *will* in unreal conditional sentences.

- If George had gone to college, he **would have** studied hard.

Use **might have** or **could have** in the result clause if the result is <u>not certain</u>. Do not use *may* or *can*.

- If George had gone to college, he **might have** become an architect.

OR

- If George had gone to college, he **could have** become an architect.

You can also use **could have** in the result clause to express **ability**.

- If George had become an architect, he **could have** designed a bridge.

4. You can begin conditional sentences with the *if* clause or the result clause. The meaning is the same.

- **If he had won a million dollars,** he would have traveled around the world.

OR

- He would have traveled around the world **if he had won a million dollars**.

▶ **BE CAREFUL!** Use a comma between the two clauses only when the *if* clause comes first.

5. Past unreal conditionals are often used to **express regret** about what really happened in the past.

- **If I had known** Mary lived alone, I **would have invited** her to my holiday dinner.
  (I regret that I didn't invite her.)

6. Use **wish + past perfect** to express **regret or sadness** about things in the past that you wanted to happen but didn't.

- George **wishes** he **had studied** architecture.
  (He didn't study architecture, and now he thinks that was a mistake.)

Focused Practice

1 | DISCOVER THE GRAMMAR

Read the numbered statements. Decide if the sentences that follow are true (T) or false (F).

1. If I had had time, I would have watched *It's a Wonderful Life*.

     ___T___ **a.** I didn't have time to watch *It's a Wonderful Life*.

     ___F___ **b.** I watched *It's a Wonderful Life*.

2. She would've watched the movie last night if she hadn't seen it before.

     _____ **a.** She watched the movie last night.

     _____ **b.** She saw the movie before.

3. I would have recorded the movie if my DVD recorder had not stopped working.

     _____ **a.** I recorded the movie.

     _____ **b.** My DVD recorder broke.

4. If George Bailey hadn't been depressed, he wouldn't have wanted to jump off the bridge.

     _____ **a.** George was depressed.

     _____ **b.** George wanted to jump off the bridge.

5. If George hadn't saved his brother's life, his brother wouldn't have become a war hero.

     _____ **a.** George didn't save his brother's life.

     _____ **b.** George's brother became a war hero.

6. George wouldn't have met Mary if he had left town.

     _____ **a.** George met Mary.

     _____ **b.** George left town.

7. George would have been happy if he had liked his job.

     _____ **a.** George wasn't happy.

     _____ **b.** George liked his job.

George and Mary

8. George says, "I wish I had traveled around the world."

     _____ **a.** George feels sad that he hasn't traveled around the world.

     _____ **b.** George has traveled around the world.

2 | GEORGE'S THOUGHTS

Complete George's thoughts about the past. Use the correct form of the words in parentheses.

1. I didn't go into business with my friend Sam. If I _____ *had gone* _____ into business
   (go)

   with him, I _____ *might have become* _____ a success.
   (may / become)

2. I couldn't go into the army because I was deaf in one ear. I _____ into
   (go)

   the army if I _____ the hearing in that ear.
   (not lose)

3. Mary and I weren't able to go on a honeymoon. We _____ away if
   (can / go)

   my father _____ sick.
   (not get)

4. My uncle lost $8,000 of the company's money. I _____ so desperate if
   (not feel)

   he _____ the money.
   (find)

5. I'm so unhappy about losing my father's business. I wish I _____

   never _____ born.
   (be)

6. Clarence showed me how the world would look without me. I _____
   (not know)

   that I was so important if Clarence _____ me.
   (not show)

7. If I _____ my brother, he _____ all those
   (not rescue)   (not save)

   lives when he was a soldier.

8. My old boss once almost made a terrible mistake. If I _____ him, he
   (not help)

   _____ to jail.
   (may / go)

9. Mary _____ happy if she _____ me.
   (not be)   (not meet)

10. Many people _____ new homes if we _____ in
    (can't / buy)   (not stay)

    business all these years.

11. Life here really _____ worse if I _____ born.
    (be)   (not be)

3 | REGRETS AND WISHES

These characters in the movie feel bad about some things. Read their regrets. Then write their wishes.

1. **Clarence (the angel):** I wasn't a first-class angel then. I didn't have much self-confidence.

   I wish I had been a first-class angel then.

   I wish I had had more self-confidence.

2. **Mr. Gower (George's childhood employer):** I hit little George when he was trying to help me. I wasn't nice to him.

   _____

   _____

3. **George:** My father had a heart attack. I had to stay and run the business.

   _____

   _____

4. **Mary (George's wife):** We weren't able to go on a honeymoon. We needed the money to save the business.

   _____

   _____

5. **Mr. Potter (the meanest person in town):** I wasn't able to trick George out of his business. He didn't accept my offer to buy his business.

   _____

   _____

6. **Billy (George's uncle):** I lost $8,000. George got into trouble with the law because of me.

   _____

   _____

7. **George's daughter:** Daddy was upset about the business. He yelled at us last night.

   _____

   _____

8. **George's friends:** We didn't know about George's troubles earlier. We didn't help him immediately.

   _____

   _____

4 | MICHAEL J. FOX

Actor Michael J. Fox starred in Back to the Future, *another movie that explores what would have happened if something in the past had been different. Read about Fox. Using the words in parentheses, combine each pair of sentences to make one past unreal conditional sentence.*

1. Michael J. Fox wasn't tall as a teenager. He didn't become a professional hockey player. (might)

   If Michael J. Fox had been tall as a teenager, he might have become a professional hockey player.

2. Fox quit high school in order to act. He didn't graduate. (would)

   _____

   _____

3. Fox moved to Los Angeles. He got several roles on TV. (might)

   _____

4. He met Tracey Pollan on the TV show *Family Ties*. They got married. (might)

   _____

5. Fox was very successful on TV. He got the leading role in *Back to the Future*. (would)

   _____

6. Actor Eric Stolz didn't remain in *Back to the Future*. Fox played the lead. (could)

   _____

7. Fox didn't have free time. He didn't watch old movies and sports on TV. (could)

   _____

8. He became ill. He didn't stay in his TV series *Spin City*. (would)

   _____

9. Fox stopped working. He wrote a book called *Lucky Man* about his life and illness. (might)

   _____

10. He developed Parkinson's disease. He started an organization to search for a cure. (would)

    _____

5 | EDITING

Read this journal entry. There are eight mistakes in the use of the past unreal conditional.
The first mistake is already corrected. Find and correct seven more.

> Tonight we rented the movie <u>Back to the Future</u>. I thought it was great,
> and I usually don't like science fiction movies. I might never ~~had~~ *have* seen it if I
> hadn't read Fox's autobiography, <u>Lucky Man</u>. His book was so good that I
> wanted to see his most famous movie. Now I wish I saw it in the theater
> when it first came out. It would have been better if we would have watched it
> on a big screen. Michael J. Fox was very good. He looked really young-just like a
> teenager. Of course, he still looks very young-I would have recognized him even
> when I hadn't known he was in the film.
>
> In the movie, Marty McFly goes back in time. He wants to change the
> past in order to improve his present life as a teenager. It's a funny idea, but
> it's very different from Fox's real philosophy. He's had a lot of problems in his
> life, but he still calls himself "Lucky Man." As a teenager, he was too small to
> become a professional hockey player-but if he hadn't looked so young, he can't
> have gotten his role in the TV hit series <u>Family Ties</u>. In Hollywood, he had to
> sell his furniture to pay his bills, but he kept trying to find acting jobs. If he
> wouldn't have, he might never have become a star. Getting Parkinson's disease
> was a terrible blow, but he has even turned that into something good. If Fox
> hasn't become sick, he might never had become so close to his family. And he
> wouldn't have started the Michael J. Fox Foundation to help find a cure.

Communication Practice

6 | LISTENING

🎧 *Some friends are discussing a party. Listen to their conversations. Then listen again and circle the letter of the sentence you heard.*

1. **a.** If I had her number, I would call her.
   b. If I'd had her number, I would've called her.

2. **a.** I would've invited him if he'd been in town.
   b. I wouldn't have invited him if he'd been in town.

3. **a.** If he'd changed jobs, he would've gotten the same benefits.
   b. If he'd changed jobs, he wouldn't have gotten the same benefits.

4. **a.** I liked it better on a big screen.
   b. I would've liked it better on a big screen.

5. **a.** I wish David had invited her.
   b. I wish David hadn't invited her.

6. **a.** I would have.
   b. I wouldn't have.

7. **a.** If I'd invited Holly, I would've invited Greg.
   b. If I'd invited Holly, I wouldn't have invited Greg.

8. **a.** If the party had been on a Saturday, they could've come.
   b. If the party hadn't been on a Saturday, they could've come.

7 | WHAT WOULD YOU HAVE DONE?

Read the following situations. In small groups, discuss what you would have done in each situation.

1. Zeke started his business making and selling energy bars* when he was a teenager. Ten years later, a large company offered to buy the business. Zeke turned the offer down because he wanted to make sure Zeke's Bars were always very high quality. If he had accepted, he could have retired rich by age 35. What would you have done?

   Example: **A:** I wouldn't have rejected it. I would've sold the business and started a new one.
   B: Not me. I would have . . .

2. A man was walking down the street when he found ten $100 bills lying on the ground. There was no one else around. He picked them up and put them in his pocket.

3. A woman came home late and found her apartment door unlocked. She was sure she had locked it. No one else had the keys. She went inside.

*Food that gives you energy and that is in the shape of a candy bar.

8 | IF ONLY . . .

With a partner, discuss a situation in your life that you regret. Describe the situation and talk about what you wish had happened and why.

Example: Someone asked me to go to a party the night before a test. I didn't like the course, and I didn't feel like studying, so I decided to go. The next day I failed the test, and I had to repeat the course. I wish I hadn't gone to the party. If I had stayed home, I would have studied for the test. If I had been prepared, I would have passed.

9 | WRITING

If you hadn't been born, what would have been different for your family, friends, teammates, or community? Choose two areas of your life to discuss and write a paragraph about all the things that would have been different. Use past unreal conditionals.

Example: Two important areas of my life are my family and my friends. I am an only child, so if I hadn't been born, my parents would have been sad. They wanted a child very much. If they hadn't had me, they might have . . .

10 | ON THE INTERNET

Do a search on a person who changed the world. Choose a person that you know about or one from the list. How would life have been different if that person hadn't been born? Discuss your findings with a classmate.

Marie Curie

Thomas Edison

Ludwig von Beethoven

Mother Teresa

Johannes Gutenberg

Marco Polo

Princess Diana

El Zahrawi

Rachel Carson

Example: **A:** If Marie Curie hadn't been born, she wouldn't have discovered helpful uses for radioactivity.
B: She wouldn't have worked with Pierre Curie.

From **Grammar** to **Writing**
Showing Cause and Effect

One way to develop a topic is to discuss its causes and effects. To show cause and effect, you can connect **sentences** with *as a result* and *therefore*. In individual sentences, you can connect **clauses** with *so*, *because*, or *if*.

Example

CAUSE	EFFECT
I was shy.	*I didn't talk in class.* $\longrightarrow$

I was shy. **As a result,** I didn't talk in class.
I was shy. **Therefore,** I didn't talk in class.
I was shy, **so** I didn't talk in class.
Because I was shy, I didn't talk in class.
If I hadn't been shy, I would have talked in class.

Punctuation Note
Use a comma after *as a result* and *therefore*. Use a comma before *so*. Use a comma after a clause beginning with *because* or *if* when it comes before the main clause.

1 | *Read this essay. Underline sentences or clauses that show a cause once. Underline sentences or clauses that show an effect twice. Circle the connecting words.*

My biggest problem in school is my fear of talking in class. My hands always shake if I answer a question or present a paper. If it is a big assignment, I even feel sick to my stomach.

There are several reasons for my problem, but my family's attitude is the most important. My family motto is, "Children should be seen, but not heard." Because my parents never ask for our opinions, we never give them. I can feel my mother's disapproval if a talkative friend visits. In addition, my parents classify their children. My older brother is the "Smart One." I am the "Creative One." I think I would do better in school if they expected more, but they don't expect much. Therefore, I have not tried very hard.

Recently I decided to do something about my problem. I discovered that I feel less nervous about giving a speech in class if I role-play my presentation with a friend. I have also joined a discussion club. As a result, I get a lot of practice talking. My problem has causes, so it must have solutions!

2 | *Connect the following sentences. Use the word(s) in parentheses.*

1. Mr. Stewart didn't help me. I never spoke in class. (if)

   If Mr. Stewart hadn't helped me, I never would have spoken in class.

2. He believed in me. I became more courageous. (because)

_____

3. We worked in groups. I got used to talking about ideas with classmates. (so)

_____

4. I have gotten a lot of practice. I feel more confident. (as a result)

_____

5. Sena didn't understand the question. She didn't raise her hand. (therefore)

_____

3 | *Before you write . . .*

1. Work with a partner. Discuss the causes of a strong feeling that you have.

   Example: I usually feel excited at the beginning of the school year.

2. Complete this outline for a cause and effect essay.

   Paragraph I   The feeling you are going to write about: _____

   One or two examples: _____

   Paragraph II   The causes and effects of the feeling:

   A. _____

   B. _____

   C. _____

   Paragraph III   How you deal with the feeling:

   A. _____

   B. _____

4 | *Write a three-paragraph essay about the causes and effects of a feeling that you have. Use your outline to organize your writing.*

5 | *Exchange essays with a different partner. Outline your partner's essay. Write questions about anything that is not clear.*

6 | *Work with your partner. Discuss each other's questions from Exercise 5. Then rewrite your own essay and make any necessary corrections.*

Review Test

| **I** | *Circle the letter of the correct word(s) to complete each sentence.* |

1. I _____ late for work if the bus doesn't arrive soon.   **A B Ⓒ D**
   - (**A**) am
   - (**B**) was
   - (**C**) 'll be
   - (**D**) 've been

2. I _____ a flight attendant if I didn't get airsick.   **A B C D**
   - (**A**) would become
   - (**B**) became
   - (**C**) become
   - (**D**) had become

3. What do you do when your bus _____ late?   **A B C D**
   - (**A**) were
   - (**B**) is
   - (**C**) would be
   - (**D**) had been

4. If the teacher cancels class today, I _____ you.   **A B C D**
   - (**A**) have joined
   - (**B**) could have joined
   - (**C**) 'll join
   - (**D**) join

5. This flight is full. _____ someone gives up a seat,
   you won't get on this flight today.   **A B C D**
   - (**A**) If
   - (**B**) Unless
   - (**C**) When
   - (**D**) Where

6. If you _____ early enough, we can't save a seat for you.   **A B C D**
   - (**A**) 'll check in
   - (**B**) check in
   - (**C**) don't check in
   - (**D**) have checked in

7. If I hadn't been fascinated with flying, I _____ a pilot.   **A B C D**
   - (**A**) would become
   - (**B**) became
   - (**C**) won't become
   - (**D**) wouldn't have become

8. I'm going to Gerry's for Thanksgiving, but I can't stand to eat turkey.   **A B C D**
   What _____ if that happened to you?
   - (**A**) would you do
   - (**B**) did you do
   - (**C**) do you do
   - (**D**) will you do

(continued)

9. If I _____ you, I'd just go for dessert.   A B C D
   (**A**) am   (**C**) were
   (**B**) was   (**D**) had been

10. I'm so busy these days. I wish I _____ more free time.   A B C D
    (**A**) had   (**C**) have
    (**B**) had had   (**D**) would have

11. What _____ if you didn't have to work for six months?   A B C D
    (**A**) would you do   (**C**) did you do
    (**B**) will you do   (**D**) have you done

12. If I were free for six months, I _____ around the world.   A B C D
    (**A**) traveled   (**C**) travel
    (**B**) 'd travel   (**D**) 'll travel

13. It's very hot. If you drink some water, you _____ better.   A B C D
    (**A**) feel   (**C**) have felt
    (**B**) felt   (**D**) might feel

14. I _____ nervous whenever I fly.   A B C D
    (**A**) would get   (**C**) 'll get
    (**B**) get   (**D**) had gotten

15. Unless the airlines _____ ticket prices, I'm not going to fly anymore.   A B C D
    (**A**) don't lower   (**C**) would lower
    (**B**) lowered   (**D**) lower

16. Your roommate is really noisy. If I _____ with him, I'd talk to him   A B C D
    about the problem.
    (**A**) lived   (**C**) live
    (**B**) 'll live   (**D**) would live

17. If he _____ soon, I'll probably move.   A B C D
    (**A**) doesn't change   (**C**) wouldn't change
    (**B**) wouldn't   (**D**) didn't change

18. What would you have done if you _____ the lottery last week?   A B C D
    (**A**) win   (**C**) 'd have won
    (**B**) 'd won   (**D**) 'll win

19. Whenever there's a thunderstorm, the cat _____ under the bed.   A B C D
    (**A**) is hiding   (**C**) hides
    (**B**) would hide   (**D**) hid

20. I didn't like the hotel. I wish we _____ to stay there.   **A   B   C   D**
    (**A**) haven't decided   (**C**) didn't decide
    (**B**) hadn't decided   (**D**) won't decide

21. Mary _____ the exam unless she had hired a tutor.   **A   B   C   D**
    (**A**) couldn't have passed   (**C**) couldn't pass
    (**B**) can't pass   (**D**) could pass

22. When Carlos has a headache, he _____ some tea.   **A   B   C   D**
    (**A**) would drink   (**C**) 's drunk
    (**B**) drank   (**D**) drinks

23. If Sami doesn't call soon, we _____ without him.   **A   B   C   D**
    (**A**) 're going to leave   (**C**) 'd leave
    (**B**) left   (**D**) 'd have left

II *Complete this conversation with the correct form of the verbs in parentheses.*

A: We had a great time at Drew's house Sunday. Why didn't you come?

B: I had to study for Spanish.

A: If you _____ *had come* _____ with us, you _____ an
            1. (come)   **2. (see)**
awesome movie.

B: Yeah? What?

A: We rented *Back to the Future*. It's about a kid who time-travels back to his parents'

high-school days. He changes his own future. It's so cool. At the end, his parents . . .

B: Wait—don't tell me. If you _____ me the ending, you
                                              3. (tell)
_____ it for me. I want to see it myself.
       4. (spoil)

A: OK. But have you ever thought about that?

B: About what?

A: About how things could be different. You grew up here in Baileyville, and you're almost

an adult now. But what _____ your childhood _____ like if
                                                              5. (be)
you _____ in a different family?
       6. (be born)

(continued)

B: Let's see. If I _____ a different family, I
                                    7. (have)

_____ here in Baileyville.
            8. (not grow up)

A: And if you _____ here, I _____ you.
                      9. (not grow up)   10. (not meet)

B: That's true. But getting back to the here-and-now, how did you do on the Spanish test?

A: I flunked. I wish I _____ that course. I'm going to fail.
                              11. (not take)

B: You just don't study enough. If you _____ more, you
                                                12. (study)

_____ this course easily this semester.
            13. (pass)

A: That's easy for you to say. You always get A's.

B: Sometimes I don't. It's not automatic. I _____ A's unless I
                                                        14. (not get)

_____ .
            15. (study)

A: I suppose you're right.

B: If I _____ you, I _____ to get better
              16. (be)   17. (try)

grades. It's important for your future.

III   *Complete this news article with the correct form of the verbs in parentheses. Choose the affirmative or the negative.*

WHAT WOULD YOU DO?

By Dewitt Rite

Imagine that you are unemployed and have a family to support. What

_____*would*_____ you _____*do*_____ if you _____ a wallet in the
                              1. (do)   2. (find)

street? _____ you _____ the money if you _____
                3. (keep)   4. (know)

no one would ever find out?

When Lara Williams faced that situation last week, she brought the wallet to the police,

who traced it to Mr. and Mrs. Asuki, tourists from Japan. The Asukis were pleasantly

surprised to see the wallet—and their money—again. "If we _____ the money
                                                                5. (get)

back, we _____ money for the rest of our trip. It _____ a long
              6. (borrow)   7. (take)

time to pay back that debt," beamed Mrs. Asuki.

The police officer who handled the situation was not surprised, however. "Most people are honest," commented Lieutenant Kronsky. "If they _____, our job
8.(be)
_____ even harder than it is."
9.(be)

Did Mrs. Williams have a hard time making her decision? "Frankly, yes. We need the money. I _____ Mr. Asuki's wallet in the gutter unless I _____
10.(see)   11.(look)
down just at that moment. For a little while, it seemed like fate had sent it to us. But each time I _____ a difficult decision to make, I always _____ the
12.(have)   13.(discuss)
problem with my husband. We both knew what was right in this situation. We always tell our kids, if something _____ to you, _____ it. Our kids
14.(belong)   15.(return)
_____ the rules unless we _____ the rules ourselves."
16.(follow)   17.(obey)

The Asukis have offered the Williamses a reward, and a friendship has sprung up between the two families. "If the Williams family ever _____ to Japan, they
18.(come)
_____ our guests," said Mr. and Mrs. Asuki.
19.(be)

IV *Rewrite each sentence or group of sentences as a wish.*

1. I want spring vacation to last six months.

 I wish spring vacation lasted six months.

2. I didn't buy business-class tickets. I'm sorry I didn't.

_____

3. Oh, no. The in-flight movie is *Back to the Future IV*. I hate that one.

_____

4. I'm sorry that we went to Disney World on vacation.

_____

5. The beach is a better place to go.

_____

6. Florida's nice. I'd like to live there.

_____

7. Maybe my office can transfer me to Orlando.

_____

V | *Each sentence has four underlined words or phrases. The four underlined parts of the sentences are marked A, B, C, or D. Circle the letter of the <u>one</u> underlined part that is NOT CORRECT.*

1. <u>Whenever</u> we <u>will get</u> a long <u>holiday</u>, my family <u>takes</u> a trip.　　　　A Ⓑ C D
　　　A　　　　　B　　　　　　C　　　　　　　　D

2. We <u>always</u> <u>went</u> camping <u>if</u> we don't <u>get</u> a lot of time off.　　　　　A B C D
　　　　　A　　　B　　　　C　　　　　D

3. <u>Unless</u> we <u>had</u> <u>gone</u> to Florida last year, I wouldn't <u>had known</u> how　　　A B C D
　　　A　　　B　　C　　　　　　　　　　　　　　　　D

　　great Disney World was.

4. If I <u>am</u> older, I <u>would</u> <u>try</u> <u>to get</u> a job in Florida.　　　　　　　A B C D
　　　　A　　　　　B　　　C　　D

5. We <u>could</u> <u>had</u> seen <u>more</u> if the lines <u>had been</u> shorter.　　　　　A B C D
　　　　A　　B　　　　C　　　　　　　D

6. I <u>wish</u> my friend <u>could have</u> <u>came</u> with us when we <u>went</u> last year.　　A B C D
　　　A　　　　　　B　　　　C　　　　　　　　D

7. <u>Unless</u> you're interested in the movies, you <u>can</u> <u>visit</u> Universal Studios　　　　
　　　A　　　　　　　　　　　　　　　　B　　C

　　and <u>see</u> all the movie sets.　　　　　　　　　　　　　　　A B C D
　　　　D

8. <u>If</u> you stay a <u>week</u>, you <u>would</u> <u>have</u> more time to do things.　　　　A B C D
　　A　　　　　B　　　　　C　　D

▶ *To check your answers, go to Answer Key on page RT-5.*

PART X

Indirect Speech and Embedded Questions

Grammar in Context

BEFORE YOU READ

🎧 *Look at the photo and read what the woman is saying. Is it ever all right to tell a lie? If so, in what situations? Read this magazine article about lying.*

THE TRUTH ABOUT LYING

BY JENNIFER MORALES

At 9:00, a supervisor from Rick Spivak's bank telephoned and **said Rick's credit card payment was late**. **"The check is in the mail,"** Rick **replied** quickly. At 11:45, Rick left for a 12 o'clock meeting across town. Arriving late, Rick **told his client that traffic had been bad**. That evening, Rick's fiancée, Ann, came home with a new haircut. Rick hated it. **"It looks great,"** he **said**.

Three lies in one day! Does Rick have a problem? Or is he just an ordinary guy? Each time, he **told himself that sometimes the truth causes too many problems**. Most of us tell white lies—harmless untruths that help us avoid trouble. These are our four most common reasons:

He **said my hair looked great this way!**

◆ To get something more quickly or to avoid unpleasant situations: **"I have to have that report by 5:00 today,"** or **"I tried to call you, but your cell phone was turned off."**

◆ To appear nicer or more interesting to a new friend or to feel better about yourself: **"I run a mile every day,"** or **"I'm looking better these days."**

◆ To make a polite excuse: **"I'd love to go to your party, but I have to work."**

◆ To protect someone else's feelings: **"Your hair looks great that way!"**

Is telling lies a new trend? In one survey, the majority of people **said that people were more honest in the past**. Nevertheless, lying wasn't really born yesterday. In the 18th century, the French philosopher Vauvenargues told the truth about lying when he **wrote, "All men are born truthful and die liars."**

AFTER YOU READ

Find the situations in the article. Check the person's exact words.

1. The supervisor at Rick's bank (to Rick):
   - ☐ "His credit card payment was late."
   - ☐ "Your credit card payment is late."

2. Rick (to his client):
   - ☐ "Traffic had been bad."
   - ☐ "Traffic was bad."

3. Many people (to a new friend):
   - ☐ "You run a mile every day."
   - ☐ "I run a mile every day."

4. People answering a survey question:
   - ☐ "That people were more honest ten years ago."
   - ☐ "People were more honest ten years ago."

Grammar Presentation

DIRECT AND INDIRECT SPEECH

Direct Speech		
Direct Statement	**Subject**	**Reporting Verb**
"The check **is** in the mail," "The haircut **looks** great," "The traffic **was** bad,"	he	**said**.

Indirect Speech				
Subject	**Reporting Verb**	**Noun/ Pronoun**	**Indirect Statement**	
He	**told**	the bank Ann her	**(that)**	the check **was** in the mail. the haircut **looked** great. the traffic **had been** bad.
	said			

GRAMMAR NOTES	EXAMPLES
1. Direct speech (also called *quoted speech*) states the exact words that a speaker used. In writing, put quotation marks before and after the speech you are quoting.	• **"The check is in the mail,"** he said. • **"I like that tie,"** she told him.
The quotation can go at the beginning or at the end of the sentence.	• He said, **"The traffic is bad."** <div align="center">OR</div>• **"The traffic is bad,"** he said.

2. Indirect speech (also called *reported speech*) reports what a speaker said without using the exact words.	• He said **the check was in the mail**. • She told him **she liked that tie**.
The word *that* can introduce indirect speech.	• He said *that* **the check was in the mail**. • She told him *that* **she liked that tie**.
▶ **BE CAREFUL!** Do not use quotation marks when writing indirect speech.	• She said **she had to work**. NOT She said ~~"she had to work."~~

3. Reporting verbs (such as *say* or *tell*) are usually in the simple past for both direct and indirect speech.	**DIRECT SPEECH** • "It's a great haircut," he **said**. **INDIRECT SPEECH** • He **said** it was a great haircut. • He **told** her that it was a great haircut.
USAGE NOTE: When you mention the listener, it is more common to use *tell* than *said*.	• "I'm sorry to be late," Rick **told** *Ann*.
▶ **BE CAREFUL!** Do not use *tell* when you don't mention the listener.	• He **said** he had been sick. NOT He ~~told~~ he had been sick.

4. When the reporting verb is in the simple past (*said, told*) in indirect speech, we often **change the verb tense** the speaker used.	
The simple present becomes the simple past.	**DIRECT SPEECH** • "I only *buy* shoes on sale," she **said**. **INDIRECT SPEECH** • She **said** she only *bought* shoes on sale.
The simple past becomes the past perfect.	**DIRECT SPEECH** • "I *found* a great store," she **said**. **INDIRECT SPEECH** • She **said** she *had found* a great store.

5. You do not have to change the tense when you report:

    a. something that was **just said**.

> **A:** **I'm** tired from all this shopping.
>
> **B:** What did you say?
>
> **A:** I **said** I**'m** tired.
>
> OR
>
>   I **said** I *was* tired.

    b. something that is **still true**.

> - Rick **said** the bank *wants* a check.
>
>   OR
>
> - Rick **said** the bank *wanted* a check.

    c. a **general truth** or **scientific law**.

> - Mrs. Smith **told** her students that water *freezes* at 0° Celsius.
>
>   OR
>
> - Mrs. Smith **told** her students that water *froze* at 0° Celsius.

---

6. When the reporting verb is in the <u>simple present</u>, **do not change the verb tense** in indirect speech.

USAGE NOTE: In newspapers, magazines, and on the TV and radio news, reporting verbs are often in the simple present.

> **DIRECT SPEECH**
>
>   **Ann:** I *run* a mile every day.
>
> **INDIRECT SPEECH**
>
> - Ann **says** that she *runs* a mile every day. NOT Ann says that she ~~ran~~ a mile every day.
>
> - Fifty-seven percent of women **report** that they always *tell* the truth.

---

7. In **indirect speech**, make changes in **pronouns and possessives** to keep the speaker's <u>original meaning</u>.

> - Rick told Ann, "**I** like **your** haircut."
>
> - Rick told Ann that *he* liked *her* haircut.

Reference Notes
For the **punctuation rules for direct speech**, see Appendix 26 on page A-13.
For additional **tense changes in indirect speech**, see Unit 26, page 382.
For a list of **reporting verbs**, see Appendix 13 on page A-5.

Focused Practice

1 | DISCOVER THE GRAMMAR

Read this magazine article about lying on the job. Circle the reporting verbs. Underline the examples of direct speech once. Underline the examples of indirect speech twice.

> "Lying during a job interview is risky business," says Martha Toledo, director of the management consulting firm Maxwell. "The truth has a funny way of coming out." Toledo tells the story of one woman applying for a job as an office manager. The woman told the interviewer that she had a B.A. degree. Actually, she was eight credits short. She also said that she had made $50,000 at her last job. The truth was $10,000 less. "Many firms really do check facts," warns Toledo. In this case, a call to the applicant's company revealed the discrepancies.
>
> Toledo relates a story about another job applicant, George. During an interview, George reported that he had quit his last job. George landed the new job and was doing well until the company hired another employee, Pete. George and Pete had worked at the same company. Pete eventually told his boss that his old company had fired George.

2 | CONFESSIONS

Grammar Notes 3, 6–7

Complete the student's essay with the correct words.

Once when I was a teenager, I went to my Aunt Leah's house. Aunt Leah collected pottery, and

as soon as I got there, she _____told_____ me she _____ to show me
           1. (said / told)   **2. (wants / wanted)**

_____ new bowl. She _____ she _____ just bought it.
3. (my / her)   **4. (said / told)**   **5. (has / had)**

It was beautiful. When Aunt Leah went to answer the door, I picked up the bowl to examine it. It

slipped from my hands and smashed to pieces on the floor. As Aunt Leah walked back into the

room, I screamed and _____ that the cat had just broken _____ new
          6. (said / told)   **7. (her / your)**

bowl. Aunt Leah got this funny look on her face and _____ me that it really
                                      8. (said / told)

_____ very important.
9. (isn't / wasn't)

I didn't sleep at all that night, and the next morning I called my aunt and _____
                                                  10. (said / told)

her that I had broken _____ bowl. She said _____ 'd known that all
             11. (her / your)   **12. (I / she)**

along. We still laugh about the story today.

3 | TO BE HONEST

Look at the pictures. Rewrite the statements as indirect speech. Use **said** *as the reporting verb and make necessary changes in the verbs and pronouns.*

1.

She said it was her own recipe.

2.

_____

3.

_____

4.

_____

5.

_____

6.

_____

4 | THEN SHE SAID

Rewrite Lisa and Ben's conversation using indirect speech. Use the reporting verbs in parentheses. Make necessary changes in the verbs and pronouns.

1. LISA: I just heard about a job at a scientific research company.

(tell) *She told him she had just heard about a job at a scientific research company.*

2. BEN: Oh, I majored in science at Florida State.

(say) *He said that he had majored in science at Florida State.*

3. LISA: The starting salary is good.

(say) _____

4. BEN: I need more money.

(say) _____

5. LISA: They want someone with some experience as a programmer.

(say) _____

6. BEN: Well, I work as a programmer for Data Systems.

(tell) _____

7. LISA: Oh—they need a college graduate.

(say) _____

8. BEN: Well, I graduated from Florida State.

(tell) _____

9. LISA: But they don't want a recent graduate.

(say) _____

10. BEN: I got my degree four years ago.

(tell) _____

11. LISA: It sounds like the right job for you.

(tell) _____

12. BEN: I think so too.

(say) _____

5 | EDITING

Read this article. There are eight mistakes in the use of direct and indirect speech. The first mistake is already corrected. Find and correct seven more.

WARNING!!!! THIS MESSAGE IS A HOAX!!!!!

Everyone gets urgent e-mail messages. They tell you that Bill

            wants

Gates now ~~wanted~~ to give away his money—to YOU! They say

you that a popular floor cleaner kills family pets. They report that

your computer monitor had taken photographs of you. Since I'm

a good-hearted person, I used to forward these e-mails to all my

friends. Not long ago, a very annoyed friend explains that the

story about killer bananas was a hoax (an untrue story). He told

me about these common telltale signs of hoaxes:

  ! The e-mail always says that it was very urgent. It has lots of

     exclamation points.

  ! It tells that it is not a hoax and quotes important people.

     (The quotations are false.)

  ! It urges you to send the e-mail to everyone you know.

He also told that *Hoaxbusters* (http://hoaxbusters.org) had lists of

Internet hoaxes. You can avoid the embarrassment of forwarding

all your friends a false warning. So, before *you* announce that

sunscreen had made people blind, check out the story on

Hoaxbusters!

Communication Practice

6 | LISTENING

🎧 *Read Lisa's weekly planner. Then listen to the conversations. Lisa wasn't always honest. Listen again and notice the differences between what Lisa said and the truth. Then write sentences about Lisa's white lies.*

SATURDAY		MONDAY
Morning		**Morning**
Afternoon		**Afternoon**
Evening *6:00 date with Ben!*	*6:00 Vegetarian Society meeting*	**Evening**
	7:30 dinner with Chris	
SUNDAY	*sleep late!*	**TUESDAY**
Morning *9:00 ~~aerobics class~~*		**Morning**
Afternoon	*4:00 weekly staff meeting – present sales report*	**Afternoon**
Evening		**Evening**

1. *She said her parents were in town, but she has a date with Ben.*

2. _____

3. _____

4. _____

7 | WHY LIE?

Review the four reasons for lying described in "The Truth About Lying" on page 368. Work in small groups. Is it OK to lie in these four circumstances? Give examples from your own experience to support your ideas.

Example: Once my friend told me that my haircut looked great, but it really looked awful. I think she should have told me the truth. Now it's hard for me to believe anything she says.

8 | HONESTY QUESTIONNAIRE

Complete the questionnaire. Then work in groups. Summarize your group's results and report them to the rest of the class.

	Always	Usually	Sometimes	Rarely	Never
1. I tell the truth to my friends.					
2. I tell the truth to my family.					
3. It's OK to lie on the job.					
4. "White lies" protect people's feelings.					
5. Most people are honest.					
6. It's best to tell the truth.					
7. I tell people my real age.					
8. My friends are honest with me.					
9. It's difficult to tell a convincing lie.					
10. Politicians are honest.					
11. Doctors tell their patients the whole truth.					
12. I answer questionnaires honestly.					

Example: Five of us said that we usually told the truth.
Only one of us said it was always best to tell the truth.

9 | TO TELL THE TRUTH

Play this game as a class. Three "contestants" leave the room. They choose one experience to report to the class. Only one contestant has actually had the experience. The other two must tell convincing lies to make the class believe that they have had the experience.

After the contestants choose the experience, they go back into the room and sit in front of the class. Each contestant states the experience. Then class members ask each contestant detailed questions about it.

Example: CONTESTANT A: Once I climbed a 10,000-meter-high mountain.
CONTESTANT B: Once I climbed a 10,000-meter-high mountain.
CONTESTANT C: Once I climbed a 10,000-meter-high mountain.
CLASS MEMBER: Contestant A, how long did it take you?
Contestant B, how long did it take *you*?
Contestant C, how many people were with you?

After each contestant has answered questions, the class decides which contestant is telling the truth. Class members explain which statements convinced them that a contestant was lying or telling the truth.

Example: I believed Contestant A because she said that it had taken her two days.
I think Contestant C was lying. He said he'd climbed the mountain alone.

10 | QUOTABLE QUOTES

*In groups, discuss these famous quotations about lying. Do you agree with them? Give examples to support your opinion. Use **says** to report the proverbs and **said** to report the ideas of individuals.*

All men are born truthful and die liars.
— *Vauvenargues (French philosopher, 1715–1747)*

> **Example:** Vauvenargues said that all men are born truthful and die liars. I agree because babies don't lie, but children and adults do.

A half truth is a whole lie.
— *Jewish proverb*

A little inaccuracy saves tons of explanation.
— *Saki (British short-story writer, 1870–1916)*

A liar needs a good memory.
— *Quintilian (first-century Roman orator)*

The man who speaks the truth is always at ease.
— *Persian proverb*

The cruelest lies are often told in silence.
— *Robert Louis Stevenson (Scottish novelist, 1850–1894)*

11 | WRITING

Read the conversation between Rick and Ann. Then write a paragraph reporting what they said. Use direct and indirect speech.

RICK: Hi, honey. Sorry I'm late.

ANN: That's all right. I made liver and onions. It's almost ready.

RICK: *(looking upset)* It smells great, honey. It's one of my favorites.

ANN: You look upset!

RICK: I'm OK. I had a rough day at work. Oh, I stopped and bought some frogs' legs for dinner on Wednesday. It's my turn to cook.

ANN: *(looking upset)* That's interesting. I look forward to trying them.

> **Example:** Rick came home and said he was sorry he was late. Ann said that was all right.

12 | ON THE INTERNET

🌐 *A hoax is an untrue story or a trick that makes people believe something that is untrue. There are many e-mail hoaxes on the Internet. Do a search on **Internet hoaxes** and find some common hoaxes. Report them to a group.*

> **Example:** One e-mail hoax said that an Internet site had everybody's passport information. Another one said people had caught a terrible disease by breathing fresh air.

Indirect Speech: Tense Changes

BEFORE YOU READ

Look at the photos on this page and the next. What is happening? What do you think the title of the article means? Read this article from a news magazine.

THE FLOOD OF THE CENTURY

Central Europe

July was hot and dry. Then, in August, the skies opened. Writing from Berlin on August 13, 2002, journalist John Hooper reported **that it had been raining for more than 24 hours straight**. A huge weather system was dumping rain on eastern and central Europe. Berliners worried not only about their own city but also about Prague and Dresden, the homes of priceless art and architectural treasures. Hooper noted **that evacuations had already started in Prague and were beginning in Dresden**.

As Hooper wrote his story, 50,000 residents were streaming out of Prague, and the 16th century Charles Bridge was in danger of collapsing. Still, Mayor Igor Nemec told reporters **that the historic Old Town should remain safe**. Dr. Irena Kopencova wasn't that optimistic. She was sloshing through the National Library of the Czech Republic in rubber boots, grabbing old manuscripts. She said sadly **that many original copies of the most treasured poems in the Czech language had been lost**.

(continued)

Prague under water

THE FLOOD OF THE CENTURY

A few days later, Dresden was battling its worst flood since 1501. Heiko Ringel stopped stacking sandbags to talk to reporter Julian Coman of the *News Telegraph*. Ringel didn't live in Dresden anymore, but he said **he was back in his hometown that summer to help**. Why? He couldn't stand seeing all that history swept away. He said **it would have been too cruel to bear**. "Dresden and Prague are the twin jewels of Central Europe."

All over Dresden, museum staff rushed items to the top floors. Egyptian stone tablets lay jumbled with Roman statues,

Saving art

and masterpieces by Rembrandt were stacked 10 deep on top of paintings by Rubens. Museum director Martin Rohl still worried. He told Coman **that with another few feet of water, nothing would be safe**.

The danger didn't stop tourism. "Flood tourists" moved from city to city gaping at the flood of the century. One speculated **that it might even be the flood of the millennium**. John Hooper didn't agree. He thought climate change was causing these events, and believed that they would get worse. His headline announced **that summer 2002 would go down in history as the time weather had changed forever**.

Was Hooper right? Were the floods of 2002 just the beginning of worse and worse disasters caused by global warming? Or were they "normal disasters" that we should expect once every 100 years? Right after the floods, statistical studies claimed **that floods were not getting worse, but that flood damage was increasing**. They concluded **that people ought to stop building so close to water**. Then, in 2003, thousands died in Europe in a heat wave that even statistics could not call "normal." By 2004, more and more scientists were warning **that governments had to do something about climate change**. The summers of 2002 and 2003 had already shown us how much we could lose if we don't listen.

AFTER YOU READ

Check the exact words that people in the article said or wrote.

1. John Hooper said:

☐ "It had been raining for more than 24 hours."

☐ "It has been raining for more than 24 hours."

2. Heiko Ringel said:

☐ "I'm back in my hometown this summer to help."

☐ "He's back in his hometown this summer to help."

3. Martin Rohl said:

☐ "With another few feet of water, nothing was safe."

☐ "With another few feet of water, nothing will be safe."

4. Scientists said:

☐ "Governments have to do something about climate change."

☐ "Governments had to do something about climate change."

Grammar Presentation

INDIRECT SPEECH: TENSE CHANGES

Direct Speech			Indirect Speech			
Subject	**Reporting Verb**	**Direct Statement**	**Subject**	**Reporting Verb**	**Noun/ Pronoun**	**Indirect Statement**
He	said,	"I **live** in Dresden." "I **moved** here in June." "I**'m looking** for an apartment." "I**'ve started** a new job." "I**'m going to stay** here." "I**'ll invite** you for the holidays." "We **can go** to museums." "I **may look** for a roommate." "I **should get back** to work." "I **have to finish** my report." "You **must come** to visit." "We **ought to see** each other more often."	He	told	Jim me you him her us them	he **lived** in Dresden. he **had moved** there in June. he **was looking** for an apartment. he **had started** a new job. he **was going to stay** there. he **would invite** me/us for the holidays.
				said		(that) we **could go** to museums. he **might look** for a roommate. he **should get back** to work. he **had to finish** his report. I/we **had to come** to visit. we **ought to see** each other more often.

GRAMMAR NOTES   **EXAMPLES**

---

1. As you learned in Unit 25, when the reporting verb is in the <u>simple past</u>, the **verb tense** in the indirect speech statement often **changes**.

DIRECT SPEECH		INDIRECT SPEECH
Simple present	→	Simple past
Present progressive	→	Past progressive
Simple past	→	Past perfect
Present perfect	→	Past perfect

DIRECT SPEECH	INDIRECT SPEECH
He said, "It**'s** cloudy."	He said it **was** cloudy.
She said, "A storm **is coming**."	She said a storm **was coming**.
He said, "Klaus **called**."	He said that Klaus **had called**.
She told him, "I**'ve heard** the news."	She told him that she**'d heard** the news.

---

2. Modals often change in indirect speech.

DIRECT SPEECH		INDIRECT SPEECH
will	→	***would***
can	→	***could***
may	→	***might***
must	→	***had to***

DIRECT SPEECH	INDIRECT SPEECH
I said, "The winds **will be** strong."	I said the winds **would be** strong.
"You **can stay** with us," they told us.	They told us we **could stay** with them.
He said, "The storm **may last** all night."	He said that the storm **might last** all night.
"You **must leave**," he told us.	He told us that we **had to leave**.

---

3. The following **do not change** in indirect speech:

a. *should, could, might,* and *ought to*

b. the past perfect

c. the present and past unreal conditional

d. past modals

DIRECT SPEECH	INDIRECT SPEECH
"You **should listen** to the news," he told us.	He told us that we **should listen** to the news.
"I **had moved** here a week before the flood," he said.	He said that he **had moved** here a week before the flood.
"If I **knew**, I **would tell** you," said Jim.	Jim said if he **knew**, he **would tell** me.
"If I **had known**, I **would have told** you," said Jim.	He said that if he **had known,** he **would have told** me.
"I **should have left**."	He said that he **should have left**.
"We **couldn't have known**."	They said they **couldn't have known**.

4. Change time words in indirect speech to keep the speaker's <u>original meaning</u>.

DIRECT SPEECH		INDIRECT SPEECH
now	→	*then*
today	→	*that day*
tomorrow	→	*the next day*
yesterday	→	*the day before*
this week / month / year	→	*that week / month / year*
last week / month / year	→	*the week / month / year before*
next week / month / year	→	*the following week / month / year*

Uta to Klaus:
- "I just got home **yesterday**. I'll start cleaning up **tomorrow**."

Klaus to Heiko (a few days later):
- Uta told me she had just gotten home **the day before**. She said she would start cleaning up **the next day**.

Lotte to her mother (right after the storm):
- "Our home won't be repaired until **next month**."

The family newsletter (two months later):
- Lotte reported that their home wouldn't be repaired until **the following month**.

5. Change *here* and *this* in indirect speech to keep the speaker's <u>original meaning</u>.

DIRECT SPEECH		INDIRECT SPEECH
here	→	*there*
this	→	*that*

Jim (in Athens) to Erica (in Berlin):
- I love it **here**. **This** climate is great.

Erica to Susan (both in Berlin):
- Jim said he loved it **there**. He told me that **that** climate was great.

Reference Note
For a list of **reporting verbs**, see Appendix 13 on page A-5.

Focused Practice

1 | DISCOVER THE GRAMMAR

Read the sentences in indirect speech. Then circle the letter of the direct speech that is being reported.

1. The local weather forecaster said that it was going to be a terrible storm.
   a. "It was going to be a terrible storm."
   b. "It's going to be a terrible storm."
   c. "It was a terrible storm."

2. She said the winds might reach 60 kilometers per hour.
   a. "The winds reached 60 kilometers per hour."
   b. "The winds would reach 60 kilometers per hour."
   c. "The winds may reach 60 kilometers per hour."

(continued)

3. She said there would be more rain the next day.

   a. "There will be more rain the next day."

   b. "There would be more rain tomorrow."

   c. "There will be more rain tomorrow."

4. She told people that they should try to leave the area.

   a. "You should try to leave the area."

   b. "You should have tried to leave the area."

   c. "You would leave the area."

5. She reported that people were leaving the city.

   a. "People are leaving the city."

   b. "People were leaving the city."

   c. "People left the city."

6. She said that they could expect a lot of damage.

   a. "We could expect a lot of damage."

   b. "We could have expected a lot of damage."

   c. "We can expect a lot of damage."

7. She said that the floods were the worst they had had there.

   a. "The floods are the worst we have here."

   b. "The floods are the worst we have had here."

   c. "The floods are the worst we have had there."

8. She told them that the emergency relief workers had arrived the day before.

   a. "Emergency relief workers arrived the day before."

   b. "Emergency relief workers arrived yesterday."

   c. "Emergency relief workers arrived today."

9. She reported that the president would be there to inspect the damage.

   a. "The president will be here to inspect the damage."

   b. "The president will be there to inspect the damage."

   c. "The president would be there to inspect the damage."

10. She said that if they hadn't had time to prepare, the danger would have been even greater.

    a. "If we hadn't had time to prepare, the danger would have been even greater."

    b. "If we don't have time to prepare, the danger will be even greater."

    c. "If we didn't have time to prepare, the danger would be even greater."

2 | RUMORS

You are in Berlin. Imagine you heard these rumors yesterday, and you are reporting them today. Use **They said** *to report the rumors.*

1. "The storm changed direction last night."

   They said that the storm had changed direction the night before.

2. "It's going to pass north of here."

   _____

3. "The gas station ran out of gasoline this afternoon."

   _____

4. "It's not really a hurricane, just a big storm."

   _____

5. "They've closed the bridge because of rising water."

   _____

6. "They won't restore the electricity until tomorrow."

   _____

7. "They can't reopen the schools for at least a week."

   _____

8. "You ought to use bottled water for a few days."

   _____

3 | FIGHTING FLOODS

🎧 *Read this interview between radio station WWEA and meteorologist Dr. Ronald Myers.*

WWEA: Exactly how common are floods?

MYERS: Floods are the most common of all natural disasters except fire. They are also the most widespread.

WWEA: What causes them?

MYERS: Usually they are the result of intense, heavy rainfall. But they can also be caused by melting snow. Another cause is unusually high tides in coastal areas.

WWEA: And what causes these high tides?

MYERS: Severe winds over the ocean surface cause high tides. Often the winds are part of a hurricane.

WWEA: What is a *flash flood*? Is it just a very bad flood?

MYERS: No. A flash flood comes with little or no warning. Because of this, it's the most dangerous type of flood. In fact, flash floods cause almost 75 percent of all flood-related deaths.

(continued)

WWEA: That's terrible. Is there anything that can be done?

MYERS: We've made progress in predicting floods. But we must get better at predicting flash floods.

WWEA: Is there anything that can be done to actually prevent floods?

MYERS: People must improve their protection of the Earth and the environment. When we replace grass and soil with roads and buildings, the ground loses its ability to absorb rainfall. This can lead to flooding. In addition, many scientists believe that global warming is causing an increase in the number of floods.

WWEA: So the answer lies in better prediction and better treatment of the Earth?

MYERS: Exactly. We can't completely stop floods from happening. It's part of nature. But we *can* help to predict them and to prevent their number from increasing.

Now read the following statements. For each statement write **That's right** *or* **That's wrong** *and report what Dr. Myers said.*

1. Floods are not very common.

   That's wrong. He said floods were the most common of all natural disasters except fire.

2. They are very widespread.

   _____

3. Floods are usually caused by melting snow.

   _____

4. A flash flood is just a very bad flood.

   _____

5. A flash flood is the most dangerous type of flood.

   _____

6. Flash floods cause 25 percent of all flood-related deaths.

   _____

7. We have made progress in predicting floods.

   _____

8. People are doing a good job of protecting the Earth and the environment.

   _____

9. Replacing grass and dirt with roads and buildings can lead to flooding.

   _____

10. Many scientists believe that global warming is causing an increase in the number of floods.

    _____

11. We can completely stop floods from happening.

    _____

4 | WEATHER REPORTS

Klaus and Eva live in Germany. Read the information that Klaus got during the day. Then write what people said. Use direct speech.

Klaus's mother called. She told him that she was listening to the weather report. She said that she was worried about Klaus and Eva. She told him that if they weren't so stubborn they'd pack up and leave right then.

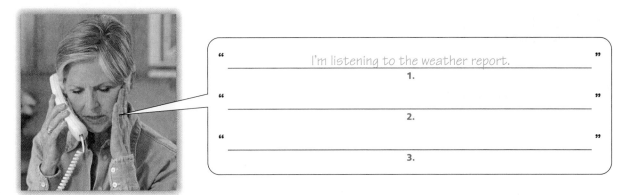

" I'm listening to the weather report. "

_____
1.

" "

_____
2.

" "

_____
3.

Klaus's father gave him some good advice. He said he'd had some experience with floods. He said Klaus and Eva had to put sandbags in front of their doors. He also told Klaus that they ought to fill the sinks and bathtubs with clean water. He said they should buy a lot of batteries.

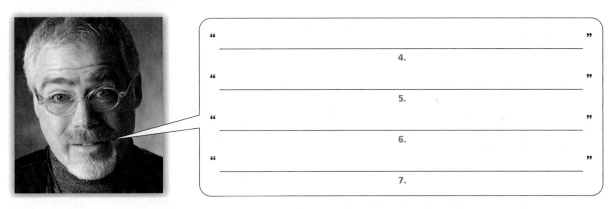

" "

_____
4.

" "

_____
5.

" "

_____
6.

" "

_____
7.

Stefan called. He and Uta are worried. Their place is too close to the river. They said that they couldn't stay there, and they told Klaus that they wanted to stay with him and Eva. They said they were leaving that night. They told Klaus they should have called him and Eva sooner.

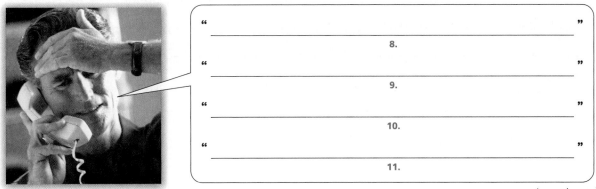

" "

_____
8.

" "

_____
9.

" "

_____
10.

" "

_____
11.

(continued)

Klaus listened to the weather advisory in the afternoon. The forecaster said the storm would hit that night. She warned that the rainfall was going to be very heavy, and she said that the storm might last for several hours.

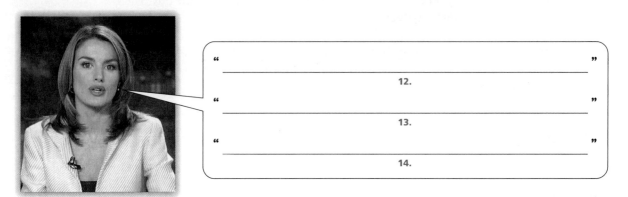

"_____"
12.

"_____"
13.

"_____"
14.

5 | EDITING

Read this student's report. There are nine mistakes in the use of indirect speech. The first mistake is already corrected. Find and correct eight more.

What is it like to live through a flood? For my report, I interviewed the

Nemec family, who experienced last month's floods in our city. They reported

that ~~we~~ *they* had experienced fear and sadness. On September 14, the family went to

a movie. Jerzy, a high school student, said they can't drive the car home

because their street was flooded. He told it had happened in only three hours.

Mrs. Nemec said that all their belongings were ruined, but that their cat has

gone to an upstairs bedroom. They were sad about losing so many things, but

she said she will have been much sadder to lose the family pet. Jerzy's father

also said it had been a complete mess here, and the family had worked all this

week to clean out the house. Anna, who is in junior high school, wanted to keep

her old dollhouse. It had belonged to her mother and her mother's mother. At

first, her father told her that she can't keep it because seeing it would just

make her sad. Anna replied that she saw memories in that dollhouse—not just

broken wood. In the end, they kept it. Mrs. Nemec said that Anna had taught

them something important today.

Communication Practice

6 | LISTENING

🎧 *Work in groups of four. Listen to the weather advisory. Listen again and check the correct information. It's all right to leave something blank. After you listen, pool your information.*

Schools

1. Today schools ☑ closed at 10:00. ☐ will close at 1:00.

2. Students and teachers ☐ should stay at school. ☐ should go home immediately.

3. Tomorrow schools ☐ will open. ☐ may stay closed.

Roads

4. Road conditions ☐ are safe. ☐ are dangerous.

5. Drivers must ☐ drive slowly. ☐ pick up passengers.

6. Everyone should ☐ avoid driving. ☐ continue driving.

Public Offices

7. Libraries ☐ will stay open. ☐ will close at 1:00.

8. Post offices ☐ will stay open until 5:00. ☐ will close early.

9. Government offices ☐ will be closed tomorrow. ☐ will remain open tomorrow.

Businesses

10. Banks ☐ will close at noon. ☐ will stay open until 3:00.

11. Gas stations ☐ will close at noon. ☐ will stay open until evening.

12. Supermarkets ☐ are open now. ☐ are closed now.

Now compare your information with what other group members heard. Complete any missing information in your chart. Then listen again and check your answers.

Example: A: She said that schools would close at 1:00.
B: That's not right. She said that schools had closed at 10:00.

7 | TELEPHONE GAME

Work in groups of six to ten students. Student A whispers something in the ear of Student B. Student B reports (in a whisper) what he or she heard to Student C. Each student reports to the next student in a whisper and may only say the information once. Expect surprises— people often hear things inaccurately or report them differently from what was said. The last student tells the group what he or she heard.

Example: A: There won't be any class tomorrow.
B: He said that there wouldn't be any class tomorrow.
C: She said that there'd be a guest in class tomorrow.

8 | INTERVIEW

Use the questions below to interview three of your classmates. Report your findings to the class.

Have you ever experienced an extreme weather condition or other natural phenomenon such as the following?

a hurricane or typhoon	a flood
very hot weather	a sandstorm
very cold weather	an earthquake
a drought	other: _____

- How did you feel?
- What did you do to protect yourself?
- What advice would you give to someone in the same situation?

Example: Arielle told me she had experienced a very hot summer when temperatures reached over 40°C. She told me that she had felt sick a lot of the time. She said she had stayed indoors until evening every day. Arielle told me that everyone should move slowly and drink a lot of liquids in hot weather.

9 | WRITING

Write a paragraph reporting someone else's experience in an extreme weather condition or natural phenomenon. You can use information from your interview in Exercise 8, or you can interview another person. Use indirect speech.

Example: My friend Julie told me about a dust storm in Australia. She said that one afternoon, the sky had gotten very dark and the wind had started to blow hard. Her mother told her that they all had to go inside right away and close all the windows. Then . . .

10 | ON THE INTERNET

Do a search to find tomorrow's weather forecast for your city or town. Take notes. Report to your classmates two days from now. What did the forecast say? Was it accurate?

Example: The forecast said it would be partly cloudy in the morning and that the sun was going to come out in the afternoon. It was cloudy in the morning, but then it rained.

Indirect Instructions, Commands, Requests, and Invitations

Grammar in Context

BEFORE YOU READ

🎧 *Look at the photo. What time is it? Where is the man? How does he feel? Why does he feel that way? Read this transcript of a radio interview with the director of a sleep clinic.*

HERE'S TO YOUR HEALTH

THE SNOOZE NEWS

CONNIE: Good morning! This is Connie Sung, bringing you "Here's to Your Health," a program about today's health issues. This morning, we've invited Dr. Thorton Ray **to talk to us about insomnia**. Dr. Ray is the director of the Sleep Disorders Clinic. Welcome to the show!

DR. RAY: Thanks, Connie. It's great to be here.

CONNIE: Your book *Night Shift* will be coming out soon. In it, you tell people **to pay more attention to sleep disorders**. What's the big deal about losing a little sleep?

DR. RAY: I always tell people **to think of the biggest industrial disaster that they've ever heard about**. Usually it was caused at least in part by sleep deprivation. Then I ask them **to think about what can happen if they drive when they're tired**. Every year, up to 200,000 automobile accidents in this country are caused by drowsy drivers.

CONNIE: Wow! That *is* a big problem.

DR. RAY: And a costly one. We figure that fatigue costs businesses about $70 million a year.

(continued)

HERE'S TO YOUR HEALTH

CONNIE: That's astounding! But getting back to the personal level, if I came to your clinic, what would you advise me **to do**?

DR. RAY: First, I would find out about some of your habits. If you drank coffee or cola late in the day, I would tell you **to stop**. Caffeine interferes with sleep.

CONNIE: What about old-fashioned remedies like warm milk?

DR. RAY: Actually, a lot of home remedies do make sense. We tell patients **to have a high-carbohydrate snack like a banana before they go to bed**. Warm milk helps too. But I'd advise you **not to eat a heavy meal before bed**.

CONNIE: My doctor told me **to get more exercise,** but when I run at night, I have a hard time getting to sleep.

DR. RAY: It's true that if you exercise regularly, you'll sleep better. But we always tell patients **not to exercise too close to bedtime**.

CONNIE: My mother always said **to get up and scrub the floor when I couldn't sleep**.

DR. RAY: That works. I advised one patient **to balance his checkbook**. He went right to sleep, just to escape from the task.

CONNIE: Suppose I try these remedies and they don't help?

DR. RAY: We often ask patients **to come and spend a night at our sleep clinic**. Our equipment monitors the patient through the night. In fact, if you're interested, we can invite you **to come to the clinic for a night**.

CONNIE: Maybe I should do that.

"I couldn't sleep."

AFTER YOU READ

Check the things that Dr. Ray suggests for people with insomnia.

☐ **1.** Stop drinking coffee and cola late in the day.

☐ **2.** Eat a heavy meal before going to bed.

☐ **3.** Get more exercise.

☐ **4.** Exercise right before bedtime.

☐ **5.** Get up from bed and balance your checkbook.

☐ **6.** Spend the night at the sleep clinic.

Grammar Presentation

INDIRECT INSTRUCTIONS, COMMANDS, REQUESTS, AND INVITATIONS

Direct Speech		
Subject	**Reporting Verb**	**Direct Speech**
He	said,	"**Drink** warm milk." "**Don't drink** coffee." "Can you **turn out** the light, please?" "Why don't you **visit** the clinic?"

Indirect Speech			
Subject	**Reporting Verb**	**Noun/ Pronoun**	**Indirect Speech**
He	told advised asked	Connie her	**to drink** warm milk. **not to drink** coffee. **to turn out** the light.
	said		
	invited	her	**to visit** the clinic.

GRAMMAR NOTES

1. In indirect speech, use the **infinitive** (*to* + **base form** of the verb) for:

  a. instructions

  b. commands

  c. requests

  d. invitations

EXAMPLES

DIRECT SPEECH	INDIRECT SPEECH
"Come early," said the doctor.	The doctor said **to come** early.
"Lie down."	The doctor told her **to lie down**.
"Could you please arrive by 8:00?"	He asked her **to arrive** by 8:00.
"Could you join us for dinner?"	They invited us **to join** them for dinner.

2. Use a **negative infinitive** (*not* + **infinitive**) for:

  a. negative instructions

  b. negative commands

  c. negative requests

DIRECT SPEECH	INDIRECT SPEECH
"Don't eat after 9:00 P.M."	He told me **not to eat** after 9:00 P.M.
"Don't wake Cindy!"	Mrs. Bartolotta told me **not to wake** Cindy.
"Please don't set the alarm."	Jean-Pierre asked me **not to set** the alarm.

Reference Note
For a list of **reporting verbs,** see Appendix 13 on page A-5.

Focused Practice

1 | DISCOVER THE GRAMMAR

Connie Sung decided to write an article about her visit to Dr. Ray's clinic. Read her notes for the article. Underline the indirect instructions, commands, requests, and invitations. Circle the reporting verbs that introduce them.

2/18	11:00 A.M. The clinic called and (asked) me to arrive at 8:30 tonight. They told me to bring my nightshirt and toothbrush. They told me people also liked to bring their own pillow, but I decided to travel light.
	8:30 P.M. I arrived on schedule. My room was small but cozy. Only the video camera and cable told me I was in a sleep clinic. Juan Estrada, the technician on duty, told me to relax and watch TV for an hour.
	9:30 P.M. Juan came back and got me ready for the test. He pasted 12 small metal disks to my face, legs, and stomach. I asked him to explain, and he told me that the disks, called electrodes, would be connected to a machine that records electrical activity in the brain. I felt like a Martian in a science fiction movie.
	11:30 P.M. Juan came back and asked me to get into bed. After he hooked me up to the machine, he instructed me not to leave the bed that night. I fell asleep easily.
2/19	7:00 A.M. Juan came to awaken me and to disconnect the wires. He invited me to join him in the next room, where he had spent the night monitoring the equipment. I looked at the pages of graphs and wondered aloud whether Juan and Dr. Ray would be able to read my weird dream of the night before. Juan laughed and told me not to worry. "These just show electrical impulses," he assured me.
	8:00 A.M. Dr. Ray reviewed my data with me. He told me I had healthy sleep patterns, except for some leg movements during the night. He told me to get more exercise, and I promised I would.

2 | DEAR HELEN

Read the questions to Helen, a newspaper columnist specializing in health matters, and report her instructions. Use the reporting verbs in parentheses.

Q: I have trouble getting to sleep every night.—MIKE LANDERS, DETROIT

A: Don't drink anything with caffeine after 2:00 P.M. Try exercising regularly, early in the day.

1. (tell) *She told him not to drink anything with caffeine after 2:00 P.M.*

2. (say) *She said to try exercising regularly, early in the day.*

Q: What can I do to soothe a sore throat? I never take medicine unless I have to.—ANNE BLY, TROY

A: Sip some hot herbal tea with honey. But don't drink black tea. It will make your throat dry.

3. (say) _____

4. (tell) _____

Q: I get leg cramps at night. They wake me up, and I can't get back to sleep.—LOU RICH, DALLAS

A: The next time you feel a cramp, do this: Pinch the place between your upper lip and your nose. The cramp should stop right away.

5. (say) _____

Q: Do you know of an inexpensive way to remove stains on teeth?—PETE LEE, BROOKLYN

A: Make a toothpaste of one tablespoon of baking soda and a little water. Brush as usual.

6. (tell) _____

7. (say) _____

Q: What can I do to ease an itchy poison ivy rash?—MARVIN SMITH, HARTFORD

A: Spread cool, cooked oatmeal over the rash. Also, try soaking the rash in a cool bath with a quarter cup of baking soda. Don't scratch the rash. That will make it worse.

8. (tell) _____

9. (say) _____

10. (tell) _____

Q: Bugs love me. They bite me all the time.—ED SMALL, TULSA

A: There are a few things you can do to keep bugs away. Eat onions or garlic every day. Your skin will have a slight odor that bugs hate. Or ask your doctor about a vitamin B supplement.

11. (say) _____

12. (tell) _____

IMPORTANT: CALL YOUR DOCTOR ABOUT ANY CONDITION THAT DOESN'T IMPROVE OR GETS WORSE.

3 | CONNIE'S DREAM

Connie had a dream at the sleep clinic. She wrote about it in her journal. Read her account of the dream and underline the indirect instructions, commands, requests, and invitations. Then complete the cartoon by writing what each character said.

I dreamed that a Martian came into my room. He told me to get up. Then he said to follow him. There was a spaceship outside the clinic. I asked the Martian to show me the ship, so he invited me to come aboard. Juan, the lab technician, was on the ship. Suddenly, Juan told me to pilot the ship. He ordered me not to leave the controls. Then he went to sleep. Next, Dr. Ray was at my side giving me instructions. He told me to slow down. Then he said to point the ship toward the Earth. There was a loud knocking noise as we hit the ground, and I told everyone not to panic. Then I heard Juan tell me to wake up. I opened my eyes and saw him walking into my room at the sleep clinic.

4 | EDITING

Read this entry in Zahra's journal. There are twelve mistakes in the use of indirect instructions, commands, requests, and invitations. The first mistake is already corrected. Find and correct eleven more. Don't forget to check punctuation. Mistakes with quotation marks count as one mistake for the sentence.

    In writing class today, the teacher asked Juan ^to^ read one of his stories. It was wonderful and everyone in class enjoyed it a lot. After class, the teacher invited me read a story in class next week. I don't feel ready to do this. I asked her no to call on me next week because I'm having trouble getting ideas. She told me that not to worry, and she said to wait for two weeks. I still was worried about coming up with an idea, so I decided to talk to Juan after class. I asked him tell me the source for his ideas. He was really helpful. He said that they came from his dreams! I was very surprised. He said me to keep a dream journal for ideas. Then he invited me "to read some of his journal." It was very interesting, so I asked him to give me some tips on remembering dreams. (Juan says that everyone dreams, but I usually don't remember my dreams in the morning.) Again, Juan was very helpful. He said getting a good night's sleep because the longer dreams come after a long period of sleep. He also tell me to keep my journal by the bed and to write as soon as I wake up. He said to no move from the sleeping position. He also told me not think about the day at first. (If you think about your day, you might forget your dreams.) Most important—every night he tells himself that to remember his dreams. These all sound like great ideas, and I want to try them out right away. The only problem is—I'm so excited about this, I'm not sure I'll be able to fall asleep!

Communication Practice

5 | LISTENING

⌒ *Juan went to a headache clinic. Listen to the conversation to find out what he learned there. Then listen again and check the correct column to show what they told him to do, what they told him not to do, and what they didn't mention.*

	Do	Don't Do	Not Mentioned
1. Get regular exercise.	☑	☐	☐
2. Get eight hours of sleep.	☐	☐	☐
3. Take painkillers.	☐	☐	☐
4. Use an ice pack.	☐	☐	☐
5. Massage around the eyes.	☐	☐	☐
6. Eat three big meals a day.	☐	☐	☐
7. Eat chocolate.	☐	☐	☐
8. Avoid cheese.	☐	☐	☐

6 | SIMPLE REMEDIES

What advice have you heard for the following problems? Work in pairs and talk about what to do and what not to do for them. Then report to the class.

minor kitchen burns   a cold

insomnia   blisters

insect bites   poison ivy

headaches   a sore throat

snoring   other: _____

hiccups

Example: **A:** My mother always told me to hold a burn under cold water.
              B: They say not to put butter on a burn.

7 | HOME ALONE

Jeff's parents went out for the evening and left a list of instructions for him. Work in pairs. Read the list and look at the picture. Talk about which instructions Jeff followed and which ones he didn't follow. Use indirect instructions.

> Dear Jeff,
> We'll be home late. Here are a few things to remember—
>   Don't stay up after 10:00.
>   Take the garbage out.
>   Wash the dishes.
>   Do your homework.
>   Let the cat in.
>   Don't watch any horror movies. (They give you
>   nightmares—remember?)
>   Don't invite your friends over tonight.
>
>   Love,
>   Mom and Dad

Example: His parents told him not to stay up after 10:00, but it's 11:30 and he's still awake.

8 | WRITING

Write a paragraph about a dream you had or one that someone has told you about. You can even invent a dream. Use the paragraph from Connie's journal in Exercise 3 as a model. Use indirect instructions, commands, requests, and invitations.

Example: One night I dreamed that I was in my grandmother's kitchen. In my dream, I saw a beautiful, carved wooden door. My grandmother invited me to open the door. She said that there were a lot of rooms in the house, and she invited me to explore them with her.

Exchange your paragraph with a partner. Draw a sketch of your partner's dream and write the direct speech in speech bubbles. Discuss your sketch with your partner to make sure you understood the story and the indirect speech in your partner's dream.

9 | ON THE INTERNET

Do a search on a problem or something you need help doing. Choose your own problem or one of the problems listed below. Search for tips on how to solve the problem. For example, type in **tips on losing weight**. *Report your findings to the class.*

losing weight

stopping smoking

making new friends

finding a new job

saving money

Example: I looked up information on losing weight. The website said to exercise regularly. It said not to eat too much bread . . .

Indirect Questions

Grammar in Context

BEFORE YOU READ

Look at the photo and the title of the article. What do you think a stress interview is?
Read this excerpt from an article about job interviews.

The **STRESS**
Interview
By Miguel Vega

*Why can't you work under pressure?
Have you cleaned out your car recently?
Who wrote your application letter for you?*

*Do I really
want this job?*

A few weeks ago, Melissa
Morrow had an unusual job
interview. First, the interviewer
asked **why she couldn't work under
pressure**. Before she could answer, he asked **if
she had cleaned out her car recently**. Then
he wanted to know **who had written her
application letter for her**. Melissa was
shocked, but she handled herself well. She
asked the interviewer **whether he was going
to ask her serious questions**. Then she
politely ended the interview.

Melissa had had a stress interview, a type of job interview that features tough, tricky
questions, long silences, and negative evaluations of the job candidate. To the
candidate, this may seem unnecessarily nasty on the interviewer's part. However, some
positions require an ability to handle just this kind of pressure. If there is an accident at
a nuclear power plant, for example, the plant's public relations officer must remain
calm when hostile reporters ask **how the accident could have occurred**.

(continued)

The **STRESS** Interview

The uncomfortable atmosphere of a stress interview gives the potential employer a chance to watch a candidate react to pressure. In one case, the interviewer ended each interview by saying, "We're really not sure that you're the right person for this job." One excellent candidate asked the interviewer angrily **if he was sure he knew how to conduct an interview**. She clearly could not handle the pressure she would encounter as a television news anchor—the job she was interviewing for.

Stress interviews may be appropriate for some jobs, but they can also work against a company. Some good candidates may refuse the job after a hostile interview. Melissa Morrow handled her interview beautifully, but later asked herself **if she really wanted to work for that company**. Her answer was *no*.

A word of warning to job candidates: Not all tough questioning is legitimate. In some countries, certain questions are illegal unless the answers are directly related to the job. If an interviewer asks **how old you are**, **whether you are married**, or **how much money you owe**, you can refuse to answer. If you think a question is improper, ask the interviewer **how the answer specifically relates to that job**. If you don't get a satisfactory explanation, you don't have to answer the question. And remember: Whatever happens, don't lose your cool. The interview will be over before you know it!

DID YOU KNOW . . .

In some countries, employers must hire only on the basis of skills and experience. In Canada, most countries in Europe, and in the United States, for example, an interviewer cannot ask an applicant certain questions unless the information is related to the job. Here are some questions an interviewer may NOT ask:

X How old are you?

X What is your religion?

X Are you married?

X What does your husband (or wife) do?

X Have you ever been arrested?

X How many children do you have?

X How tall are you?

X Where were you born?

AFTER YOU READ

Check the questions the interviewer asked Melissa.

☐ **1.** "Why can't you work under pressure?"

☐ **2.** "Have you cleaned your car out recently?"

☐ **3.** "Is he going to ask me serious questions?"

☐ **4.** "How can the accident have occurred?"

☐ **5.** "Does she really want to work for this company?"

☐ **6.** "Are you sure you know how to conduct an interview?"

Grammar Presentation

INDIRECT QUESTIONS

Direct Speech: *Yes / No* Questions		
Subject	Reporting Verb	Direct Question
He	asked,	**"Do you have** any experience**?"** **"Can you create** spreadsheets**?"** **"Will you stay** for a year**?"**

Indirect Speech: *Yes / No* Questions				
Subject	Reporting Verb	(Noun / Pronoun)	Indirect Question	
He	asked	(Melissa) (her)	**if** **whether** **whether or not**	**she had** any experience**.** **she could create** spreadsheets**.** **she would stay** for a year**.**

Direct Speech: *Wh-* Questions About the Subject		
Subject	Reporting Verb	Direct Question
He	asked,	**"Who told you** about the job**?"** **"What happened** on **your** last job**?"**

Indirect Speech: *Wh-* Questions About the Subject			
Subject	Reporting Verb	(Noun / Pronoun)	Indirect Question
He	asked	(Bob) (him)	**who had told him** about the job**.** **what had happened** on **his** last job**.**

(continued)

Direct Speech: *Wh-* Questions About the Predicate		
Subject	**Reporting Verb**	**Direct Question**
He	asked,	"Who(m) **did you work** for**?**" "Where **do you work** now**?**" "How **are you going to get** to work**?**" "Why **have you decided to change** jobs**?**" "How much **are you making?**"

Indirect Speech: *Wh-* Questions About the Predicate			
Subject	**Reporting Verb**	**(Noun / Pronoun)**	**Indirect Question**
He	asked	(Melissa) (her)	**who(m) she had worked** for. **where she worked** now. **how she was going to get** to work. **why she had decided to change** jobs. **how much she was making.**

GRAMMAR NOTES

EXAMPLES

	DIRECT QUESTION	**INDIRECT QUESTION**
1. Use *if* or *whether* in **indirect *yes/no* questions**.	"Can you type?" she asked.	She asked me *if* **I could type**.
	"Do you know how to use a scanner?" he asked.	He wanted to know *whether* **I knew how to use a scanner**.

USAGE NOTES

Whether is more formal than *if*.

- My boss wants to know *whether* **the report is ready**.

We often use *whether or not* to report *yes/no* questions.

- He wanted to know *whether or not* **the report was ready**.

2. Use **question words** in indirect *wh-* questions.	**DIRECT QUESTION**	**INDIRECT QUESTION**
	"Where is your office?" I asked.	I asked *where* **his office was**.
	I asked, "How much is the salary?"	I asked *how much* **the salary was**.

3. Use **statement word order** (subject + verb), not question word order for:	**STATEMENT**	
	subject verb **They hired** Li.	
	DIRECT QUESTION	**INDIRECT QUESTION**
a. indirect *yes/no* questions	Did they hire Li?	I asked **if they had hired** Li.
b. indirect *wh-* questions about the predicate (usually the last part of the sentence)	Who did they hire?	I asked **who they had hired**.
c. indirect *wh-* questions about the subject (usually the first part of the sentence)	Which company hired Li?	I asked **which company had hired** Li.
▶ **BE CAREFUL!** If a direct question about the subject has the form **question word + *be* + noun**, then the indirect question has the form **question word + noun + *be***.	Who is the boss?	I asked **who the boss was**. NOT I asked who ~~was the boss~~.

4. In indirect questions:	**DIRECT QUESTION**	**INDIRECT QUESTION**
	Why did you leave?	She asked me **why I had left**.
a. do not use the auxiliary *do, does,* or *did.*		NOT She asked me why ~~did I leave~~.
b. do not end with a question mark (end with a period).		NOT She asked me why I had left~~?~~

Reference Notes

The same **verb tense changes and other changes** occur in both indirect questions and indirect statements (see Units 25 and 26).

For a list of **reporting verbs** in questions, see Appendix 13 on page A-5.

Focused Practice

1 | DISCOVER THE GRAMMAR

🎧 *Melissa Morrow is telling a friend about her job interview. Underline the indirect questions in the conversation.*

DON: So, how did the interview go?

MELISSA: It was very strange.

DON: What happened?

MELISSA: Well, it started off OK. He asked me <u>how much experience I had had</u>, and I told him I had been a public relations officer for 10 years. Let's see . . . He also asked what I would change about my current job. That was a little tricky.

DON: What did you say?

MELISSA: Well, I didn't want to say anything negative, so I told him that I was ready for more responsibility.

DON: Good. What else did he ask?

MELISSA: Oh, you know, the regular things. He asked what my greatest success had been, and how much money I was making.

DON: Sounds like a normal interview to me. What was so strange about it?

MELISSA: Well, at one point, he just stopped talking for a long time. Then he asked me all these bizarre questions that weren't even related to the job.

DON: Like what?

MELISSA: He asked me if I had cleaned out my car recently.

DON: You're kidding.

MELISSA: No, I'm not. Then he asked me why my employer didn't want me to stay.

DON: That's crazy. I hope you told him that you hadn't been fired.

MELISSA: Of course. Oh, and he asked me if I was good enough to work for his company.

DON: What did you tell him?

MELISSA: I told him that with my skills and experience I was one of the best in my field.

DON: That was a great answer. It sounds like you handled yourself very well.

MELISSA: Thanks. But now I'm asking myself if I really want this job.

DON: Take your time. Don't make any snap decisions.

Now check the direct questions that the interviewer asked Melissa.

☑ **1.** How much experience have you had?

☐ **2.** What would you change about your current job?

☐ **3.** Are you ready for more responsibility?

☐ **4.** What was your greatest success?

☐ **5.** How much are you making now?

☐ **6.** Was it a normal interview?

☐ **7.** Have you cleaned out your car recently?

☐ **8.** Have you been fired?

☐ **9.** Are you good enough to work for this company?

☐ **10.** Do you ever make snap decisions?

2 | NOSY NEIGHBOR

Grammar Notes 1–4

🎧 *Claire has an interview next week. Her neighbor, Jaime, wants to know all about it.*
Report Jaime's questions using the correct order of the words in parentheses.

JAIME: I heard you're going on an interview next week. What kind of job is it?

CLAIRE: It's for a job as an office assistant.

1. _He asked what kind of job it was._____
                          (kind of job / what / was / it)

JAIME: Oh, really? When is the interview?

CLAIRE: It's on Tuesday at 9:00.

2. _____
                          (the interview / was / when)

JAIME: Where's the company?

CLAIRE: It's downtown on the west side.

3. _____
                          (was / where / the company)

JAIME: Do you need directions?

CLAIRE: No, I know the way.

4. _____
                          (needed / if / she / directions)

JAIME: How long does it take to get there?

CLAIRE: About half an hour.

5. _____
                          (to get there / it / takes / how long)

JAIME: Are you going to drive?

CLAIRE: I think so. It's probably the fastest way.

6. _____
                          (was going / if / she / to drive)

(continued)

JAIME: Who's going to interview you?

CLAIRE: Uhmmm. I'm not sure. Probably the manager of the department.

7. _____
(was going / her / who / to interview)

JAIME: Well, good luck. When will they let you know?

CLAIRE: It will take a while. They have a lot of candidates.

8. _____
(her / they / would / when / let / know)

3 | WHO'S ASKING?   *Grammar Notes 1–4*

Read these questions, which were asked during Claire's interview. Claire asked some of the questions, and the manager, Mr. Stollins, asked others. Decide who asked each question. Then rewrite each question as indirect speech.

1. "What type of training is available for the job?"

   Claire asked what type of training was available for the job.

2. "What kind of experience do you have?"

   _____

3. "Is there opportunity for promotion?"

   _____

4. "Are you interviewing with other companies?"

   _____

5. "What will my responsibilities be?"

   _____

6. "How is job performance rewarded?"

   _____

7. "What was your starting salary at your last job?"

   _____

8. "Did you get along well with your last employer?"

   _____

9. "Do you hire many women?"

   _____

10. "Why did you apply for this position?"

    _____

11. "Have you had any major layoffs in the past few years?"

    _____

4 | EDITING

Read this memo an interviewer wrote after an interview. There are seven mistakes in the use of indirect questions. The first mistake is already corrected. Find and correct six more. Don't forget to check punctuation. Mistakes with quotation marks count as one mistake for the sentence.

May 15, 2006

TO: Francesca Giuffrida

FROM: Ken Marley

SUBJECT: Interview with Carlos Lopez

This morning I interviewed Carlos Lopez for the administrative assistant position. Since this job requires a lot of contact with the public, I did some stress questioning. I asked Mr. Lopez why
                                                       he couldn't
~~couldn't he~~ work under pressure. I also asked him why his supervisor disliked him. Finally, I inquired when he would quit the job with our company?

Mr. Lopez kept his poise throughout the interview. He answered all my questions calmly, and he had some excellent questions of his own. He asked "if we expected changes in the job." He also wanted to know how often do we evaluate employees. I was quite impressed when he asked why did I decide to join this company.

Mr. Lopez is an excellent candidate for the job, and I believe he will handle the responsibilities well. At the end of the interview, Mr. Lopez inquired when we could let him know our decision? I asked him if whether he was considering another job, and he said he was. I think we should act quickly to hire Mr. Lopez.

Communication Practice

5 | LISTENING

🎧 *You are going to hear a job interview that takes place in Canada. First read the checklist. Then listen to the interview and check the topics the interviewer asks about.*

Possible Job Interview Topics

OK to Ask

- ☐ Name
- ☐ Address
- ☐ Work experience
- ☐ Reason for leaving job
- ☑ Reason for seeking position that is open
- ☐ Salary
- ☐ Education
- ☐ Professional affiliations
- ☐ Convictions for crimes
- ☐ Skills
- ☐ Job performance
- ☐ Permission to work in Canada

Not OK to Ask *

- ☑ Age
- ☐ Race
- ☐ Sex
- ☐ Religion
- ☐ National origin
- ☐ Height or weight
- ☐ Marital status
- ☐ Information about spouse
- ☐ Arrest record
- ☐ Physical disabilities
- ☐ Children
- ☐ Citizenship
- ☐ English language skill
- ☐ Financial situation

*illegal to ask if not related to the job

Listen again and write the illegal questions the interviewer asks.

1. *How old are you?*

2. _____

3. _____

4. _____

5. _____

6. _____

7. _____

Now report the illegal questions to the class.

Example: He asked her how old she was.

6 | **ROLE PLAY: A JOB INTERVIEW**

Work in groups. Using the advertisement and the résumé, develop questions for a job interview. Half of the group should write questions for the interviewer, and the other half should write questions for the candidate. Then select two people to act out the interview for the class.

Pat Rogers
215 West Hill Drive
Baltimore, MD 21233
Telephone: (410) 555-7777
Fax: (410) 555-7932
progers@email.com

EDUCATION   **Taylor Community College**
Associate's Degree (Business) 2001

Middlesex High School
High school diploma, 1998

EXPERIENCE   **Medical receptionist**
2001–Present Responsibilities: Greet patients, make appointments,
Patients Plus answer telephones, update computer records
Baltimore, MD

1998–2001   **Admitting clerk, hospital admissions office**
Union Hospital Responsibilities: Interviewed patients for admission,
Baltimore, MD input information in computer, answered telephones

MEDICAL RECEPTIONIST for busy doctor's office. Mature individual needed to answer phones, greet patients, make appointments. Some filing and billing. Similar experience preferred. Computer skills a plus.

Now discuss each group's role-play interview as a class. Use these questions to guide your discussion. Support your ideas by reporting questions that were asked in the interview.

1. Was it a stress interview? Why or why not?

2. Did the interviewer ask any illegal questions? Which ones were illegal?

3. Which of the candidate's questions were the most useful in evaluating the job? Explain your choices.

4. Which of the interviewer's questions gave the clearest picture of the candidate? Explain your choices.

5. If you were the interviewer, would you hire this candidate? Why or why not?

6. If you were the candidate, would you want to work for this company? Why or why not?

Example: I think it was a stress interview because the interviewer asked him why he couldn't find a new job. The interviewer asked two illegal questions. She asked when the candidate was born. She also asked where the candidate was from.

7 | CURIOUS QUESTIONS

Work in pairs. What would you like to know about your partner? Make a list of questions. Ask and answer each other's questions. Then get together with another pair and report your conversations.

> **Example:** She asked me what I was going to do next semester. I told her I was going to take the advanced-level grammar class.

8 | IN YOUR EXPERIENCE

In small groups, discuss a personal experience with a school or job interview. (If you do not have a personal experience, use the experience of someone you know.) Talk about these questions:

- What did the interviewer want to find out?
- What was the most difficult question to answer? Why?
- Were there any questions that you didn't want to answer? What did you say?
- What did you ask the interviewer?

9 | WRITING

Before you look for work, it's a good idea to talk to people who are already working in jobs that might interest you. In these kinds of "informational interviews" you can ask what the tasks in that job are, why people like or dislike the work, or how much you can expect to be paid. Write a list of questions to ask in an informational interview about a job.

> **Example:** Do you like your job?
> How much vacation time do you get?

Now interview someone and write a report about the interview. Use indirect questions.

> **Example:** I interviewed Pete Ortiz, who is an assistant in the computer lab. I wanted to talk to him because I'm interested in applying for a job in the lab. I asked Pete if he liked working there, and he told me he liked it most of the time . . .

10 | ON THE INTERNET

Do a search to find an interview with a famous person. Choose two or three interesting questions that the interviewer asked. Report the questions and the answers to the class.

> **Example:** I read an interview with Turkish movie director Ferzan Ozpetek. The interviewer asked him where he got the idea for his movie *Facing Windows*. He said that he had gotten the idea from a real-life experience.

Embedded Questions

Grammar in Context

BEFORE YOU READ

🎧 *Look at the cartoon. What is the man worried about? Read this interview about tipping.*

THE TIP

In China it used to be illegal, in New Zealand it's uncommon, but in Germany it's included in the bill. In the United States and Canada it's common but illogical: You tip the person who delivers flowers, but not the person who delivers a package.

Do *you* often wonder **what to do** about tipping?

Our correspondent, Marjorie S. Fuchs, interviewed Irene Frankel, author of *Tips on Tipping*, to help us through the tipping maze.

"I wonder **how much we should give**."

MSF: Tell me **why you decided to write a book about tipping**.

IF: I began writing it for people from cultures where tipping wasn't a custom. But when I started researching, I found that Americans, too, often weren't sure **how to tip**, so *Tips* became a book for anybody living in the United States.

MSF: Does your book explain **who to tip**?

IF: Oh, absolutely. It tells you **who to tip, how much to tip, and when to tip**. Equally important, it tells you **when not to tip**.

MSF: That *is* important. Suppose I don't know **whether to tip someone**, and I left your book at home. Is it OK to ask?

(continued)

THE TIP

IF: Sure. If you don't know **whether to leave a tip**, the best thing to do is ask. People usually won't tell you **what to do**, but they *will* tell you **what most customers do**.

MSF: I always wonder **what to do when I get bad service**. Should I still tip?

IF: Don't tip the ordinary amount, but tip *something* so that the service person doesn't think that you just forgot to leave a tip.

MSF: Is there any reason **why we tip a restaurant server but not a flight attendant**?

IF: Not that I know. The rules for tipping in the United States are very illogical, and there are often contradictions in who we tip. That's why I wrote this book.

MSF: Another thing—I've never understood **why a restaurant tip depends on the amount of the bill rather than on the amount of work involved in serving the meal**. After all, bringing out a $20 dish of food involves the same amount of work as carrying out a $5 plate.

IF: You're right. It makes no sense. That's just the way it is.

MSF: One last question. Suppose I'm planning a trip to Egypt. Tell me **how I can learn about tipping customs in that country**.

IF: Usually travel agents know **what the rules are for tipping in each country**. Look up the information on the Internet if you can't find out from a travel agent or a book.

MSF: Well, thanks for all the good tips. I know our readers will find them very helpful. *I* certainly did.

IF: Thank *you*.

AFTER YOU READ

Circle the correct words to complete these embedded questions from the interview.

1. Tell me why <u>did you decide / you decided</u> to write a book about tipping.

2. It tells you when <u>no / not</u> to tip.

3. I always wonder what <u>do I do / to do</u> when I get bad service.

4. Is there any reason why <u>do we tip / we tip</u> a restaurant server but not a flight attendant?

5. Tell me how <u>I can / can I</u> learn about tipping customs in that country.

Grammar Presentation

EMBEDDED QUESTIONS

Main Clause	Embedded Question
I'm not sure He wondered	**if I left the right tip.** **whether (or not) five dollars was enough.**
Can you remember	**how much our bill was?**

Wh- Word + Infinitive	
I don't know	**how much to tip.**
Do you know	**where to leave the tip?**

GRAMMAR NOTES

EXAMPLES

1. Embedded questions are questions that are inside another sentence. An embedded question can be:

a. inside a statement

b. inside another question

▶ **BE CAREFUL!** If the embedded question is inside a <u>statement</u>, use a **period** at the end of the sentence.

If the embedded question is inside a <u>question</u>, use a **question mark** at the end of the sentence.

- I don't know **who our server is.**

- Do you remember **who our server is?**

- I wonder **if that's our server.**
  NOT I wonder if that's our server?

- Do you know **if that's our server?**

2. Use embedded questions to:

a. express something you do not know

b. ask politely for information

USAGE NOTE: Embedded questions are <u>more polite</u> than direct questions.

DIRECT QUESTION	EMBEDDED QUESTION
Why didn't he tip the mechanic?	I don't know **why he didn't tip the mechanic.**
Is the tip included?	Can you tell me **if the tip is included**?
Less formal: Does our bill include a service charge?	*More polite:* Can you tell me **if our bill includes a service charge**?

(continued)

3. Begin **embedded *yes/no* questions** with *if*, *whether*, or *whether or not*.

USAGE NOTE: ***Whether*** is more formal than *if*.

- Do you know ***if* they delivered the pizza**?

  OR

- Do you know ***whether* they delivered the pizza**?

  OR

- Do you know ***whether or not* they delivered the pizza**?

Begin **embedded *wh-* questions** with a **question word**.

- Many tourists wonder ***how much* to tip their restaurant server.**

---

4. Use **statement word order** (subject + verb), not question word order in:

	DIRECT QUESTION	EMBEDDED QUESTION
a. embedded *yes/no questions* Do not leave out *if* or *whether* in embedded *yes/no* questions.	Is it 6:00 yet?	Could you tell me **if it is** 6:00 yet? NOT Could you tell me ~~is it~~ 6:00 yet?
b. embedded *wh-* questions about the predicate (usually the last part of the sentence) Do not use the auxiliary verbs *do, does,* or *did* in embedded questions.	Why did they order pizza?	I wondered why **they ordered** pizza. NOT I wondered why ~~did they order~~ pizza.
c. embedded *wh-* questions about the subject (usually the first part of the sentence)	Who ordered pizza?	I can't remember **who ordered** pizza.
▶ **BE CAREFUL!** If a direct question about the subject has the form **question word + *be* + noun**, then the indirect question has the form **question word + noun + *be***.	Who is our waiter?	Do you know **who** our waiter **is**? NOT Do you know ~~who is our waiter~~?

5. In embedded questions, you can also use:

    a. question word + infinitive

- Let's ask where we should leave the tip.

        OR

- Let's ask **where to leave** the tip.

- I wonder whether I should leave a tip.

        OR

    b. *whether* **+ infinitive**

- I wonder **whether to leave a tip**.

▶ **BE CAREFUL!** Do not use the infinitive after *if* or *why*.

- I don't understand **why I should tip**.
  NOT I don't understand why ~~to tip~~.

---

6. Embedded questions often follow these phrases:

    I don't know . . .

    I'd like to know . . .

    Do you know . . . ?

    Can you tell me . . . ?

    I can't remember . . .

    Can you remember . . . ?

    Let's ask . . .

    We need to find out . . .

    I'd like to find out . . .

    I wonder . . .

    I'm not sure . . .

    It doesn't say . . .

    Could you explain . . . ?

    I can't imagine . . .

- ***I don't know*** what the name of the restaurant is.
- ***Can you remember*** how much the shrimp costs?
- ***Let's ask*** what today's specials are.
- ***I wonder*** what time the restaurant closes.
- ***Could you explain*** what that sign means?
- ***I can't imagine*** why this restaurant isn't more popular.

Focused Practice

1 | DISCOVER THE GRAMMAR

Read the advertisement for Tips on Tipping. *Underline the embedded questions.*

Tips on Tipping

This book is for you if . . .

you've ever avoided a situation just because you didn't know <u>how much to tip</u>.

you've ever realized (too late) that you were supposed to offer a tip.

you've ever given a huge tip and then wondered if a tip was necessary at all.

you've ever needed to know how to calculate the right tip instantly.

you're new to the United States and you're not sure who you should tip here.

you'd like to learn how tipping properly can get you the best service for your money.

What readers are saying . . .

"I can't imagine how I got along without it."

    —Chris Sarton, Minneapolis, Minnesota

"Take *Tips* along if you want a stress-free vacation."

    —Midori Otaka, Osaka, Japan

"I took my fiancée to dinner at Deux Saisons and knew exactly how to tip everyone!"

    —S. Prasad, San Francisco, California

"You need this book—whether you stay in hostels or five-star hotels."

    —Cuno Pumpin, Bern, Switzerland

Send for the ultimate guide to tipping and get all the answers to your tipping questions.

Yes! I want to learn who to tip, when to tip, and how much to tip. Please send me additional information on *Tips on Tipping*. I understand that the book will be $4.95 plus $2.00 postage and handling for each copy. (New York residents: Add sales tax.) Contact Martin Unlimited, Inc. at dmifdmif@yahoo.com.

2 | SERVICE CHARGES

Complete this travel column about tipping customs around the world. Change the direct questions in parentheses to embedded questions. Use correct punctuation.

Tipping customs vary, so travelers should find out who, where, and how much to tip. Here are some frequently asked questions.

Q: Can you tell me whether *I should tip in Canada?*
1. (Should I tip in Canada?)

A: Yes. Tipping practices in Canada are similar to those in the United States.

Q: I know that some places in France include a service charge. Could you explain

_____
2. (How can I tell if the tip is included in the bill?)

A: Look for the phrase *service compris* (service included) on the bill.

Q: I'm going to China next month. I understand that tipping used to be illegal. Do you know

_____
3. (Will restaurant servers accept tips now?)

A: Yes. You should leave 3 percent in a restaurant.

Q: On a recent trip to Iceland, I found that service people refused tips. Could you explain

_____
4. (Why did this happen?)

A: In Iceland, people often feel insulted by tips. Just say thank you—that's enough.

Q: Our family is planning a trip to Norway to visit my in-laws. My daughter doesn't know how

to ski and wants to take some lessons while we're there. I'd like to know

_____
5. (Should I tip her instructor?)

A: Tipping is rare all over Scandinavia. Take the instructor to lunch instead.

Q: I'm going to work in Japan for a year. I'm bringing a lot of luggage. Could you tell me

_____
6. (How much should I tip the airport and train porters?)

A: There's a fixed fee per bag for airport porters. No tipping is expected on trains.

Q: My husband and I are planning a trip to several cities in Australia. Please tell us

_____
7. (Who expects a tip and who doesn't?)

A: Restaurant servers expect a tip of 10 percent, but you don't need to tip taxi drivers.

3 | WHEN IN ROME . . .

Grammar Notes 1–4, 6

Two foreign exchange students are visiting Rome, Italy. Complete their conversations. Choose the appropriate questions from the list and change them to embedded questions. Use correct punctuation.

- How much are we supposed to tip the taxi driver?
- Could we rent a car and drive there?
- Do they have tour buses that go there?
- How much does the subway cost?
- How far are you going?
- How are we going to choose?
- How much does a bus tour cost?
- What did they put in the sauce?
- Where is the Forum?
- ~~Where is it?~~
- Where do they sell them?

A. **DRIVER:** Where do you want to go? The airport?

MARTINA: The Hotel Forte. Do you know _where it is?_ _____
1.

DRIVER: Sure. Get in and I'll take you there.

MARTINA: *(whispering to Miuki)* Do you know _____
2.

MIUKI: According to the book, we're supposed to leave 10–15 percent. I've got it.

B. **MARTINA:** There's so much to see in Rome. I don't know _____
1.

MIUKI: We could take a bus tour of the city first, and then decide.

MARTINA: Does the guidebook say _____
2.

MIUKI: Yeah. About $15 per person, plus tips for the guide and the driver.

C. **MARTINA:** That was delicious.

MIUKI: Let's try to find out _____
1.

MARTINA: It tasted like it had a lot of garlic and basil. I'll ask the waiter.

D. **MARTINA:** Excuse me. Can you tell me _____
1.

OFFICER: Sure. Just turn right and go straight.

E. MIUKI: Let's take the subway. Do you know _____
1.

MARTINA: It's not expensive. I don't think it depends on _____
2.

But we have to get tickets, and I'm not sure _____
3.

MIUKI: Oh. Probably right in the station or at a newsstand.

F. MARTINA: I'd like to visit Ostia Antica. It's supposed to be like the ruins at Pompeii.

MIUKI: I wonder _____
1.

MARTINA: I really don't want to go with a big group of people. What about you? Do you think

_____
2.

MIUKI: Good idea! It'll be nice to drive around and see some of the countryside too.

4 | ASKING FOR ADVICE   *Grammar Note 5*

*Complete the conversation between Martina and Miuki. Use a question word and the
infinitive form of the verbs in the box.*

figure out	get	go	invite	leave	~~wear~~

MARTINA: I can't decide _____ *what to wear* _____ Friday night.
1.

MIUKI: Your red dress. You always look great in it. By the way, where are you going?

MARTINA: Trattoria da Luigi with Janek. We're meeting there at 8:00.

MIUKI: Great! You know _____ there, don't you?
2.

MARTINA: Yes, but I'm not sure _____.
3.

MIUKI: Leave at 7:30. That'll give you enough time.

MARTINA: I'd like to take Janek someplace for dessert afterward, but I don't know

_____.
4.

MIUKI: The desserts at da Luigi's are supposed to be pretty good.

MARTINA: Oh. By the way, it's Janek's birthday, so I'm paying. But I'm still not quite sure

_____ the tip.
5.

MIUKI: Service is usually included in Italy. The menu should tell you. So, who else is going?

MARTINA: Well, I thought about asking a few people to join us, but I really didn't know

_____.
6.

MIUKI: Don't worry. I'm sure it will be fine with just the two of you.

5 | EDITING

Read this post to a travelers' website. There are ten mistakes in the use of embedded questions. The first mistake is already corrected. Find and correct nine more. Don't forget to check punctuation.

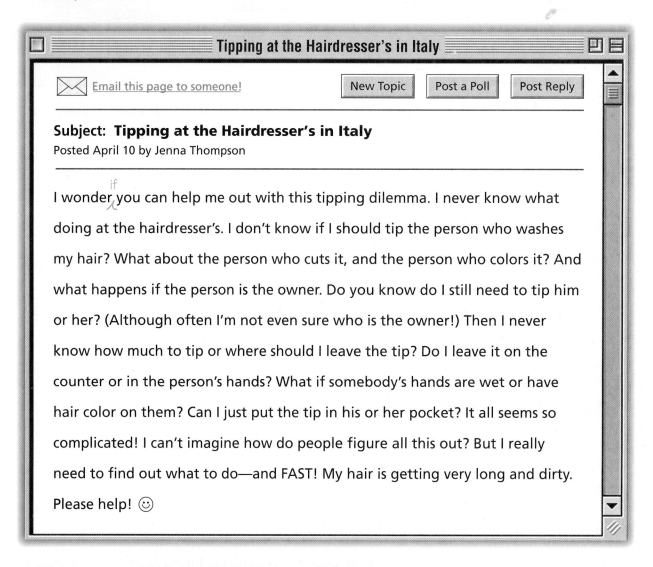

Tipping at the Hairdresser's in Italy

✉ Email this page to someone!   New Topic   Post a Poll   Post Reply

Subject: Tipping at the Hairdresser's in Italy
Posted April 10 by Jenna Thompson

I wonder ~~if~~ you can help me out with this tipping dilemma. I never know what doing at the hairdresser's. I don't know if I should tip the person who washes my hair? What about the person who cuts it, and the person who colors it? And what happens if the person is the owner. Do you know do I still need to tip him or her? (Although often I'm not even sure who is the owner!) Then I never know how much to tip or where should I leave the tip? Do I leave it on the counter or in the person's hands? What if somebody's hands are wet or have hair color on them? Can I just put the tip in his or her pocket? It all seems so complicated! I can't imagine how do people figure all this out? But I really need to find out what to do—and FAST! My hair is getting very long and dirty. Please help! ☺

Communication Practice

6 | LISTENING

🎧 *A travel agent is being interviewed on a call-in radio show. The topic is tipping. Listen to the callers' questions. Then listen again, and circle the letter of the correct response to each caller's question.*

1. Caller One
   a. Between 15 and 20 percent of the total bill.
   b. The waiter.

2. Caller Two

    a. About 15 percent of the fare.

    b. Only if you are happy with the ride.

3. Caller Three

    a. Before you leave.

    b. On the table.

4. Caller Four

    a. The person who takes you to your seat.

    b. One euro for one person. Two euros for two or more people.

5. Caller Five

    a. The manager.

    b. Don't leave a tip.

6. Caller Six

    a. $1.00.

    b. At the cashier.

7. Caller Seven

    a. Look it up on the Internet.

    b. It's included in the bill.

8. Caller Eight

    a. $1.00.

    b. The person who delivers your food.

7 | TIPPING

Work in small groups. Discuss these questions.

1. Do you think tipping is a good system? Why or why not?

2. Were you ever in a situation where you didn't know what to do about a tip? What did you do?

3. How do people tip in your country and in other countries you know?

    Example: **A:** I'm not sure whether tipping is good or not. I think people should get paid enough so that they don't have to depend on tips.

                 B: I wonder if you would still get good service if the tip were included.

                 C: Sure you would. A service charge is included in a lot of countries, and the service is still good.

8 | INFORMATION GAP: EATING OUT

Work in groups of three. Students A and B are customers in a restaurant. Student C is the server. Students A and B, look at the menu below. Student C, turn to page 426 and follow the instructions there.

Trattoria da Luigi

English version

Appetizers

Bruschetta	1.25
Roasted vegetables	3.25

FIRST COURSE

Soup of the day (*please ask*)	2.95
Caesar salad	3.25
Luigi's salad	2.95
Linguine with clam sauce	10.80
Spaghetti da Luigi	12.90

SECOND COURSE

Chicken

Chicken da Luigi	7.95
Half roasted chicken	6.95

Beef

Veal parmigiano	15.90
Steak frites	12.90

Fish

Catch of the day (*please ask*)	price varies
Shrimp marinara	15.80
Filet of sole with sauce Dijon	13.90

Side Dishes

Vegetable of the day	2.50
Roasted potatoes	2.50

Desserts

Fruit tart (in season)	4.30
Ice cream	3.40
Chocolate cake	2.50
Fresh fruit	2.95
Dessert of the day (*please ask*)	price varies

Service Charge Not Included

Student A, you are allergic to tomatoes and dairy products. Student B, you don't eat meat or chicken. Discuss the menu with your partner. Then ask your server about items on the menu and order a meal. When you get the check, figure out a 15 percent tip.

Example: **A:** Do you know what's in a Caesar salad?

B: Not really. We'll have to ask the server.
Excuse me. Can you tell us what's in the Caesar salad?

C: Sure. It has lettuce, parmesan cheese, and croutons.

9 | THE FIRST TIME IS ALWAYS THE HARDEST

Think about the first time you did something—for example, the first time you:

drove a car   traveled to a foreign country

went on a job interview   became a parent

Work in pairs. Discuss what problems you had.

Example: I remember the first time I drove a car. I didn't know how to start it.
I didn't know which gear to use. I even had to ask how to turn the wipers on . . .

10 | ROLE PLAY: INFORMATION PLEASE!

Work in pairs (A and B). Student A, you are a desk clerk at a hotel. Student B, you are a guest at the hotel. Use embedded questions to find out information about the following:

restaurants   banks

interesting sights   shopping

transportation   tipping

entertainment   laundry

Example: **A:** Can I help you?
B: Yes. Could you tell me where to find a good, inexpensive restaurant around here?
A: There are some nice restaurants around the university.

11 | WRITING

Think about a time you were traveling. Write a paragraph about a situation that confused or surprised you. Use embedded questions.

Example: When I was an exchange student in China, my Chinese friends always wanted to know how old I was. I couldn't understand why new friends needed to know my age. I wasn't sure whether to tell the truth, because I was younger than them . . .

12 | ON THE INTERNET

ⓒ *Do a search on tipping customs in a country you are interested in. Report your findings to the class.*

Example: I wanted to know if you should tip a taxi driver in Russia. I'm confused. One site said that taxi drivers do not expect tips. Another site said they expect a tip of 10 percent. I really don't know what to do!

INFORMATION GAP FOR STUDENT C

Student C, read these notes about today's menu. Answer your customers' questions. When they are done ordering, look at the menu on page 424 and write up the order and figure out the check.

Trattoria da Luigi

Appetizers
Bruschetta (toasted bread with chopped tomatoes, garlic, olive oil)
Roasted vegetables (onions, red pepper, zucchini, eggplant)

FIRST COURSE
Soup of the day
Monday: vegetable soup (carrots, peas, string beans in a tomato broth)
Tuesday: tomato soup
Wednesday: pea soup
Thursday: onion soup
Friday: fish soup
Saturday: potato soup (includes cream)

Caesar salad (lettuce, parmesan cheese,
croutons—cubes of bread toasted in olive oil and garlic)
Luigi's salad (spinach, mushrooms, tomatoes, onions)
Spaghetti da Luigi (spaghetti with spinach, fresh
tomatoes, and mushrooms in a light cream sauce)

SECOND COURSE
Chicken da Luigi (chicken baked in a tomato sauce
with olives and basil)
Steak frites (steak cooked in pan with butter,
served with french fried potatoes)
Catch of the day: grilled flounder—6.95 euros
Shrimp marinara (shrimp in tomato sauce)
Filet of sole with sauce Dijon (mustard sauce)

Side Dishes
Vegetable of the day: broccoli

Desserts
Fruit tart (cherry, apple, blueberry)
Ice cream (chocolate, strawberry, vanilla)
Fresh fruit (apples, bananas, strawberries)
Dessert of the day: strawberry shortcake (yellow cake
with fresh strawberries and whipped cream—3.25 euros)

Example: A: Do you know what's in a Caesar salad?

B: Not really. We'll have to ask the server.
Excuse me. Can you tell us what's in the Caesar salad?

C: Sure. It has lettuce, parmesan cheese, and croutons.

From **Grammar** to **Writing**
Using Direct and Indirect Speech

A letter of complaint often includes both direct and indirect speech to describe a problem. We use direct speech only when it is important (for 100 percent accuracy) to report someone's exact words or to communicate a speaker's attitude. Otherwise, we use indirect speech.

1 *Read this letter of complaint. Underline all the examples of indirect speech once. Underline all the examples of direct speech twice.*

Computer Town, Inc.
Customer Service Department
One Swell Way
Dallas, TX 75201

Dear Customer Service Manager:

In September 2004, I purchased a computer from your company. After the one-year warranty expired, I bought an extended service contract every year. I always received a renewal notice in the mail that told me that my policy was going to expire in a few weeks. This year, however, I did not receive the notice, and, as a result, I missed the deadline.

Upon realizing this mistake, I immediately called your company and asked if I could renew the service contract. The representative said, "It's too late, Miss." He said that if I wanted to extend my contract, they would have to send someone to my home to inspect my computer. He also told me I would have to pay $160 for this visit. He said that my only other option was to ship my computer back to the company for inspection. I told him that neither of these options was acceptable.

When I asked him why I hadn't been notified that my contract was going to expire, he said, "We don't send notices out anymore." I said that I wanted to make a complaint. He said, "Don't complain to me. I don't even park the cars of the people who make these decisions."

I think that your representatives should be more polite when speaking to customers. I also think that your customers should have

(continued)

been told that they would no longer receive renewal notices in the
mail. That way, I would not have missed the deadline. I would,
therefore, greatly appreciate it if I could have my service contract
renewed without having to go through the inconvenience and expense
of having my computer inspected.

   Thank you for your attention.

Sincerely yours,

Anne Marie Clarke

Anne Marie Clarke
Customer No. 5378593

2 | *Look at the letter in Exercise 1. Circle the correct words to complete these sentences.*
Give an example of each item.

1. The word *that* often introduces <u>direct</u> /(indirect) speech.

   He told me that I would have to pay $160 for this visit.

   _____

2. Use quotation marks for <u>direct</u> / <u>indirect</u> speech.

   _____

   _____

3. Put final punctuation <u>inside</u> / <u>outside</u> the quotation marks.

   _____

   _____

4. Don't use a comma before <u>direct</u> / <u>indirect</u> speech.

   _____

   _____

5. Capitalize the first word of <u>direct</u> / <u>indirect</u> speech.

   _____

   _____

6. You can leave out the <u>word *that*</u> / <u>question word</u> when it introduces a reported

   <u>statement</u> / <u>question</u>.

   _____

   _____

7. The writer used <u>direct</u> / <u>indirect</u> speech to show that the representative on the phone was rude.

   _____

3 | *Before you write . . .*

1. Think of an incident you would like to complain about, or make one up.

2. Work with a partner. Discuss each other's incidents and ask questions. Talk about where to use direct speech most effectively.

4 | *Write your letter of complaint. Remember to use indirect speech, and, if appropriate, direct speech. Be sure to capitalize and punctuate correctly.*

5 | *Exchange letters with a different partner. Then answer the following questions.*

	Yes	No
1. Do you understand the writer's complaint?	☐	☐
2. Did the writer choose direct speech to show the other person's attitude?	☐	☐
3. Did the writer choose direct speech for 100 percent accuracy?	☐	☐
4. Did the writer use quotation marks for direct speech only?	☐	☐
5. Is the direct speech punctuated correctly?	☐	☐

6 | *Work with your partner. Discuss each other's editing questions from Exercise 5. Then rewrite your own letter and make any necessary corrections.*

Review Test

I *Karen and Jon had a party a week ago. Karen is telling a friend about the conversations she had before the party. Read what people actually said. Then circle the correct word(s) to complete each reported sentence.*

1. "We'd like you and Bill to come to a party at our apartment this Friday."

   I invited Maria and Bill <u>came /</u> <u>to come</u> to a party at our apartment <u>last / this</u> Friday.
                                 a.   **b.**

2. "It'll be a housewarming for our new apartment."

   I told them it <u>would be / will be</u> a housewarming for <u>our / their</u> new apartment.
                              a.   **b.**

3. "We'll be a little late."

   Maria <u>said / told</u> me that <u>they / we</u> would be a little late.
               a.   **b.**

4. "What time is your party going to start?"

   Sheila <u>said / asked</u> what time our party <u>is / was</u> going to start.
                 a.   **b.**

5. "Should I bring something?"

   She asked if <u>I / she</u> <u>should bring / should have brought</u> something.
                       a.   **b.**

6. "Thanks, Sheila, but that's OK. Don't bring anything."

   I thanked her, but I <u>told / said</u> her <u>not to bring / didn't bring</u> anything.
                            a.   **b.**

7. "Hi, Karen. I've been planning to call you and Jon for a long time."

   Tory told me he <u>'s been planning / 'd been planning</u> to call <u>us / you</u> for a long time.
                                  a.   **b.**

8. "I don't know how to get to your place."

   He said he <u>didn't know how / doesn't know how</u> to get to <u>your / our</u> place.
                          a.   **b.**

9. "Is there a bus stop nearby?"

   He <u>said / asked</u> <u>was there / if there was</u> a bus stop nearby.
               a.   **b.**

(continued)

10. "Don't be afraid of getting lost."

I told Tory <u>not to be / be</u> afraid of getting lost.
    a.

11. "Take the Woodmere Avenue bus."

I <u>invited / told</u> him <u>take / to take</u> the Woodmere Avenue bus.
    a.   b.

12. "I'm sorry, Karen. I can't come tomorrow night."

Nita said that she <u>can't / couldn't</u> come <u>the following night / tomorrow night</u>.
                    a.   b.

13. "My cousin from Detroit is arriving today."

She told me her cousin from Detroit <u>is / was</u> arriving <u>today / that day</u>.
                                    a.   b.

14. "Bring your cousin along."

I <u>said / told</u> Nita to bring <u>her / your</u> cousin along.
    a.   b.

15. "The weather bureau has issued a storm warning for tonight."

Jon told me that the weather bureau <u>has issued / had issued</u> a storm warning for <u>tonight / that night</u>.
                                    a.   b.

16. "Schools will close early today."

The forecaster said that schools <u>would /will</u> close early <u>today / that day</u>.
                                a.   b.

17. "Motorists must drive with extreme caution."

She said that motorists <u>must have driven / had to drive</u> with extreme caution.
                        a.

18. "I love snow."

Jon always <u>tells / says</u> that he <u>loves / loved</u> snow.
            a.   b.

19. "Would you please shovel the driveway?"

The next morning I asked <u>you / him</u> <u>to shovel / if he had shoveled</u> the driveway.
                        a.   b.

20. "Where are my boots?"

He <u>told / asked</u> me where <u>were his boots / his boots were</u>.
    a.   b.

II Each sentence has four underlined words or phrases. The four underlined parts of the sentences are marked A, B, C, or D. Circle the letter of the <u>one</u> underlined part that is NOT CORRECT.

1. I <u>wonder</u> <u>how much</u> <u>should I</u> <u>tip</u> the driver for a trip to the airport.
     A   B   C   D
        A   B   C D
    A   B (C) D

2. Bob <u>said</u> <u>don't</u> forget <u>to bring</u> my bathing suit <u>because</u> they have a pool.
      A   B   C   D
    A   B   C   D

3. The <u>forecaster</u> <u>said</u>, "<u>The</u> weather <u>was going</u> to be great tomorrow."
      A   B   C   D
    A   B   C   D

4. <u>Cindy asked</u> Paz <u>if he knew</u> the phone number of the restaurant or
    A   B

   <u>if</u> <u>should she</u> look it up.
   C   D
    A   B   C   D

5. She <u>wasn't sure</u> <u>if</u> or not <u>she</u> <u>needed</u> an umbrella.
       A   B   C   D
    A   B   C   D

6. The bus driver <u>said</u> me I <u>should</u> <u>get off</u> at Pine Street and <u>walk</u> to Oak.
           A   B   C   D
    A   B   C   D

7. Juan <u>said</u> that <u>if</u> he <u>had known</u>, he <u>would</u> told me the way.
       A   B   C   D
    A   B   C   D

8. <u>When</u> I <u>talked</u> to Pat last month, she <u>told</u> she <u>was leaving</u>.
    A   B   C   D
    A   B   C   D

9. It <u>was snowing</u> last night when Vick <u>called</u> me from Florida and <u>told</u>
    A   B   C

   me he loved the warm weather down <u>here</u>.
                                      D
    A   B   C   D

10. My doctor <u>told me</u> <u>to</u> <u>wearing</u> a hat whenever I <u>go</u> into the sun.
            A   B   C   D
    A   B   C   D

III Read the direct speech. Circle the letter of the correct word(s) to complete the same speech reported the following day.

1. "You look beautiful in that dress."
    A   B   C (D)
   She told me _____ beautiful in that dress.
   (**A**) you look   (**C**) I'll look
   (**B**) you looked   (**D**) I looked

2. "Have you met Bill and Maria yet?"
    A   B   C   D
   Harry asked me _____ Bill and Maria yet.
   (**A**) if I met   (**C**) did I meet
   (**B**) have I met   (**D**) if I had met

(continued)

3. "Is Tory coming tonight?"   **A B C D**

   I asked Jon _____ Tory was coming that night.

   (**A**) whether   (**C**) when

   (**B**) did   (**D**) is

4. "I'm not sure."   **A B C D**

   He told me _____ sure.

   (**A**) I wasn't   (**C**) he isn't

   (**B**) he wasn't   (**D**) I'm not

5. "Why don't you ride home with us?"   **A B C D**

   Bill invited me _____ home with them.

   (**A**) why I didn't ride   (**C**) to ride

   (**B**) not to ride   (**D**) riding

6. "It may snow tonight."   **A B C D**

   He said it might snow _____.

   (**A**) tomorrow night   (**C**) at night

   (**B**) that night   (**D**) tonight

7. "Call me tomorrow."   **A B C D**

   Karen said _____ her the next day.

   (**A**) to call   (**C**) call

   (**B**) me to call   (**D**) I will call

8. "We ought to get together more often."   **A B C D**

   We all said that we _____ together more often.

   (**A**) had better get   (**C**) ought to get

   (**B**) ought to have gotten (**D**) should have gotten

9. "Don't drive fast."   **A B C D**

   Jon told Maria _____ fast.

   (**A**) to not drive   (**C**) they don't drive

   (**B**) don't drive   (**D**) not to drive

10. "I had a great time."   **A B C D**

    Bill told Jon _____ had had a great time.

    (**A**) I   (**C**) you

    (**B**) he   (**D**) Jon

IV *Report the conversation that Nita and Jon had at the party last week. Use the verbs in parentheses.*

1. **NITA:** How long have you and Karen been living here?

   (ask) *Nita asked how long Jon and Karen had been living there.*

2. **JON:** We moved in three weeks ago.

   (tell)_____

3. **NITA:** Do you like this place better than your old apartment?

   (ask)_____

4. **JON:** We like it a lot more.

   (say)_____

5. **JON:** When did your cousin arrive from Detroit?

   (ask)_____

6. **NITA:** He just came yesterday.

   (tell)_____

7. **JON:** It's been an incredible winter.

   (say)_____

8. **NITA:** The roads may close again with this storm.

   (say)_____

9. **JON:** Don't drive tonight.

   (say)_____

10. **JON:** Stay here with your cousin.

    (say)_____

11. **NITA:** We should try to make it home.

    (tell)_____

12. **NITA:** I have to walk my dog early tomorrow morning.

    (say)_____

V *Read this draft of a news story. There are nine mistakes in the use of direct and indirect speech and embedded questions. The first mistake is already corrected. Find and correct eight more. Don't forget to check punctuation. Mistakes with quotation marks count as one mistake for the sentence.*

Motorists returning home during last night's snow storm were pleasantly surprised.

Early yesterday afternoon, forecasters had predicted that Route 10 ~~will~~ *would* close because of high

winds. However, all major highways remained open last night. One woman, stopping for a

newspaper on Woodmere Avenue at about midnight, told this reporter that she and her

cousin have almost decided to stay with a friend tonight, rather than drive home. Her cousin

told me that I had just arrived from Detroit, where the storm hit first. He said "that it had

been a big one." School children seemed especially pleased. Yesterday morning, most schools

announced that they will close at 1:00 P.M. Several kids at James Fox Elementary reported

that they are planning to spend that afternoon sledding and having snowball fights.

Many people are wondering how could weather forecasters have made such a big

mistake. Carla Donati, the weather reporter for WCSX, said that they really were not sure

why this had happened? The National Weather Service has not commented.

▶ *To check your answers, go to the Answer Key on page RT-6.*

APPENDICES

1 | Irregular Verbs

Base Form	Simple Past	Past Participle
arise	arose	arisen
awake	awoke	awoken
be	was/were	been
beat	beat	beaten/beat
become	became	become
begin	began	begun
bend	bent	bent
bet	bet	bet
bite	bit	bitten
bleed	bled	bled
blow	blew	blown
break	broke	broken
bring	brought	brought
build	built	built
burn	burned/burnt	burned/burnt
burst	burst	burst
buy	bought	bought
catch	caught	caught
choose	chose	chosen
cling	clung	clung
come	came	come
cost	cost	cost
creep	crept	crept
cut	cut	cut
deal	dealt	dealt
dig	dug	dug
dive	dived/dove	dived
do	did	done
draw	drew	drawn
dream	dreamed/dreamt	dreamed/dreamt
drink	drank	drunk
drive	drove	driven
eat	ate	eaten
fall	fell	fallen
feed	fed	fed
feel	felt	felt
fight	fought	fought
find	found	found
fit	fit/fitted	fit
flee	fled	fled
fling	flung	flung
fly	flew	flown
forbid	forbade/forbid	forbidden
forget	forgot	forgotten
forgive	forgave	forgiven
freeze	froze	frozen
get	got	gotten/got

Base Form	Simple Past	Past Participle
give	gave	given
go	went	gone
grind	ground	ground
grow	grew	grown
hang	hung	hung
have	had	had
hear	heard	heard
hide	hid	hidden
hit	hit	hit
hold	held	held
hurt	hurt	hurt
keep	kept	kept
kneel	knelt/kneeled	knelt/kneeled
knit	knit/knitted	knit/knitted
know	knew	known
lay	laid	laid
lead	led	led
leap	leaped/leapt	leaped/leapt
leave	left	left
lend	lent	lent
let	let	let
lie *(lie down)*	lay	lain
light	lit/lighted	lit/lighted
lose	lost	lost
make	made	made
mean	meant	meant
meet	met	met
pay	paid	paid
prove	proved	proved/proven
put	put	put
quit	quit	quit
read /rid/	read /rɛd/	read /rɛd/
ride	rode	ridden
ring	rang	rung
rise	rose	risen
run	ran	run
say	said	said
see	saw	seen
seek	sought	sought
sell	sold	sold
send	sent	sent
set	set	set
sew	sewed	sewn/sewed
shake	shook	shaken
shave	shaved	shaved/shaven
shine *(intransitive)*	shone/shined	shone/shined
shoot	shot	shot

(continued)

Base Form	Simple Past	Past Participle		Base Form	Simple Past	Past Participle
show	showed	shown		strike	struck	struck/stricken
shrink	shrank/shrunk	shrunk/shrunken		swear	swore	sworn
shut	shut	shut		sweep	swept	swept
sing	sang	sung		swim	swam	swum
sink	sank/sunk	sunk		swing	swung	swung
sit	sat	sat		take	took	taken
sleep	slept	slept		teach	taught	taught
slide	slid	slid		tear	tore	torn
speak	spoke	spoken		tell	told	told
speed	sped/speeded	sped/speeded		think	thought	thought
spend	spent	spent		throw	threw	thrown
spill	spilled/spilt	spilled/spilt		understand	understood	understood
spin	spun	spun		upset	upset	upset
spit	spit/spat	spat		wake	woke	woken
split	split	split		wear	wore	worn
spread	spread	spread		weave	wove/weaved	woven/weaved
spring	sprang	sprung		weep	wept	wept
stand	stood	stood		win	won	won
steal	stole	stolen		wind	wound	wound
stick	stuck	stuck		withdraw	withdrew	withdrawn
sting	stung	stung		wring	wrung	wrung
stink	stank/stunk	stunk		write	wrote	written

2 | Non-Action Verbs

EMOTIONS	MENTAL STATES		WANTS AND PREFERENCES	APPEARANCE AND VALUE	POSSESSION AND RELATIONSHIP
admire	agree	know	desire	appear	belong
adore	assume	mean	hope	be	contain
appreciate	believe	mind	need	cost	have
care	consider	presume	prefer	equal	own
detest	disagree	realize	want	look *(seem)*	possess
dislike	disbelieve	recognize	wish	matter	
doubt	estimate	remember		represent	
envy	expect	see *(understand)*	**PERCEPTION AND**	resemble	
fear	feel *(believe)*	suppose	**THE SENSES**	seem	
hate	find *(believe)*	suspect	feel	signify	
like	guess	think *(believe)*	hear	weigh	
love	hesitate	understand	notice		
miss	hope	wonder	observe		
regret	imagine		perceive		
respect			see		
trust			smell		
			sound		
			taste		

3 | Verbs Followed by the Gerund (Base Form of Verb + -ing)

acknowledge	celebrate	dislike	forgive	miss	recall	risk
admit	consider	endure	give up *(stop)*	postpone	recommend	suggest
advise	delay	enjoy	imagine	practice	regret	support
appreciate	deny	escape	justify	prevent	report	tolerate
avoid	detest	explain	keep *(continue)*	prohibit	resent	understand
can't help	discontinue	feel like	mention	propose	resist	
can't stand	discuss	finish	mind *(object to)*	quit		

4 | Verbs Followed by the Infinitive (*To* + Base Form of Verb)

agree	can('t) wait	expect	hurry	neglect	promise	volunteer
appear	choose	fail	intend	offer	refuse	wait
arrange	consent	grow	learn	pay	request	want
ask	decide	help	manage	plan	seem	wish
attempt	demand	hesitate	mean *(intend)*	prepare	struggle	would like
can('t) afford	deserve	hope	need	pretend	swear	yearn

5 | Verbs Followed by Objects and the Infinitive

advise	choose*	forbid	invite	persuade	require	want*
allow	convince	force	need*	promise*	teach	warn
ask*	enable	get*	order	remind	tell	wish*
cause	encourage	help*	pay*	request	urge	would like*
challenge	expect*	hire	permit			

*These verbs can also be followed by the infinitive without an object (EXAMPLE: *ask to leave* or *ask someone to leave*).

6 | Verbs Followed by the Gerund or the Infinitive

begin	continue	hate	love	remember*	stop*
can't stand	forget*	like	prefer	start	try

*These verbs can be followed by either the gerund or the infinitive but there is a big difference in meaning. *(see Unit 9)*

7 | Verb + Preposition Combinations

admit to	choose between /	dream about/of	look forward to	resort to
advise against	among	feel like/about	object to	succeed in
apologize for	complain about	go along with	pay for	talk about
approve of	count on	insist on	plan on	think about
believe in	deal with	keep on	rely on	wonder about

8 | Adjective + Preposition Expressions

accustomed to	awful at	content with	fond of	opposed to	satisfied with	terrible at
afraid of	bad at	curious about	glad about	pleased about	shocked at/by	tired of
amazed at/by	bored with/by	different from	good at	ready for	sick of	used to
angry at	capable of	excited about	happy about	responsible for	slow at	worried about
ashamed of	careful of	famous for	interested in	sad about	sorry for/about	
aware of	concerned about	fed up with	nervous about	safe from	surprised at/about/by	

9 | Adjectives Followed by the Infinitive

EXAMPLE: I'm **happy to hear** that.

afraid	anxious	depressed	disturbed	encouraged	happy	pleased	reluctant	surprised
alarmed	ashamed	determined	eager	excited	hesitant	proud	sad	touched
amazed	curious	disappointed	easy	fortunate	likely	ready	shocked	upset
angry	delighted	distressed	embarrassed	glad	lucky	relieved	sorry	willing

10 | Irregular Comparisons of Adjectives, Adverbs, and Quantifiers

ADJECTIVE	ADVERB	COMPARATIVE	SUPERLATIVE
bad	badly	worse	worst
far	far	farther/further	farthest/furthest
good	well	better	best
little	little	less	least
many/a lot of	—	more	most
much*/a lot of	much*/a lot	more	most

*Much is usually only used in questions and negative statements.

11 | Adjectives That Form the Comparative and Superlative in Two Ways

ADJECTIVE	COMPARATIVE	SUPERLATIVE
common	commoner/more common	commonest/most common
cruel	crueler/more cruel	cruelest/most cruel
deadly	deadlier/more deadly	deadliest/most deadly
friendly	friendlier/more friendly	friendliest/most friendly
handsome	handsomer/more handsome	handsomest/most handsome
happy	happier/more happy	happiest/most happy
likely	likelier/more likely	likeliest/most likely
lively	livelier/more lively	liveliest/most lively
lonely	lonelier/more lonely	loneliest/most lonely
lovely	lovelier/more lovely	loveliest/most lovely
narrow	narrower/more narrow	narrowest/most narrow
pleasant	pleasanter/more pleasant	pleasantest/most pleasant
polite	politer/more polite	politest/most polite
quiet	quieter/more quiet	quietest/most quiet
shallow	shallower/more shallow	shallowest/most shallow
sincere	sincerer/more sincere	sincerest/most sincere
stupid	stupider/more stupid	stupidest/most stupid
true	truer/more true	truest/most true

12 | Participial Adjectives

-ed	-ing	-ed	-ing	-ed	-ing
alarmed	alarming	disturbed	disturbing	moved	moving
amazed	amazing	embarrassed	embarrassing	paralyzed	paralyzing
amused	amusing	entertained	entertaining	pleased	pleasing
annoyed	annoying	excited	exciting	relaxed	relaxing
astonished	astonishing	exhausted	exhausting	satisfied	satisfying
bored	boring	fascinated	fascinating	shocked	shocking
confused	confusing	frightened	frightening	surprised	suprising
depressed	depressing	horrified	horrifying	terrified	terrifying
disappointed	disappointing	inspired	inspiring	tired	tiring
disgusted	disgusting	interested	interesting	touched	touching
distressed	distressing	irritated	irritating	troubled	troubling

13 | Reporting Verbs

STATEMENTS

acknowledge	complain	note	state
add	conclude	observe	suggest
admit	confess	promise	tell
announce	declare	remark	warn
answer	deny	repeat	whisper
argue	exclaim	reply	write
assert	explain	report	yell
believe	indicate	respond	
claim	maintain	say	
comment	mean	shout	

INSTRUCTIONS, COMMANDS, REQUESTS, AND INVITATIONS

advise	invite
ask	order
caution	say
command	tell
demand	urge
instruct	warn

QUESTIONS

ask
inquire
question
want to know
wonder

14 | Time Word Changes in Indirect Speech

DIRECT SPEECH		INDIRECT SPEECH
now	→	then
today	→	that day
tomorrow	→	the next day OR the following day OR the day after
yesterday	→	the day before OR the previous day
this week/month/year	→	that week/month/year
last week/month/year	→	the week/month/year before
next week/month/year	→	the following week/month/year

15 | Phrases Introducing Embedded Questions

I don't know . . .
I don't understand . . .
I wonder . . .
I'm not sure . . .
I can't remember . . .
I can't imagine . . .
It doesn't say . . .

I'd like to know . . .
I want to understand . . .
I'd like to find out . . .
We need to find out . . .
Let's ask . . .

Do you know . . . ?
Do you understand . . . ?
Can you tell me . . . ?
Could you explain . . . ?
Can you remember . . . ?
Would you show me . . . ?
Who knows . . . ?

allow oneself	be proud of oneself	enjoy oneself	keep oneself (busy)	remind oneself
amuse oneself	behave oneself	feel sorry for oneself	kill oneself	see oneself
ask oneself	believe in oneself	forgive oneself	look after oneself	take care of oneself
avail oneself of	blame oneself	help oneself	look at oneself	talk to oneself
be hard on oneself	cut oneself	hurt oneself	prepare oneself	teach oneself
be oneself	deprive oneself of	imagine oneself	pride oneself on	tell oneself
be pleased with oneself	dry oneself	introduce oneself	push oneself	treat oneself

17 | Transitive Phrasal Verbs

(s.o. = someone   s.t. = something)
- **separable phrasal verbs** show the object between the verb and the particle: *call s.o. up.*
- **verbs which must be separated** have an asterisk (*): *do s.t. over**
- **inseparable phrasal verbs** show the object after the particle: carry on s.t.

Remember: You can put a **noun object** between the verb and the particle of **separable** two-word verbs (**call** *Jan* **up** OR **call up** *Jan*). You <u>must</u> put a **pronoun object** between the verb and the particle of separable verbs (**call** *her* **up** NOT ~~call up~~ *her*).

PHRASAL VERB	MEANING	PHRASAL VERB	MEANING
ask s.o. **over***	*invite to one's home*	cut s.t. **off**	*1. stop the supply of*
block s.t. **out**	*stop from passing through (light/ noise)*		*2. remove by cutting*
		cut s.t. **out**	*remove by cutting*
blow s.t. **out**	*stop burning by blowing air on it*	cut s.t. **up**	*cut into small pieces*
blow s.t. **up**	*1. make explode*	do s.t. **over***	*do again*
	2. fill with air (a balloon)	do s.o. or s.t. **up**	*make more beautiful*
	3. make something larger (a photo)	draw s.t. **together**	*unite*
bring s.t. **about**	*make happen*	dream s.t. **up**	*invent*
bring s.o. or s.t. **back**	*return*	drink s.t. **up**	*drink completely*
bring s.o. **down***	*depress*	drop s.o. or s.t. **off**	*take someplace*
bring s.t. **out**	*introduce (a new product/book)*	drop out of s.t.	*quit*
bring s.o. **up**	*raise (children)*	empty s.t. **out**	*empty completely*
bring s.t. **up**	*bring attention to*	end up with s.t.	*have an unexpected result*
build s.t **up**	*increase*	fall for s.o.	*feel romantic love for*
burn s.t. **down**	*burn completely*	fall for s.t.	*be tricked by, believe*
call s.o. **back***	*return a phone call*	figure s.o. or s.t. **out**	*understand (after thinking about)*
call s.o. **in**	*ask for help with a problem*	fill s.t. **in**	*complete with information*
call s.t. **off**	*cancel*	fill s.t. **out**	*complete (a form)*
call s.o. **up**	*contact by phone*	fill s.t. **up**	*fill completely*
carry on s.t.	*continue*	find s.t. **out**	*learn information*
carry s.t. **out**	*conduct (an experiment/a plan)*	fix s.t. **up**	*redecorate (a home)*
cash in on s.t.	*profit from*	follow **through with** s.t.	*complete*
charge s.t. **up**	*charge with electricity*	get s.t. **across**	*get people to understand an idea*
check s.t. **out**	*examine*	get off s.t.	*leave (a bus/a train/a phone call)*
cheer s.o. **up**	*cause to feel happier*	get on s.t.	*board (a bus/a train/a phone call)*
clean s.o. or s.t. **up**	*cleam completely*	get out of s.t.	*leave (a car/taxi)*
clear s.t. **up**	*explain*	get s.t. **out of** s.t.*	*benefit from*
close s.t. **down**	*close by force*	get **through with** s.t.	*finish*
come off s.t.	*become unattached*	get to s.o. or s.t.	*1. reach s.o. or s.t.*
come up with s.t.	*invent*		*2. upset s.o.*
count on s.o. or s.t.	*depend on*	get **together with** s.o.	*meet*
cover s.o. or s.t. **up**	*cover completely*	give s.t. **away**	*give without charging money*
cross s.t. **out**	*draw a line through*	give s.t. **back**	*return*
cut s.t. **down**	*1. bring down by cutting (a tree)*	give s.t. **out**	*distribute*
	2. reduce		

PHRASAL VERB	MEANING
give s.t. **up**	quit, abandon
go after s.o. or s.t.	try to get or win, pursue
go along with s.t.	support
go over s.t.	review
hand s.t. **in**	give work (to a boss/ teacher), submit
hand s.t. **out**	distribute
hang s.t. **up**	put on a hook or hanger
help s.o. **out**	assist
hold s.t. **on**	keep attached
keep s.o. or s.t. **away**	cause to stay at a distance
keep s.t. **on***	not remove (a piece of clothing/jewelry)
keep s.o. or s.t. **out**	prevent from entering
keep up with s.o. or s.t.	go as fast as
lay s.o. **off**	end employment
lay s.t. **out**	1. arrange according to a plan
	2. spend money
leave s.t. **on**	1. not turn off (a light/radio)
	2. not remove (a piece of clothing/jewelry)
leave s.t. **out**	not include, omit
let s.o. **down**	disappoint
let s.o. or s.t. **in**	allow to enter
let s.o. **off**	1. allow to leave (a bus/car)
	2. not punish
let s.o. or s.t. **out**	allow to leave
light s.t. **up**	illuminate
look after s.o. or s.t.	take care of
look into s.t.	research
look s.o. or s.t. **over**	examine
look s.t. **up**	try to find (in a book/on the Internet)
make s.t. **up**	create
miss out on s.t.	lose the chance for something good
move s.t. **around***	change the location
pass s.t. **out**	distribute
pass s.o. or s.t. **up**	decide not to use, reject
pay s.o. or s.t. **back**	repay
pick s.o. or s.t. **out**	1. choose
	2. identify
pick s.o. or s.t. **up**	lift
pick s.t. **up**	1. buy, purchase
	2. get (an idea/an interest)
	3. answer the phone
point s.o. or s.t. **out**	indicate
put s.t. **away**	put in an appropriate place
put s.t. **back**	return to its original place
put s.o. or s.t. **down**	stop holding
put s.o. **off**	discourage
put s.t. **off**	delay
put s.t. **on**	cover the body (with clothes or jewelry)
put s.t. **together**	assemble
put s.t. **up**	erect
run into s.o.	meet accidentally
see s.t. **through***	complete
send s.t. **back**	return
send s.t. **out**	mail
set s.t. **off**	cause to explode

PHRASAL VERB	MEANING
set s.t. **up**	1. prepare for use
	2. establish (a business/an organization)
settle on s.t.	choose s.t. after thinking about many possibilities
show s.o. or s.t. **off**	display the best qualities
show up on s.t.	appear
shut s.t. **off**	stop (a machine/light)
sign s.o. **up** (for s.t.)	register
start s.t. **over***	start again
stick with/**to** s.o. or s.t.	not quit, not leave, persevere
straighten s.t. **up**	make neat
switch s.t. **on**	start (a machine/light)
take s.t. **away**	remove
take s.o. or s.t. **back**	return
take s.t. **down**	remove
take s.t. **in**	1. notice, understand, and remember
	2. earn (money)
take s.t. **off**	remove
take s.o. **on**	hire
take s.t. **on**	agree to do
take s.t. **out**	borrow from a library
take s.t. **up**	begin a job or activity
talk s.o. **into***	persuade
talk s.t. **over**	discuss
team up with s.o.	start to work with
tear s.t. **down**	destroy
tear s.t. **up**	tear into small pieces
think back on s.o. or s.t.	remember
think s.t. **over**	consider
think s.t. **up**	invent
throw s.t. **away/out**	discard, put in the trash
touch s.t. **up**	improve by making small changes
try s.t. **on**	put clothing on to see if it fits
try s.t. **out**	use to see if it works
turn s.t. **around***	change the direction so the front is at the back
turn s.o. **down**	reject
turn s.t. **down**	1. lower the volume (a TV/radio)
	2. reject (a job/an idea)
turn s.t. **in**	submit, give work (to a boss/ teacher)
turn s.o. or s.t. **into***	change from one form to another
turn s.o. **off***	[slang] destroy interest
turn s.t. **off**	stop (a machine), extinguish (a light)
turn s.t. **on**	start (a machine/light)
turn s.t. **over**	turn something so the top side is at the bottom
turn s.t. **up**	make louder (a TV/radio)
use s.t. **up**	use completely, consume
wake s.o. **up**	awaken
watch out for s.o. or s.t.	be careful about
work s.t. **off**	remove by work or activity
work s.t. **out**	solve, understand
write s.t. **down**	write on a piece of paper
write s.t. **up**	write in a finished form

PHRASAL VERB	MEANING
act up	cause problems
blow up	explode
break down	stop working (a machine)
break out	happen suddenly
burn down	burn completely
call back	return a phone call
catch on	become popular
cheer up	make happier
clean up	clean completely
clear up	become clear
close down	stop operating
come about	happen
come along	come with, accompany
come around	happen
come back	return
come down	become less (price)
come in	enter
come off	become unattached
come out	appear
come up	arise
dress up	wear special clothes
drop in	visit by surprise
drop out	quit
eat out	eat in a restaurant
empty out	empty completely
end up	1. do something unexpected or unintended
	2. reach a final place or condition
fall off	become detached
find out	learn information
follow through	complete
fool around	act playful
get ahead	make progress, succeed
get along	have a good relationship
get back	return
get by	survive
get off	1. leave (a bus, the Internet)
	2. end a phone conversation
get on	enter, board (a bus, a train)
get through	finish
get together	meet
get up	get out of bed, arise
give up	quit
go away	leave a place or person

PHRASAL VERB	MEANING
go back	return
go down	become less (price, number), decrease
go off	explode (a gun/fireworks)
go on	continue
go out	leave
go over	succeed with an audience
go up	1. be built
	2. become more (price, number), increase
grow up	become an adult
hang up	end a phone call
hold on	1. wait
	2. not hang up the phone
keep away	stay at a distance
keep on	continue
keep out	not enter
keep up	go as fast
lie down	recline
light up	illuminate
look out	be careful
make up	end a disagreement, reconcile
miss out	lose the chance for something good
pay off	be worthwhile
pick up	improve
play around	have fun
run out	not have enough
show up	appear
sign up	register
sit down	take a seat
slip up	make a mistake
stand up	rise
start over	start again
stay up	remain awake
straighten up	make neat
take off	depart (a plane)
turn out	have a particular result
turn up	appear
wake up	stop sleeping
watch out	be careful
work out	1. be resolved
	2. exercise

A. SOCIAL MODALS AND EXPRESSIONS

FUNCTION	MODAL OR EXPRESSION*	TIME	EXAMPLES
Ability	can can't	Present	• Sam **can swim**. • He **can't skate**.
	could could not	Past	• We **could swim** last year. • We **couldn't skate**.
	be able to* not be able to*	All verb forms	• Lea **is able to run** fast. • She **wasn't able to run** fast last year.
Advice	should shouldn't ought to** had better** had better not**	Present or Future	• You **should study** more. • You **shouldn't miss** class. • We **ought to leave**. • We**'d better go**. • We**'d better not stay**.
Advisability in the Past and **Regret or Blame**	should have should not have ought to have could have might have	Past	• I **should have become** a doctor. • I **shouldn't have wasted** time. • He **ought to have told** me. • She **could have gone** to college. • You **might have called**. I waited for hours.
Necessity	have to* not have to*	All verb forms	• He **has to go** now. • He **doesn't have to go** yet. • I **had to go** yesterday. • I **will have to go** soon.
	have got to* must	Present or Future	• He**'s got** to leave! • You **must use** a pen for the test.
Permission	can	Present or Future	• **Can** I **sit** here? • **Can** I **call** tomorrow? • Yes, you **can**.
	can't could may		• No, you **can't**. Sorry. • **Could** he **leave** now? • **May** I **borrow** your pen? • Yes, you **may**.
	may not		• No, you **may not**. Sorry.
Prohibition	must not can't	Present or Future	• You **must not drive** without a license. • You **can't drive** without a license.
Requests	can	Present or Future	• **Can** you **close** the door, please? • Sure, I **can**.
	can't could will would		• Sorry, I **can't**. • **Could** you please **answer** the phone? • **Will** you **wash** the dishes, please? • **Would** you please **mail** this letter?

*The meaning of this expression is similar to the meaning of a modal. Unlike a modal, it has -*s* for third person singular.

**The meaning of this expression is similar to the meaning of a modal. Like a modal, it has no -*s* for third person singular.

B. Logical Modals and Expressions

Function	Logical Modal or Expression	Time	Examples
Impossibility	can't	Present or Future	• That **can't be** Ana. She left for France yesterday. • It **can't snow** tomorrow. It's going to be too warm.
	couldn't		• He **couldn't be** guilty. He wasn't in town when the crime occurred. • The teacher **couldn't give** the test tomorrow. Tomorrow's Saturday.
	couldn't have	Past	• You **couldn't have failed**. You studied so hard.
Possibility	must must not have to* have got to* may	Present	• This **must be** her house. Her name is on the door. • She **must not be** home. I don't see her car. • She **has to know** him. They went to school together. • He **'s got to be** guilty. We saw him do it. • She **may be** home now.
	may not might might not could	Present or Future	• It **may not rain** tomorrow. • Lee **might be sick** today. • He **might not come** to class. • They **could be** at the library. • It **could rain** tomorrow.
	may have may not have might have might not have could have	Past	• They **may have left** already. I don't see them. • They **may not have arrived** yet. • He **might have called**. I'll check my phone messages. • He **might not have left** a message. • She **could have forgotten** to mail the letter.

*The meaning of this expression is similar to the meaning of a modal. Unlike a modal, it has -s for third person singular.

20 | Irregular Plural Nouns

Singular	Plural	Singular	Plural	Singular	Plural	Singular	Plural
analysis	analyses	half	halves	person	people	deer	deer
basis	bases	knife	knives	man	men	fish	fish
crisis	crises	leaf	leaves	woman	women	sheep	sheep
hypothesis	hypotheses	life	lives	child	children		
		loaf	loaves	foot	feet		
		shelf	shelves	tooth	teeth		
		wife	wives	goose	geese		
				mouse	mice		

1. Add **-s** for most verbs.

work	work**s**
buy	buy**s**
ride	ride**s**
return	return**s**

2. Add **-es** for verbs that end in **-ch**, **-s**, **-sh**, **-x**, or **-z**.

watch	watch**es**
pass	pass**es**
rush	rush**es**
relax	relax**es**
buzz	buzz**es**

3. Change the **y** to **i** and add **-es** when the base form ends in a consonant + **y**.

study	stud**ies**
hurry	hurr**ies**
dry	dr**ies**

Do not change the **y** when the base form ends in a vowel + **y**. Add **-s**.

play	play**s**
enjoy	enjoy**s**

4. A few verbs are irregular.

be	**is**
do	**does**
go	**goes**
have	**has**

1. Add **-ing** to the base form of the verb.

read	read**ing**
stand	stand**ing**

2. If a verb ends in a **silent -e**, drop the final **-e** and add **-ing**.

leave	leav**ing**
take	tak**ing**

3. In one-syllable verbs, if the last three letters are a consonant-vowel-consonant combination (CVC), double the last consonant before adding **-ing**.

```
C V C
↓ ↓ ↓
s i t        sit**ting**

C V C
↓ ↓ ↓
p l a n      plan**ning**
```

Do not double the last consonant in words that end in **-w**, **-x**, or **-y**.

sew	sew**ing**
fix	fix**ing**
play	play**ing**

4. In verbs of two or more syllables that end in a consonant-vowel-consonant combination, double the last consonant only if the last syllable is stressed.*

admít	admit**ting**	(The last syllable is stressed.)
whísper	whisper**ing**	(The last syllable is not stressed, so don't double the **-r**.)

5. If a verb ends in **-ie**, change the **ie** to **y** before adding **-ing**.

die	d**ying**

*The symbol ′ shows main stress.

23 | Spelling Rules for the Simple Past of Regular Verbs

1. If the verb ends in a consonant, add **-ed**.

return	return**ed**
help	help**ed**

2. If the verb ends in **-e**, add **-d**.

live	live**d**
create	create**d**
die	die**d**

3. In one-syllable words, if the last three letters are a consonant-vowel-consonant combination (CVC), double the last consonant before adding **-ed**.

C V C
↓ ↓ ↓
h o p   hop**ped**

C V C
↓ ↓ ↓
p l a n   plan**ned**

Do not double the last consonant of one-syllable words ending in **-w**, **-x**, or **-y**.

bow	bow**ed**
mix	mix**ed**
play	play**ed**

4. In words of two or more syllables that end in a consonant-vowel-consonant combination, double the last consonant only if the last syllable is stressed.*

prefér	prefer**red** (The last syllable is stressed, so double the **r**.)
vísit	visit**ed** (The last syllable is not stressed, so don't double the **t**.)

5. If the verb ends in a consonant + **y**, change the **y** to **i** and add **-ed**.

worry	worr**ied**
cry	cr**ied**

6. If the verb ends in a vowel + **y**, add **-ed**. (Do not change the **y** to **i**.)

play	play**ed**
annoy	annoy**ed**
Exceptions:	lay—laid, pay—paid, say—said

*The symbol ′ shows main stress.

24 | Spelling Rules for the Comparative (-er) and Superlative (-est) of Adjectives

1. Add **-er** to one-syllable adjectives to form the comparative. Add **-est** to one-syllable adjectives to form the superlative.

cheap	cheap**er**	cheap**est**
bright	bright**er**	bright**est**

2. If the adjective ends in **-e**, add **-r** or **-st**.

nice	nice**r**	nice**st**

3. If the adjective ends in a consonant + **y**, change **y** to **i** before you add **-er** or **-est**.

pretty	prett**ier**	prett**iest**	
Exception:	shy	shy**er**	shy**est**

4. In one-syllable words, if the last three letters are a consonant-vowel-consonant combination (CVC), double the last consonant before adding **-er** or **-est**.

C V C
↓ ↓ ↓
b i g   big**ger**   big**gest**

Do not double the consonant in words ending in **-w** or **-y**.

slow	slow**er**	slow**est**
gray	gray**er**	gray**est**

25 | Spelling Rules for Adverbs Ending in -ly

1. Add **-ly** to the corresponding adjective.

nice	nice**ly**
quiet	quiet**ly**
beautiful	beautiful**ly**

2. If the adjective ends in a consonant + **y**, change the **y** to **i** before adding **-ly**.

easy	eas**ily**

3. If the adjective ends in **-le**, drop the **e** and add **-y**.

possible	possib**ly**

Do not drop the **e** for other adjectives ending in **-e**.

extreme	extreme**ly**
Exception:	true	tru**ly**

4. If the adjective ends in **-ic**, add **-ally**.

basic	basic**ally**
fantastic	fantastic**ally**

26 | Direct Speech: Punctuation Rules

Direct speech may either follow or come before the reporting verb. When direct speech follows the reporting verb:

a. Put a comma after the reporting verb.

b. Use opening quotation marks (") before the first word of the direct speech.

c. Begin the quotation with a capital letter.

d. Use the appropriate end punctuation for the direct speech. It may be a period (.), a question mark (?), or an exclamation point (!).

e. Put closing quotation marks (") after the end punctuation of the quotation.

Examples: He said, "I had a good time."
She asked, "Where's the party?"
They shouted, "Be careful!"

When direct speech comes before the reporting verb:

a. Begin the sentence with opening quotation marks (").

b. Use the appropriate end punctuation for the direct speech. If the direct speech is a statement, use a comma (,). If the direct speech is a question, use a question mark (?). If the direct speech is an exclamation, use an exclamation point (!).

c. Use closing quotation marks after the end punctuation for the direct speech (").

d. Begin the reporting clause with a lowercase letter.

e. Use a period at the end of the main sentence (.).

Examples: "I had a good time," he said.
"Where's the party?" she asked.
"Be careful!" they shouted.

27 | Pronunciation Table

These are the pronunciation symbols used in this text. Listen to the pronunciation of the key words.

VOWELS				CONSONANTS			
Symbol	Key Word	Symbol	Key Word	Symbol	Key Word	Symbol	Key Word
i	beat, feed	ə	banana, among	p	pack, happy	ʃ	ship, machine, station, special, discussion
ɪ	bit, did	ɚ	shirt, murder	b	back, rubber		
eɪ	date, paid	aɪ	bite, cry, buy, eye	t	tie	ʒ	measure, vision
ɛ	bet, bed	aʊ	about, how	d	die	h	hot, who
æ	bat, bad	ɔɪ	voice, boy	k	came, key, quick	m	men
ɑ	box, odd, father	ɪr	beer	g	game, guest	n	sun, know, pneumonia
ɔ	bought, dog	ɛr	bare	tʃ	church, nature, watch		
oʊ	boat, road	ɑr	bar	dʒ	judge, general, major	ŋ	sung, ringing
ʊ	book, good	ɔr	door	f	fan, photograph	w	wet, white
u	boot, food, student	ʊr	tour	v	van	l	light, long
ʌ	but, mud, mother			θ	thing, breath	r	right, wrong
				ð	then, breathe	y	yes, use, music
				s	sip, city, psychology	t̬	butter, bottle
				z	zip, please, goes		

28 | Pronunciation Rules for the Simple Present: Third-Person Singular (*he, she, it*)

1. The third person singular in the simple present always ends in the letter **-s**. There are three different pronunciations for the final sound of the third person singular.

/s/	/z/	/ɪz/
talk**s**	love**s**	danc**es**

2. The final sound is pronounced /s/ after the voiceless sounds /**p**/, /**t**/, /**k**/, and /**f**/.

top	to**ps**
get	ge**ts**
take	ta**kes**
laugh	lau**ghs**

3. The final sound is pronounced /**z**/ after the voiced sounds /**b**/, /**d**/, /**g**/, /**v**/, /**ð**/, /**m**/, /**n**/, /**ŋ**/, /**l**/, and /**r**/.

describe	descri**bes**
spend	spen**ds**
hug	hu**gs**
live	li**ves**
bathe	ba**thes**
seem	see**ms**
remain	remai**ns**
sing	si**ngs**
tell	te**lls**
lower	lowe**rs**

4. The final sound is pronounced /**z**/ after all vowel sounds.

agree	agr**ees**
try	tr**ies**
stay	st**ays**
know	kn**ows**

5. The final sound is pronounced /**ɪz**/ after the sounds /**s**/, /**z**/, /**ʃ**/, /**ʒ**/, /**tʃ**/, and /**dʒ**/. /**ɪz**/ adds a syllable to the verb.

relax	rela**xes**
freeze	free**zes**
rush	ru**shes**
massage	massa**ges**
watch	wa**tches**
judge	ju**dges**

6. ***Do*** and ***say*** have a change in vowel sound.

do	/**du**/	does	/**dʌz**/
say	/**sɛɪ**/	says	/**sɛz**/

29 | Pronunciation Rules for the Simple Past of Regular Verbs

1. The regular simple past always ends in the letter **-d**. There are three different pronunciations for the final sound of the regular simple past.

/t/	/d/	/ɪd/
race**d**	live**d**	attend**ed**

2. The final sound is pronounced /**t**/ after the voiceless sounds /**p**/, /**k**/, /**f**/, /**s**/, /**ʃ**/, and /**tʃ**/.

hop	ho**pped**
work	wor**ked**
laugh	lau**ghed**
address	addre**ssed**
publish	publi**shed**
watch	wa**tched**

3. The final sound is pronounced /**d**/ after the voiced sounds /**b**/, /**g**/, /**v**/, /**z**/, /**ʒ**/, /**dʒ**/, /**m**/, /**n**/, /**ŋ**/, /**l**/, /**r**/, and /**ð**/.

rub	ru**bbed**
hug	hu**gged**
live	li**ved**
surprise	surpri**sed**
massage	massa**ged**
change	chan**ged**
rhyme	rhy**med**
return	retur**ned**
bang	ba**nged**
enroll	enro**lled**
appear	appea**red**
bathe	ba**thed**

4. The final sound is pronounced /**d**/ after all vowel sounds.

agree	agr**eed**
play	pl**ayed**
die	d**ied**
enjoy	enj**oyed**
snow	sn**owed**

5. The final sound is pronounced /**ɪd**/ after /**t**/ and /**d**/. /**ɪd**/ adds a syllable to the verb.

start	star**ted**
decide	deci**ded**

	USE FOR . . .	**EXAMPLE**
capital letter	• the pronoun *I*	Tomorrow **I** will be here at 2:00.
	• proper nouns	His name is **Karl**. He lives in **Germany**.
	• the first word of a sentence.	**When** does the train leave? **At** 2:00.
apostrophe (')	• possessive nouns	Is that **Marta's** coat?
	• contractions	**That's** not hers. **It's** mine.
comma (,)	• after items in a list	He bought **apples, pears, oranges,** and **bananas**.
	• before sentence connectors *and*, *but*, *or*, and *so*	They watched TV, **and** she played video games.
	• after the first part of a sentence that begins with *because*	*Because* **it's raining,** we're not walking to work.
	• after the first part of a sentence that begins with a preposition	*Across from* **the post office,** there's a good restaurant.
	• after the first part of a sentence that begins with a time clause or an *if* clause	*After* **he arrived,** we ate dinner. *If* **it rains,** we won't go.
	• before and after a non-identifying adjective clause in the middle of a sentence	Tony, **who lives in Paris,** e-mails me every day.
	• before a non-identifying adjective clause at the end of a sentence	I get e-mails every day from Tony, **who lives in Paris**.
exclamation mark (!)	• at the end of a sentence to show surprise or a strong feeling	You're here! That's great! Stop! A car is coming!
period (.)	• at the end of a statement	Today is Wednesday.
question mark (?)	• at the end of a question	What day is today?

GLOSSARY OF GRAMMAR TERMS

action verb   a verb that describes an action.
- Alicia **ran** home.

active sentence   a sentence that focuses on the agent (the person or thing doing the action).
- **Ari kicked** the ball.

addition   a clause or a short sentence that follows a statement and expresses similarity to or contrast with the information in the statement.
- Pedro is tall, **and so is Alex**.
- Trish doesn't like sports. **Neither does her sister**.

adjective   a word that describes a noun or pronoun.
- It's a **good** plan, and it's not **difficult**.

adjective clause   a clause that identifies or gives additional information about a noun.
- The woman **who called you** didn't leave her name.
- Samir, **who you met yesterday,** works in the lab.

adverb   a word that describes a verb, an adjective, or another adverb.
- She drives **carefully**.
- She's a **very** good driver.
- She drives **really** well.

affirmative   a statement or answer meaning **yes**.
- He **works**. (affirmative statement)
- **Yes**, he **does**. (affirmative short answer)

agent   the person or thing doing the action in a sentence. In passive sentences, the word **by** is used before the agent.
- This magazine is published **by National Geographic**.

article   a word that goes before a noun. The **indefinite** articles are **a** and **an**.
- I ate **a** sandwich and **an** apple.

The **definite** article is **the**.
- I didn't like **the** sandwich. **The** apple was good.

auxiliary verb   (also called **helping verb**) a verb used with a main verb. **Be**, **do**, and **have** are often auxiliary verbs. Modals (**can**, **should**, **may**, **must** . . .) are also auxiliary verbs.
- I **am** exercising right now.
- I **should** exercise every day.
- **Do** you like to exercise?

base form   the simple form of a verb without any endings (-s, -ed, -ing) or other changes.
- **be**, **have**, **go**, **drive**

clause   a group of words that has a subject and a verb. A sentence can have one or more clauses.
- We are leaving now. (one clause)
- If it rains, we won't go. (two clauses)

common noun   a word for a person, place, or thing (but not the name of the person, place, or thing).
- Teresa lives in a **house** near the **beach**.

comparative   the form of an adjective or adverb that shows the difference between two people, places, or things.
- Alain is **shorter** than Brendan. (adjective)
- Brendan runs **faster** than Alain. (adverb)

conditional sentence   a sentence that describes a condition and its result. The sentence can be about the past, the present, or the future. The condition and result can be real or unreal.
- If it **rains**, I **won't go**. (future, real)
- If it **had rained**, I **wouldn't have gone**. (past, unreal)

continuous   See **progressive**.

contraction   a short form of a word or words. An apostrophe (') replaces the letter or letters.
- **she's** = she is
- **can't** = cannot

count noun a noun you can count. It has a singular and a plural form.

- one **book**, two **books**

definite article *the*. This article goes before a noun that refers to a specific person, place, or thing.

- *Please bring me **the book** on **the table**. I'm almost finished reading it.*

dependent clause (also called **subordinate clause**) a clause that needs a main clause for its meaning.

- ***If I get home early**, I'll call you.*

direct object a noun or pronoun that receives the action of a verb.

- *Marta kicked **the ball**. I saw **her**.*

direct speech language that gives the exact words a speaker used. In writing, quotation marks come before and after the speaker's words.

- ***"I saw Bob yesterday,"** she said.*
- ***"Is he in school?"***

embedded question a question that is inside another sentence.

- *I don't know **where the restaurant is**.*
- *Do you know **if it's on Tenth Street**?*

formal language used in business situations or with adults you do not know.

- *Good afternoon, Mr. Rivera. Please have a seat.*

gerund a word formed with **verb + -ing** that can be used as a subject or an object.

- ***Swimming** is great exercise.*
- *I enjoy **swimming**.*

helping verb See **auxiliary verb**.

identifying adjective clause a clause that identifies which member of a group the sentence is about.

- *There are ten students in the class. The student **who sits in front of me** is from Russia.*

***if* clause** the clause that states the condition in a conditional sentence.

- ***If I had known you were here**, I would have called you.*

imperative a sentence that gives a command or instructions.

- ***Hurry!***
- ***Don't touch that!***

indefinite article *a* or *an*. These articles go before a noun that does not refer to a specific person, place, or thing.

- *Can you bring me **a book**? I'm looking for something to read.*

indefinite pronoun a pronoun such as ***someone**, **something**, **anyone**, **anything**, **anywhere**, **no one**, **nothing**, **everyone**,* and ***everything***. An indefinite pronoun does not refer to a specific person, place, or thing.

- ***Someone** called you last night.*
- *Did **anything** happen?*

indirect object a noun or pronoun (often a person) that receives something as the result of the action of the verb.

- *I told **John** the story.*
- *He gave **me** some good advice.*

indirect speech language that reports what a speaker said without using the exact words.

- *Ann said **she had seen Bob the day before**.*
- *She asked **if he was in school**.*

infinitive *to* + **base form** of the verb.

- *I want **to leave** now.*

infinitive of purpose *(in order) to* + **base form** of the verb. This form gives the reason for an action.

- *I go to school **in order to learn** English.*

informal language used with family, friends, and children.

- *Hi, Pete. Sit down.*

information question See *wh*- **question**.

inseparable phrasal verb a phrasal verb whose parts must stay together.

- *We **ran into** Tomás at the supermarket. (NOT: We ~~ran Tomás into~~ . . .)*

intransitive verb a verb that does not have an object.

- *She **paints**.*
- *We **fell**.*

irregular a word that does not change its form in the usual way.

- **Go** *is an* **irregular** *verb. Its simple past* (**went**) *does not end in* -ed.

main clause a clause that can stand alone as a sentence.

- **I called my friend Tom**, *who lives in Chicago.*

main verb a verb that describes an action or state. It is often used with an auxiliary verb.

- *Jared is* **calling**.
- *Does he* **call** *every day?*

modal a type of auxiliary verb. It goes before a main verb and expresses ideas such as ability, advice, permission, and possibility. **Can**, **could**, **will**, **would**, **may**, **might**, **should**, and **must** are modals.

- **Can** *you swim?*
- *You really* **should** *learn to swim.*

negative a statement or answer meaning **no**.

- *He* **doesn't** *work.* (negative statement)
- **No**, *he* **doesn't**. (negative short answer)

non-action verb a verb that does not describe an action. It describes such things as thoughts, feelings, and senses.

- *I* **remember** *that word.*
- *Chris* **loves** *ice cream.*
- *It* **tastes** *great.*

non-count noun a noun you usually do not count (**air**, **water**, **rice**, **love** . . .). It has only a singular form.

- *The* **rice** *is delicious.*

nonidentifying adjective clause (also called **nonrestrictive adjective clause**) a clause that gives additional information about the noun it refers to. The information is not necessary to identify the noun.

- *My sister Diana,* **who usually hates sports**, *recently started tennis lessons.*

nonrestrictive adjective clause See **nonidentifying adjective clause**.

noun a word for a person, place, or thing.

- *My* **sister**, **Anne**, *works in an* **office**.
- *She uses a* **computer**.

object a noun or a pronoun that receives the action of a verb.

- *Layla threw* **the ball**.
- *She threw* **it** *to* **Tom**.

object pronoun a pronoun (**me**, **you**, **him**, **her**, **it**, **us**, **them**) that receives the action of the verb.

- *I gave* **her** *a book.*
- *I gave* **it** *to* **her**.

object relative pronoun a relative pronoun that is an object in an adjective clause.

- *I'm reading a book* **that** *I really like.*

paragraph a group of sentences, usually about one topic.

particle a word that looks like a preposition and combines with a main verb to form a phrasal verb. It often changes the meaning of the main verb.

- *He looked the word* **up**. (He looked for the meaning of the word in the dictionary.)

passive causative a sentence formed with **have** or **get** + **object** + **past participle**. It is used to talk about services that you arrange for someone to do for you.

- *She* **had the car checked** *at the service station.*
- *He's going to* **get his hair cut** *by André.*

passive sentence a sentence that focuses on the object (the person or thing receiving the action). The passive is formed with **be** + **past participle**.

- **The ball was kicked** *by Ari.*

past participle a verb form (**verb** + **-ed**). It can also be irregular. It is used to form the present perfect, past perfect, and future perfect. It can also be an adjective.

- *We've* **lived** *here since April.*
- *They had* **spoken** *before.*
- *She's* **interested** *in math.*

phrasal verb (also called **two-word verb**) a verb that has two parts (**verb** + **particle**). The meaning is often different from the meaning of its separate parts.

- *He* **grew up** *in Texas.* (became an adult)
- *His parents* **brought** *him* **up** *to be honest.* (raised)

phrase   a group of words that forms a unit but does not have a main verb. Many phrases give information about time or place.

- *Last year*, we were living *in Canada*.

plural   two or more.

- There *are* three *people* in the restaurant.
- *They are* eating dinner.
- *We* saw *them*.

possessive   nouns, pronouns, or adjectives that show a relationship or show that someone owns something.

- Zach is *Megan's* brother. (possessive noun)
- Is that car *his*? (possessive pronoun)
- That's *his* car. (possessive adjective)

predicate   the part of a sentence that has the main verb. It tells what the subject is doing or describes the subject.

- My sister *works for a travel agency*.

preposition   a word that goes before a noun or a pronoun to show time, place, or direction.

- I went *to* the bank *on* Monday. It's *next to* my office.

A preposition also goes before nouns, pronouns, and gerunds in expressions with verbs and adjectives.

- We rely *on* him.
- She's accustomed *to* getting up early

progressive   (also called **continuous**) the verb form **be + verb + -ing**. It focuses on the continuation (not the completion) of an action.

- She*'s reading* the paper.
- We *were watching* TV when you called.

pronoun   a word used in place of a noun.

- That's my brother. You met *him* at my party.

proper noun   a noun that is the name of a person, place, or thing. It begins with a capital letter.

- *Maria* goes to *Central High School*.
- It's on *High Street*.

punctuation   marks used in writing (period, comma, . . .) that make the meaning clear. For example, a period (.) shows the end of a sentence. It also shows that the sentence is a statement, not a question.

quantifier   a word or phrase that shows an amount (but not an exact amount). It often comes before a noun.

- Josh bought *a lot of* books last year.
- He doesn't have *much* money.

question   See *yes / no question* and *wh- question*.

question word   See *wh- word*.

quoted speech   See **direct speech**.

real conditional sentence   a sentence that talks about general truths, habits, or things that happen again and again. It can also talk about things that will happen in the future under certain circumstances.

- If it rains, he takes the bus.
- If it rains tomorrow, we'll take the bus with him.

regular   a word that changes its form in the usual way.

- *Play* is a *regular* verb. Its simple past form *(played)* ends in *-ed*.

relative pronoun   a word that connects an adjective clause to a noun in the main clause.

- He's the man *who* lives next door.
- I'm reading a book *that* I really like.

reported speech   See **indirect speech**.

reporting verb   a verb such as *said*, *told*, or *asked*. It introduces direct and indirect speech. It can also come after the quotation in direct speech.

- She *said*, "I'm going to be late."   OR   "I'm going to be late," she *said*.
- She *told* me that she was going to be late.

restrictive adjective clause   See **identifying adjective clause**.

result clause   the clause in a conditional sentence that talks about what happens if the condition occurs.

- If it rains, *I'll stay home*.
- If I had a million dollars, *I would travel*.
- If I had had your phone number, *I would have called you*.

sentence   a group of words that has a subject and a main verb.

- *Computers are* very useful.

separable phrasal verb a phrasal verb whose parts can separate.

- Tom **looked** the word **up** in a dictionary.
- He **looked** it **up**.

short answer an answer to a *yes / no* question.

A: *Did you call me last night?*
B: *No, I didn't.* OR *No.*

singular one.

- They have a **sister**.
- **She** works in a **hospital**.

statement a sentence that gives information. In writing, it ends in a period.

- Today is Monday.

stative verb See **non-action verb**.

subject the person, place, or thing that the sentence is about.

- **Ms. Chen** teaches English.
- **Her class** is interesting.

subject pronoun a pronoun that shows the person (**I**, **you**, **he**, **she**, **it**, **we**, **they**) that the sentence is about.

- **I** read a lot.
- **She** reads a lot too.

subject relative pronoun a relative pronoun that is the subject of an adjective clause.

- He's the man **who** lives next door.

subordinate clause See **dependent clause**.

superlative the form of an adjective or adverb that is used to compare a person, place, or thing to a group of people, places, or things.

- Cindi is **the shortest** player on the team. (adjective)
- She dances **the most gracefully**. (adverb)

tag question a statement + tag. The **tag** is a short question at the end of the statement. Tag questions check information or comment on a situation.

- You're Jack Thompson, **aren't you?**
- It's a nice day, **isn't it?**

tense the form of a verb that shows the time of the action.

- **simple present**: Fabio **talks** to his friend every day.
- **simple past**: Fabio **talked** to his teacher yesterday.

third-person singular the pronouns **he**, **she**, and **it** or a singular noun. In the simple present, the third-person-singular verb ends in **-s** or **-es**.

- Tomás **works** in an office. (Tomás = he)

three-word verb a phrasal verb + preposition.

- Slow down! I can't **keep up with** you.

time clause a clause that begins with a time word such as **when**, **before**, **after**, **while**, or **as soon as**.

- I'll call you **when I get home**.

transitive verb a verb that has an object.

- She **likes** apples.

two-word verb See **phrasal verb**.

unreal conditional sentence a sentence that talks about unreal conditions and their unreal results. The condition and its result can be untrue, imagined, or impossible.

- If I were a bird, I would fly around the world.
- If you had called, I would have invited you to the party.

verb a word that describes what the subject of the sentence does, thinks, feels, senses, or owns.

- They **run** two miles every day.
- She **loved** that movie.
- He **has** a new camera.

***wh-* question** (also called **information question**) a question that begins with a *wh-* word. You answer a *wh-* question with information.

A: *Where* are you going?
B: *To the store.*

***wh-* word** a question word such as **who**, **what**, **when**, **where**, **which**, **why**, **how**, and **how much**. It can begin a *wh-* question or an embedded question.

- **Who** is that?
- **What** did you see?
- **When** does the movie usually start?
- I don't know **how much** it costs.

***yes / no* question** a question that begins with a form of **be** or an auxiliary verb. You can answer a *yes / no* question with *yes* or *no*.

A: *Are* you a student?
B: *Yes*, I am. OR *No*, I'm not.

REVIEW TESTS ANSWER KEY

Note: In this answer key, where the contracted verb form is given, it is the preferred form, though the full form is also acceptable. Where the full verb form is given, it is the preferred form, though the contracted form is also acceptable.

I (Units 1–4)

2. are discussing	**12.** sounds
3. Are you thinking	**13.** has accepted
	14. think
4. wondered	**15.** means
5. love	**16.** roasted
6. agree	**17.** had become
7. argue	**18.** stood
8. claim	**19.** talked
9. has	**20.** was
10. used	**21.** seems
11. called	**22.** is

II (Units 1–4)

1. b. 's been happening
  c. have
  d. moved
  e. bought
  f. had been looking
  g. had been planning
  h. decided
  i. is
  j. Have you ever been
  k. have

2. a. tried
  b. 've already eaten
  c. smell
  d. 'm thinking
  e. saw
  f. looked

3. a. Have you met
  b. calls
  c. What does she do
  d. was working
  e. laid off
  f. lost
  g. have been cutting
  h. liked
  i. 's trying

4. a. Have Al and Jack
  b. got
  c. 're staying
  d. sounds

  e. need
  f. have been
  g. met
  h. are they doing
  i. 're taking
  j. have been learning

III (Units 1–4)

2. A	**6.** D	**9.** C	**12.** C
3. C	**7.** B	**10.** D	**13.** A
4. A	**8.** C	**11.** C	**14.** D
5. B			

IV (Units 1–4)

2. mentioned	**13.** got
3. don't look	**14.** didn't mind
4. guess	**15.** was
5. did . . . decide	**16.** met
6. was	**17.** 've wanted OR 've been wanting
7. loved	
8. was	**18.** understand
9. had read	**19.** have . . . had
10. knew	**20.** 've been following
11. wanted	**21.** haven't been able to
12. 're attending OR 've been attending	**22.** worry

V (Units 1–4)

have been staying
Jack and I ~~are staying~~ at the Splendor for almost a week already. We've been spending a lot of time at the beach swimming and water-skiing, and

've been taking
I ~~was taking~~ scuba lessons in the hotel pool for

I was planning OR *I'd been planning* OR *I planned*
several days now. Yesterday, ~~I've been planning~~ to take my first dive from a boat. Unfortunately, by

had changed
the time we left shore, the weather ~~has changed~~. We had to cancel the dive. This morning it was still a little cloudy, so we did something different. We

decided
~~were deciding~~ to visit the Castle, an old pirate stronghold in Hideaway Bay. We had both read a little about it before we left, and it really sounded

fascinating. So we've ~~rented~~ a motorbike and took

we rented

off. They ~~aren't having~~ any road signs here outside

don't have

of town, so by the time we found the Castle,

we'd been driving

~~we've been driving~~ for about an hour. It was fun,

though. When we were ~~seeing~~ the Castle, dark

saw

clouds were drifting over it. It really looked spooky
and beautiful.

Well, the weather has cleared, and Jack ~~gets~~

is getting

ready to go for a dive. I think I'll join him.

PART II

I (Unit 5)

2. I'll mail
3. We're going to go
4. They're going to crash
5. I'm graduating
6. I get
7. I'll see
8. I finish, I start
9. I won't be, I'll take
10. you do

II (Units 5–6)

2. you'll have been studying
3. I'll have graduated
4. what'll you be doing
5. I'll be looking
6. I won't have graduated
7. I'm going to be getting ready
8. you'll be sitting
9. I go
10. I get
11. you'll have found
12. I'm learning
13. you'll be starting

III (Units 5–6)

2. A	5. A	8. C
3. D	6. B	9. A
4. B	7. D	10. C

IV (Units 5–6)

2. won't be driving OR aren't going to be driving
3. 'll have driven
4. won't be polluting OR aren't going to be polluting
5. won't be spending OR aren't going to be spending
6. will . . . be taking OR are . . . going to be taking
7. 'll be working OR 's going to be working

8. 'll have completed
9. 'll have been teaching OR 'll have taught
10. won't have graded

V (Units 5–6)

2. A	4. B	6. D
3. C	5. A	7. B

PART III

I (Unit 7)

2. is
3. Doesn't . . . produce
4. Aren't . . . planting   OR   Don't . . . plant
5. exports
6. hasn't . . . been
7. visited
8. Didn't . . . name
9. doesn't use
10. Don't . . . speak

II (Unit 7)

2. hasn't he	7. Aren't
3. have they	8. shouldn't we
4. Didn't	9. Won't
5. had they	10. won't we
6. do they	11. Isn't

III (Units 7–8)

2. A	4. B	6. A	8. B	10. A
3. C	5. D	7. A	9. C	

IV (Unit 8)

2. Neither does	7. am too
3. So does	8. doesn't either
4. did too	9. Neither should
5. was too	10. So am
6. So would	

V (Units 7–8)

I'm a pretty bad letter writer, ~~amn't~~ I? How are

aren't

you? You didn't mention Marta in your last letter.

Aren't

~~Don't~~ you roommates anymore? My new
roommate's name is Rafaella. We have a lot in

am I

common. She's 18, and so ~~I am~~. She lived in
Chicago, and, of course, I did too. We have the
same study habits too. She doesn't stay up late,

do

and neither ~~don't~~ I.

Luckily, there are some important differences
too. You remember what my room looked like at

don't

home, ~~didn't~~ you? Well, I'm not very neat, but
Rafaella is. I can't cook, but she can ~~too~~. So life is

don't

improving. You have a break soon, ~~do~~ you? Why
don't you come for a visit? I know the three of us
would have a good time.

PART IV

I **(Units 9–10)**

2. C	**6.** D	**10.** C	**14.** D
3. A	**7.** B	**11.** B	**15.** A
4. D	**8.** A	**12.** B	
5. C	**9.** D	**13.** C	

II **(Units 9–10)**

2. driving	**13.** having to
3. suspending	**14.** feeling OR to feel
4. to drive	**15.** to prevent OR prevent
5. to drive	
6. being	**16.** not to use
7. passing	**17.** to buckle up
8. not to take	**18.** ride
9. to give	**19.** driving
10. pay	**20.** behave
11. to be	**21.** saving
12. obeying	**22.** to make

III **(Units 9–10)**

2. A	**4.** C	**6.** A	**8.** A
3. D	**5.** B	**7.** D	

IV **(Units 9–10)**

2. urges Alicia to ask
3. lets students stay
4. doesn't mind my daughter's (OR daughter) recording
5. appreciates the teacher's (OR teacher) being
6. are used to Ms. Allen's (OR Ms. Allen) demanding
7. makes them take
8. gets them to help
9. wants them to do
10. are happy with her teaching

V **(Units 9–10)**

2. is letting OR is going to let OR will let Caryn use
3. afford to buy
4. persuaded Caryn to take
5. invited Jason to join
6. quit eating OR has quit eating
7. offered to lift
8. suggested turning on
9. made Dan show him OR her
10. denied calling Caryn

PART V

I **(Units 11–12)**

2. out	**7.** with
3. up	**8.** out
4. over	**9.** out
5. over	**10.** over
6. in	**11.** up

12. down, up	**18.** off
13. up	**19.** through with
14. in	**20.** away
15. up with	**21.** off
16. out	**22.** up, back
17. back	

II **(Units 11–12)**

2. C	**6.** D	**10.** D	**14.** B
3. D	**7.** B	**11.** D	**15.** B
4. A	**8.** C	**12.** C	
5. B	**9.** C	**13.** A	

III **(Units 11–12)**

2. call it off
3. carry it out
4. switched it on
5. get along with John OR him
6. keep away from them
7. put it back
8. taken them off
9. wake her up
10. work them out

IV **(Units 11–12)**

2. A	**5.** D	**8.** D	**11.** D
3. D	**6.** D	**9.** D	**12.** D
4. A	**7.** A	**10.** B	

V **(Units 11–12)**

2. Please don't throw them away.
3. The teacher turned down my topic proposal (OR turned my topic proposal down).
4. All forms must be turned in by April 8.
5. They could blow up.
6. Don't give up hope.
7. You left it out.
8. The students didn't let me down.
9. Can someone point out what the mistake is?
10. Don't just show up without one.

PART VI

I **(Units 13–14)**

2. who	**8.** who
3. who	**9.** that
4. where	**10.** which
5. whose	**11.** when
6. which	**12.** when
7. which	

II **(Units 13–14)**

2. She lives in the house which (OR that) is across the street.
3. This is the time of year when (OR that) she always goes away.

4. She travels with her older sister, who lives in Connecticut.

5. This year they're taking a trip with the car that (OR which) she just bought.

6. They're going to Miami, where they grew up.

7. They have a lot of relatives in Florida, who(m) they haven't seen in years.

8. The family is going to have a reunion, which they've been planning all year.

9. They'll be staying with their Aunt Sonya, whose house is right on a canal.

10. They really need this vacation, which they've been looking forward to all year.

III **(Units 13–14)**

2. C	**6.** B	**10.** C
3. C	**7.** A	**11.** C
4. C	**8.** B	
5. B	**9.** C	

IV **(Units 13–14)**

2. D	**5.** B	**8.** C
3. B	**6.** C	**9.** B
4. C	**7.** D	**10.** C

V **(Units 13–14)**

There is an old German proverb that says,

which OR *that* OR no relative pronoun

"Friendship is a plant ~~who~~ we must often water." This means that we have to nurture our relationships to make them grow and flourish. A relationship that you neglect will wilt and die.

When I was ten, my family moved from Germany to the United States. There I had a "friend" (whom I will call Jack) who ~~he~~ never invited me to do things with him. Jack lived in a

which OR *that* OR no relative pronoun

house ~~where~~ I never got to see even though it was just a few blocks away from mine. He had family and friends whom I never met. Of course, today I realize that Jack really wasn't a friend at all. He was what in Germany is called a *Bekannter*—

know

someone who you ~~knows~~—an acquaintance. And for an acquaintance, his behavior was fine. I got

when OR no relative pronoun

confused on the day ~~where~~ Jack referred to me as his friend.

"Friend" is a word that has a different set of expectations for me. In Germany, that word is

whom

reserved for people with ~~that~~ one is really close. I learned through the experience with Jack that although you can translate a word from one language to another, the meaning can still be different. Today I have friends from many

whose

countries. I also have many acquaintances ~~who~~ friendships I have learned to value too.

PART VII

I **(Units 15–17)**

2. couldn't	**9.** might have	
3. could have	**10.** must have	
4. can't	**11.** must not have	
5. must not	**12.** could have	
6. 's got to	**13.** shouldn't have	
7. has to	**14.** shouldn't have	
8. should	**15.** 'd better not	

II **(Units 15–17)**

2. may not have been
3. could have been
4. couldn't have been
5. should have studied
6. could . . . have done
7. shouldn't have missed
8. ought to have copied
9. must have come

III **(Units 15–17)**

2. I should've watched the show about Easter Island.

3. It must've been very interesting.

4. The local library ought to have bought books about Easter Island.

5. Sara should've reminded me about it.

6. John could've told me about it.

7. He must not have remembered our conversation about it.

8. My roommate might've invited me to the party.

9. John might not have gotten an invitation.

10. He couldn't have forgotten our date.

IV **(Units 15–17)**

2. B	**5.** D	**8.** B
3. A	**6.** B	**9.** C
4. C	**7.** C	**10.** A

V **(Units 15–17)**

better not

What a day! I guess I'd ~~not better~~ stay up so late

have

anymore. This morning I should ~~of~~ gotten up much earlier. When I got to the post office, the lines were

waited

already long. I must have ~~wait~~ at least half an hour.

fire

My boss was furious that I was late. He might ~~fires~~ me for lateness—even though I couldn't have worked during that time anyway. The computers were down again! We must ~~had~~ *have* lost four hours because of that. While the system was down, some

of us were able ^*to* go out to lunch. Later, we all felt

sick. It had to ~~has~~ *have* been the food—we all ate the same thing. On the way home, I got stuck in

traffic. A trip that should ^*have* taken twenty minutes took forty-five. Tomorrow's Saturday. I just might

~~sleeping~~ *sleep* until noon.

PART VIII

I (Units 18–19)
2. leave
3. were mailed
4. have
5. were made
6. were confirmed
7. need
8. be met
9. rent
10. just handed
11. were sent
12. was done

II (Unit 19)
2. might be delivered
3. 'll be read
4. 'll be satisfied
5. have to be packed OR will have to be packed
6. ought to be told
7. could be extended
8. should be painted
9. has to be serviced
10. can be arranged

III (Units 18–20)
2. C	6. D	10. A
3. A	7. B	11. D
4. B	8. A	
5. A	9. C	

IV (Unit 20)
2. have OR get . . . cleaned
3. have OR get . . . looked at
4. have OR get . . . painted
5. had OR got . . . designed
6. have OR get . . . delivered
7. have OR get . . . made up
8. have OR get . . . catered
9. Have OR Get . . . sent

V (Units 18–20)
2. is grown
3. are employed by the sugar industry
4. is exported
5. is struck by hurricanes
6. was popularized by Bob Marley
7. 's listened to (by people)

VI (Units 18–20)
2. C	4. A	6. A
3. D	5. D	7. D

PART IX

I (Units 21–24)
2. A	8. A	14. B	20. B
3. B	9. C	15. D	21. A
4. C	10. A	16. A	22. D
5. B	11. A	17. A	23. A
6. C	12. B	18. B	
7. D	13. D	19. C	

II (Units 21–24)
2. would have seen
3. tell
4. 'll spoil
5. would . . . have been
6. 'd been born
7. 'd had
8. wouldn't have grown up
9. hadn't grown up
10. wouldn't have met
11. hadn't taken
12. studied OR study
13. 'd pass OR 'll pass
14. don't get OR wouldn't get
15. study OR studied
16. were
17. 'd try

III (Units 21–24)
2. found
3. Would . . . keep
4. knew
5. hadn't gotten
6. would've borrowed
7. would've taken
8. weren't
9. would be
10. wouldn't have seen
11. had looked
12. have
13. discuss
14. doesn't belong
15. return

16. won't follow

17. obey

18. comes

19. 'll be

IV (Units 23–24)

2. I wish I had bought business-class tickets.

3. I wish the in-flight movie weren't *Back to the Future IV*.

4. I wish we hadn't gone to Disney World on vacation.

5. I wish we had gone (OR could have gone) to the beach.

6. I wish I (OR we lived) in Florida.

7. I wish my office could transfer me to Orlando.

V (Units 21–24)

2. B	**5.** B	**7.** A
3. D	**6.** C	**8.** C
4. A		

PART X

I (Units 25–28)

1. b. last

2. a. would be	**b.** our
3. a. told	**b.** they
4. a. asked	**b.** was
5. a. she	**b.** should bring
6. a. told	**b.** not to bring
7. a. 'd been planning	**b.** us
8. a. didn't know how	**b.** our
9. a. asked	**b.** if there was
10. a. not to be	
11. a. told	**b.** to take
12. a. couldn't	**b.** the following night
13. a. was	**b.** that day
14. a. told	**b.** her
15. a. had issued	**b.** that night
16. a. would	**b.** that day
17. a. had to drive	
18. a. says	**b.** loves
19. a. him	**b.** to shovel
20. a. asked	**b.** his boots were

II (Units 25–29)

2. B	**5.** B	**8.** C
3. D	**6.** A	**9.** D
4. D	**7.** D	**10.** C

III (Units 25–28)

2. D	**5.** C	**8.** C
3. A	**6.** B	**9.** D
4. B	**7.** A	**10.** B

IV (Units 25–28)

2. Jon told her (that) they had moved in three weeks before.

3. Nita asked if (OR whether) they liked (OR like) that place better than their old apartment.

4. Jon said (that) they liked (OR like) it a lot more.

5. Jon asked (her) when her cousin had arrived from Detroit.

6. Nita told him (that) he had just come the day before.

7. Jon said (that) it had been (OR has been) an incredible winter.

8. Nita said (that) the roads might close again with that storm.

9. Jon said not to drive that night.

10. Jon said to stay there with her cousin.

11. Nita told him (that) they should try to make it home.

12. Nita said (that) she had to walk her dog early the next morning.

V (Units 25–29)

Motorists returning home during last night's snow storm were pleasantly surprised. Early yesterday afternoon, forecasters had predicted that Route 10 ~~will~~ *would* close because of high winds. However, all major highways remained open last night. One woman, stopping for a newspaper on Woodmere Avenue at about midnight, told this reporter that she and her cousin ~~have~~ *had* almost decided to stay with a friend ~~tonight~~ *that night* OR *last night*, rather than drive home.

Her cousin told me that ~~I~~ *he* had just arrived from Detroit, where the storm hit first. He said ~~"that it had been a big one."~~ *that it had been a big one.* School children seemed especially pleased. Yesterday morning, most schools announced that they ~~will~~ *would* close at 1:00 P.M. Several kids at James Fox Elementary reported that they ~~are~~ *were* planning to spend that afternoon sledding and having snowball fights.

Many people are wondering how ~~could~~ weather forecasters *could* have made such a big mistake. Carla Donati, the weather reporter for WCSX, said that they were not sure why this had happened. The National Weather Service has not commented.

INDEX

This Index is for the full and split editions. All entries are in the full book. Entries for Volume A of the split edition are in black. Entries for Volume B are in color.

Notes

Notes

4/2011